U0866854

新曲綫 New Curves | 用心雕刻每一本……
http://site.douban.com/110283/
http://weibo.com/nccpub

用心字里行间　雕刻名著经典

商务印书馆（成都）有限责任公司出品

信息、会计和理财

第 7 版，双语教学版

〔美〕威廉·普赖德　罗伯特·休斯　杰克·卡普尔　著
孔小磊　译注

商务印书馆
2025年·北京

Information, Accounting, and Finance, 7th Edition

William M. Pride   Robert J. Hughes   Jack R. Kapoor

Copyright © 2023 Cengage Learning, Inc.
The Commercial Press is authorized by Cengage Learning to publish and distribute exclusively this custom reprint edition. This edition is authorized for sale in the People's Republic of China only (excluding Hong Kong, Macao SAR and Taiwan). Unauthorized export of this edition is a violation of the Copyright Act. No part of this publication may be reproduced or distributed by any means, or stored in a database or retrieval system, without the prior written permission of the publisher.
978-0-357-71794-3
Cengage
200 Pier 4 Boulevard
Boston, MA 02210
USA

此客户定制影印版由圣智学习出版公司授权商务印书馆独家出版发行。此版本仅限在中华人民共和国境内（不包括中国香港、澳门特别行政区及中国台湾）销售。未经授权的本书出口将被视为违反版权法的行为。未经出版者预先书面许可，不得以任何方式复制或发行本书的任何部分。
本书封面贴有Cengage Learning防伪标签，无标签者不得销售。

Contents 目录

Chapter 4: Exploring Social Media and e-Business 101

探索社交媒体和电子商业

Acknowledgments 致谢

The quality of this book and its supplements program has been helped immensely by the insightful and rich comments of a special set of instructors. Their thoughtful and helpful comments had real impact in shaping the final product. We wish to thank:

Ken Anglin, *Minnesota State University, Mankato*
Ellen A. Benowitz, *Mercer County Community College*
Michael Bento, *Owens Community College*
Laura Bulas, *Central Community College, NE*
Brennan Carr, *Long Beach City College*
Paul Coakley, *The Community College of Baltimore County*
Jean Condon, *Mid-Plains Community College*
Mary Cooke, *Surry Community College*
Dean Danielson, *San Joaquin Delta College*
Gary Donnelly, *Casper College*
Karen Edwards, *Chemeketa Community College*
Donna K. Fisher, *Georgia Southern University*
Mark Fox, *Indiana University South Bend*
Connie Golden, *Lakeland Community College*
Karen Gore, *Ivy Tech Community College—Evansville*
John Guess, *Delgado Community College*
Tom Hendricks, *Oakland Community College*
Robert James, *Macomb Community College*
Eileen Kearney, *Montgomery Community College*
Mary Beth Klinger, *College of Southern Maryland*
Natasha Lindsey, *University of North Alabama*
Emilio Lopez, *Dallas College*
Robert Lupton, *Central Washington University*
John Mago, *Anoka Ramsey Community College*
Pamela G. McElligott, *St. Louis Community College Meramec*
Myke McMullen, *Long Beach City College*
Carol Miller, *Community College of Denver*
Diane Minger, *Dallas College*
Jaideep Motwani, *Grand Valley State*
Mark Nagel, *Normandale Community College*
Dyan Pease, *Sacramento City College*
Jeffrey D. Penley, *Catawba Valley Community College*
Angela J. Rabatin, *Prince George's Community College*
Anthony Racka, *Oakland Community College—Auburn Hills Campus*
Dwight Riley, *Dallas College*
Carol Rowey, *Community College of Rhode Island*
Christy Shell, *Houston Community College*
Cindy Simerly, *Lakeland Community College*
Yolanda I. Smith, *Northern Virginia Community College*
Gail South, *Montgomery College*
Rieann Spence-Gale, *Northern Virginia Comm. College—Alexandria Campus*
Kurt Stanberry, *University of Houston, Downtown*
John Striebich, *Monroe Community College*
Keith Taylor, *Lansing Community College*
Tricia Troyer, *Waubonsee Community College*
Leo Trudel, *University of Maine - Fort Kent*
Anne Williams, *Gateway Community College*
Kevin Wortley, *Dallas College*

We want to thank the following people for their professional and technical assistance: Gwyn Walters, Klarisa Posada, Ashley Nguyen, Kelsey Reddick, Brenda Aram, Theresa Kapoor, David Pierce, Kathryn Thumme, Karen Tucker, Dave Kapoor, Susan Fant, and Jeff Penley.

Many talented professionals at Cengage Learning have contributed to the development of *Foundations of Business, 7e*. We are especially grateful to Erin Joyner, Thais Alencar, Joe Sabatino, Heather Thompson, Clara Kuhlman, Allie Janneck, Stephanie Hall, Megan Guiliani, Angela Sheehan, Sara Greenwood, Hannah May, Amanda Ryan, Tony Winslow, Cara Suriyamongkol, and Nick Perez. Their inspiration, patience, support, and friendship are invaluable.

W. M. P.
R. J. H.
J. R. K.

About the Authors 作者介绍

William M. Pride
Texas A&M University

William M. Pride is Professor of Marketing at Mays Business School, Texas A&M University. He received his PhD from Louisiana State University. He is the author of Cengage Learning's *Marketing*, 20th edition, a market leader. Dr. Pride's research interests are in advertising, promotion, and distribution channels.

Dr. Pride's research articles have appeared in major journals in the fields of advertising and marketing, such as *Journal of Marketing*, *Journal of Marketing Research*, *Journal of the Academy of Marketing Science*, and the *Journal of Advertising*. Dr. Pride is a member of the American Marketing Association, Academy of Marketing Science, Society for Marketing Advances, and the Marketing Management Association. Dr. Pride has taught Principles of Marketing and other marketing courses for more than 45 years at both the undergraduate and graduate levels.

Robert J. Hughes
Dallas College - Richland Campus

Robert J. Hughes (EdD, University of North Texas) specializes in business administration and college instruction. He has taught Introduction to Business for more than 35 years both on campus and online for Richland College—one of seven campuses that are part of the Dallas College System. In addition to *Business* and *Foundations of Business*, published by Cengage Learning, he has authored college textbooks in personal finance and business mathematics; served as a content consultant for two popular national television series, *It's Strictly Business* and *Dollars & Sense: Personal Finance for the 21st Century*; and is the lead author for a business math project utilizing computer-assisted instruction funded by the ALEKS Corporation. He is also active in many academic and professional organizations and has served as a consultant and investment advisor to individuals, businesses, and charitable organizations. Dr. Hughes is the recipient of three different Teaching in Excellence Awards at Richland College. According to Dr. Hughes, after 35 years of teaching Introduction to Business, the course is still exciting: "There's nothing quite like the thrill of seeing students succeed, especially in a course like Introduction to Business, which provides the foundation for not only academic courses, but also life in the real world."

Jack R. Kapoor
College of DuPage

Jack R. Kapoor (EdD, Northern Illinois University) has been a Professor of Business and Economics in the Business and Technology Division at the College of DuPage, where he has taught Introduction to Business, Marketing, Management, Economics, and Personal Finance since 1969. He previously taught at Illinois Institute of Technology's Stuart School of Management, San Francisco State University's School of World Business, and other colleges. Professor Kapoor was awarded the Business and Services Division's Outstanding Professor Award for 1999–2000. He served as an Assistant National Bank Examiner for the U.S. Treasury Department and as an international trade consultant to Bolting Manufacturing Co., Ltd., Mumbai, India.

Dr. Kapoor is known internationally as a coauthor of several textbooks in Business and Personal Finance, including Business MindTap (Cengage Learning), has served as a content consultant for two popular national television series, *Dollars & Sense: Personal Finance for the 21st Century* and *The Business File: An Introduction to Business*, and developed two full-length audio courses in business and personal finance. He has been quoted in many national newspapers and magazines, including *USA Today*, *U.S. News & World Report*, the *Chicago Sun-Times*, *Crain's Small Business*, the *Chicago Tribune*, and other publications.

Dr. Kapoor has traveled around the world and has studied business practices in capitalist, socialist, and communist countries.

Information, Accounting, and Finance

Chapter

1

Exploring the World of Business and Economics

探索商业和经济世界

Why Should You Care?

Studying business will help you choose a career, become a successful employee or manager, start your own business, and become a more informed consumer and better investor.

Learning Objectives

Once you complete this chapter, you will be able to:

1-1 Discuss what you must do to be successful in today's business world.

1-2 Identify the potential risks and rewards of business.

1-3 Describe the two types of economic systems: capitalism and command economy.

1-4 Identify the ways to measure economic performance.

1-5 Examine the different phases in the typical business cycle.

1-6 Outline the four types of competition.

1-7 Summarize the development of American business and the challenges that businesses and society will encounter in the future.

Inside Business 商业透视：特斯拉在竞争中领先

Tesla Races Ahead of the Competition

Today Tesla is a household name around the world. Because the company is now the leader in electric vehicles (EVs), it has also become one of the most valuable companies in the world. Although Tesla is relatively young compared to General Motors, Ford, Toyota, and other competitors, the car manufacturer's commitment to innovation and sustainability has propelled it to the front of the pack. Even though Toyota is much larger than Tesla in terms of sales, Tesla's market capitalization has surpassed the Japanese carmaker, demonstrating that investors see a bright future ahead for the electric car company. For any company traded on the stock exchange, market capitalization is calculated by multiplying the current market value for a share of the company's stock by the total number of shares that have been issued. At the time of publication, Tesla was valued at almost $800 billion—not bad for a relative newcomer to the automobile industry.

While Tesla didn't invent the electric car, it set the standard for what an EV should be. The Tesla Roadster was the first highway-legal production vehicle that used lithium-ion batteries, giving it a longer driving range than other EVs on the market. With superior distance and speed and longer battery life, Tesla managed to make its products appealing to a wide range of customers. As Tesla makes record sales and expands globally, it's clear the company's early bet on EVs has paid off.

Tesla's robust supply chain has driven down battery costs, making it even more challenging for other manufacturers to catch up. Even though other automakers including BMW, Ford, General Motors, Mercedes Benz, Nissan, Volkswagen, and some companies you probably don't recognize are investing heavily in EVs, a Tesla automobile is the one that customers want. It's so popular that customers often have to wait for delivery for popular models. While Tesla does face competition from traditional automakers as well as electric car startups, the difference could be that other companies still think of EVs as an afterthought.[1]

Did you know?

Tesla's market capitalization is worth more than Ford and General Motors combined.

Wow! What a challenging world we live in. Just for a moment, think about how the world has changed in the last few years. The United States has experienced a pandemic, non-essential businesses were closed in many states, the unemployment rate increased, and the stock market took a nosedive and then recovered all in a short period of time. Even though the economy has shown signs of improvement, there are still problems and many people worry about the future of the nation and the economy. Simply put, many individuals, business leaders, and politicians worry that the future of the nation's economy could be a bumpy road that leads to another recession.

Regardless of the current state of the economy, keep in mind that our economy continues to adapt and change to meet the challenges of an ever-changing world and to provide opportunities for those who want to achieve success. Our economic system also provides an amazing amount of freedom that allows businesses like Tesla—the company profiled in the Inside Business opening case for this chapter—to adapt to satisfy the needs of customers. To meet increased consumer demands for an electric automobile, the company's managers, engineers, and employees were able to design and build an automobile that consumers really wanted. After initial success, Tesla—a newcomer in the automobile industry—continues to innovate and create new models with self-driving capability. As a result, the company is now profitable and is one of the most valuable companies in the world.

Within certain limits, imposed mainly to ensure public safety, the owners of a business can produce any legal good or service they choose and attempt to sell it at the price they set. This system of business, in which individuals decide what to produce, how to produce it, and at what price to sell it, is called **free enterprise**. Our free-enterprise system ensures, for example, that Amazon.com can sell everything from books, televisions, and toys to computers, cameras, and clothing. Our system gives Amazon's owners and stockholders the right to make a profit from the company's success. It gives Amazon's management the right to compete with bookstore rival Barnes & Noble and retailers Walmart, Best Buy, and Macy's. It also gives you—the consumer—the right to choose.

In this chapter, we look briefly at what business is and how it became that way. First, we discuss what you must do to be successful in the world of business and explore some important reasons for studying business. Second, we define *business,* noting how business organizations satisfy their customers' needs and earn profits. Third, we examine how capitalism and command economies answer four basic economic questions. Next, our focus shifts to how the nations of the world measure economic performance, the phases in a typical business cycle, and the four types of competitive situations. Finally, we look at the events that helped shape today's business system, the current business environment, and the challenges that businesses face.

在不断变化的商业世界中展望未来

1-1 Your Future in the Changing World of Business

Learning Objective

1-1 Discuss what you must do to be successful in today's business world.

The key word in this heading is *changing*. When faced with the COVID-19 pandemic that raced through the world, small business owners, employees, managers, and investors began to ask the question: What effect will non-essential business closures and record high unemployment rates have on the economy? More specifically, many people wanted to know, how does this affect me both now and in the future? Although this is a fair question, it is difficult to answer. For an employee just starting a career or for a college student preparing for a career, the question is even more difficult to answer. Now, as the United States and the world adjust to life after the COVID-19 pandemic and the economy shows signs of recovery, there are opportunities out there for people who are willing to work hard, continue to learn, and possess the ability to adapt to change. Let's begin this course with three basic concepts.

- What do you want?
- Why do you want it?
- Write it down!

Joe Dudley, one of the world's most respected Black business owners, offers the preceding advice to anyone who wants to succeed in business. His advice can help you achieve success. What is so amazing about Dudley's success is that he started a manufacturing business in his own kitchen, with his wife and children serving as the new firm's only employees. He went on to develop his own line of haircare and cosmetic products sold directly to cosmetologists, barbers, beauty schools, and consumers in the United States and in foreign countries. Today, after a lot of hard work and a strong work ethic, Mr. Dudley has built a well-recognized and respected company in the competitive cosmetics industry. He is not only a successful business owner but also a winner of the Horatio Alger Award—an award given to outstanding individuals who have succeeded in the face of adversity.[2]

Although many people would say that Joe Dudley was just lucky or happened to be in the right place at the right time, the truth is that he became a success because he had a dream and worked to turn the dream into a reality. He would be the first to tell you that you have the same opportunities he had. According to Mr. Dudley, "Success is a journey, not just a destination."[3]

Whether you want to obtain part-time employment to pay college and living expenses, begin your career as a full-time employee, or start a business, you must

自由企业
free enterprise the system of business in which individuals are free to decide what to produce, how to produce it, and at what price to sell it

bring something to the table that makes you different from the next person. Employers and our economic system are more demanding than ever before. Ask yourself: What can I do that will make employers want to pay me a salary? What skills do I have that employers need? With these two questions in mind, we begin the next section with another basic question: Why study business?

为什么学习商学

1-1a **Why Study Business?**

The potential benefits of higher education are enormous. To begin with, there are economic benefits. Over their lifetimes, college graduates on average earn much more than high school graduates. Although lifetime earnings are substantially higher for college graduates, so are annual income amounts (refer to Figure 1-1). In addition to higher income, you will find at least four compelling reasons for studying business.

For Help in Choosing a Career What do you want to do with the rest of your life? Like many people, you may find it a difficult question to answer. This business course will introduce you to a wide array of employment opportunities. In private enterprise, these range from small, local businesses owned by one individual to large companies such as American Express and Microsoft owned by thousands of stockholders. There are also employment opportunities with federal, state, county, and local governments and with charitable organizations such as Habitat for Humanity, the Red Cross, and Save the Children. For help in deciding which career might be right for you, read Appendix A "Careers in Business," which appears on the text website.

In addition to career information in Appendix A, a number of websites provide information about career development. To click your career into high gear, you can also use online networking. Websites like Facebook, Twitter, LinkedIn, and other social media sites can help you locate job openings and help prospective employers to find you. To make the most of online networking, begin by identifying and joining sites where you can connect with potential employers, former classmates, and others who may have or may hear of job openings. Next, be sure your online profile, photographs, and posts communicate your abilities and interests. Finally, be ready to respond quickly when you spot a job opening.

One thing to remember as you think about what your ideal career might be is that people often choose a career that is a reflection of what they value and consider most important. What will give one individual personal satisfaction may not satisfy another. For example, one person may dream of a career as a successful corporate executive with a large salary and job security in marketing or technology or financial services. Another person may choose a career that has more modest monetary rewards but that provides the opportunity to help others. What you choose to do with your life will be based on what you feel is most important. And *you* are a very important part of that decision.

Figure 1-1 Who Makes the Most Money?

Education makes a difference. Dollar amounts represent the average annual salary for full-time workers in each household.

Source: "Educational Attainment of Householder—Households with Householder 25 Years Old and Over by Median and Mean Income," The U.S. Census Bureau.

Exploring Careers

职业探索：Z世代寻求职场多样性

Gen Z Seeks Workplace Diversity

When it comes to finding the perfect employer, Generation Z (people born between 1997 and 2012) prioritizes workplace diversity. According to a survey by Tallo, an online platform for students and job seekers, nearly 70 percent say they would be more likely to accept a job offer if the recruiters and materials representing the company were ethnically and racially diverse. In fact, some would even decline a job offer if the firm fell short on these factors. Workplace diversity—the differences among people in a workforce owing to factors such as age, race, ethnicity, gender, sexual orientation, and ability—is a top priority for Gen Z.

Gen Z—the most diverse generation ever—has surpassed Millennials (people born between 1981 and 1996) to become the largest generation. The effects of their entry into the workplace are already felt by companies around the world. Diversity for Gen Z goes beyond race and gender to encompass gender identity and orientation.

Companies that reflect diversity, equity, and inclusion in their branding and marketing materials will be more likely to attract fresh talent. Firms should be prepared to embed these values at the heart of the organization rather than making surface-level claims. With Gen Z on the hunt for organizations that reflect their values and beliefs, the burden is on employers to prioritize diversity issues.

Sources: Based on information in Tamara E. Holmes, "Diverse Workforce a Top Draw for Nearly 7 in 10 Members of Generation Z," *Yahoo Finance*, November 4, 2020; Deloitte, "Understanding Generation Z in the Workplace"; Sheryl Estrada, "Workplace D&I in 2021 Will Keep External Community in Mind," *HR Dive*, January 13, 2021.

To Be a Successful Employee Deciding on the type of career you want is only the first step. To get a job in your chosen field and to be successful at it, you will have to develop a plan, or a road map, that ensures you have the skills and knowledge the job requires. Think about what you'd look for if you were hiring an employee and strive to be that kind of person. You will also be expected to have the ability to work well with many types of people in a culturally diverse workforce. **Cultural** (or **workplace**) **diversity** refers to a system that recognizes and respects the differences among people because of their age, race, ethnicity, gender, sexual orientation, and ability.

This course and the other college courses you take, your instructors, and all of the resources available at your college or university can help you acquire the skills and knowledge you will need for a successful career. But don't underestimate your part in making your dream a reality. In addition to job-related skills and knowledge, employers will also look for the following characteristics when hiring a new employee or promoting an existing employee:

- Honesty and integrity
- Willingness to work hard
- Dependability
- Time management skills
- Self-confidence
- Motivation
- Willingness to learn
- Communication skills
- Professionalism

文化（或职场）多样性
cultural (or **workplace**) **diversity** a system that recognizes and respects the differences among people because of their age, race, ethnicity, gender, sexual orientation, and ability

The road to success can take many different paths! While many people want immediate success, it's important to chart a path that leads to life-long success. It helps to remember what Joe Dudley, the founder of Dudley Beauty Products said: "Success is a journey, not just a destination."

Employers will also be interested in any work experience you may have had in cooperative work/school programs, during summer vacations, or in part-time jobs during the school year. Experience—even part-time work experience—can make a difference when it is time to apply for the job you really want.

Many employees want to become managers because managers often receive higher salaries and can earn promotions within an organization. To be effective, managers must be able to perform four basic management functions: planning, organizing, leading and motivating, and controlling. To successfully perform these management functions, managers must also be able to work effectively with individual employees, other managers within the firm, and people outside the firm. In addition to the four management functions just mentioned, a successful manager will need many of the same characteristics that an employee needs to be successful.

To Start Your Own Business Some people prefer to work for themselves, and they open their own businesses. To be successful, business owners must possess many of the same characteristics that successful employees and managers have, and they must be willing to work hard and put in long hours.

It also helps if a small-business owner has an idea that will provide a product or service that customers want. At the age of 16, Palmer Luckey began building virtual reality headsets in his garage after school and work. While the first prototypes based on his ideas were crude by today's standards, the product showed a great deal of promise. After further development, refinements, and more ideas, the product—now called Oculus—was a success in the marketplace. How successful? Answer: so successful that Facebook paid $2 billion to acquire the company.[4]

Unfortunately, many business firms fail. In fact, only about 50 percent survive the first five years. Typical reasons for business failures include undercapitalization (not enough money), poor business location, poor customer service, unqualified or untrained employees, fraud, lack of a proper business plan, and failure to seek outside professional help. The material in this course will help you to overcome many of these problems.

To Become a Better Informed Consumer and Investor The world of business surrounds us. You cannot buy a home, a new Ford Escape Hybrid from the local Ford dealer, a pair of jeans at Gap Inc., or a hot dog from a street vendor without entering into a business transaction. Because you no doubt will engage in business transactions almost every day of your life, one very good reason for studying business is to become a more fully informed consumer.

Many people also rely on a basic understanding of business to help them invest for the future. According to Julie Stav, Hispanic stockbroker turned radio and YouTube personality and the author of *Get Your Share: A Guide to Striking It Rich in the Stock Market* and other personal finance help books, it is important to learn the basics about the economy and business, stocks, mutual funds, and other alternatives before investing your money. She also believes that it is never too early to start investing.[5] Although this is an obvious conclusion, just dreaming of being rich does not make it happen. In fact, like many facets of life, it takes planning and determination to establish the type of investment program that will help you accomplish your financial goals.

给商科学生的特别提示

1-1b **Special Note to Business Students**

It is important to begin reading this text with one thing in mind: *This business course does not have to be difficult.* We have done everything possible to eliminate the problems that you encounter in a typical class. All of the features in each chapter have been evaluated and recommended by instructors with years of teaching experience. In addition, business students—just like you—were asked to critique each chapter component. Based on this feedback, the text includes the following features:

- *Learning objectives* appear at the beginning of each chapter.
- *Inside Business* is a chapter-opening case that highlights how successful, real-world companies do business on a day-to-day basis.
- *Margin notes* are used throughout a chapter to reinforce both learning objectives and key terms.
- *Boxed features* in each chapter highlight how managers, employees, and entrepreneurs can be both ethical and successful. Topics discussed in the boxed features include ethics and social responsibility, suggestions for entrepreneurs, technology and innovation, environmental issues, and exploring different career options.
- *Concept Checks* at the end of each major section within a chapter help you test your understanding of the main issues just discussed.
- *End-of-chapter materials* provide a chapter summary, a list of key terms, discussion questions, and a case about a successful, real-world company.
- The last section of every chapter is entitled *Building Skills for Career Success* and includes exercises devoted to enhancing your social media skills, building team skills, and researching different careers.
- *End-of-part materials* provide a continuing case about Graeter's Ice Cream, a company that operates a chain of retail outlets in the Cincinnati, Ohio, area and sells to Kroger Stores and other retailers and consumers throughout the country. Also, at the end of each major part is an exercise designed to help you develop the components included in a typical business plan.

We've worked hard to make sure this edition reflects what is happening in the world and our nation. We wanted you to know how changes in the economy and world events, and yes, even a pandemic can impact not only business, but also you as a student and a consumer. Just as important, we wanted to create a text and student learning materials that help you be successful.

Because a text should always be evaluated by the students and professors who use it, we would welcome and sincerely appreciate your comments and suggestions. Please feel free to contact us by using one of the following e-mail addresses:

Bill Pride: w-pride@tamu.edu
Bob Hughes: Hughespublishing@outlook.com
Jack Kapoor: kapoorj@att.net

✓ Concept Check

- What reasons would you give if you were advising someone to study business?
- What factors affect a person's choice of careers?
- Once you have a job, what steps can you take to be successful?

企业的定义

1-2 Business: A Definition

Learning Objective

1-2 Identify the potential risks and rewards of business.

Business is the organized effort of individuals to produce and sell, for a profit, the goods and services that satisfy society's needs. The general term *business* refers to all such efforts within a society (as in "American business"). However, *a business* is a particular organization, such as a Kroger grocery store or a Cracker Barrel Old Country Store. To be successful, a business must perform three activities. It must be organized, it must satisfy needs, and it must earn a profit.

个体有组织的努力

1-2a The Organized Effort of Individuals

For a business to be organized, it must combine four kinds of resources: material, human, financial, and informational. *Material* resources include the raw materials used in manufacturing processes. For example, Mrs. Fields Cookies needs flour, sugar, butter, eggs, and other raw materials to produce the food products it sells worldwide. Material resources can also include buildings and machinery—sometimes referred to as the capital resources needed to produce goods and services. In addition, a company needs human, financial, and informational resources. *Human* resources are the people who furnish their labor to the business in return for wages. The *financial* resource is the money required to pay employees, purchase materials, and generally keep the business operating. *Information* is the resource that tells the managers of the business how effectively the other three resources are being combined and used (refer to Figure 1-2).

Today, businesses are usually organized as one of three specific types. *Service businesses* produce services, such as haircuts, legal advice, or tax preparation. H&R Block provides tax preparation and software and digital products to both businesses and consumers in the United States and around the world. *Manufacturing businesses* process various material resources into tangible goods, such as automobiles and trucks, clothing, or computers. Intel, for example, produces computer chips and other technology components that, in turn, are sold to companies that manufacture computers. Finally, some firms called *marketing intermediaries* buy products from manufacturers and then resell them. Sony Corporation is a manufacturer that produces stereo equipment, televisions, cameras, and other electronic products. These products may be sold to a marketing intermediary—often referred to as a retailer—such as Best Buy or Walmart, which then resells the manufactured goods to consumers in their retail stores.

Figure 1-2 Combining Resources

A business must combine all four resources effectively to be successful.

商业
business the organized effort of individuals to produce and sell, for a profit, the goods and services that satisfy society's needs

While most people think of retailers as the "store around the corner," today many consumers prefer to shop online. For example, there was a dramatic increase in the number of customers shopping online during the COVID-19 pandemic. While people still needed food, cleaning supplies, toilet paper, and other essential items, they were afraid to venture out to shop at local retailers because of the fear of contracting the virus. As an alternative, they used the internet to order merchandise online and then had their purchases delivered to their home or used "curbside" delivery. As a result, major retailers including Walmart, Amazon, Target, Home Depot, Lowe's, and smaller retailers saw increases in the number of online sales.

To take advantage of the opportunities to sell goods and services online, there are retailers that exist only on the internet and more traditional business firms that sell goods and services in both their brick-and-mortar stores *and* online. For example, Etsy is a highly successful internet retailer. The secret of Etsy's success is that the company provides an online site for buyers looking for unique or custom-made items not found in typical retail stores. Macy's, on the other hand, sells merchandise in both its stores and online. For our purposes, **e-business** can be defined as the organized effort of individuals to produce and sell for a profit, the goods and services that satisfy society's needs *through the facilities available on the internet.* While very similar to the definition of business, an e-business is different because of the last seven words—*through the facilities available on the internet.* e-Business—a topic we will continue to explore throughout this text—has become an accepted method of conducting business and a way for businesses to increase sales and profits and reduce expenses.

满足需求

1-2b Satisfying Needs

The ultimate objective of every firm must be to satisfy the needs of its customers. People generally do not buy goods and services simply to own them; they buy goods and services to use them in order to satisfy their particular needs. In fact, a large number of start-up businesses fail because customers don't need or want what the business is selling. Many experts suggest that talking to customers to determine what needs they have is an essential step that many would-be business owners ignore. In other situations, would-be business owners don't consider if competitors are already meeting the needs of customers in a specific geographic area. Even an

电子商业
e-business the organized effort of individuals to produce and sell for a profit, the goods and services that satisfy society's needs *through the facilities available on the internet*

Oh, thank heaven for 7-Eleven!® This 7-Eleven store in Osaka, Japan, is just one convenience store, but it is part of a company that has over 70,000 stores in 17 different countries. Started in 1927, today 7-Eleven is the largest chain of convenience stores in the world and is built on a basic principle: "Give the customers what they want, when and where they want it."

existing business can fail if it doesn't adapt to changing customer needs and its products or services no longer meet customer needs.

Different people have different needs. Some of us may feel the need for transportation is best satisfied by an air-conditioned BMW with navigation system, turbo V8 engine, stereo system, heated and cooled seats, automatic transmission, power windows, and remote-control side mirrors. Others may believe that a Chevrolet Spark with a four-cylinder engine and manual transmission will do just fine. Both products are available to those who want them, along with a wide variety of other products that satisfy the need for transportation.

When businesses understand their customers' needs and work to satisfy those needs, they are usually successful. Back in 1962, Sam Walton opened his first discount store in Rogers, Arkansas. Although the original store was quite different from the Walmart superstores you see today, the basic ideas of providing customer service and offering goods that satisfied needs at low prices are part of the reason why this firm has grown to become the largest retailer in the world.

企业利润
1-2c Business Profit

A business receives money (sales revenue) from its customers in exchange for goods or services. It must also pay out money to cover the expenses involved in doing business. If the firm's sales revenues are greater than its expenses, it has earned a profit. More specifically, as shown in Figure 1-3, **profit** is what remains after all business expenses have been deducted from sales revenue.

A negative profit, which results when a firm's expenses are greater than its sales revenue, is called a *loss*. A business cannot continue to operate at a loss for an indefinite period of time. Management and employees must find some way to increase sales revenues and reduce expenses to return to profitability. If some specific actions are not taken to eliminate losses, a firm may be forced to close its doors or file for bankruptcy protection. For example, many businesses including JCPenney, Neiman Marcus, J. Crew, and Hertz were forced to file bankruptcy in 2020 because each firm had lower sales revenues and experienced a loss caused by the COVID-19 pandemic. Fortunately, many of the firms that filed for bankruptcy protection were able to reorganize and continue to operate.

Although many people—especially stockholders and business owners—believe that profit is literally the bottom line or most important goal for a business, many stakeholders may be just as concerned about a firm's social responsibility and environmental record. The term **stakeholders** is used to describe all the different people or groups of people who are affected by an organization's policies, decisions, and activities. Many corporations, for example, are careful to point out their efforts to sustain the planet, participate in the green ecological movement, and help people to live better lives in an annual social responsibility report. In its latest report, General Mills describes how it contributed over $93 million in 2019 (the last year that complete statistics are available) to a wide variety of charitable causes, including support for programs that feed the hungry and for nonprofit organizations, schools, and communities in the United States and around the globe.[6]

Figure 1-3 The Relationship Between Sales Revenue and Profit

Profit is what remains after all business expenses have been deducted from sales revenue.

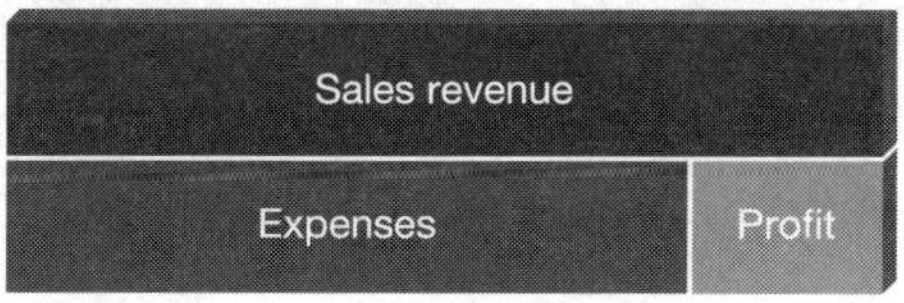

利润
profit what remains after all business expenses have been deducted from sales revenue

利益相关者
stakeholders all the different people or groups of people who are affected by an organization's policies, decisions, and activities

✓ Concept Check

- Describe the four resources that must be combined to organize and operate a business.
- What is the difference between a manufacturing business, a service business, and a marketing intermediary?
- Explain the relationship among profit, business risk, and the satisfaction of customers' needs.

The profit earned by a business becomes the property of its owners. Thus, in one sense, profit is the reward business owners receive for producing goods and services that customers need and want. Profit is also the payment that business owners receive for assuming the considerable risks of business ownership. One of these is the risk of not being paid. Everyone else—employees, suppliers, and lenders—must be paid before the owners.

A second risk that owners must consider is the risk of losing whatever they have invested into the business. A business that cannot earn a profit is very likely to fail, in which case the owners lose whatever money, effort, and time they have invested.

To satisfy society's needs and make a profit, a business must operate within the parameters of a nation's economic system. In the next section, we define economics and describe two different types of economic systems.

经济制度的类型

1-3 Types of Economic Systems

Learning Objective

1-3 Describe the two types of economic systems: capitalism and command economy.

Economics is the study of how wealth is created and distributed. By *wealth,* we mean "anything of value," including the goods and services produced and sold by business. *How wealth is distributed* simply means "who gets what." Experts often use economics to explain the choices we make and how these choices change as we cope with the demands of everyday life. In simple terms, individuals, businesses, governments, and society must make decisions that reflect what is important to each group at a particular time. For example, suppose you want to take a weekend trip to some exotic vacation spot, and you also want to begin an investment program. Because of your financial resources, though, you cannot do both, so you must decide what is most important. Business firms, governments, and to some extent society face the same types of decisions. Each group must deal with scarcity when making important decisions. In this case, *scarcity* means "lack of resources"—money, time, natural resources, and so on—that are needed to satisfy a want or need.

经济学
economics the study of how wealth is created and distributed

微观经济学
microeconomics the study of the decisions made by individuals and businesses

Today, experts often study economic problems from two different perspectives: microeconomics and macroeconomics. **Microeconomics** is the study of the decisions made by individuals and businesses. Microeconomics, for example, examines how the prices of homes affect the number of homes individuals will buy. On the other hand,

Who owns Dairy Queen? There's a chance you've purchased shakes or burgers at DQ, but do you know who owns the restaurant chain? The restaurant chain is part of a multinational corporation—Berkshire Hathaway—a company that owns dozens and dozens of successful companies and was started by Warren Buffett. Today Berkshire Hathaway *and* Dairy Queen meet customer needs, earn profits, and employ thousands of employees because they thrive in a nation with a capitalistic economy.

macroeconomics is the study of the national economy and the global economy. Macroeconomics examines the economic effect of national income, unemployment, inflation, taxes, government spending, interest rates, and similar factors on a nation and society.

The decisions that individuals, business firms, government, and society make, and the way in which people deal with the creation and distribution of wealth determine the kind of economic system, or **economy**, that a nation has.

Over the years, the economic systems of the world have differed in essentially two ways: (1) the ownership of the factors of production and (2) how they answer four basic economic questions that direct a nation's economic activity.

Factors of production are the inputs and resources used to produce goods and services. There are four such factors:

- *Land and natural resources*—elements that can be used in the production process to make appliances, automobiles, and other products. Typical examples include crude oil, forests, minerals, land, water, and even air.
- *Labor*—the time and effort that we use to produce goods and services. It includes human resources—people with skills, knowledge, training, and experiences. Examples include managers and employees.
- *Capital*—facilities, equipment, machines, tools, and man-made items used in the production of goods and services and the operation of businesses. For example, the manufacturing equipment in a Pepperidge Farm production facility or a computer used in the corporate offices of McDonald's are both types of capital. Although most people think of money as capital, it is not one of the basic four factors of production because it is a financial resource used to obtain the factors of production necessary to conceptualize, create, and produce goods and services.
- *Entrepreneurship*—the activity that conceptualizes, creates, and organizes land and natural resources, labor, and capital. It is the willingness to take risks and the knowledge and ability to use the other factors of production efficiently. An **entrepreneur** is a person who risks time, effort, and money to start and operate a business.

A nation's economic system determines how the factors of production are used to meet the needs of society. Today, two different economic systems exist: capitalism

宏观经济学
macroeconomics the study of the national economy and the global economy

经济
economy the way in which people deal with the creation and distribution of wealth

生产要素
factors of production inputs and resources used to produce goods and services

企业家
entrepreneur a person who risks time, effort, and money to start and operate a business

Is this so-much hot air?
No, not really. Fueled by environmental concerns, more and more businesses in industrialized nations are using wind and solar power for their energy needs. Today both wind and solar power are sources of clean and cost-effective energy leading some experts to suggest there's a new natural resource in town.

Entrepreneurial Success

创业成功：下一波创业浪潮来了

The Next Wave of Entrepreneurs Is Here

During the COVID-19 pandemic, the United States experienced the highest unemployment rate since 1929, and that indirectly led to a boom in entrepreneurship. Based on data from the U.S. Census Bureau, new business formations during the pandemic jumped dramatically, reaching a record high.

Since business creation has historically declined during periods of recession, professionals are optimistic about this new wave of entrepreneurship. The sharp increase in applications to form businesses also suggests that the labor market will recover more quickly from the COVID-19 recession than the Great Recession of 2008. After all, new, successful businesses will need to hire employees.

Recessions often give rise to new types of businesses as innovative entrepreneurs capitalize on new opportunities. The Great Recession of 2008, for example, gave birth to the gig economy as unemployed individuals looked for temporary, flexible, or freelance jobs for alternative ways to make money. Apps like Airbnb and Uber became immensely popular. Now, consumer demand suggests several products and services such as home improvement, pet products, home beauty products, gaming, and fitness and health that may offer new business opportunities to meet the needs of customers.

The COVID-19 pandemic disrupted business operations, shifted consumer behavior, and created new opportunities. As a result, entrepreneurs will have to look outside the box to match customer needs with their internal core strengths. As new start-ups emerge, only time will tell which ones will enjoy long-term success.

Sources: Based on information in Michael Sasso and Alexandre Tanzi, "Covid Recession Spawning Entrepreneurs in U.S. Amid Joblessness," *Bloomberg*, October 14, 2020; Adam Singolda, "Op-Ed: Analysis of 8 Billion Page Views Shows Where the Next Hot Start-up Can Thrive," *CNBC*, May 12, 2020; Dr. Anthony M. Criniti, IV, "How to Become a Successful Entrepreneur During the Pandemic," *The Entrepreneur*, July 28, 2020.

and command economies. The way each system answers the four basic economic questions listed below determines which type of economy a nation has.

1. *What* goods and services—and how much of each—will be produced?
2. *How* will these goods and services be produced?
3. *For whom* will these goods and services be produced?
4. *Who* owns and who controls the major factors of production?

资本主义

1-3a Capitalism

Capitalism is an economic system in which individuals own and operate the majority of businesses that provide goods and services. Capitalism stems from the theories of the Scottish economist Adam Smith. In his book *Wealth of Nations,* published in 1776, Smith argued that a society's interests are best served when the individuals within that society are allowed to pursue their own self-interest. According to Smith, when individuals act to improve their own fortunes, they indirectly promote the good of their community and the people in that community. Smith went on to call this concept the "invisible hand." The **invisible hand** is a term created by Adam Smith to describe how an individual's own personal gain benefits others and a nation's economy. For example, the only way a small-business owner who produces shoes can increase personal wealth is to sell shoes to customers. To become even more prosperous, the small-business owner must hire workers to produce even more shoes. According to the invisible hand, people in the small-business owner's community not only would have shoes but also would have jobs working for the shoemaker. Thus, the success of people in the community and, to some extent, the nation's economy are tied indirectly to the success of the small-business owner.

资本主义
capitalism an economic system in which individuals own and operate the majority of businesses that provide goods and services

看不见的手
invisible hand a term created by Adam Smith to describe how an individual's personal gain benefits others and a nation's economy

Adam Smith's capitalism is based on the following fundamental issues—also refer to Figure 1-4.

1. The creation of wealth is the concern of private individuals, not the government.
2. Individuals must own private property and the resources used to create wealth.
3. Economic freedom ensures the existence of competitive markets that allow both sellers and buyers to enter and leave the market as they choose.
4. The role of government should be limited to providing defense against foreign enemies, ensuring internal order, and furnishing public works and education.

One factor that Smith felt was extremely important was the role of government. He believed that government should act only as rule maker and umpire. The French term *laissez-faire* describes Smith's capitalistic system and implies that there should be no government interference in the economy. Loosely translated, this term means "let them do" (as they choose).

Adam Smith's laissez-faire capitalism is also based on the concept of a market economy. A **market economy** (sometimes referred to as a *free-market economy*) is an economic system in which businesses and individuals decide what to produce and buy, and the market determines prices and quantities sold. In today's competitive world, a business like Ford Motor Company must decide *what* type of automobiles it will sell, *how* the automobiles will be produced, and *for whom* the automobiles will be produced. *You,* the consumer, must decide if you will buy a Ford product or an automobile manufactured by another company. Prices are determined by the interaction of consumers and businesses in the marketplace.

美国的资本主义

1-3b Capitalism in the United States

Our economic system is rooted in the laissez-faire capitalism of Adam Smith. However, our real-world economy is not as laissez-faire as Smith would have liked because government participates as more than umpire and rule maker. Our economy is, in fact, a **mixed economy**, one that exhibits elements of both capitalism and socialism.

In a mixed economy, the four basic economic questions discussed at the beginning of this section (*what, how, for whom,* and *who*) are answered through the interaction of households, businesses, and governments. The interactions among these three groups are shown in Figure 1-5.

Households Households, made up of individuals, are the consumers of goods and services as well as owners of some of the factors of production. As *resource owners,* people should be free to determine how their resources are used and also to enjoy the income and wages, rents, interest, and other benefits derived from ownership of their resources. For example, members of households provide businesses with labor. In return, businesses pay wages, which households receive as income.

As *consumers,* household members spend their income to purchase the goods and services produced by business. Today, almost 70 percent of our nation's total production consists of **consumer products**—goods and services purchased by

Figure 1-4 Basic Assumptions of Adam Smith's Laissez-Faire Capitalism

市场经济
market economy an economic system in which businesses and individuals decide what to produce and buy, and the market determines prices and quantities sold.

混合经济
mixed economy an economy that exhibits elements of both capitalism and socialism

消费品
consumer products goods and services purchased by individuals for personal consumption

Figure 1-5 The Circular Flow in Our Mixed Economy

Our economic system is guided by the interaction of buyers and sellers, with the role of government being taken into account.

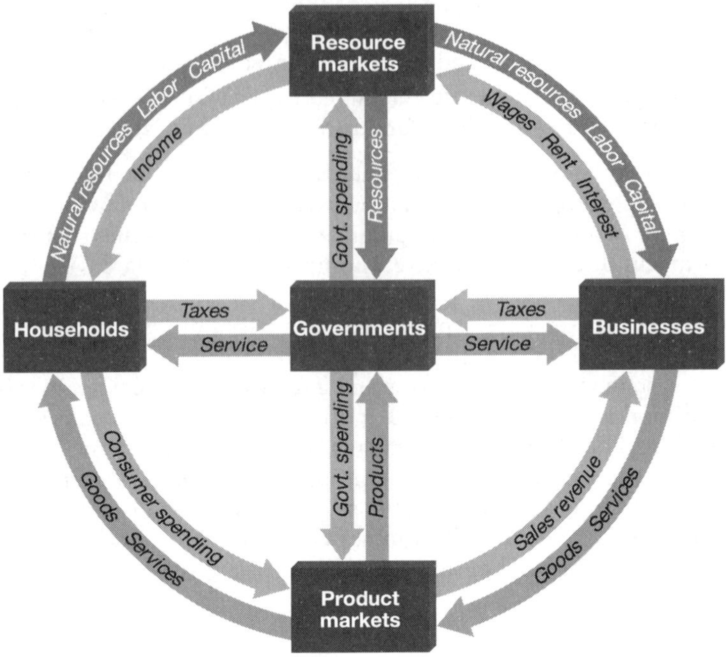

individuals for personal consumption.[7] This means that consumers, as a group, are the biggest customers of American business. Consumer spending is a very important component for the financial health of any nation. Consider what happened in the first six months of 2020 in the United States. When the nation experienced the first cases of the COVID-19 virus, consumer spending began to slow down. Then the situation got even worse when non-essential businesses including restaurants, theaters, and some retailers closed down in March and April in many states. When this happened, many consumers were advised (or told) to stay home, and they began to save money and buy only essential items. The combination of fear of losing their job or reduced hours on the job and not knowing how long the pandemic would last caused a huge drop in consumer spending and an economic downturn. Fortunately, consumer spending and the economy began to turn around in the summer of 2020 as businesses began to reopen, and early research indicated that a vaccine that could protect people from the virus and decrease the number of deaths would be available by the end of the year.

Businesses Like households, businesses are engaged in two different exchanges. They exchange money for resources, labor, and capital and use these resources to produce goods and services. Then they exchange their goods and services for sales revenue. This sales revenue, in turn, is exchanged for additional resources, which are used to produce and sell more goods and services.

When business profits are distributed to business owners, these profits become household income. (Business owners are, after all, members of households.) When the economy is running smoothly, households are willing to invest their money in businesses. They can do so directly by buying stocks issued by businesses, by purchasing shares in mutual funds that purchase stocks in businesses, or by lending money to businesses. They can also invest indirectly by placing their money in bank accounts. Banks and other financial institutions then invest money as part of their normal business operations. Thus, business profits, too, are retained in the business system, and the circular flow in Figure 1-5 is complete. How, then, does government fit in?

Governments The numerous government services are important but they (1) would either not be produced by private business firms or (2) would be produced only for those who could afford them. Typical services include national defense, police, fire protection, education, and construction of roads and highways. To pay for all these services, governments collect a variety of taxes from households (such as personal income taxes and sales taxes) and from businesses (corporate income taxes).

Figure 1-5 shows this exchange of taxes for government services. It also shows government spending of tax dollars for resources and products required to provide these services.

Actually, with government included, our circular flow looks more like a combination of several flows. In reality, it is. The important point is that together the various flows make up a single unit—a complete economic system that provides answers to the basic economic questions. Simply put, the system works.

计划经济

1-3c Command Economies

A **command economy** is an economic system in which the government decides *what* goods and services will be produced, *how* they will be produced, *for whom* available goods and services will be produced, and *who* owns and controls the major factors of production. Today, two types of economic systems—*socialism* and *communism*—serve as examples of command economies.

Socialism In a socialist economy, the key industries are owned and controlled by the government. Land, buildings, and raw materials may also be the property of the state in a socialist economy. Depending on the country, private ownership of smaller businesses is permitted to varying degrees. Usually, people may choose their own occupations, although many work in state-owned industries. Today, China, New Zealand, Canada, Sweden, and Norway are often referred to as socialist nations because they have adopted *some* socialist policies and welfare programs.

What to produce and how to produce it often are determined in accordance with national goals, which are based on projected needs and the availability of resources. The distribution of goods and services—who gets what—is also controlled by the state to the extent that it controls taxes, rents, and wages. Among the professed aims of socialist countries are the equitable distribution of income, the elimination of poverty, and the distribution of social services (such as medical care) to all who need them. The disadvantages of socialism include increased taxation and loss of incentive and motivation for both individuals and business owners.

Communism If Adam Smith was the father of capitalism, Karl Marx was the father of communism. In his writings during the mid-1800s, Marx advocated a classless society whose citizens together owned all economic resources. All workers would then contribute to this *communist* society according to their ability and would receive benefits according to their need.

Since the breakup of the Soviet Union and economic reforms in China and most of the Eastern European countries, the best remaining example of communism is DPRK. Today, the basic four economic questions (what, how, for whom, and who) are answered through centralized government plans. Emphasis is placed on the production of goods and services the government needs rather than on the needs of consumers, so there are frequent shortages of consumer goods.

✓ Concept Check

- What are the four basic economic questions? How are they answered in a capitalist economy?
- Describe the four basic assumptions required for a laissez-faire capitalist economy.
- Why is the American economy called a mixed economy?
- How does capitalism differ from socialism and communism?

计划经济

command economy an economic system in which the government decides *what* goods and services will be produced, *how* they will be produced, *for whom* available goods and services will be produced, and *who* owns and controls the major factors of production

衡量经济表现

1-4 Measuring Economic Performance

Learning Objective

1-4 Identify the ways to measure economic performance.

Consider for just a moment the following questions:

- Are U.S. workers as productive as workers in other countries?
- Is the gross domestic product for the United States increasing or decreasing?
- How does inflation affect the prices that consumers pay for products and services?

Information needed to answer these questions is easily obtainable from many sources. More important, the answers to these and other questions can be used to gauge the economic health of the nation.

生产力在全球市场中的重要性

1-4a The Importance of Productivity in the Global Marketplace

One way to measure a nation's economic performance is to assess its productivity. While there are other definitions of productivity, for our purposes, **productivity** is the average level of output per worker per hour. An increase in productivity results in economic growth because a larger number of goods and services are produced by a given labor force. To see how productivity affects you and the economy, consider the following three questions:

Question: *How does an increase in productivity affect the economy?*

Answer: Because of increased productivity, it takes fewer workers to produce more goods and services. As a result, employers can reduce costs, earn more profits, and may sell their products or services for less. Finally, productivity growth helps American business to compete more effectively with other nations in a global, competitive world.

Question: *Is an increase in productivity always good?*

Answer: Fewer workers producing more goods and services can lead to lower salary expenses for employers and higher unemployment rates for workers. In this case, increased productivity is good for employers but not good for unemployed workers.

生产力 / 生产率
productivity the average level of output per worker per hour

How do you improve productivity? Most experts agree the most important factors needed to improve worker productivity are workers who feel appreciated and valued for the contributions they make to the organization, and being part of an inclusive team. In fact, sharing ideas and different opinions and being part of "the team" are often the foundation for improving a company's productivity.

Question: *How does a nation improve productivity?*

Answer: Reducing costs and enabling employees to work more efficiently are at the core of all attempts to improve productivity. Increased productivity is one of the key factors that account for an increase in a nation's gross domestic product.

国内生产总值

1-4b The Nation's Gross Domestic Product

In addition to productivity, a measure called *gross domestic product* can be used to measure the economic well-being of a nation. **Gross domestic product (GDP)** is the total dollar value of all goods and services produced by all people within the boundaries of a country during a specified time period—usually a one-year period. For example, the values of automobiles produced by employees in an American-owned General Motors plant and a Japanese-owned Toyota plant *in the United States* are both included in the GDP for the United States. The U.S. GDP was $20.9 trillion in 2020.[8] (*Note:* At the time of publication, 2020 was the last year for which statistics were available.)

The GDP figure facilitates comparisons between the United States and other countries because it is the standard used in international guidelines for economic accounting. It is also possible to compare the GDP for one nation over several different time periods. This comparison—often called the GDP growth rate—allows observers to determine the extent to which a nation is experiencing economic growth on an annual or quarterly basis. For example, government economic experts project the U.S. GDP will grow approximately 2 percent each year from 2019 to 2029.[9]

To make accurate comparisons of the GDP for different years, we must adjust the dollar amounts for inflation. **Inflation** is a general rise in the level of prices. (The opposite of inflation is deflation.) **Deflation** is a general decrease in the level of prices. By using inflation-adjusted figures, we are able to measure the *real* GDP for a nation. In effect, it is now possible to compare the goods and services produced by a nation in constant dollars—dollars that will purchase the same amount of goods and services. Figure 1-6 depicts the GDP of the United States in current dollars

Figure 1-6 GDP in Current Dollars and in Inflation-Adjusted Dollars

The change in GDP and real GDP for the United States from one year to another year can be used to measure economic growth.

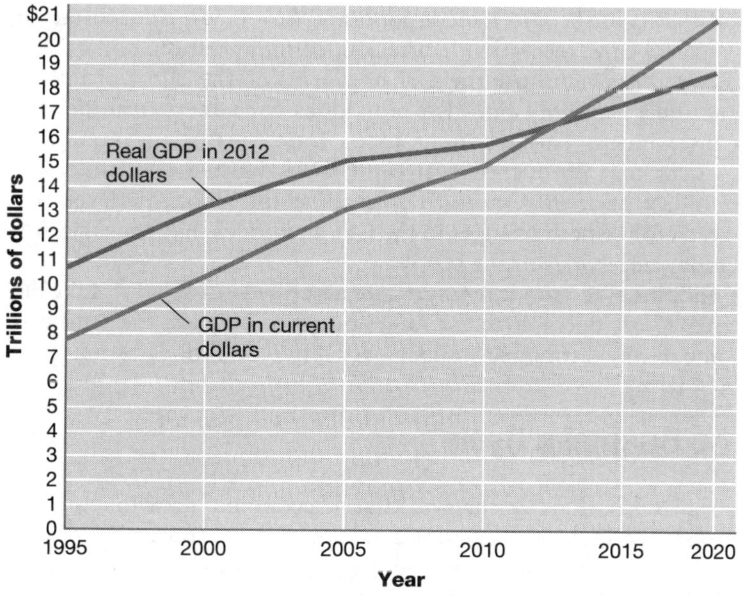

Source: U.S. Bureau of Economic Analysis website at www.bea.gov (accessed January 28, 2021).

国内生产总值
gross domestic product (GDP) the total dollar value of all goods and services produced by all people within the boundaries of a country during a specified time period—usually a one-year period

通货膨胀
inflation a general rise in the level of prices

通货紧缩
deflation a general decrease in the level of prices

Table 1-1 Common Measures Used to Evaluate a Nation's Economic Health

Economic Measure	Description
1. Balance of trade	The difference between the value of a nation's exports and a nation's imports over a specific period of time.
2. Consumer confidence index	A measure of how optimistic or pessimistic consumers are about the nation's economy. This measure is usually reported on a monthly basis.
3. Corporate profits	The total amount of profits made by corporations over selected time periods.
4. Inflation rate	An economic statistic that tracks the increase in prices of goods and services over a period of time. This measure is usually reported monthly and calculated on an annual basis.
5. National income	The total income earned by various components of the economy, including employees, interest and rental income, profits from businesses, and other types of income.
6. New housing starts	The total number of new homes started during a specific time period.
7. Prime interest rate	The lowest interest rate that banks charge their most credit-worthy customers.

and the real GDP in inflation-adjusted dollars. Note that between 1995 and 2020, America's real GDP grew from almost $10.7 trillion to $18.8 trillion.[10]

衡量一国经济的其他重要经济指标

1-4c Other Important Economic Indicators That Measure a Nation's Economy

In addition to productivity, GDP, and real GDP, other economic measures exist that can be used to evaluate a nation's economy. One very important statistic is the unemployment rate. The **unemployment rate** is the percentage of a nation's labor force unemployed at any time. Although the unemployment rate for the United States is typically about 4 to 6 percent, it peaked during the COVID-19 pandemic when the unemployment rate reached almost 15 percent when non-essential businesses were closed in many states. By the end of 2020, the unemployment rate had dropped to just over 6 percent. This is an important statistic—especially if you are unemployed.

The **consumer price index (CPI)** is a monthly index that measures the changes in prices of a fixed basket of goods purchased by a typical consumer in an urban area. Goods listed in the CPI include food and beverages, transportation, housing, clothing, medical care, recreation, education, communication, and other goods and services. Economists often use the CPI to determine the effect of inflation on not only the nation's economy but also individual consumers. Another index is the producer price index. The **producer price index (PPI)** is a monthly index that measures prices that producers receive for their finished goods. Because changes in the PPI reflect price increases or decreases at the wholesale level, the PPI is an accurate predictor of both changes in the CPI and prices that consumers will pay for many everyday necessities in the future.

Some additional economic measures are described in Table 1-1. Like the measures for GDP, real GDP, unemployment rate, and price indexes, these measures can be used to compare one economic statistic over different periods of time.

✓ Concept Check

- How does an increase in productivity affect business?
- What is the difference between the gross domestic product and the real gross domestic product? Why are these economic measures significant?
- How does inflation affect the prices you pay for goods and services?
- How is the producer price index related to the consumer price index?

失业率
unemployment rate the percentage of a nation's labor force unemployed at any time

消费者价格指数
consumer price index (CPI) a monthly index that measures the changes in prices of a fixed basket of goods purchased by a typical consumer in an urban area

生产者价格指数
producer price index (PPI) a monthly index that measures prices that producers receive for their finished goods

经济周期

1-5 The Business Cycle

Learning Objective

1-5 Examine the different phases in the typical business cycle.

All industrialized nations of the world seek economic growth, full employment, and price stability. However, a nation's economy fluctuates rather than grows at a steady pace every year. In fact, if you were to graph the economic growth rate for a country like the United States over a long period of time, it would resemble a roller-coaster ride with peaks (high points) and troughs (low points). These fluctuations

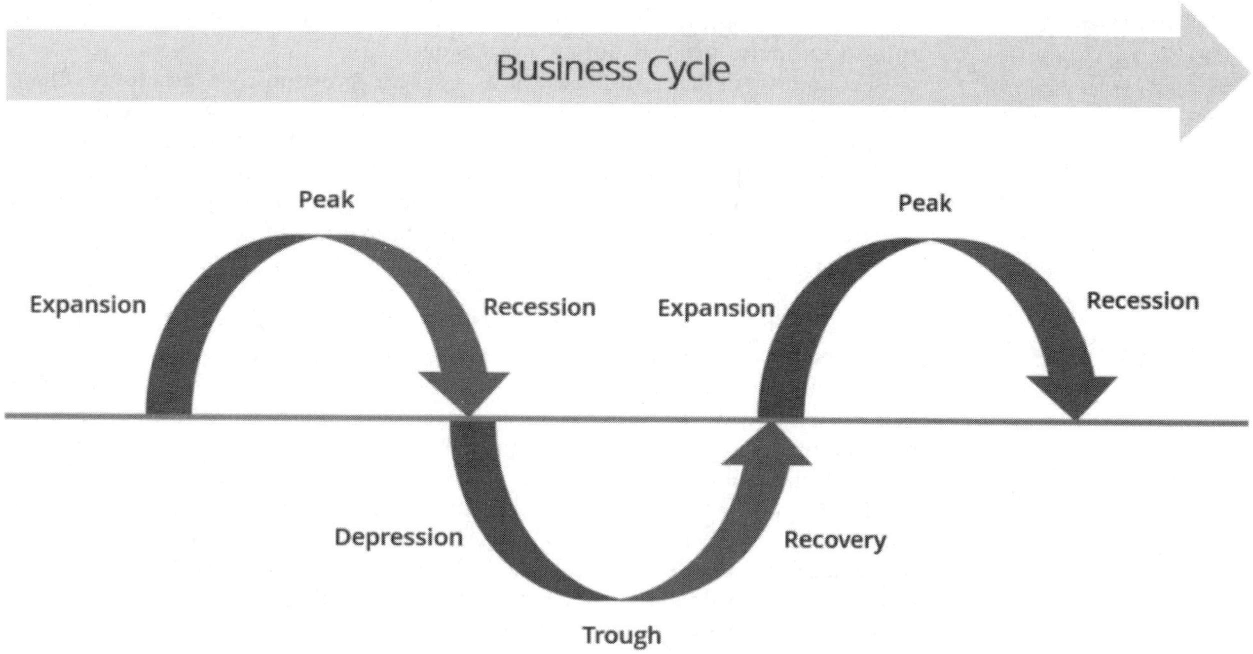

are generally referred to as the **business cycle**, that is, the recurrence of periods of growth and recession in a nation's economic activity.

At the time of publication, the U.S. economy is showing signs of improvement after the effects of a global pandemic. Key economic indicators including the gross domestic product, the stock market, and consumer spending have improved, and the unemployment rate has decreased. And yet, there are concerns about the size of the national debt—a topic described later in this section. There are also concerns about the effect of possible changes by the Biden administration and how those changes could affect individuals, businesses, and the nation's economy. In addition, many experts worry about the economies of foreign nations around the globe and social unrest throughout the world.

The changes that result from either economic growth or an economic downturn affect the demand for products and services that consumers are willing to buy and, as a result, the amount of products and services produced by business firms. Generally, the business cycle consists of four phases: the peak (sometimes called prosperity), recession, the trough, and recovery (sometimes called expansion).

During the *peak period* (prosperity), the economy is at its highest point and unemployment is low. Total income is relatively high. As long as the economic outlook remains prosperous, consumers are willing to buy products and services. In fact, businesses often expand and offer new products and services during the peak period to take advantage of consumers' increased buying power.

Generally, economists define a **recession** as two or more consecutive three-month periods of decline in a country's GDP. Although the recession of 2020 lasted only a few months before the economy began to recover, most recessions are longer. For example, the Great Recession of 2008 lasted 18 months. During a recession, it is typical for the unemployment rate to increase and consumer buying power to

经济周期
business cycle the recurrence of periods of growth and recession in a nation's economic activity

经济衰退
recession two or more consecutive three-month periods of decline in a country's GDP

decline. As buying power declines, consumers tend to purchase essential items and are reluctant to purchase frivolous or non-essential items. In response to a recession, many businesses focus on producing the products and services that provide the most value to their customers. Companies and government at all levels often postpone or go slow on major projects during a recession.

Economists define a **depression** as a severe recession that lasts longer than a typical recession and has a larger decline in business activity when compared to a recession. A depression is characterized by extremely high unemployment rates, low wages, reduced purchasing power, lack of confidence in the economy, a decline in stock values, and a general decrease in business activity. While the United States has experienced many recessions, there have only been a few economic depressions. The worst depression, often called "the Great Depression," began in 1929 lasted over ten years.

The third phase of the business cycle is the *trough*. The trough of a recession or depression is the turning point when a nation's production and employment bottom out and reach their lowest levels. Some experts believe that effective use of monetary and fiscal policies can speed up recovery and reduce the amount of time the economy is in recession. **Monetary policies** are the Federal Reserve's actions to promote maximum employment, stabilize prices, and increase or decrease interest rates. Through **fiscal policy**, the government can influence the amount of savings and expenditures by altering the tax structure and changing the levels of government spending. For example, during the 2020 pandemic crisis both the Federal Reserve's monetary policies (lower interest rates) and the government's fiscal policies (stimulus packages) were used to stabilize the economy.

One of the concerns about the government's recent stimulus programs is the national debt. Although the federal government collects almost $4 trillion in annual revenues, the government usually spends more than it receives, resulting in a **federal deficit**. For example, the government had a federal deficit for each year between 2002 and 2020. The total of all federal deficits is called the **national debt**. Today, the U.S. national debt is over $27 trillion or approximately $83,000 for every man, woman, and child in the United States.[11]

Recovery (or *expansion*) is the movement of the economy from the trough, when a nation's production and employment bottom out and reach their lowest levels, to the next peak in a business cycle. For example, the recession that began in December 2008 lasted 18 months while the recovery that followed the 2008 recession lasted 128 months until February 2020.[12] During the recovery stage of a business cycle, high unemployment rates decline, income increases, and both the ability and the willingness to buy rise for consumers, businesses, and governments.

> **✓ Concept Check**
>
> - What are the four phases in the typical business cycle?
> - At the time you are studying the material in this chapter, which phase of the business cycle do you think the U.S. economy is in? Justify your answer.
> - How can the Federal Reserve and government use monetary policy and fiscal policy to reduce the effects of an economic crisis?

经济萧条
depression a severe recession that lasts longer than a typical recession and has a larger decline in business activity when compared to a recession

货币政策
monetary policies Federal Reserve's actions to promote maximum employment, stabilize prices, and increase or decrease interest rates.

财政政策
fiscal policy government influence on the amount of savings and expenditures; accomplished by altering the tax structure and by changing the levels of government spending

联邦赤字
federal deficit a shortfall created when the federal government spends more in a fiscal year than it receives

国债
national debt the total of all federal deficits

竞争的类型

1-6 Types of Competition

> **Learning Objective**
>
> **1-6** Outline the four types of competition.

Our capitalist system ensures that individuals and businesses make the decisions about what to produce, how to produce it, and what price to charge for the product. Mattel, Inc., for example, can introduce new versions of its famous Barbie doll, license the Barbie name, change the doll's price and method of distribution, and attempt to produce and market Barbie in other countries or over the internet at www.mattel.com. Our system also allows customers the right to choose between Mattel's products and those produced by competitors.

As a consumer, you get to choose which products or services you want to buy. Competition like that between Mattel and other toy manufacturers is a necessary and extremely important by-product of capitalism. Business **competition** is essentially a rivalry among businesses for sales to potential customers. In a capitalistic economy, competition also ensures that a firm will survive only if it serves its customers well by providing products and services that meet needs. Economists recognize

竞争
competition rivalry among businesses for sales to potential customers

four different degrees of competition ranging from ideal, complete competition to no competition at all. These are perfect competition, monopolistic competition, oligopoly, and monopoly. For a quick overview of the different types of competition, including numbers of firms and examples for each type, look at Table 1-2.

完全竞争

1-6a Perfect Competition

Perfect (or **pure) competition** is the market situation in which there are many buyers and sellers of a product, and no single buyer or seller is powerful enough to affect the price of that product. As pointed out in Table 1-2, real-world examples of perfect competition are corn, wheat, peanuts, and many agricultural products. For perfect competition to exist, there are five very important concepts.

- We are discussing the market for a single product, such as bushels of wheat.
- There are no restrictions on firms entering the industry.
- All sellers offer essentially the same product for sale.
- All buyers and sellers know everything there is to know about the market (including, in our example, the prices that all sellers are asking for their wheat).
- The overall market is not affected by the actions of any one buyer or seller.

When perfect competition exists, every seller should ask the same price that every other seller is asking. Why? Because if one seller wanted 50 cents more for their products than all the others, that seller would not be able to sell a single product. Buyers could—and would—do better by purchasing the same products from the competition. On the other hand, a firm willing to sell below the going price would sell all its products quickly. However, that seller would lose sales revenue (and profit) because buyers are willing to pay more.

In perfect competition, the price of each product is determined by the actions of all buyers and all sellers together through the forces of supply and demand.

The Basics of Supply and Demand The **supply** of a particular product is the quantity of the product that producers are willing to sell at each of various prices. Producers are rational people, so we would expect them to offer more of a product for sale at higher prices and to offer less of the product at lower prices, as illustrated by the supply curve in Figure 1-7.

The **demand** for a particular product is the quantity that buyers are willing to purchase at each of various prices. Buyers, too, are usually rational, so we would expect them—as a group—to buy more of a product when its price is low and to buy less of the product when its price is high, as depicted by the demand curve in Figure 1-7.

The Equilibrium, or Market, Price There is always one certain price at which the demand for a product is equal to the quantity of that product produced. Suppose

Table 1-2 Four Different Types of Competition

The number of firms determines the degree of competition within an industry.

Type of Competition	Number of Business Firms or Suppliers	Real-World Examples
1. Perfect	Many	Corn, wheat, peanuts, many agricultural products
2. Monopolistic	Many	Clothing, shoes
3. Oligopoly	Few	Automobiles, airlines
4. Monopoly	One	Many local public utilities, software protected by copyright

完全竞争
perfect (or **pure) competition** the market situation in which there are many buyers and sellers of a product, and no single buyer or seller is powerful enough to affect the price of that product

供给
supply the quantity of a product that producers are willing to sell at each of various prices

需求
demand the quantity of a product that buyers are willing to purchase at each of various prices

Figure 1-7 Supply Curve and Demand Curve

The interaction of a supply curve and a demand curve is called the equilibrium or market price. This interaction indicates a single price and quantity at which suppliers will sell products and buyers will purchase them.

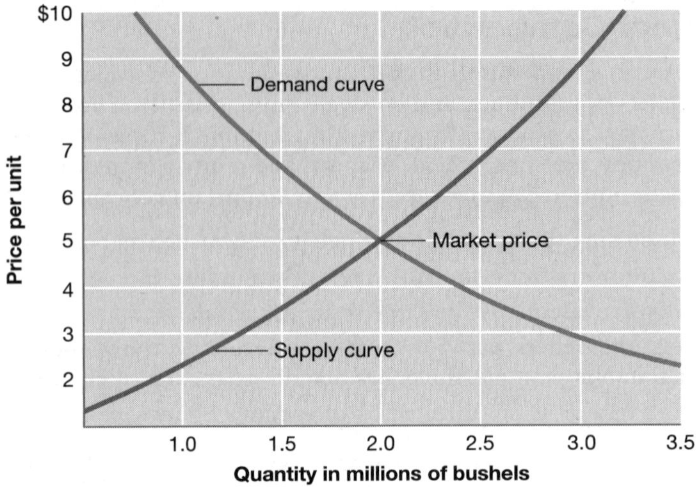

that producers are willing to *supply* two million bushels of wheat at a price of $5 per bushel and that buyers are willing to *purchase* two million bushels at a price of $5 per bushel. As shown in Figure 1-7, supply and demand are in balance, or in equilibrium, at the price of $5. Economists call this price the *market price*. The **market price** of any product is the price at which the quantity demanded is exactly equal to the quantity supplied.

In theory and in the real world, market prices are affected by anything that affects supply and demand. The *demand* for wheat, for example, might change if researchers suddenly discovered that it offered a previously unknown health benefit. Then buyers would demand more wheat at every price. Or the *supply* of wheat might change if new technology permitted the production of greater quantities of wheat from the same amount of acreage. Other changes that can affect the market price of wheat are shifts in buyer tastes, the development of new products, fluctuations in income owing to inflation or recession, or even changes in the weather that affect the production of wheat.

Perfect competition is quite rare in today's world. Many real markets, however, are examples of monopolistic competition.

垄断竞争

1-6b Monopolistic Competition

Monopolistic competition is a market situation in which there are many buyers along with a relatively large number of sellers. Real-world examples of products sold in a monopolistically competitive market include clothing, shoes, soaps, furniture, and many consumer items. The various products available in this type of competitive market are similar in nature, and they are all intended to satisfy the same basic need. However, each seller attempts to make its product different from the others by providing unique product features, an attention-getting brand name, unique packaging, or services such as free delivery or a lifetime warranty.

Product differentiation is the process of developing and promoting differences between a company's products and all competitive products. It is a fact of life for the producers of many consumer goods, from soaps to clothing to furniture to shoes. A furniture manufacturer such as Bush Industries sees what looks like a mob of competitors, all trying to chip away at its share of the ready-to-assemble furniture

市场价格
market price the price at which the quantity demanded is exactly equal to the quantity supplied

垄断竞争
monopolistic competition a market situation in which there are many buyers along with a relatively large number of sellers who differentiate their products from the products of competitors

产品差异化
product differentiation the process of developing and promoting differences between a company's products and all competitive products

How does competition affect a retailer like Macy's? For Macy's, competition is a way of life. Executives know they must compete with Dillard's, Target, Walmart, Amazon, and other retailers—all businesses that sell clothing and many other products. Each retailer uses product differentiation to differentiate its merchandise from competitors on the basis of price, quality, brand names, customer service, and other factors that can entice a customer to shop at one store instead of a competitor.

market. By differentiating each of its products from all similar products produced by competitors, Bush Industries obtains some limited control over the market price of its product.

寡头垄断

1-6c Oligopoly

An **oligopoly** is a market (or industry) situation in which there are few sellers. Generally, these sellers are quite large, and sizable investments are required to enter into their market. Examples of oligopolies are the automobile, airline, car rental, cereal, and farm implement industries.

Because there are few sellers in an oligopoly, the market actions of each seller can have a strong effect on competitors' sales and prices. For instance, when General Motors began offering cash incentives to encourage consumers to purchase new Chevrolet and GMC trucks at the beginning of 2021, Ford, Nissan, and Toyota began offering similar incentives and for the same reasons—to attract new-car buyers and to retain their market share. In the absence of much price competition, product differentiation becomes the major competitive weapon; this is very evident in the advertising of the major automobile manufacturers.

垄断

1-6d Monopoly

A **monopoly** is a market (or industry) with only one seller, and customers can only buy the product or service from that seller. In a monopoly, there is no close substitute for the product or service. Because only one business is the seller of a product or service, it would seem that it has complete control over price. However, no business can set its price at some astronomical amount just because there is no competition; the business would soon find that it has no customers or sales revenue either. Instead, the business in a monopoly position must consider the demand for its product and set the price at the most profitable level.

寡头垄断
oligopoly a market (or industry) in which there are few sellers

垄断
monopoly a market (or industry) with only one seller, and customers can only buy the product or service from that seller

Classic examples of monopolies in the United States are public utilities, including companies that provide local gas, water, sewer services, or electricity. Each utility firm operates in a *natural monopoly*, an industry that requires huge start-up costs that act as a deterrent for potential competitors. Natural monopolies are permitted to exist, but they operate under the scrutiny and control of various state and federal agencies. Although many public utilities are still classified as natural monopolies, there is increased competition in many areas of the country. For example, consumers now have a choice when selecting a company that provides electrical service to both homes and businesses in many areas of the country.

A legal monopoly—sometimes referred to as a *limited monopoly* or *statutory monopoly*—is created when a government entity issues a license, franchise, copyright, patent, or trademark. Because Microsoft owns the trademarks on its popular logos, it can control how both trademarks and logos are used by other businesses or individuals. Except for natural monopolies and legal monopolies, federal antitrust laws discourage or prohibit both monopolies and attempts to form monopolies in order to ensure that competitive markets exist and customers have a choice for products or services they need or want to purchase.

✓ Concept Check

- Is competition good for business? Is it good for consumers?
- Explain how the equilibrium or market price of a product is determined.
- Compare the four forms of competition.

当代的美国商业

1-7 American Business Today

Learning Objective

1-7 Summarize the development of American business and the challenges that businesses and society will encounter in the future.

Although our economic system is far from perfect, it provides Americans with a high standard of living compared with people in other countries throughout the world. **Standard of living** is a loose, subjective measure of how well off an individual or a society is, mainly in terms of want satisfaction through goods and services. Also, our economic system offers solutions to many of the problems that plague society and provides opportunities for people who are willing to work and to continue learning.

To understand the current business environment and the challenges ahead, it helps understand how business developed.

早期的商业发展

1-7a Early Business Development

Our American business system has its roots in the knowledge, skills, and values that the earliest settlers brought to this country. The first settlers in the United States were concerned mainly with providing themselves with basic necessities—food, clothing, and shelter. Almost all families lived on farms, and the entire family worked at the business of surviving. They used their surplus of agricultural products for trading, mainly by barter, among themselves and with the English trading ships that called at the colonies. As this trade increased, small businesses began to appear. Some settlers were able to use their skills and their excess time to work under the domestic system of production. The **domestic system** was a method of manufacturing in which an entrepreneur distributed raw materials to various homes, where families would process them into finished goods. The entrepreneur then offered the goods for sale.

Then, in 1793, a young English apprentice mechanic named Samuel Slater opened a textile mill in Pawtucket, Rhode Island, to spin raw cotton into thread. Slater's textile mill was America's first use of the **factory system** of manufacturing, in which all the materials, machinery, and workers required to manufacture a product are assembled in one place. The Industrial Revolution in America was born.

A manufacturing technique called *specialization* was used to improve productivity. **Specialization** is the separation of a manufacturing process into distinct tasks and the assignment of different tasks to different individuals.

Entrepreneurs continued to invent new machinery during the 1800s. Often, historians call this time period the golden age of invention and innovation. At the same time, new means of transportation greatly expanded the domestic markets for American products. Certainly, many basic characteristics of our modern business system took form during this time period.

生活水平
standard of living a loose, subjective measure of how well off an individual or a society is, mainly in terms of want satisfaction through goods and services

家庭生产制度
domestic system a method of manufacturing in which an entrepreneur distributed raw materials to various homes, where families would process them into finished goods to be offered for sale by the entrepreneur

工厂制度
factory system a system of manufacturing in which all the materials, machinery, and workers required to manufacture a product are assembled in one place

专业化
specialization the separation of a manufacturing process into distinct tasks and the assignment of different tasks to different individuals

20 世纪的商业发展

1-7b Business Development in the 1900s

Industrial growth and prosperity continued well into the 20th century. Henry Ford's moving automotive assembly line, which brought the work to the worker, refined the concept of specialization and helped spur on the mass production of consumer goods. Fundamental changes occurred in business ownership and management as well. No longer were the largest businesses owned by one individual; instead, more companies were owned by stockholders who were willing to invest in—but not to operate—a business.

To understand the major events that shaped the United States during the 20th century, it helps to remember that the economy was compared to a roller-coaster ride earlier in this chapter—periods of economic growth followed by periods of economic slowdown. The following are major events that shaped the nation's economy during the period from 1910 to 2000:

- The 1929 stock market crash and the Great Depression
- Federal government involvement in business in order to stimulate the economy, reduce unemployment, and ease the problems during the Great Depression
- World War I, World War II, the Korean War, and the Vietnam War
- Rapid economic growth and higher standard of living during the 1950s and 1960s
- The social responsibility movement during the 1960s
- A shortage of crude oil and higher prices for most goods in the mid-1970s
- High inflation, high interest rates, and reduced business profits during the last part of the 1970s and early 1980s
- Sustained economic growth in the 1990s

Unfortunately, by the last part of the 1990s, an increasing number of business failures, higher interest rates, and concerns about the financial markets and the economy were signs that larger economic problems were on the way.

Think for a moment what Henry Ford would think about today's automated factories. It's fair to assume he would be amazed at how manufacturing has developed in just over 100 years. While today's factories are definitely more advanced, don't underestimate the significance of Ford's assembly line back in 1913. Simply put, it not only changed the way automobiles like the one in this photo were manufactured, but it also led to changes in the way just about everything else was manufactured.

新世纪：2000 年及以后

1-7c A New Century: 2000 and Beyond

According to many economic experts, the first part of the 21st century might be characterized as the best of times and the worst of times rolled into one package. On the plus side, technology became available at an affordable price. Both individuals and businesses could now access information with the click of a button. They also could buy and sell merchandise online as e-commerce became a new type of retailing.

In addition to information technology, the growth of service businesses also changed the way American firms do business in the 21st century. Because service businesses employ over 80 percent of the nation's workforce, we now have a service economy.[13] A **service economy** is an economy in which more effort is devoted to the production of services than to the production of goods. Typical service businesses include restaurants, dry cleaners, real estate, movie theaters, repair companies, and other services.

On the negative side, it is hard to watch television, surf the Web, listen to the radio, or read the newspaper without hearing news about the economy, social and political unrest in the world, and lingering health and economic problems caused by the COVID-19 pandemic. Because many economic indicators suggest that either current or future problems could affect the nation's economy, there is still a certain amount of pessimism surrounding the nation's economy and the global economy. In addition, there are other concerns including social unrest; political uncertainty on the national, state, and local levels; global terrorism; and the threat of wars around the globe.

当前的商业环境

1-7d The Current Business Environment

Before reading on, answer the following question:

In today's competitive business world, which of the following environments affects business?

a. The competitive environment
b. The global environment
c. The technological environment
d. The economic environment
e. All of the above

Correct Answer: e. All the environments listed in the above question affect business today.

The Competitive Environment As noted earlier in this chapter, competition is a basic component of capitalism. Every day, business owners must figure out what makes their businesses successful and how the goods and services they provide are different from the competition. Often, the answer is contained in the basic definition of business provided on page 9. Just for a moment, review the definition:

> *Business is the organized effort of individuals to produce and sell, for a profit, the goods and services that satisfy society's needs.*

In the definition of business, note the phrase *satisfy society's needs*. These three words say a lot about how well a successful firm competes with competitors. If you meet customer needs, then you have a better chance at success.

服务经济
service economy an economy in which more effort is devoted to the production of services than to the production of goods

The Global Environment Related to the competitive environment is the global environment. Not only do American businesses have to compete with other American businesses, but they also must compete with businesses from all over the globe.

Technology, technology, and more technology!
What would happen if you didn't have your cell phone or if you couldn't use a computer for the next 24 hours? For many people, it would be catastrophic. For businesses, it would be just as bad. Many businesses rely on technology to operate. Without technology to process customer payments, track inventory, maintain accounting records, and other critical business activities, it would be impossible to function. For many businesses, it could mean they might have to "close the doors" until their technology was restored.

Firms in other countries including China, Japan, India, Germany, Vietnam, and most of the remaining European and Asian countries around the world also compete with U.S. firms. There was once a time when the label "Made in the United States" gave U.S. businesses an inside edge both at home and in the global marketplace. Today, because business firms in other countries manufacture and sell goods, the global marketplace has never been more competitive.

While many foreign firms are attempting to sell goods and services to U.S. customers, U.S. firms are also increasing both sales and profits by selling goods and services to customers in other countries. In fact, there are many "potential" customers in developing nations that will buy goods and services manufactured by U.S. firms. For example, Procter & Gamble sells laundry detergent, soap, health and grooming products, and baby products in Asia, Europe, India, the Middle East, Africa, Latin America, and North America. And Procter & Gamble is not alone. Unilever, DuPont, Johnson & Johnson, General Motors, and many more U.S. companies are also selling goods and services to customers in countries all over the globe.

The Technological Environment The technological environment for U.S. businesses has never been more challenging. Changes in communication with customers, manufacturing equipment, and distribution of products are all examples of how technology has changed everyday business practices. For example, many businesses are now using social media to provide customers with information about products and services. For our purposes **social media** is defined as online interaction that allows people and businesses to communicate and share ideas, personal information, and information about products or services. Because of rapid developments in social media and the increased importance of technology and information, businesses will need to spend additional money to keep abreast of an ever-changing technological environment and even more money to train employees to use the new technology.

New and creative ways to use technology are also changing the way that products are now manufactured and distributed to customers. Today, many manufacturers are using sophisticated automated equipment to improve employee productivity,

社交媒体
social media the online interaction that allows people and businesses to communicate and share ideas, personal information, and information about products or services

Technology and Innovation

技术与创新：当今最大的技术趋势

Today's Biggest Tech Trends

The technological environment is ever-changing, and it's critical for businesses to keep pace or risk being left behind. The biggest trends in today's tech world include artificial intelligence, blockchain technology, and extended reality.

Artificial intelligence (AI) involves computers performing tasks that traditionally require human intelligence. Since programming an AI-based system is cost-prohibitive for most organizations, many professionals will interact with the technology through available platforms, such as e-mail marketing software. Additionally, automation in manufacturing and supply chains is greatly improving with the use of AI and robotics. With the number of AI providers growing, adoption of the technology will continue to increase for years to come.

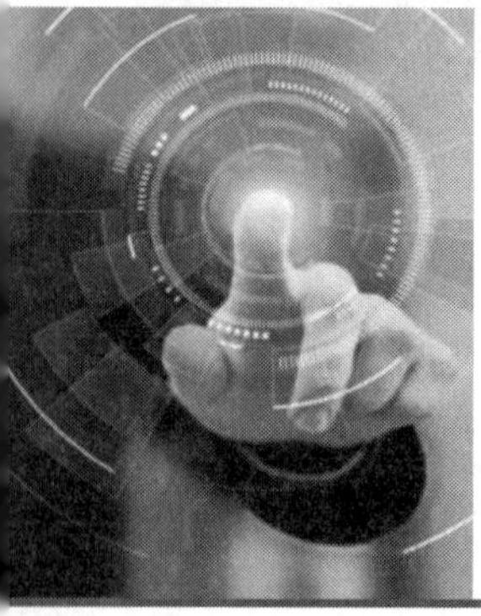

Blockchain, a secure digital ledger, has many applications, from supply chain management to cryptocurrency. The hype around blockchain has been around for years, but now there is an emerging shared belief that blockchain technology will become a top strategic priority for many businesses and organizations. Popular uses for the technology include recording transactions, data validation, data access, data sharing, and identity protection.

Extended reality (XR) encompasses technologies that create an immersive or all-in experience, namely virtual reality (VR) and augmented reality (AR). Many consumers have interacted with VR and AR in the form of video games and smartphone features such as VR headsets or social media apps, but XR has even more unlocked potential. Businesses that get a better handle on XR will discover new methods of customer engagement.

AI, blockchain, and XR are just a few of the technologies shaking up the world of business. Keeping up with key trends and investing in new technologies that add value to the business will help organizations stay ahead of the curve. Knowledge and experience about emerging technologies will also help workers and job seekers advance their careers.

Sources: Based on information in Deloitte, "C-Suite Briefing: 5 Blockchain Trends for 2020," March 2020; Bernard Marr, "The 7 Biggest Technology Trends in 2020 Everyone Must Get Ready for Now," *Forbes*, September 30, 2019; Anis Uzzaman, "Top Business and Technology Trends in 2021," *Inc.*, December 15, 2020.

increase product quality, and lower expenses. Technology has also changed the way customers purchase products and the way those products are delivered. For example, if you purchase merchandise on Amazon's e-commerce website, you don't necessarily wait days to receive your merchandise. Depending on your location and if the merchandise is available, your purchase could be delivered the same day. While this type of technology-driven delivery system is expensive, it is one reason why Amazon has grown to be one of the largest retailers in the world.

The Economic Environment The economic environment must always be considered when making business decisions. This fact is especially important when the nation's economy takes a nosedive or an individual firm's sales revenues and profits are declining. Consider what happened when non-essential businesses were ordered to close in many states because of the COVID-19 pandemic. Both small and large non-essential businesses had no sales revenues and had to use cash reserves to pay expenses. In many cases employees were placed on leave or lost their jobs. As businesses began to reopen, customers began to buy products and services, and businesses brought back furloughed employees or hired new employees.

可持续性
sustainability the ability to create and maintain conditions under which present and future generations can exist in productive harmony, and permit fulfilling the social, economic, and other requirements of future and present generations

In addition to economic pressures, today's socially responsible managers and business owners must be concerned about the concept of sustainability. According to the U.S. Environmental Protection Agency, **sustainability** is the ability to create and maintain conditions under which present and future generations can exist in productive harmony, and permit fulfilling the social, economic, and other requirements of future and present generations.[14] Although the word *green* used to mean a color in a box of crayons, today green means a new way of doing business. As a result, a combination of forces, including economic factors, growth in population, increased energy use, and concerns for the environment, is changing the way individuals live and businesses operate.

When you look back at the original question we asked at the beginning of this section, clearly, each different type of environment—competitive, global, technological, and economic—affects the way a business does *business*. As a result, there are always opportunities for improvement and challenges that must be considered.

未来面临的挑战

1-7e The Challenges Ahead

There it is—the American business system in brief.

When it works well, it provides a standard of living that few countries can match and many opportunities for personal advancement for those willing to work hard and continue to learn. However, like every other system devised by humans, it is not perfect. Our capitalist economic system may give us prosperity, but it also gave us the Great Depression of the 1930s, the economic problems of the 1970s and the early 1980s, and a volatile stock market, high unemployment, and business failures caused by the COVID-19 pandemic.

Obviously, the system can be improved. Certainly, there are plenty of people who are willing to tell us exactly what they think the American economy needs. However, these people often provide us only with conflicting opinions. Who is right and who is wrong? Even the experts cannot agree.

The experts do agree, however, that several key issues will challenge our economic system (and our nation) over the next decade. Some of the questions to be resolved include:

- How can we deal with social unrest, discrimination, and inequality in society?
- How can we create a more stable economy and create new, quality jobs for the unemployed?
- How can we reduce the number of low-income workers and increase the number of middle- and higher-income workers?
- How can we use research and technology to make American workers more productive and American firms more competitive in the global marketplace?
- How can we preserve the benefits of competition and small business in our American economic system?
- How do we reduce the national debt and stimulate business growth?
- How can we conserve natural resources and sustain our environment?
- How can we meet the needs of low-income families, single parents, older Americans, and the less fortunate who need healthcare and social programs to exist?

The answers to these questions are anything but simple. While there have been (and always will be) challenges for a nation like the United States, Americans have always been able to solve many of their problems through ingenuity and creativity. Now, as we continue the journey through the 21st century, we need that same ingenuity and creativity not only to solve our current problems but also to compete in the global marketplace and build a nation and economy for future generations.

The American business system is not perfect by any means, but it does work reasonably well. We discuss some of its problems in Chapter 2 as we examine the topics of social responsibility and business ethics.

✓ Concept Check

- How does your standard of living affect the products or services you buy?
- What is the difference between the domestic system and the factory system?
- Choose one of the environments that affect business or society and explain how it affects a small electronics manufacturer located in Portland, Oregon.
- What do you consider the most important challenge that will face people in the United States in the years ahead?

Summary　小 结

1-1 Discuss what you must do to be successful in today's business world.

When faced with the COVID-19 pandemic that raced through the world, small business owners, employees, managers, investors, and a large number of people began to ask the question: What effect will non-essential business closures and record high unemployment rates have on the economy? More specifically, many people asked, how does this affect me both now and in the future? Although this is a fair question, it is difficult to answer. Certainly, for a college student taking business courses or an employee just starting a career, the question is even more difficult to answer. And yet there are still opportunities out there for people who are willing to work hard, continue to learn, and possess the ability to adapt to change. By studying business, you can become a better employee or manager or you may decide to start your own business. You can also become a better consumer and investor.

1-2 Identify the potential risks and rewards of business.

Business is the organized effort of individuals to produce and sell, for a profit, the goods and services that satisfy society's needs. Four kinds of resources— material, human, financial, and informational—must be combined to start and operate a business. The three general types of businesses are service businesses, manufacturers, and marketing intermediaries. Today, marketing intermediaries sell goods and services in brick-and-mortar stores, online, or both. Profit is what remains after all business expenses are deducted from sales revenue. It is the payment that owners receive for assuming the risks of business—primarily the risks of not receiving payment and of losing whatever has been invested in the firm. Although many people believe that profit is literally the bottom line or most important goal for a business, the ultimate objective of a successful business is to satisfy the needs of its customers. In addition to profit, many corporations are careful to point out their efforts to sustain the planet, participate in the green ecological movement, and help people to live better lives.

1-3 Describe the two types of economic systems: capitalism and command economy.

Economics is the study of how wealth is created and distributed. An economic system must answer four questions: *What* goods and services will be produced? *How* will they be produced? *For whom* will they be produced? And *Who* owns and who controls the major factors of production? The factors of production are land and natural resources, labor, capital, and entrepreneurship. Capitalism (on which our economic system is based) is an economic system in which individuals own and operate the majority of businesses that provide goods and services. Capitalism stems from the theories of Adam Smith. Smith's pure laissez-faire capitalism is an economic system based on the assumptions described in Figure 1-4.

Our economic system today is a mixed economy and exhibits elements of both capitalism and socialism. In the circular flow that characterizes our business system (refer to Figure 1-5), households and businesses exchange resources, labor, and capital for goods and services, using money as the medium of exchange. In a similar manner, the government collects taxes from businesses and households and purchases products and resources with which to provide services.

In a command economy, government, rather than individuals, owns many of the factors of production and provides the answers to the three other economic questions. Socialist and communist economies are—at least in theory—command economies.

1-4 Identify the ways to measure economic performance.

One way to evaluate the performance of an economic system is to assess changes in productivity, which is the average level of output per worker per hour. Gross domestic product (GDP) can also be used to measure a nation's economic health and is the total dollar value of all goods and services produced by all people within the boundaries of a country during a one-year period. It is also possible to adjust GDP for inflation and thus to measure real GDP. Other economic indicators include a nation's balance of trade, consumer confidence index, consumer price index (CPI), corporate profits, inflation rate, national income, new housing starts, prime interest rate, producer price index (PPI), and unemployment rate.

1-5 Examine the different phases in the typical business cycle.

A nation's economy fluctuates rather than grows at a steady pace every year. These fluctuations are generally referred to as the business cycle. Generally, the business cycle consists of four states: the peak (sometimes called prosperity), recession, the trough, and recovery (sometimes called expansion). Some experts believe that effective use of monetary policy (the Federal Reserve's decisions to promote maximum employment, stabilize prices, and increase or decrease interest rates) and fiscal policy (the government's influence on the amount of savings and expenditures) can speed up recovery.

A federal deficit occurs when the government spends more than it receives in taxes and other revenues. At the time of publication, the national debt is over $27 trillion or approximately $83,000 for every man, woman, and child in the United States.

1-6 Outline the four types of competition.

Competition is essentially a rivalry among businesses for sales to potential customers. In a capitalist economy, competition works to ensure the efficient and effective operation of business. Competition also ensures that a firm will survive only if it serves its customers well by providing goods and services that meet their needs. Economists recognize four degrees of competition. Ranging from most to least competitive, the four degrees are perfect competition, monopolistic competition, oligopoly, and monopoly. The factors of supply and demand generally influence the price that customers pay producers for goods and services.

1-7 Summarize the development of American business and the challenges that businesses and society will encounter in the future.

To understand the major events that shaped the United States, it helps to remember that the economy was compared to a roller-coaster ride earlier in this chapter—periods of economic growth followed by periods of economic slowdown. Events and a changing business environment including the Great Depression, government involvement in business, wars, rapid economic growth, the social responsibility movement, a shortage of crude oil, high inflation, high interest rates, reduced business profits, increased use of technology, and social media all have shaped business and the economy.

Now more than ever before, the way a business operates is affected by the competitive environment, global environment, technological environment, and economic environment. As a result, business has a number of opportunities for improvement and challenges for the future.

Key Terms 关键术语

You should now be able to define and give an example relevant to each of the following terms:

free enterprise
cultural (or workplace) diversity
business
e-business
profit
stakeholders
economics
microeconomics
macroeconomics
economy
factors of production
entrepreneur
capitalism
invisible hand
market economy
mixed economy
consumer products
command economy
productivity
gross domestic product (GDP)
inflation
deflation
unemployment rate
consumer price index (CPI)
producer price index (PPI)
business cycle
recession
depression
monetary policies
fiscal policy
federal deficit
national debt
competition
perfect (or pure) competition
supply
demand
market price
monopolistic competition
product differentiation
oligopoly
monopoly
standard of living
domestic system
factory system
specialization
service economy
social media
sustainability

Discussion Questions 讨论题

1. What factors caused American business to develop into a mixed economic system rather than some other type of economic system?
2. Does an individual consumer really have a voice in answering the four basic economic questions described on page 14?
3. Is gross domestic product a reliable indicator of a nation's economic health? What might be a better indicator?
4. Discuss this statement: "Business competition encourages improved product quality and increased customer satisfaction."
5. Is government participation in our business system good or bad? What factors can be used to explain your position.
6. Choose one of the challenges listed on page 31 and describe possible ways in which business and society could help to solve or eliminate the problem in the future.

Case 1 案例 1：Zoom 成功的关键

The Keys to Zoom's Success

Zoom—a video conference technology company based in San Jose, California—not only broke into a highly competitive industry, but it also became an industry leader. Zoom's success can be attributed to good leadership, a growing market, a customer orientation, accessibility, and the ability to secure funding.

Eric Yuan is the CEO and founder of Zoom. He got the idea for the company when he was in college in the 1980s and regularly took a 10-hour train ride to visit his then-girlfriend. He knew there had to be an easier way to see her. At the time, video communication was a distant dream as widespread consumer internet use was still years away. After relocating from China to the United States in 1997, Yuan landed a software developer job at Webex, an online communications company, in the midst of the so-called dot-com boom. The dot-com era was marked by a period of rapid growth in internet use. While excessive investor speculation of internet firms caused a stock market bubble that would eventually burst, Webex remained strong. When Cisco acquired Webex in 2007 for $3.2 billion, Yuan became the vice president of engineering, overseeing more than 800 employees. Yuan, however, wasn't happy with the company's online service, which often cut in and out and lacked various modern features. His calls to update the platform were ignored, so he left in 2011 to build a cloud-based video-conferencing tool of the future that prioritized customers and their needs.

Zoom, founded in 2011, entered the video communications market at a time when consumer and business demand for video conference products was increasing. It was around the same time that Apple introduced FaceTime and Skype was acquired by Microsoft for $8.5 billion. Almost a decade later when the COVID-19 pandemic struck, the demand for Zoom's products accelerated as the need to communicate from a distance became more prevalent than ever.

Yuan decided that his company's vision would be "video is the new voice" and its goal would be to deliver happiness. It's this customer orientation that has contributed to Zoom's success. From Yuan's experience at his previous company, he knew consistent and quality video connections should be a priority. To add to that, Zoom offers 24/7 customer service, which Yuan would often take part in during Zoom's early years. Yuan would reach out to any individual who canceled their service. This focus on customer service is a large reason behind Zoom's high customer satisfaction ratings.

Another key element in Zoom's success is accessibility. When it launched, Zoom had several competitive advantages. For instance, its software identified the user's device, eliminating the need for multiple versions of the software. Additionally, it had high security protections in place that kept bugs out. But perhaps most important to the customer, Zoom was able to operate on slow internet connections. From the start, Zoom was easy to use, and this holds true today. Case in point, when someone is invited to a Zoom meeting, they need only to click a link to attend. Even if users choose to register for a basic account, it's free to host up to 100 participants with an unlimited number of meetings. Premium features are available on Pro, Business, and Enterprise accounts at competitive rates. This is known as a "freemium" pricing model. By offering free entry-level access, Zoom has opened up its platform to the masses and lowered barriers to product trial.

Many start-ups struggle to find financing. Initial funding for Zoom came from Webex executives who knew Yuan and believed in his ability to build a quality product. Though Zoom didn't see profits for many years, investors kept investing because of the platform's promising future. When Zoom made its initial public offering (IPO) on the Nasdaq stock market, it was already growing and profitable, a rarity for tech companies. With an IPO price of $36 per share, Zoom was valued at $9.2 billion. Now, the video communications company is valued at close to $100 billion.

Yuan's ability to identify a growing market and create a superior product that was easy to use led to Zoom's present-day success. The COVID-19 pandemic only accelerated Zoom's path to the front of the pack. As people worked from home, students attended school online, and friends gathered for virtual happy hours, Zoom emerged as the go-to service. Looking to the future, Zoom is focusing on new products and winning over large clients. Maintaining its customer orientation and continuing to innovate will better prepare Zoom for future growth opportunities and challenges.[15]

Questions

1. What entrepreneurial traits did Eric Yuan—the founder of Zoom—have that enabled him to turn an idea into a very successful company in a very competitive market?
2. One of the benchmarks of a successful business is satisfying the needs of its customers. How is Zoom meeting the needs of its customers?
3. One reason Zoom has been successful is that it is easy to use. What other factors have made Zoom a popular choice for video conferencing?

Building Skills for Career Success 为成功的职业生涯培养技能

1. Social Media Exercise

Today, many companies use Facebook, Twitter, Instagram, and other social media sites in addition to their corporate website. Think of three of your favorite car companies and conduct a quick search using a search engine like Google or Yahoo! Then answer the following:

1. Name the social networks for each company.
2. Compare each of their Facebook pages. How many "likes" does each company have? Are there multiple pages for the company? How much interaction (or engagement) is on each Facebook page?
3. What business goals do you think each company is trying to reach through their Facebook presence?

2. Building Team Skills

Over the past few years, employees have been expected to function as productive team members instead of working alone. People often believe that they can work effectively in teams, but many people find working with a group to be a challenge.

College classes that function as teams are more interesting and more fun to attend, and students generally learn more about the topics in the course. One way to begin creating a team is to learn something about each student in the class. This helps team members to feel comfortable with each other and fosters a sense of trust.

Assignment

1. Find a partner, preferably someone you do not know.
2. Each partner has two to three minutes to answer the following questions:
   a. What is your name, and where do you work?
   b. What interesting or unusual thing have you done in your life? (Do not talk about work or college; rather, focus on such things as hobbies, travel, family, and sports.)
   c. Why are you taking this course, and what do you expect to learn? (Satisfying a degree requirement is not an acceptable answer.)
3. Introduce your partner to the class. Use one to two minutes, depending on the size of the class.

3. Researching Different Careers

In this chapter, *entrepreneurship* is defined as the willingness to take risks and the knowledge and ability to use the other factors of production efficiently. An *entrepreneur* is a person who risks time, effort, and money to start and operate a business. Some people believe that these terms apply only to small businesses. However, employees with entrepreneurial attitudes are often viewed as more valuable and can advance more rapidly in large companies.

Assignment

1. Use the internet or go to the local library and research how large firms, especially large corporations, are rewarding employees who have entrepreneurial skills.
2. Find answers to the following questions:
   a. Why is an entrepreneurial attitude important in large corporations today?
   b. What makes an entrepreneurial employee different from other employees?
   c. How are these employees being rewarded, and are the rewards worth the effort?
3. Write a two-page report that summarizes your findings.

Chapter 2

Ethics and Social Responsibility in Business
商业伦理与社会责任

Why Should You Care?

Business ethics and social responsibility issues have become extremely relevant in today's business world. Business schools teach business ethics to prepare managers to be more responsible. Corporations are developing ethics and social responsibility programs to help meet these needs in the workplace.

Learning Objectives

Once you complete this chapter, you will be able to:

2-1 Define *business ethics.*

2-2 Identify the types of ethical concerns that arise in the business world.

2-3 Discuss the factors that affect the level of ethical behavior in organizations.

2-4 Explain how organizations can encourage ethical decision making in business.

2-5 Describe how our current views on the social responsibility of business have evolved.

2-6 List the responsibilities businesses have to the public, especially with regard to consumer rights and public health.

2-7 Analyze how present employment practices are being used to counteract past abuses.

2-8 Describe the major environmental issues and businesses' response to them.

2-9 Identify the steps a business must take to implement a program of social responsibility.

Inside Business 商业透视：美国普渡制药的营销策略加剧了阿片类药物危机

Marketing Tactics at Purdue Fueled the Opioid Crisis

The opioid crisis has killed more than 450,000 people in the United States since 1999 largely due to illegal and misleading marketing. Purdue Pharma LP, a privately held pharmaceutical company, reached an $8.34 billion settlement for its marketing and distribution of OxyContin, an addictive painkiller, after years of state and federal investigations. Purdue is not the only company implicated in the crisis. Manufacturer Johnson & Johnson and distributors McKesson, Cardinal Health, and AmerisourceBergen have also faced legal action.

Ethical misconduct at Purdue included illegal kickbacks, funding pain treatment groups, misrepresentations made to the Drug Enforcement Administration (DEA), and marketing messages that minimized the addictive nature of OxyContin. The drugmaker used marketing data to target physicians who were the highest opioid prescribers as well as physicians in states with lighter prescription regulations. After compiling detailed prescriber profiles, Purdue would attempt to influence the physicians' prescribing patterns. In two instances, Purdue paid doctors to influence them to write more opioid prescriptions. Additionally, the company made false claims about the safety of the product.

Purdue's unethical and illegal actions had a direct impact on society, fueling the opioid crisis and a culture of corruption throughout its supply chain. Purdue has since made changes in leadership, operations, governance, and oversight to keep the company in compliance with the law. Purdue's owners, the Sackler family, created an image of philanthropy and avoided being publicly tied to the opioid crisis. Now, many prominent institutions will no longer accept donations from the family. However, neither the Sackler family nor top Purdue executives will face prison time as a result of the settlement.[1]

Did you know?

Purdue Pharma's corporate values are integrity, courage, innovation, and collaboration.

Obviously, organizations want to be seen as responsible corporate citizens and recognize the need to harmonize their operations with environmental demands and other social concerns. However, as shown in the opening vignette, not all firms have adopted a mindset that includes social responsibility and ethics in their strategies, decisions, and activities. Some managers still regard such business programs as a poor investment, in which the cost is not worth the return. Other managers—indeed, most managers—view the cost of these programs as a necessary business expense, similar to wages or rent.

Most managers today are finding ways to balance an agenda of socially responsible activities with the drive to generate profits. This also happens to be a good way for organizations to demonstrate their values and to attract like-minded employees, customers, and shareholders. In a highly competitive global business environment, an increasing number of companies are seeking to set themselves apart by developing a reputation for ethical and socially responsible behavior.

We begin this chapter by defining *business ethics* and examining ethical issues. Next, we look at the standards of behavior in organizations and how ethical behavior can be encouraged. We then turn to the topic of social responsibility. We explore the evolution of the idea of social responsibility, compare and contrast two present-day models of social responsibility, and present arguments for and against increasing the social responsibility of business. We then explore business responsibilities toward the public. Next, we discuss how social responsibility in business has affected employment practices and environmental concerns. Finally, we consider the commitment and planning that go into a firm's program of social responsibility.

商业伦理的定义

2-1 Business Ethics Defined

Learning Objective

2-1 Define *business ethics.*

Ethics is the study of right and wrong and of the morality of the choices individuals make. An ethical decision or action is one that is "right" according to some standard of behavior. When there is strong consensus regarding a particular unethical action, society may demand laws to prohibit it. **Business ethics** is the application of moral standards to business situations. Recent court cases involving unethical behavior have helped make business ethics a matter of public concern. In one such case, concert promoter Billy McFarland was convicted of fraud, sentenced to six years in prison, and ordered to pay millions in restitution for bilking concert goers and investors of the Fyre Festival. Concert goers, who had paid as much as $100,000 to attend, were led to expect to hobnob with celebrities and models while enjoying lavish accommodations and popular bands, but found nothing of the kind when they arrived. McFarland also faces numerous lawsuits related to the ill-fated festival, and several celebrities who endorsed it on social media were fined.[2] While all unethical business actions do not result in fines and jail time, they do harm others by eroding trust in business decisions and decision makers. Regardless of their legality, all business decisions can be judged as right or wrong.

✓ Concept Check

- What is meant by business ethics?
- How do business ethics differ from personal ethics?

商业中的伦理问题

2-2 Ethical Issues in Business

Learning Objective

2-2 Identify the types of ethical concerns that arise in the business world.

Ethical issues often arise out of a business's relationships with investors, customers, employees, creditors, suppliers, or competitors. Each of these stakeholder groups has specific concerns and usually exerts pressure on the organization's managers. Investors, for example, want management to make sensible financial decisions that will boost sales, profits, and returns on their investments. Customers expect a firm's products to be safe, reliable, and reasonably priced. Employees demand to be treated fairly in hiring, promotion, and compensation decisions. Creditors require accounts to be paid on time and the accounting information furnished by the firm to be accurate. Competitors expect the firm's competitive practices to be fair and honest. Chick-fil-A, for example, sued 17 chicken suppliers, including Tyson Foods, Perdue Farms, and Pilgrim's Pride, accusing them of price-fixing—colluding to keep the prices it pays for poultry artificially high. The fast-food restaurant chain contends that the suppliers engaged in anticompetitive behavior by conspiring to share confidential bidding and pricing information in order to sustain higher chicken prices, resulting in consumers paying more for inferior chicken. A court will have to resolve the dispute.[3]

Businesspeople face ethical issues every day, and some of these issues can be difficult to assess. Although some types of issues arise infrequently, others occur regularly. Let's take a closer look at several ethical issues.

公平和诚实

2-2a Fairness and Honesty

Fairness and honesty in business are two important ethical concerns. Besides obeying all laws and regulations, businesspeople are expected to refrain from knowingly deceiving, misrepresenting, or intimidating others. The consequences of failing to do so can be expensive. For example, NeuroMetrix, Inc., paid more than $4 million to settle Federal Trade Commission (FTC) charges that it deceptively promoted its Quell electrical nerve stimulation device. The commission claimed the company misled customers when it falsely touted the device as "clinically proven" and "Food and Drug Administration (FDA) cleared" for treating pain, when it was neither. In addition to the fine, the company and its marketers were ordered not to make any further false or misleading claims about the product.[4]

伦理
ethics the study of right and wrong and of the morality of the choices individuals make

商业伦理
business ethics the application of moral standards to business situations

If consumers feel they have been deceived or that companies have been unfair, they will take their business elsewhere and may even ask regulators to intervene. For instance, the Securities and Exchange Commission (SEC) charged the stock-trading app Robinhood with giving customers misleading information about the actual costs of trading with the app and failing to obtain the best reasonably available terms to execute their orders. The SEC blamed the app for depriving customers of $34 million in total. Robinhood paid $65 million to settle the case and updated its procedures to ensure that it executes the best trades possible for its users.[5]

组织关系

2-2b **Organizational Relationships**

Businesspeople may be tempted to place their personal welfare above the welfare of others or the welfare of the organization. As an example, Kristin M. Lapree was convicted of misappropriating more than $700,000 of funds while she worked as the business manager of Wisconsin-based Rettler Corporation. She was sentenced to six years in prison and ordered to pay restitution.[6] Aside from the legality of such actions, they may threaten the livelihood of employees and the business itself and harm relations with customers, suppliers, and others.

Relationships among co-workers often create ethical problems. Unethical behavior in these areas includes taking credit for others' ideas or work, not meeting one's commitments in a mutual agreement, and pressuring others to behave unethically. Managers and executives have even more power to pressure others due to their ability to provide rewards and sanctions. Consider Wells Fargo, which suffered incalculable damage to its reputation after investigators revealed that managers had pressured employees to achieve unrealistic sales quotas, which led many bank employees to open fake accounts for customers without their knowledge. The company ultimately paid billions of dollars to settle criminal and civil charges; several of its executives also face charges as a result of the scandal.[7] The Global Business Ethics Survey reported that 22 percent of workers around the world say

Ethics violations Ethics violations can be more than humiliating. Ethics violators sometimes go to prison, pay large fines, lose their jobs, lose their families, and pay expensive legal fees.

they feel pressured to compromise their organization's ethics guidelines and policies, or to break the law; in North America, that value is 31 percent.[8]

One issue related to fairness and honesty is **plagiarism**—knowingly taking someone else's words, ideas, or other original material without acknowledging the source. When exposed, the consequences of plagiarism can be grave. For example, the U.S. Army War College rescinded the master's degree that it had awarded U.S. Senator John Walsh after an academic review by the college determined that Walsh had copied significant parts of his final paper from other sources. Walsh withdrew from his reelection campaign soon after the scandal.[9]

When misconduct occurs in business, investors also suffer. Investors and owners must be able to trust that companies are acting in their best interests and reporting their activities truthfully. They have the right to expect that all actions by a firm contribute toward a return on their investment. Two issues that raise flags for investors are executive compensation packages that are out of line with performance and the conflict of interest that may occur when a chief executive officer also sits on the board of directors—the group that oversees the CEO. In recent years, investors have protested high executive compensation, particularly when those executives do not generate strong profits for the owners. Shareholders have voted against executive compensation packages at a number of companies, including Electronic Arts, Ameriprise, Disney, and more.[10] Activist investors have also protested companies whose CEOs also sit on the board of directors, which can result in a conflict of interest when the CEO's performance is under review.

利益冲突

2-2c Conflicts of Interest

A **conflict of interest** results when businesspeople take advantage of a situation for their own personal interest rather than for the employer's interest. Examples of situations involving conflicts of interest generally involve an employee who has divided loyalties, such as a manager who is dating a subordinate, an employee with a close relative who works for a competitor, a purchasing manager who chooses to do business with another firm in which he is an investor, or a firm that advises clients without informing them that it has a relationship with some of the products it recommends. Even the appearance of a conflict of interest can jeopardize a businessperson's credibility. As an example, Louis DeJoy came under fire for failing to divest his ownership shares of XPO Logistics—where he previously served as CEO and chairman—when he was appointed Postmaster General by then President Donald Trump. His continued equity stake in XPO, a transportation and logistics firm that has million-dollar contracts with the U.S. Postal Service, created a conflict of interest for him when making shipping decisions for the federal agency. After the backlash, DeJoy agreed to sell his XPO stock.[11] In such cases, consumers and taxpayers have the right to know whether the head of a major government agency may be favoring certain contractors over others in order to benefit financially.

Conflicts of interest may occur when payments and gifts make their way into business deals. Although bribes—gifts, favors, or payments offered with the intent of influencing an outcome—are often part of business negotiations overseas, it is illegal for American businesspersons and companies to use bribes in the United States or abroad. Defending against bribery charges can be costly and affect future business negotiations. A wise rule to remember is that anything given to a person that might unfairly influence that person's business decision is a bribe, and all bribes are unethical.

剽窃
plagiarism knowingly taking someone else's words, ideas, or other original material without acknowledging the source

利益冲突
conflict of interest when businesspeople take advantage of a situation for their own personal interest rather than for the employer's interest

At Procter & Gamble (P&G), all employees are obligated to act solely in the best interests of the company. P&G defines a conflict of interest as when an employee has a personal relationship or financial or other interest that could interfere with this obligation, or when employees use their position with the company for personal gain. The company requires employees to disclose all potential conflicts of interest and to take prompt actions to eliminate a conflict when the company asks them to do so. Generally, P&G prohibits employees from receiving gifts, entertainment, or other gratuities from people with whom the company does business because doing so could imply an obligation on the part of the company and potentially pose a conflict of interest.[12]

沟通

2-2d **Communications**

Business communications, especially advertising, can present ethical questions. False and misleading advertising is illegal and unethical, and it can infuriate customers. For example, angry consumers filed suit against the Folger Coffee Company, arguing that 30.5 ounce canisters of Folgers ground coffee claim to contain enough to make 240 servings, but actually hold just 173 servings when prepared according to the instructions on the canister. Disgruntled consumers have filed similar lawsuits against other coffee makers.[13] In another example, the Federal Trade Commission fined Williams-Sonoma $1 million and ordered the retailer to stop claiming that some products sold in Williams-Sonoma and Pottery Barn stores are "Made in USA," when they contained significant imported components.[14] Sponsors of advertisements aimed at children must be especially careful to avoid misleading messages. Advertisers of health-related products also must take precautions to guard against deception when using such descriptive terms as *low fat, fat free,* and *light.* In fact, the Federal Trade Commission has issued guidelines on the use of these labels.

✓ Concept Check

- What are the different types of ethical concerns that may arise in the business world?
- Explain and give an example of how advertising can present ethical questions.

Entrepreneurial Success

创业成功：与社交媒体建立健康的关系

Building a Healthy Relationship with Social Media

Social media has long been criticized for its negative impact on society. For example, algorithms are often designed to manipulate users to stay on social networks as long as possible. It has also had immeasurable implications for data privacy. But despite these downfalls, social media still holds value for entrepreneurs as a source of inspiration, tools, insights, and community. With just a few simple changes, entrepreneurs can build a healthier relationship with social media.

For startups, establishing a brand on social media is critical, and an opportunity exists for creative, thoughtful engagement. However, it's important to be in control of your tech environment. Many apps allow users to reduce their screen time. A tool called Mailbrew rounds up social feeds and email newsletters into a single daily digest, and an app called Freedom blocks distracting apps on desktop and mobile devices to help users be more productive. Utilizing such resources can help you become the master of your devices.

Entrepreneurs can also set a positive example for their team members by promoting work-life balance and setting clear parameters for "on" and "off" times. Many entrepreneurs work around the clock, so it can be challenging to step away from the laptop and call it a day. But, by protecting off hours, entrepreneurs can cultivate a more productive work environment. In the end, unplugging can be positive for mental health and help people replenish their energy.

It's up to the next generation of business owners to disrupt the social media cycle. Rather than calling it quits, entrepreneurs can redefine their connection with their devices and build a healthier relationship with social media.

Sources: Based on information in Aytekin Tank, "How Entrepreneurs Can Harness The Power of Social Media for Good," *Entrepreneur*, October 22, 2020; Adi Robertson, "Telling People to Delete Facebook Won't Fix the Internet," *The Verge*, September 4, 2020.

影响伦理行为的因素

2-3 Factors Affecting Ethical Behavior

Learning Objective

2-3 Discuss the factors that affect the level of ethical behavior in organizations.

Is it possible for an individual with strong moral values to make ethically questionable decisions in a business setting? What factors affect a person's inclination to make either ethical or unethical decisions in a business organization? Although the answers to these questions are not entirely clear, three general sets of factors do appear to influence the standards of behavior in an organization.[15] As shown in Figure 2-1, these include individual factors, social factors, and opportunities.

影响伦理的个体因素

2-3a Individual Factors Affecting Ethics

Several factors influence an individual's ethical choices and behavior in an organization, including personal knowledge, values, and goals. How much an individual knows about an issue is one factor. A decision maker with a greater amount of knowledge regarding a situation may take steps to avoid ethical problems, whereas a less-informed person may unknowingly make choices that could lead to ethical problems. Individuals' moral values and central, value-related attitudes also clearly influence their business behavior and choices. Most organizations do not try to change an employee's personal ethics but instead strive to hire people with good character and values that complement their own. The actions of specific individuals in scandal-plagued companies, such as Wells Fargo, Volkswagen, Theranos, Turing Pharmaceuticals, and Enron, often raise questions about individuals' personal character and integrity. Finally, most people join organizations to accomplish personal goals. The types of personal goals an individual aspires to and how they choose to pursue them have a significant impact on that individual's behavior in an organization.

影响伦理的社会因素

2-3b Social Factors Affecting Ethics

Many social factors can affect ethical behavior within a firm, including cultural norms, actions and decisions of co-workers, values and attitudes of "significant others," and the use of the internet. A person's behavior in the workplace, to some degree, is determined by cultural norms, and these social factors vary from one culture to another. For example, in some countries it is acceptable and ethical for customs agents to receive gratuities for performing ordinary, legal tasks that are a part of their jobs, whereas in other countries these practices would be viewed as unethical and perhaps illegal. The actions and decisions of co-workers may also shape a person's sense of business ethics. For example, if your co-workers peruse YouTube and Instagram on company time and at company expense, you might come to view that behavior as acceptable and ethical because everyone does it. The moral values and attitudes of "significant others"—spouses, friends, and relatives,

Figure 2-1 Factors That Affect the Level of Ethical Behavior in an Organization

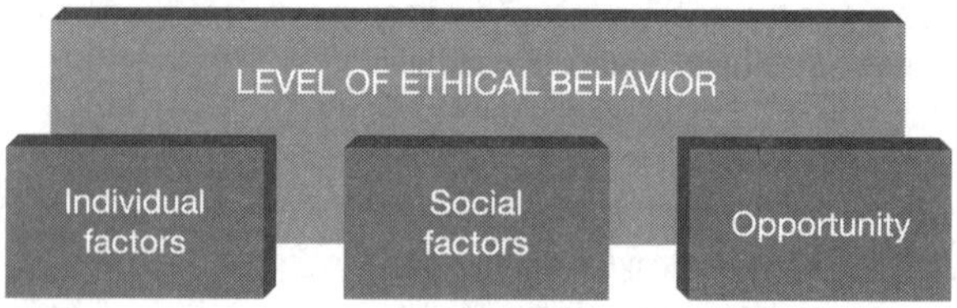

Source: Based on O. C. Ferrell and Larry Gresham, "A Contingency Framework for Understanding Ethical Decision Making in Marketing," *Journal of Marketing* (Summer 1985), 89.

for instance—also can affect an employee's perception of what is ethical and unethical behavior in the workplace.

The internet also presents challenges for firms whose employees enjoy easy access through convenient high-speed connections at work. An employee's behavior online can be viewed as offensive to co-workers and possibly lead to lawsuits against the firm if employees engage in unethical behavior on controversial websites not related to their job. Moreover, if an employee posts controversial content on social media using their employer's email, Instagram, or Twitter account, that content may run counter to the company's core values and reflect negatively on the company. Interestingly, one recent survey of employees found that most workers assume that their use of technology at work will be monitored. A large majority of employees approved of most monitoring methods such as monitoring faxes and email, tracking Web use, and even recording telephone calls.

机会是影响伦理的因素

2-3c **Opportunity as a Factor Affecting Ethics**

Several factors related to opportunity affect ethics in an organization. *Opportunity* refers to the amount of freedom an organization affords an employee to behave unethically if he or she makes that choice. If the employee is rewarded in some way for an unethical choice—receiving praise or a bonus, for example—or fails to suffer any kind of consequence, he or she is more likely to make that same choice in the future. In some organizations, certain company policies and procedures reduce the opportunity to be unethical. For example, at some fast-food restaurants, one employee takes your order and receives your payment, and another fills the order. This procedure reduces the opportunity to be unethical because the person handling the money is not dispensing the product, and the person giving out the product is not handling the money.

The existence of codes of ethics and other policies on ethics, as well as the importance management places on these policies are other elements of opportunity (codes of ethics are discussed in more detail in the next section). The degree of enforcement of company policies, procedures, and ethical codes is a major force affecting opportunity. When employees see that violations are dealt with consistently and firmly, they are less likely to act unethically knowing that doing so will bring repercussions.

Now that we have considered some of the factors believed to influence the level of ethical behavior in the workplace, let us explore what can be done to encourage ethical behavior and to discourage unethical behavior.

✓ Concept Check

- Describe several individual factors that influence the level of ethical behavior in an organization.
- Explain several social factors that affect ethics in an organization.
- How does opportunity influence the level of ethical behavior in the workplace?

鼓励符合伦理的行为

2-4 Encouraging Ethical Behavior

Learning Objective

2-4 Explain how organizations can encourage ethical decision making in business.

Most authorities agree that there is room for improvement in business ethics. A more problematic question is: Can business be made more ethical in the real world? The majority opinion on this issue suggests that government, trade associations, and individual firms indeed can promote acceptable levels of ethical behavior.

政府在鼓励伦理行为方面的作用

2-4a **Government's Role in Encouraging Ethics**

The government can encourage ethical behavior in business by enacting more stringent regulations and laws. One example is the landmark **Sarbanes-Oxley Act of 2002**, which provides sweeping legal protection for those who report corporate misconduct. Among other things, the law deals with corporate responsibility,

2002 年萨班斯－奥克斯利法案
Sarbanes-Oxley Act of 2002 provides sweeping legal protection for employees who report corporate misconduct

Sarbanes-Oxley Act The Sarbanes-Oxley Act of 2002 includes tough provisions to deter and punish corporate and accounting fraud and corruption. The legislation passed with unanimous support.

conflicts of interest, and corporate accountability. However, rules require enforcement, and the unethical businessperson frequently seems to "slip something by" without getting caught. Increased regulation may help, but it cannot solve the entire ethics problem.

行业协会在鼓励伦理行为方面的作用

2-4b Trade Associations' Role in Encouraging Ethics

Trade associations can and often do provide ethical guidelines for their members. These organizations, which operate within particular industries, are in an excellent position to exert pressure on members to stop engaging in questionable business practices that may harm all firms in the industry. For example, a pharmaceutical trade group adopted a new set of guidelines intended to end the extravagant dinners and expensive gifts sales representatives often give to physicians to persuade them to prescribe a particular medicine. However, enforcement and authority vary from association to association. Because trade associations exist for the benefit of their members, harsh measures may be self-defeating. Trade associations must also ensure that their codes do not contain provisions that may run afoul of antitrust laws.

公司在鼓励伦理行为方面的作用

2-4c Individual Companies' Role in Encouraging Ethics

Enforced codes of ethics are perhaps the most effective way to encourage ethical behavior within organizations. A **code of ethics** is a written guide to acceptable and ethical behavior as defined by an organization; it outlines uniform policies, standards, and punishments for violations. Because a code of ethics informs employees what is expected of them and what will happen if they violate the rules, it can go a long way toward encouraging ethical behavior. However, codes cannot possibly cover every situation. Companies also must create an environment in which employees recognize the importance of complying with the written code. Managers must provide direction by fostering communication, actively modeling and encouraging ethical decision making, and training employees to make ethical decisions. However, codes that are not enforced are likely to be viewed as lip service by employees and other stakeholders. Figure 2-2 offers snippets of some of the guiding principles behind well-known companies' codes of ethics.

伦理准则
code of ethics a guide to acceptable and ethical behavior as defined by the organization

Figure 2-2 Defining Acceptable Behavior at Starbucks, Nike, and Apple

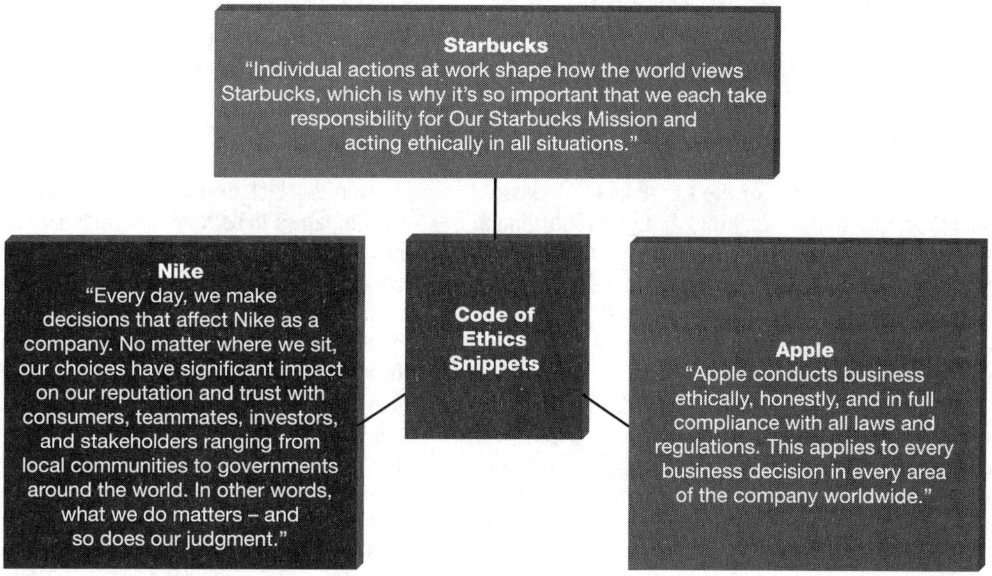

Sources: Starbucks, "Business Ethics and Compliance: Standards of Business Conduct"; Nike, "Inside the Lines: The NIKE Code of Ethics"; Apple, "Business Conduct: The Way We Do Business Worldwide".

Beginning in the 1980s, an increasing number of organizations created and implemented ethics codes. Today, about 95 percent of *Fortune* 1000 firms have a formal code of ethics or conduct. For example, the ethics code of Starbucks defines the firm's mission and values and includes provisions relating to policies and procedures; laws and regulations; relationships with customers, suppliers, competitors, and the community; conflicts of interest; handling of proprietary information; and more. Starbucks' code also details how employees can express concerns or find guidance in ambiguous situations and even provides a graphical decision-making framework that employees can apply to difficult decisions.[16]

In the wake of a number of corporate scandals and the Sarbanes-Oxley Act, many large companies now have created a new executive position, the chief ethics (or compliance) officer. Assigning an ethics officer who guides ethical conduct provides employees someone to consult if they are not sure of the right thing to do. An ethics officer meets with employees and top management to provide ethical advice, establishes and maintains an anonymous confidential service to answer questions about ethical issues, and takes action on ethics code violations.

Sometimes even employees who want to act ethically may find it difficult to do so. Unethical practices can become ingrained in an organization. Employees with high personal ethics may then take a controversial step called *whistle-blowing*. **Whistle-blowing** is informing the press or government officials about unethical practices within an organization. Consider Teresa Ross, who brought a lawsuit against Group Health Cooperative (GHC, now Kaiser Foundation Health Plan's Washington subsidiary) under the False Claims Act, which permits whistle-blowers to sue companies they believe have defrauded the government. Ross, who worked as Director of Risk Adjustment Services for the healthcare firm, believed that GHC was defrauding Medicare by inflating or altering patients' diagnoses in order to receive

举报

whistle-blowing informing the press or government officials about unethical practices within one's organization

Exploring Careers

职业探索：首席伦理官的兴起

The Rise of the Chief Ethics Officer

With artificial intelligence (AI) applications spreading throughout the business world, executives now rank ethics issues as one of the top risks of AI. Bias, for instance, can find its way into AI algorithms, which can lead to discrimination. This mounting concern has contributed to the rise of the chief ethics officer. Ethics officers are executives who provide oversight to guide the organization through legal and ethical standards.

Though the role does not have a set job description like other C-suite roles, some companies are looking to the chief ethics officer to ensure AI algorithms are fair and unbiased. AI has been integrated into a variety of functions, from recruiting and contact tracing to facial recognition and email marketing. Candidates for the chief ethics officer role may have a background in business law and human resources, though some tech departments are hiring dedicated AI ethics officers.

Due to a lack of regulation for AI development, it's up to companies to set their own standards and policies. The ethics officer can assess risks, create a code of ethics, conduct internal training programs, ensure compliance with regulations, monitor ongoing ethical conduct, and act on violations of the company's ethics code. In addition to AI, other tech issues to consider are privacy, data collection, and security. The chief ethics officer can play a critical part in eliminating bias, guarding against unintended consequences, and holding individuals and organizations accountable.

Sources: Based on information in "Rise of the Chief Ethics Officer," *Forbes*, March 27, 2019; Geoff Nudelman, "20 Minutes With: Hypergiant Industries' Chief Ethics Officer Will Griffin on Diversity and Ethics in Technology," *Barron's*, September 7, 2020; Merve Hickok, "What Does an AI Ethicist Do? A Guide for the Why, the What, and the How," *Medium*, April 27, 2020.

higher payments. The company eventually settled the case with the Department of Justice for $6.3 million. Ross was awarded about $1.5 million for blowing the whistle.[17]

Whistle-blowing, however, can have serious repercussions for employees: Those who "blow the whistle" may face retaliation and sometimes even lose their jobs. The Sarbanes-Oxley Act of 2002 protects whistle-blowers who report corporate misconduct. Any executive who retaliates against a whistle-blower can be held criminally liable and imprisoned for up to ten years. Federal employees who report misconduct are likewise protected by the Whistleblower Protection Act of 1989.

When companies set up anonymous hotlines to advise employees who are unsure how to handle ethically questionable situations, employees actually may be more likely to engage in whistle-blowing. When firms instead create an environment that educates employees and nurtures ethical behavior, fewer ethical problems arise. Ultimately, the need for whistle-blowing is greatly reduced.

It is difficult for an organization to develop ethics codes, programs, and procedures to deal with all relationships and every situation. Michael Josephson, an expert on workplace ethics, says, "The objective of such programs is to establish a business culture in which it's easier to do the right thing than the wrong thing, and where concerned co-workers and vigilant supervisors repress illegal or improper conduct that can potentially endanger or embarrass the company."[18] When no company policies or procedures exist or apply, a quick test to determine if a behavior is ethical is to see if others—co-workers, customers, and suppliers—approve of it. Ethical decisions will always withstand scrutiny. Openness and communication about choices will often build trust and strengthen business relationships. Table 2-1 provides some general guidelines for making ethical decisions.

✓ Concept Check

- How can the government encourage the ethical behavior of organizations?
- What is the role of trade associations in encouraging ethics?
- What is whistle-blowing? Who protects the whistle-blowers?

Table 2-1 Guidelines for Making Ethical Decisions

1. Listen and learn	Recognize the problem or decision-making opportunity that confronts your company, team, or unit. Don't argue, criticize, or defend yourself—keep listening and reviewing until you are sure that you understand others.
2. Identify the ethical issues	Examine how co-workers and consumers are affected by the situation or decision at hand. Examine how you feel about the situation, and attempt to understand the viewpoint of those involved in the decision or in the consequences of the decision.
3. Create and analyze options	Try to put aside strong feelings such as anger or a desire for power and prestige and come up with as many alternatives as possible before developing an analysis. Ask everyone involved for ideas about which options offer the best long-term results for you and the company. Then decide which option will increase your self-respect even if, in the long run, things don't work out the way you hope they will.
4. Identify the best option from your point of view	Consider it and test it against some established criteria, such as respect, understanding, caring, fairness, honesty, and openness.
5. Explain your decision and resolve any differences that arise	This may require neutral arbitration from a trusted manager or taking "time out" to reconsider, consult, or exchange written proposals before a decision is reached.

Source: Based on information in Tom Rusk with D. Patrick Miller, "Doing the Right Thing," *Sky* (Delta Airlines), August 1993, 18–22.

社会责任

2-5 Social Responsibility

Learning Objective

2-5 Describe how our current views on the social responsibility of business have evolved.

社会责任

social responsibility the recognition that business activities have an impact on society and the consideration of that impact in business decision making

Social responsibility is the recognition that business activities have an impact on society and the consideration of that impact in business decision making. Alphabet and its subsidiary Google, for example, have pledged to donate $14.5 million to support initiatives to combat racial injustice, inequity, and violence, including grants to the Center for Policing Equity and Equal Justice Initiative.[19] Obviously, social responsibility costs money. It is perhaps not so obvious—except in isolated cases—that social responsibility is also good business. Many companies contribute resources, knowledge, and products as well as money to help neighbors and others during times of crisis. For example, Procter & Gamble's orange Loads of Hope trucks are a welcome sight during disaster relief efforts. Residents in disaster areas can drop off loads of dirty laundry at the mobile laundromats, and volunteers use Tide products and high-efficiency machines to wash, dry, and even fold their clothes. Thus far, the program has helped nearly 48,000 families and brought a sense of normalcy and hope back to survivors so that they can focus on more pressing matters.[20] Efforts like these bring positive associations for brands that can help them stand out in a competitive market. Customers eventually find out which firms act responsibly and which do not. Just as easily as they can purchase a product made by a company that is socially responsible, they can choose against buying from the firm that is not.

Even small businesses can develop social responsibility programs. For example, P. Terry's, which operates 19 fast-food hamburger stands in Central Texas, donates 100 percent of its profits from one day each quarter to a local charity. The company, which has donated more than $1 million to local nonprofits, lets customers know about upcoming charity days through its social media accounts.[21] In general, people are more likely to want to work for and buy from such organizations.

Social responsibility is good business. Natural disasters create opportunities for companies to engage in socially responsible behavior. Procter & Gamble's Loads of Hope program takes in disaster survivors' dirty laundry and returns it to them clean and folded, allowing them to deal with more important problems.

Table 2-2 10 Best Corporate Citizens

1. Owens Corning
2. Citi
3. General Mills
4. Cisco
5. HP
6. Intel
7. Ecolab
8. General Motors
9. Hess
10. Accenture

Source: "100 Best Corporate Citizens of 2020," *3BL Media*.

Increasingly, companies large and small are striving to be good corporate citizens. **Corporate citizenship** is adopting a strategic approach to fulfilling economic, ethical, environmental, and social responsibilities. This requires balancing the needs, desires, and demands of a diverse group of stakeholders including investors, employees, customers, regulators, competitors, neighborhoods and communities, and social activists. Consider Chris Kempczinski, president and CEO of McDonald's, who views the company's role in society as going beyond feeding Big Macs to customers: "What we realized is that for 65 years, McDonald's purpose has been to both feed and foster communities. To our franchisees, suppliers and employees, the words 'billions served' aren't just about the burgers and fries we serve, but the tens of thousands of communities around the world that we serve." One way the company does that is through its longtime sponsorship of Ronald McDonald House Charities, which helps support the families of sick and injured children during treatment.[22] Table 2-2 lists the best corporate citizens as evaluated by 3BL Media.

企业社会责任的演变

2-5a The Evolution of Social Responsibility in Business

Business is far from perfect in many respects, but its record of social responsibility today is much better than that in past decades. In fact, present demands for social responsibility have their roots in outraged reactions to the abusive business practices of the early 1900s.

During the first quarter of the 20th century, businesses were free to operate pretty much as they chose. Government protection of workers and consumers was minimal. As a result, people either accepted what business had to offer or they did without. Working conditions often were deplorable by today's standards. The average workweek in most industries exceeded 60 hours, no minimum-wage law existed, and employee benefits were almost nonexistent. Workplaces were crowded and unsafe, and industrial accidents were the rule rather than the exception. To improve working conditions, employees organized and joined labor unions. During the early 1900s, however, businesses—with the help of government—were able to use court orders, brute force, and even the few existing antitrust laws to defeat union attempts to improve working conditions.

During this period, consumers generally were subject to the doctrine of **caveat emptor**, a Latin phrase meaning "let the buyer beware." In other words, "what you see is what you get," and if it is not what you expected, too bad. Although victims of unscrupulous business practices could take legal action, going to court was very expensive, and consumers rarely won their cases. Moreover, no consumer groups or government agencies existed to publicize their consumers' grievances or to hold sellers accountable for their actions.

Before the 1930s, most people believed that competition and the action of the marketplace would, in time, correct abuses. Government, therefore, became involved in day-to-day business activities only in cases of obvious abuse of the free-market system. Six of the most important business-related federal laws passed between 1887 and 1914 are described in Table 2-3. As you can see, these laws were aimed more at encouraging competition than at correcting abuses, although two of them did deal with the purity of food and drug products.

The collapse of the stock market on October 29, 1929, triggered the Great Depression. Factory production fell by almost half, and up to 25 percent of the nation's workforce was unemployed. Public pressure soon mounted for the government to "do something" about the economy and about worsening social conditions. Soon after Franklin D. Roosevelt became president in 1933, he instituted programs to restore the economy and improve social conditions. The government passed laws to correct what many viewed as the monopolistic abuses of big business, and provided various social services for individuals. These massive federal programs became the foundation for increased government involvement in the dealings between business and society.

企业公民
corporate citizenship adopting a strategic approach to fulfilling economic, ethical, environmental, and social responsibilities

买者自慎
caveat emptor a Latin phrase meaning "let the buyer beware"

Table 2-3 Early Government Regulations That Affected American Business

Government Regulation	Major Provisions
Interstate Commerce Act (1887)	First federal act to regulate business practices; provided regulation of railroads and shipping rates
Sherman Antitrust Act (1890)	Prevented monopolies or mergers where competition was endangered
Pure Food and Drug Act (1906)	Established limited supervision of interstate sales of food and drugs
Meat Inspection Act (1906)	Provided for limited supervision of interstate sales of meat and meat products
Federal Trade Commission Act (1914)	Created the Federal Trade Commission to investigate illegal trade practices
Clayton Antitrust Act (1914)	Eliminated many forms of price discrimination that gave large businesses a competitive advantage over smaller firms

As government involvement has increased, so has everyone's awareness of the social responsibility of business. Today's business owners are concerned about the return on their investment, but at the same time most of them demand ethical behavior from employees. In addition, employees demand better working conditions, and consumers want safe, reliable products. Various advocacy groups echo these concerns and also call for careful consideration of the Earth's delicate ecological balance. Therefore, managers must operate in a complex business environment—one in which they are just as responsible for their managerial actions as for their actions as individual citizens. Interestingly, today's high-tech and internet-based firms fare relatively well when it comes to environmental issues, worker conditions, animal testing, and charitable donations.

社会责任的两种观点

2-5b Two Views of Social Responsibility

Government regulation and public awareness are *external* forces that have increased the social responsibility of business. However, business decisions are made within the firm—there, social responsibility begins with the attitude of management. Two contrasting philosophies, or models, define the range of management attitudes toward social responsibility.

According to the traditional concept of business, a firm exists to produce quality goods and services, earn a reasonable profit, and provide jobs. In line with this concept, the **economic model of social responsibility** holds that society will benefit most when business is left alone to produce and market profitable products that society needs. The economic model has its origins in the 18th century, when businesses were owned primarily by entrepreneurs or owner-managers. Competition was vigorous among small firms, and short-run profits and survival were the primary concerns. To the manager who adopts this traditional attitude, social responsibility is someone else's job. After all, stockholders invest in a corporation to earn a return on their investment, not because the firm is socially responsible, and the firm is legally obligated to act in the economic interest of its stockholders. Moreover, profitable firms pay federal, state, and local taxes that are used to meet the needs of society. Thus, managers who concentrate on profit believe that they fulfill their social responsibility indirectly through the taxes paid by their firms. As a result, social responsibility becomes the problem of the government, various environmental groups, charitable foundations, and similar organizations.

In contrast, some managers believe that they have a responsibility not only to stockholders but also to customers, employees, suppliers, and the general public. This broader view is referred to as the **socioeconomic model of social responsibility**, which places emphasis not only on profits but also on the impact of business decisions on society.

社会责任的经济模式
economic model of social responsibility the view that society will benefit most when business is left alone to produce and market profitable products that society needs

社会责任的社会经济模式
socioeconomic model of social responsibility the concept that business should emphasize not only profits but also the impact of its decisions on society

Recently, increasing numbers of managers and firms have adopted the socioeconomic model, and they have done so for at least three reasons. First, business is dominated by the corporate form of ownership, and the corporation is a creation of society. If a corporation does not perform as a good citizen, society can and will demand changes. Second, many firms have begun to take pride in their social responsibility records, among them Starbucks, HP, Colgate-Palmolive, and Coca-Cola. Of course, many other corporations are much more socially responsible today than they were ten years ago. Third, many businesspeople believe that it is in their best interest to take the initiative in this area. The alternative may be legal action brought against the firm by some special-interest group; in such a situation, the firm may lose control of its activities.

社会责任的利弊

2-5c The Pros and Cons of Social Responsibility

Business owners, managers, customers, and government officials have debated the pros and cons of the economic and socioeconomic models for years. Each side seems to have four major arguments to reinforce its viewpoint.

Proponents of the socioeconomic model maintain that a business must do more than simply seek profits. To support their position, they offer the following arguments:

1. Because business is a part of our society, it cannot ignore social issues.
2. Business has the technical, financial, and managerial resources needed to tackle today's complex social issues.
3. By helping resolve social issues, business can create a more stable environment for long-term profitability.
4. Socially responsible decision making by firms can prevent increased government intervention, which would force businesses to do what they fail to do voluntarily.

These arguments are based on the assumption that a business has a responsibility not only to its stockholders but also to its customers, employees, suppliers, and the general public.

Opponents of the socioeconomic model argue that business should do what it does best: earn a profit by manufacturing and marketing products that people want. Those who support this position argue as follows:

1. Business managers are responsible primarily to stockholders, so management must be concerned with providing a return on owners' investments.
2. Corporate time, money, and talent should be used to maximize profits, not to solve society's problems.
3. Social problems affect society in general, so individual businesses should not be expected to solve these problems.
4. Social issues are the responsibility of government officials who are elected for that purpose and who are accountable to the voters for their decisions.

These arguments obviously are based on the assumption that the primary objective of business is to earn profits and that government and social institutions should deal with social problems.

Today, few firms are either purely economic or purely socioeconomic in outlook; most have chosen some middle ground between the two extremes. However, our society generally seems to want—and even to expect—some degree of social responsibility from business. Thus, within this middle ground, businesses are leaning toward the socioeconomic view. In the next several sections, we look at some results of this movement in four specific areas: the public, employment practices, the environment, and implementation of social responsibility programs.

✓ Concept Check

- What is social responsibility? How can business be socially responsible?
- Outline the historical evolution of business social responsibility.
- Explain two views on the social responsibility of business.
- What are the arguments for and against increased social responsibility?

企业的公共责任

2-6 Public Responsibilities of Business

In recent years, more businesses have adopted the idea that they have basic responsibilities to the public, particularly to consumers and public health.

> **Learning Objective**
>
> **2-6** List the responsibilities businesses have to the public, especially with regard to consumer rights and public health.

消费者权益保护

2-6a Consumerism

Consumerism consists of all activities undertaken to protect the rights of consumers. The fundamental issues pursued by the consumer movement fall into three categories: environmental protection, product performance and safety, and information disclosure. Although consumerism has been with us to some extent since the early 19th century, the consumer movement became stronger in the 1960s. It was then that President John F. Kennedy declared that the consumer was entitled to a new "Bill of Rights."

The Basic Rights of Consumers President Kennedy's Consumer Bill of Rights asserted that consumers have a right to safety, to be informed, to choose, and to be heard. Two additional rights added since 1975 are the right to consumer education and the right to courteous service. These six rights are the basis of much of the consumer-oriented legislation passed during the last 55 years. These rights also provide an effective outline of the objectives and accomplishments of the consumer movement.

The consumers' right to safety means that the products they purchase must be safe for their intended use, must include thorough and explicit directions for proper use, and must be tested by the manufacturer to ensure product quality and reliability. Federal agencies, such as the Food and Drug Administration and the Consumer Product Safety Commission, have the power to force businesses that make or sell defective products to take corrective actions such as offering refunds, recalling defective products, issuing public warnings, and reimbursing consumers—all of which can be expensive. Moreover, consumers and the government have been winning an increasing number of product-liability lawsuits against sellers of defective products. The amount of the awards in these suits has been increasing steadily. For example, a Florida man won $41.1 million when he sued R.J. Reynolds Tobacco Company and Phillip Morris USA, claiming that for decades they had concealed the hazards of smoking, which led him to develop severe COPD.[23] Yet another major reason for improving product safety is consumers' demand for safe products. People simply will stop buying a product they believe is unsafe or unreliable.

消费者权益保护
consumerism all activities undertaken to protect the rights of consumers

The right to be informed means that consumers must have access to complete information about a product before they buy it. Detailed information about ingredients and nutrition must be provided on food containers, information about fabrics and laundering methods must be attached to clothing, and lenders must disclose the true cost of borrowing the money they make available to customers who purchase merchandise on credit. In addition, manufacturers must inform consumers about the potential dangers of using their products. Manufacturers that fail to provide such information can be held responsible for personal injuries suffered because of their products. For example, Maytag provides customers with a lengthy booklet that describes how they should use their new washing

The right to safety The Consumer Bill of Rights asserts buyers' basic rights. The right to safety means that products must be safe for their intended use and tested by the producer to ensure product quality and safety.

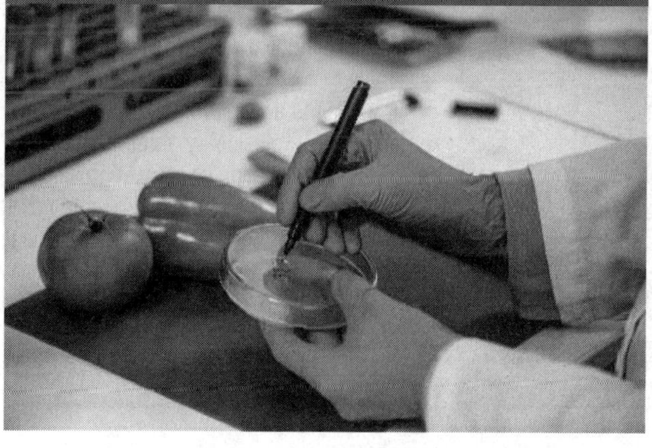

machines. Sometimes such warnings seem excessive, but they are necessary if user injuries (and resulting lawsuits) are to be avoided.

The right to choose means that consumers must have a choice of products, offered by different manufacturers and sellers, to satisfy a particular need. The government has done its part by encouraging competition through antitrust legislation. The greater the competition, the greater is the choice available to consumers. Competition and the resulting freedom of choice provide additional benefits for customers by reducing prices. For example, when personal computers were introduced, they cost more than $5,000. Thanks to intense competition and technological advancements, personal computers today can be purchased for less than $500.

The right to be heard means that someone will listen and take appropriate action when customers complain. In fact, management began to listen to consumers after World War II, when competition between businesses that manufactured and sold consumer goods increased. One way that firms gained a competitive edge was to listen to consumers and provide the products they said they wanted and needed. Today, businesses are listening even more attentively, and many larger firms have consumer relations departments that can be contacted easily via email and social media. Other groups listen, too. Most large cities and some states have consumer affairs offices to act on citizens' complaints.

In 1975, President Gerald Ford added to the Consumer Bill of Rights *the right to consumer education,* which entitles people to be fully informed about their rights as consumers. In 1994, President Bill Clinton added a sixth right, *the right to service,* which entitles consumers to convenience, courtesy, and responsiveness from manufacturers and sellers of consumer products.

Ethics and Social Responsibility

商业伦理与社会责任：谷歌被控违反反垄断法

Google Sued for Antitrust Violations

Google, the world's largest search engine and one of the largest companies in the United States, faces a series of lawsuits centered around anticompetitive behavior. The Department of Justice and 11 state attorneys general filed a lawsuit against the company to prevent it from using anticompetitive practices to maintain its monopolies in the search and search advertising markets. Anticompetitive behavior negatively affects both consumers and competitors. Among other things, stifling competition inhibits innovation and reduces the options available to consumers.

Complaints against the tech giant include entering into exclusionary agreements that prohibit preinstallation of competing search services and using monopoly profits to pay for preferential treatment for its products. Google has responded to the lawsuit, saying it believes there is nothing wrong with its business agreements. A separate case from more than 30 states alleges Google uses its general search monopoly to discriminate against vertical search companies like Yelp and Kayak. A third lawsuit from a smaller group of states alleges Google uses its position in the advertising marketplace to create unfair conditions for advertisers and publishers, taking in a higher percentage of online ad spending.

Though on a surface level it may seem Google is being targeted for being successful, the accusations made against the company are serious. The distinction between competitive behavior and anticompetitive behavior is that being competitive relates to efforts taken to become the best while being anticompetitive relates to suppressing the competition. Antitrust laws are intended to promote competition and protect consumers. Lawsuits such as the ones Google faces stand to reshape the tech industry.

Sources: Based on information in Department of Justice, "Justice Department Sues Monopolist Google For Violating Antitrust Laws," October 20, 2020; Gilad Edelman, "Google's Antitrust Cases: A Guide for the Perplexed," *Wired*, December 18, 2020; Federal Trade Commission, "Guide to Antitrust Laws".

Major Consumerism Forces The major forces in consumerism are individual consumer advocates and organizations, consumer education programs, and consumer laws. Consumer advocates take it upon themselves to protect the rights of consumers. They band together into consumer organizations, either independently or under government sponsorship. They write letters and advocate for stricter legislation concerning practices that may harm consumers. In Europe, for example, some consumer groups have complained to regulators that Amazon's Prime membership service is difficult to cancel, manipulating users into sticking with a plan they no longer want. Public Citizen, a consumer group in the United States, has made a similar complaint to the Federal Trade Commission.[24] Some consumer advocates and organizations encourage consumers to boycott products and businesses to which they have objections.

Educating consumers to make wiser purchasing decisions is perhaps one of the most far-reaching aspects of consumerism. Increasingly, consumer education is becoming a part of high school and college curricula and adult education programs. These programs cover many topics—for instance, what major factors should be considered when buying specific products, such as insurance, real estate, automobiles, appliances and furniture, clothes, and food; the provisions of certain consumer-protection laws; and the sources of information that can help individuals become knowledgeable consumers.

Major advances in consumerism have come through federal legislation. Some laws enacted in the last 60 years to protect your rights as a consumer are listed and described in Table 2-4.

Most businesspeople now realize that they ignore consumer issues only at their own peril. Managers know that improper handling of consumer complaints can result in lost sales, bad publicity, and lawsuits.

公共健康

2-6b Public Health

Many people believe that businesses have a basic responsibility to contribute to the general well-being of the public, starting with ensuring that their products do not harm anyone. Beyond this basic responsibility, however, there is disagreement as to how far businesses' responsibility to public health should extend, especially about issues such as obesity, smoking, heart disease, alcohol use, and even smartphone use while driving. These issues are not black and white, but exploring them can help us find balance among the desires and demands of various stakeholders.

Obesity has become a major public health topic in recent years, with more than one-third of adult Americans being categorized as obese. Other countries are experiencing similar trends. People who are obese or significantly overweight face higher rates of diabetes, strokes, heart disease, and some types of cancer, and the swelling numbers of these illnesses place a great burden on the healthcare system, the costs of which are borne by society. Public health advocates have called for companies—particularly those that market sugary drinks and fast food—to modify their products or at least their advertising in an effort to reduce the consumption of these products, which have been shown to contribute to rising rates of obesity. Perhaps as a result, some producers of these products have suffered losses and are responding with new ideas and products. Coca-Cola, for example, discontinued hundreds of brands, including some with higher levels of sugar, such as Odwalla. In recent years, the beverage giant has introduced or acquired new beverage brands such as Fairlife milk, Simply juices, and Topo Chic mineral waters that have less sugar and/or provide health benefits.[25] Other companies, including Panera and Starbucks, are posting the calories in their offerings right on their menus and apps to help people make better choices.

Another major public health topic facing business relates to smoking and tobacco products. The relationship between smoking—even secondhand smoke—and cancer has been well documented, but some consumers still demand to buy cigarettes and tobacco

Table 2-4 **Major Federal Legislation Protecting Consumers Since 1960**

Legislation	Major Provisions
Federal Hazardous Substances Labeling Act (1960)	Required warning labels on household chemicals if they were highly toxic
Kefauver-Harris Drug Amendments (1962)	Established testing practices for drugs and required manufacturers to label drugs with generic names in addition to trade names
Cigarette Labeling Act (1965)	Required manufacturers to place standard warning labels on all cigarette packages and advertising
Fair Packaging and Labeling Act (1966)	Called for all products sold across state lines to be labeled with net weight, ingredients, and manufacturer's name and address
Motor Vehicle Safety Act (1966)	Established standards for safer cars
Truth in Lending Act (1968)	Required lenders and credit merchants to disclose the full cost of finance charges in both dollars and annual percentage rates
Credit Card Liability Act (1970)	Limited credit card holder's liability to $50 per card and stopped credit card companies from issuing unsolicited cards Required credit bureaus to provide credit reports to consumers regarding their own credit files; also provided for correction of incorrect information
Consumer Product Safety Commission Act (1972)	Established an abbreviated procedure for registering certain generic drugs
Fair Credit Billing Act (1974)	Amended the Truth in Lending Act to enable consumers to challenge billing errors
Equal Credit Opportunity Act (1974)	Provided equal credit opportunities for all individuals regardless of sex or marital status Provided for minimum disclosure standards for written consumer-product warranties for products that cost more than $15
Amendments to the Equal Credit Opportunity Act (1976, 1994)	Prevented discrimination based on race, creed, color, religion, age, and income when granting credit
Fair Debt Collection Practices Act (1977)	Outlawed abusive collection practices by third parties
Nutrition Labeling and Education Act (1990)	Required the Food and Drug Administration to review current food labeling and packaging focusing on nutrition label content, label format, ingredient labeling, food descriptors and standards, and health messages
Telephone Consumer Protection Act (1991)	Prohibited the use of automated dialing and prerecorded voice calling equipment to make calls or deliver messages
Consumer Credit Reporting Reform Act (1997)	Placed more responsibility for accurate credit data on credit issuers; required creditors to verify that disputed data are accurate and to notify a consumer before reinstating the data
Children's Online Privacy Protection Act (2000)	Placed parents in control over what information is collected online from their children younger than 13 years; required commercial website operators to maintain the confidentiality, security, and integrity of personal information collected from children
Do Not Call Implementation Act (2003)	Directed the FCC and the FTC to coordinate so that their rules are consistent regarding telemarketing call practices including the Do Not Call Registry and other lists, as well as call abandonment
Credit Card Accountability, Responsibility, and Disclosure Act (2009)	Provided the most sweeping changes in credit card protections since the Truth in Lending Act of 1968
Dodd-Frank Wall Street Reform and Consumer Protection Act of 2010	Promoted the financial stability of the United States by improving accountability and responsibility in the financial system; established a new Consumer Financial Protection Agency to regulate home mortgages, car loans, and credit cards; became Public Law on July 21, 2010

products. While most people agree that businesses should not knowingly sell products that harm customers, what should they do when consumers continue to demand those products? CVS Health earned significant publicity several years ago when it announced that it would stop selling cigarettes in its stores, even though it lost $2 billion in revenue from doing so.[26] In recent years, the rise of vaping has further compounded the issue. Marketers of e-cigarettes and vaping products insist that their products are safer than cigarettes and even tout them as a method to stop smoking. Health advocates, however, say they are still harmful, and worry that the vapors—which often come in flavors such as bubblegum and pina colada—may be especially attractive to minors. Some cities have banned e-cigarettes along with conventional ones, and federal regulators are studying the devices to determine whether further regulation is needed.

One growing concern is the use of smartphones and smartphone apps while driving. Should cell phone service providers take steps to prevent customers from texting and using apps that distract from driving or merely advise them to refrain from these activities? AT&T launched its "It Can Wait" promotion campaign to ask customers to avoid texting while driving, and more than 38 million users pledged not to. The cell phone service provider asked customers to use the hashtag #X to alert their friends and followers that they are about to be unreachable on social media because they are driving.[27] There are other issues businesses face with regard to public health, including labeling products that contain genetically modified organisms (GMOs), making questionable claims about the health benefits of supplements and ingredients, where and how to provide affordable housing for the homeless, and many more.

✓ Concept Check

- Describe the six basic rights of consumers.
- What are the major forces in consumerism today?
- What are some of the federal laws enacted in the last 60 years to protect your rights as a consumer?
- What are some of the issues businesses must consider with regard to public health?

对员工的责任

2-7 Responsibilities to Employees

Learning Objective

2-7 Analyze how present employment practices are being used to counteract past abuses.

Everyone should have the opportunity to land a job for which they are qualified and to be rewarded on the basis of ability and performance. This is a fundamental issue for Americans, and it also makes good business sense. Yet, over the years, this opportunity has been denied to members of various racial, religious, political, national, and other underrepresented groups, and members of these groups are often singled out for unfavorable treatment in the workplace.

The federal government responded to the outcry of minority groups during the 1960s and 1970s by passing a number of laws forbidding discrimination in the workplace. Yet, more than 50 years after passage of the Civil Rights Act of 1964, abuses still exist. An example is the disparity in income levels for Whites, Blacks, Hispanics, and Asians, as illustrated in Figure 2-3. Lower incomes and higher unemployment rates also characterize Native Americans, people with disabilities, and women. Responsible managers have instituted a number of programs to counteract the results of discrimination.

平权行动计划

2-7a Affirmative Action Programs

An **affirmative action program** is a plan designed to increase the number of employees from underrepresented groups at all levels within an organization. Employers with federal contracts of more than $50,000 per year must have written affirmative action plans. The objective of such programs is to ensure that members of underrepresented groups are represented within the organization in approximately the same proportion as in the surrounding community. If 25 percent of the electricians in a geographic area in which a company is located are Black, then approximately 25 percent of the electricians it employs also should be Black. Affirmative action plans encompass all areas of human resources management: recruiting, hiring, training, promotion, and pay.

平权行动计划

affirmative action program a plan designed to increase the number of employees from underrepresented groups at all levels within an organization

Unfortunately, affirmative action programs have been plagued by two problems. The first involves quotas. In the beginning, many firms pledged to recruit and hire a

Figure 2-3 Comparative Income Levels

Real Median Household Income by Race and Hispanic Origin: 1967 to 2019

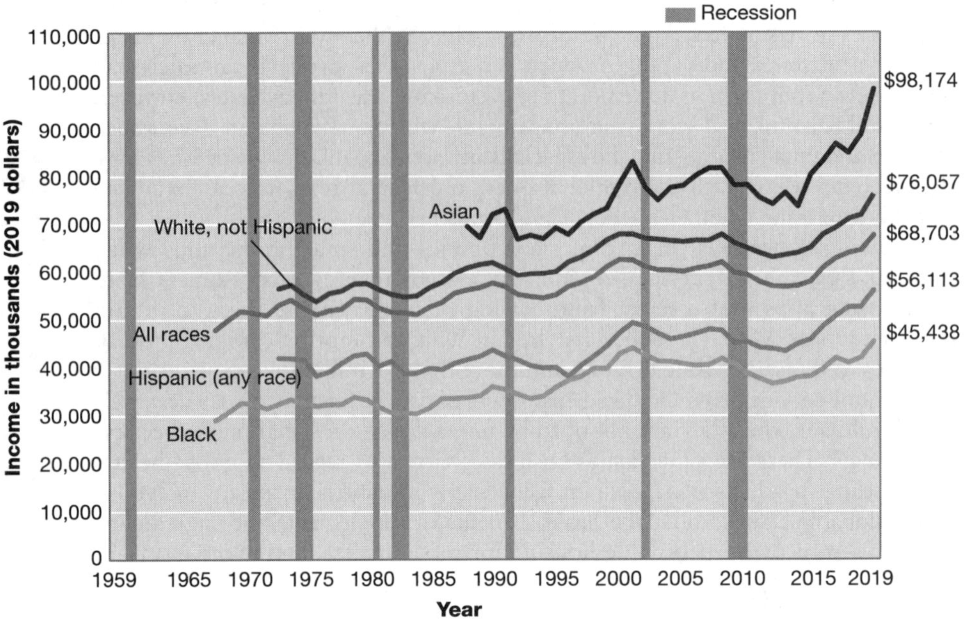

Note: The data for 2017 and beyond reflect the implementation of an updated processing system. The data for 2013 and beyond reflect the implementation of the redesigned income questions. The data points are placed at the midpoints of the respective years. Median household income data are not available prior to 1967.

Source: U.S. Census Bureau, Current Population Survey, 1968 to 2020 Annual Social and Economic Supplements.

certain number of people from underrepresented groups by a specific date. To achieve this goal, they were forced to consider only applicants from underrepresented groups for job openings; if they hired nonminority workers, they would be defeating their own purpose. However, the courts have ruled that such quotas are unconstitutional even though their purpose is commendable. They are, in fact, a form of discrimination called *reverse discrimination.*

平等就业机会委员会
Equal Employment Opportunity Commission (EEOC) a government agency with the power to investigate complaints of employment discrimination and the power to sue firms that practice it

The second problem is that although most such programs have been reasonably successful, not all businesspeople are in favor of affirmative action programs. Managers not committed to these programs can "play the game" and still discriminate against workers. To help solve this problem, Congress created (and later strengthened) the **Equal Employment Opportunity Commission (EEOC)**, a government agency with the power to investigate complaints of employment discrimination and sue firms that practice it.

Workplace diversity A company with a diverse workforce benefits in a number of ways.

The threat of legal action has persuaded some corporations to amend their hiring and promotional policies, but the discrepancy between men's and women's salaries still exists, as illustrated in Figure 2-4. For more than 60 years, women have consistently earned only about 80 cents for each dollar earned by men.

长期失业者培训计划
2-7b Training Programs for the Hard-Core Unemployed

For some firms, social responsibility extends far beyond placing a help-wanted advertisement in the local newspaper. These firms have assumed the task of helping

Figure 2-4 Relative Earning of Male and Female Workers

The ratio of women's to men's annual full-time earnings was 80% in 2019, up from 74% first reached in 1996.

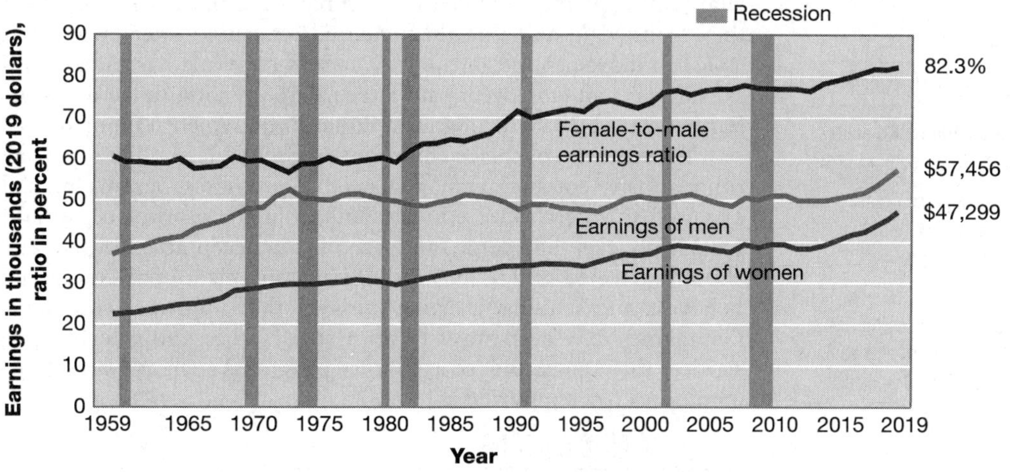

Note: The data for 2017 and beyond reflect the implementation of the redesigned income questions. The data for 2013 and beyond reflect the implementation of the redesigned income questions. The data points are placed at the midpoints of the respective years. Data on earnings of full-time, year-round workers are not readily available before 1960. Data are for people aged 14 and older for years prior to 1980.

Source: U.S. Census Bureau, Current Population Survey, 1961 to 2020 Annual Social and Economic Supplements.

the **hard-core unemployed**, workers with little education or vocational training and a long history of unemployment. These individuals may not have gained employable skills and education due to disabilities, systemic racism, economic factors, or personal issues. For example, Midas Hospitality, a hotel development and management firm, teamed up with the Boone Center, Inc., a vocational training facility for adults with intellectual and developmental disabilities, to create a program to prepare students for hotel housekeeping jobs in the St. Louis area.[28] In the past, such workers often were turned down routinely by personnel managers, even for the most menial jobs.

减少性骚扰和虐待行为的计划

2-7c Programs to Reduce Sexual Harassment and Abusive Behavior

Another hot button issue in the workplace is addressing sexual harassment, bullying, and other abusive behaviors. The Workplace Bullying Institute (WBI) defines bullying in the workplace as repeated work sabotage; verbal abuse; and/or abusive conduct that is threatening, humiliating, or intimidating. The stress of bullying can result in physical and mental health issues that can ultimately cost employers many hours of lost worker productivity as well as lower morale and higher turnover. The WBI has found that 19 percent of respondents to a survey have suffered abusive conduct at work; 19 percent say they have witnessed it in the workplace.[29] Other researchers have found much higher rates of bullying. Moreover, research by the WBI suggests that half of victims do not report their bullying out of fear of further harassment because their bully is in a position of power.[30] Even football players can be subject to bullying in the workplace: Former Miami Dolphins tackle Jonathan Martin left the team because he felt he could not continue to do his job in the face of repeated bullying from other teammates.[31]

When bullying takes on sexual overtones, it becomes sexual harassment, which the U.S. Equal Employment Opportunity Commission defines as unwelcome sexual advances, requests for sexual favors, and other verbal or physical harassment of a physical nature. Unlike bullying, sexual harassment is illegal.[32] It can also result in poor morale, high turnover, and expensive lawsuits. For example, two women filed

长期失业者
hard-core unemployed workers with little education or vocational training and a long history of unemployment

a $500 million class-action lawsuit against McDonald's, claiming that the sexual harassment they endured at corporate-owned restaurants in Florida created a "hostile work environment" for all women working in those stores. In addition to those charges, the women claimed the company did not act to stop the harassment when they reported it, and that they endured retaliation after their complaints.[33] With the #MeToo movement heightening awareness of sexual harassment in the workplace, it's no surprise that employers paid a record $68 million to survivors of workplace sexual harassment in 2019 through the Equal Employment Opportunity Commission.[34]

To create a workplace environment that stifles bullying, sexual harassment, and other abusive conduct, managers need to provide programs, much like the ones that are used to foster more ethical conduct in the workplace. In addition to creating formal policies that define and prohibit unacceptable abusive conduct, companies should strive to create an antibullying organizational culture by modeling good behavior and sending a strong message that improper conduct will be punished. Companies may even want to go a step further and offer training and additional services through employee assistance programs such as counseling to ensure that all employees feel supported.[35]

✓ Concept Check

- What is an affirmative action program? What is its purpose?
- Why did Congress create (and later strengthen) the Equal Employment Opportunity Commission?
- How can businesses reduce sexual harassment and abusive behavior at the workplace?

对环境的责任

2-8 Responsibilities to the Environment

Learning Objective

2-8 Describe the major environmental issues and businesses' response to them.

According to a report published by the U.S. Sentencing Commission, the most common federal offense committed by organizations is not fraud or money laundering but environmental crime. Environmental offenses made up nearly a third of all crimes committed by organizations, followed by fraud at 21 percent and food/drug crimes at 12.2 percent. Seventy percent of the environmental crimes were water-related, 16.7 percent affected wildlife, 8.3 percent involved hazardous materials, and 5 percent were air-related.[36]

A growing social consciousness by the public and some business managers, fostered by government legislation, has led to major efforts to reduce environmental pollution, conserve natural resources, and reverse some of the worst damage caused by past negligence in this area.

环境问题

2-8a Environmental Issues

A significant environmental issue is the amount of waste produced by businesses and society. For example, by some estimates, the United States throws out one-third of all the food produced, and grocery stores are responsible for as much as 10 percent of that. One reason for the large amount of grocery waste is consumer expectations: Consumers bypass fruits and vegetables that do not appear to be perfect, so supermarkets discard any produce that doesn't meet that expectation, even when that produce is otherwise safe and healthy.[37] The disposal problem has grown over the past few years because modern technology has continued to produce increasing amounts of chemical and radioactive waste. U.S. manufacturers produce an estimated 40 to 60 million tons of contaminated oil, solvents, acids, and sludge each year. Service businesses, utility companies, hospitals, and other industries also dump vast amounts of wastes into the environment. While companies today strive to reduce waste from operations as much as possible, much still winds up in landfills. A shortage of landfills, owing to stricter regulations, makes garbage disposal a serious problem in some areas. Incinerators help to solve the landfill-shortage problem, but they bring with them their own problems. They reduce the amount of garbage and also leave tons of ash to be buried—ash that often has a higher concentration of toxicity than the original garbage. Increasingly, plastic waste winds up in the ocean, where it accumulates into huge "garbage patches" or breaks down into microplastics that harm marine life.

Another major environmental issue is **pollution**, the contamination of water, air, or land through the actions of people in an industrialized society. Pollution harms water and air quality, threatens human and animal health, degrades habitats, and contributes to climate change. Among the serious threats to people posed by pollutants are respiratory irritation, asthma, cancer, kidney and liver damage, anemia, and heart failure. Businesspeople harm the environment when they unwittingly—or knowingly—dump hazardous chemicals and waste in unapproved ways. For example, Bernhard Schulte Shipmanagement was fined $1.75 million for improperly discharging a ship's bilge waste water into Hawaiian waters and failing to log the discharge as required by law. The Singapore-based company must also implement an environmental compliance plan for all of its vessels operating in U.S. waters.[38] For decades, environmentalists have been warning us about the dangers of industrial pollution. Unfortunately, business and government leaders either ignored the problem or were not concerned about it until pollution became a threat to life and health in America.

环境立法的影响

2-8b Effects of Environmental Legislation

As in other areas of concern to our society, legislation and regulations play a crucial role in pollution control. The laws outlined in Table 2-5 reflect the scope of current environmental legislation: laws to promote clean air, clean water, and even quiet work and living environments. Of major importance was the creation of the Environmental Protection Agency (EPA), the federal agency charged with enforcing laws designed to protect the environment.

污染

pollution the contamination of water, air, or land through the actions of people in an industrialized society

Table 2-5 Summary of Major Environmental Laws

Legislation	Major Provisions
National Environmental Policy Act (1970)	Established the Environmental Protection Agency (EPA) to enforce federal laws that involve the environment
Clean Air Act Amendment (1970)	Provided stringent automotive, aircraft, and factory emission standards
Water Quality Improvement Act (1970)	Strengthened existing water pollution regulations and provided for large monetary fines against violators
Resource Recovery Act (1970)	Enlarged the solid-waste disposal program and provided for enforcement by the EPA
Water Pollution Control Act Amendment (1972)	Established standards for cleaning navigable streams and lakes and eliminating all harmful waste disposal by 1985
Noise Control Act (1972)	Established standards for major sources of noise and required the EPA to advise the Federal Aviation Administration on standards for airplanes
Clean Air Act Amendment (1977)	Established new deadlines for cleaning up polluted areas; also required review of existing air quality standards
Resource Conservation and Recovery Act (1984)	Amended the original 1976 act and required federal regulation of potentially dangerous solid-waste disposal
Clean Air Act Amendment (1987)	Established a national air quality standard for ozone
Oil Pollution Act (1990)	Expanded the nation's oil spill prevention and response activities; also established the Oil Spill Liability Trust Fund
Clean Air Act Amendments (1990)	Required that motor vehicles be equipped with onboard systems to control about 90% of refueling vapors
Food Quality Protection Act (1996)	Amended the Federal Insecticide, Fungicide and Rodenticide Act and the Federal Food Drug and Cosmetic Act; the requirements included a new safety standard—reasonable certainty of no harm—that must be applied to all pesticides used on foods
American Recovery and Reinvestment Act (2009)	Provided $7.22 billion to the EPA to protect and promote "green" jobs and a healthier environment

Pollution Oil spills can have long-lasting effects on our wildlife and other natural resources. As our population and businesses expand, the need to reduce pollution at its source becomes more important.

When they are aware of a pollution problem, many firms are proactive in addressing it rather than wait to be cited by the EPA. Other owners and managers, however, take the position that environmental standards are too strict. (Loosely translated, this means that compliance with present standards is too expensive.) Consequently, it often has been necessary for the EPA to take legal action to force firms to install antipollution equipment and to clean up waste storage areas. Americold Logistics, for example, was fined $41,500 for illegally leaking pollutants into a creek and violating its Washington state industrial stormwater permit, among other EPA charges. The company, which promptly acknowledged and acted to resolve the issues, agreed to develop and implement plans to reduce pollutants leaving its food warehouse facility.[39]

Experience has shown that the combination of environmental legislation, voluntary compliance, and EPA action can succeed in restoring the environment and keeping it clean. However, much still remains to be done.

企业对环境问题的回应

2-8c Business Response to Environmental Concerns

One of the most effective ways that companies can reduce their impact on the environment is to reduce waste from operations and other activities. Identifying and eliminating inefficiencies in production and operations is where most firms begin that process. Finding alternative uses for waste is another. For example, leftover food from supermarkets and restaurants is often donated to local food banks or sold to farmers who feed it to livestock. Most companies strive to recycle as much as possible. **Recycling** involves converting used materials into new products or components for new products in order to prevent their unnecessary disposal. Companies can recycle waste paper, glass, rubber, metals, some plastic packaging, and other materials so that they or their components can be reprocessed into new products and kept out of landfills. As an example, Madewell gives customers $20 toward a new pair of Madewell jeans when they bring in worn-out or out-of-style jeans of any brand. The clothing company donates the used denim to the Cotton's Blue Jeans Go Green program, which turns it into insulation for homes, preventing 529 tons of waste from going into a landfill thus far.[40]

回收利用
recycling converting used materials into new products or components for new products in order to prevent their unnecessary disposal

Another way businesses strive to be more environmentally conscious is through the use of "greener" forms of power to counter their use of huge quantities of energy during operations and other activities. Companies can audit their operations to identify places where more efficient and environmentally friendly products can be used to save energy, such as using LED light bulbs—which reduce heat as well as power use—and even natural sunlight to light workplaces. Many companies are turning to alternative forms of power generation,

Reducing dependence on fossil fuels Today's businesses (and consumers) are more open to alternative sources of energy because they are concerned about the negative impact of conventional energy sources.

Sustaining the Planet

保护地球：可持续发展有利可图吗

Is Sustainability Profitable?

Sustainability has taken the spotlight as environmental consciousness grows among consumers, business professionals, and investors. Though sustainability was once an afterthought for many organizations, more than ever shoppers are looking for products and brands that align with their values. Long story short: sustainability leads to profitability.

In the not-too-distant past, it was difficult to convince investors that sustainability and profitability were linked. Now, with many companies aligning executive bonuses with sustainability targets, there's a growing consensus that environmental, social, and governance practices are strategic priorities. This shift has caused businesses to evaluate their supply chains, from materials to transportation, to find opportunities to limit their environmental impact. Environmental goals often include water reduction, zero waste to landfill, and lowering carbon energy use. Additionally, companies can focus on making products more durable, reusable, repairable, and recyclable.

Investors, who now see that the future is green, often have specific environmental expectations and put pressure on companies to evolve. Many organizations have reaped the benefits of leading with sustainability. According to *The Wall Street Journal*, the most sustainably managed companies in the world include Sony (hardware), Philips (medical equipment), Cisco Systems (hardware), Merck (biotechnology and pharmaceuticals), and Iberdrola (electric utilities and power generators). These organizations have all prioritized environmental concerns while maintaining high profits, showing that sustainability can play a critical role in an organization's future success.

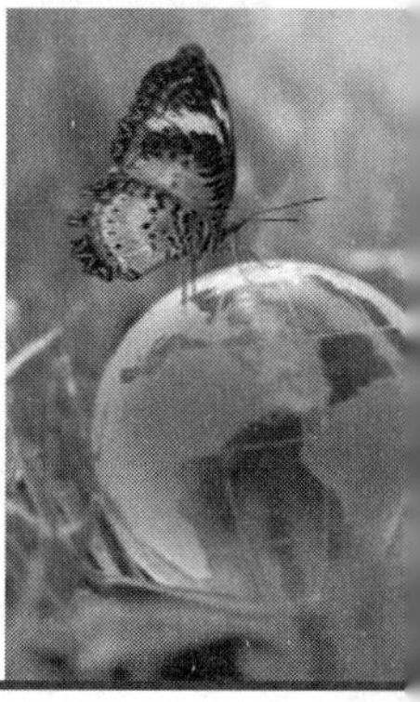

Sources: Based on information in Dieter Holger and Olivia Bugault, "CEOs Increasingly See Sustainability as Path to Profitability," *The Wall Street Journal*, October 12, 2020; Fabiana Negrin Ochoa, Dieter Holger, Maitane Sardon, and Catherine Lindsay, "The 100 Most Sustainably Managed Companies in the World," *The Wall Street Journal*, October 13, 2020.

including solar and wind power which do not rely on diminishing sources of fossil fuels. New Belgium Brewing in Fort Collins, Colorado, became the first company to be 100 percent powered by the wind, but many other companies have followed suit. A number of Fortune 500 businesses, including Google, Apple, Starbucks, Cisco, and Bank of America, get 100 percent of their electricity from renewable energy sources such as wind and solar.[41]

Recognizing public demand for greater environmental responsibility, more and more firms are adopting environmentally friendly practices and products that are less harmful to the environment. **Green marketing** is the process of creating, making, delivering, and promoting products that are environmentally safe. It may include making modifications to products, manufacturing processes, packaging, and/or promotion activities to make or deliver products that are better for the environment. Chipotle Mexican Grill, for example, built its reputation as a green marketer by abiding by its "Cultivate a Better World" mission, which requires using real ingredients that "are responsibly sourced and classically cooked with people, animals and the environment in mind." To live by that mission, the company strives to use only natural animal products (treated humanely and fed a vegetarian diet that does not include growth hormones or antibiotics), organic ingredients, and where possible, local sources. It also educates consumers and other stakeholders about its efforts through a Real Foodprint tracker on its app as well as a regularly released Sustainability Report that details its sustainability goals and progress in reaching them. It is significant that Chipotle has not yet achieved all its sustainability goals, but its mission guides the firm in all decision making and activities.[42]

Recognizing that consumers increasingly prefer to purchase from businesses that make recycling, green energy, and sustainability a strategic priority, companies are increasingly touting their green efforts. However, green marketers must take care to ensure that their claims are backed by evidence that shows a significant

绿色营销
green marketing the process of creating, making, delivering, and promoting products that are environmentally safe

environmental benefit and does not mislead consumers or they may run afoul of the Federal Trade Commission.[43] Companies that take their green marketing efforts too far, without relevance or support for their environmental claims risk being labeled guilty of *green washing*.

As we have seen, more businesses are trying harder to make their activities and products sustainable going forward, but what about cleaning up past environmental messes—oil spills, improperly stored industrial wastes, polluting emissions, and more—that harm the environment today? Many business leaders offer one answer: Use tax money to clean up the environment and to keep it clean. They reason that business is not the only source of pollution, so business should not be forced to absorb the entire cost of the cleanup. Environmentalists disagree. They believe that the cost of proper treatment and disposal of industrial wastes is an expense of doing business. In either case, consumers ultimately will bear a large part of the cost—either as taxes or in the form of higher prices for goods and services.

✓ Concept Check

- What are the major environmental issues facing society today?
- Summarize major provisions of federal environmental laws enacted since 1970.
- What is businesses' response to environmental concerns?

实施社会责任计划

2-9 Implementing a Program of Social Responsibility

Learning Objective

2-9 Identify the steps a business must take to implement a program of social responsibility

A firm's decision to be socially responsible is a step in the right direction—but only the first step. The business then must develop and implement a program to reach this goal. The program will be affected by the firm's size, financial resources, past record in the area of social responsibility, and competition. Above all, however, the program must have the firm's total commitment or it will fail.

An effective program for ethics and social responsibility requires time, money, and organization. In most cases, developing and implementing such a program will require four steps: securing the commitment of top executives, planning, appointing a director, and preparing a social audit.

高层管理人员的承诺

2-9a Commitment of Top Executives

Without the support of top executives, any program will soon falter and become ineffective. At CitiGroup, the board of directors maintains the Ethics, Conduct, and Culture Committee, which oversees the financial conglomerate's ethics and compliance program.[44] As evidence of their commitment to social responsibility, top managers should develop a policy statement that outlines key areas of concern. Such statements set a tone of positive support and later will serve as a guide for other employees as they become involved in the program.

规划

2-9b Planning

Next, a committee of managers should be appointed to plan the program. Whatever form their plan takes, it should deal with each of the issues described in the top managers' policy statement. If necessary, outside consultants can be hired to help develop the plan.

委任董事

2-9c Appointment of a Director

After the social responsibility plan is established, a top-level executive should be appointed to implement the organization's plan. This individual should be charged with recommending specific policies and helping individual departments to understand and live up to the social responsibilities the firm has assumed. Depending on the size of the firm, the director may require a staff to handle the program on a day-to-day basis. For example, at Cisco, Tae Yoo, Senior Vice President of Corporate Affairs, administers the technology giant's corporate social responsibility program, including applying its resources to facilitate problem solving that has positive impacts on people, society, and the Earth.[45]

社会审计

2-9d The Social Audit

At specified intervals, the program director should prepare a social audit for the firm. A **social audit** is a comprehensive report of what an organization has done and is doing with regard to social issues that affect it. This document provides the information the firm needs to evaluate and revise its social responsibility program. Typical subject areas include human resources, community involvement, the quality and safety of products, business practices, and efforts to reduce pollution and improve the environment. The information included in a social audit should be as accurate and as quantitative as possible, and the audit should reveal both positive and negative aspects of the program. Caesars Entertainment, which operates casinos, evaluates its corporate citizenship efforts annually and then issues a report describing its performance for a variety of stakeholders including employees, investors, and the media. Caesars' Corporate Citizenship Report details its performance in meeting goals in the areas of responsible gaming, employee development, environmental stewardship, and community investment.[46]

Today, many companies listen to concerned individuals within and outside the company. For example, the Citi Ethics Line listens to and acts on concerns expressed by employees and others about possible violations of company policies, laws, or regulations, such as improper or unethical business practices, as well as health, safety, and environmental issues. Employees are encouraged to communicate their concerns, as well as ask questions about ethical issues. The Ethics Line is available to all Citi employees, as well as concerned individuals outside the company.

社会审计
social audit a comprehensive report of what an organization has done and is doing with regard to social issues that affect it

✓ Concept Check

- What steps must a business take to implement a program of social responsibility?
- What is the social audit? Who should prepare a social audit for the firm?

Summary 小 结

2-1 Define *business ethics.*

Ethics is the study of right and wrong and of the morality of choices. Business ethics is the application of moral standards to business situations.

2-2 Identify the types of ethical concerns that arise in the business world.

Ethical issues arise often in business situations out of relationships with investors, customers, employees, creditors, or competitors. Businesspeople should make every effort to be fair, to consider the welfare of customers and others within the firm, to avoid conflicts of interest, and to communicate honestly.

2-3 Discuss the factors that affect the level of ethical behavior in organizations.

Individual, social, and opportunity factors all affect the level of ethical behavior in an organization. Individual factors include knowledge level, moral values and attitudes, and personal goals. Social factors include cultural norms and the actions and values of co-workers and significant others. Opportunity factors refer to the amount of leeway that exists in an organization for employees to behave unethically if they choose to do so.

2-4 Explain how organizations can encourage ethical decision making in business.

Governments, trade associations, and individual firms can establish regulations and guidelines for defining ethical behavior. Governments can pass stricter regulations and laws. Trade associations provide ethical guidelines for their members. Companies provide and enforce codes of ethics—written guides to acceptable and ethical behavior as defined by an organization—and create an atmosphere in which ethical behavior is encouraged. An ethical employee working in an unethical environment may resort to whistle-blowing to bring a questionable practice to light.

2-5 Describe how our current views on the social responsibility of business have evolved.

In a socially responsible business, management realizes that its activities have an impact on society and considers that impact in the decision-making process. Before the 1930s, workers, consumers, and government had very little influence on business activities; as a result, business leaders gave little thought to social responsibility. All this changed with the Great Depression. Government regulations, employee demands, and consumer awareness combined to create a demand that businesses act in socially responsible ways.

The basic premise of the economic model of social responsibility is that society benefits most when business is left alone to produce profitable goods and services. According to the socioeconomic model, business has as much responsibility to society as it has to its owners. Most managers adopt a viewpoint somewhere between these two extremes.

2-6 List the responsibilities businesses have to the public, especially with regard to consumer rights and public health.

Consumerism consists of all activities undertaken to protect the rights of consumers. Although concerns over consumer rights have been around to some extent since the early 19th century, the movement became more powerful in the 1960s when President John F. Kennedy initiated the Consumer Bill of Rights. The six basic rights of consumers include the right to safety, the right to be informed, the right to choose, the right to be heard, and the rights to consumer education and courteous service. Today, many people believe that businesses have a basic responsibility to contribute to the general wellbeing of the public. Other issues businesses face relate to public health, including addressing products that contribute to obesity and cancer.

2-7 Analyze how present employment practices are being used to counteract past abuses.

Legislation and public demand have prompted some businesses to correct past abuses in employment practices—mainly with regard to minority groups. Affirmative action and training of the hard-core unemployed are two types of programs that have been used successfully. Another issue in the workplace is addressing sexual harassment and other abusive behaviors, such as bullying and verbal abuse.

2-8 Describe the major environmental issues and businesses' response to them.

A growing social consciousness, fostered by government legislation, has led to major efforts to reduce waste and pollution, conserve natural resources, and reverse some of the worst damage caused by past negligence in this area. Current environmental laws, enforced by the Environmental Protection Agency, promote clean air, clean water, and even quiet work and living environments. However, much still remains to be done. Many companies are looking for ways to reduce their environmental footprint, such as improving operations to reduce waste, recycling, using alternative forms of energy, including solar and wind power, and engaging in green marketing—the process of creating, making, delivering, and promoting products that are environmentally safe.

2-9 Identify the steps a business must take to implement a program of social responsibility.

A program to implement social responsibility in a business begins with total commitment by top management. The program should be planned carefully, and a capable director should be appointed to implement it. Social audits should be prepared periodically as a means of evaluating and revising the program.

Key Terms 关键术语

You should now be able to define and give an example relevant to each of the following terms:

ethics
business ethics
plagiarism
conflict of interest
Sarbanes-Oxley Act of 2002
code of ethics
whistle-blowing
social responsibility
corporate citizenship
caveat emptor
economic model of social responsibility
socioeconomic model of social responsibility
consumerism
affirmative action program
Equal Employment Opportunity Commission (EEOC)
hard-core unemployed
pollution
recycling
green marketing
social audit

Discussion Questions 讨论题

1. When a company acts in an ethically questionable manner, what types of problems are caused for the organization and its customers?
2. What factors affect ethical behavior and choices? How can businesses use this knowledge to further ethical behavior in their organizations?
3. How can employees take an ethical stand regarding a business decision when their superior already has taken a different position?
4. How can businesses encourage employees to make ethical choices?
5. Overall, would it be more profitable for a business to follow the economic model or the socioeconomic model of social responsibility?
6. Why should business take on the task of training the hard-core unemployed?
7. To what extent should the blame for vehicular air pollution be shared by manufacturers, consumers, and government?
8. Why is there so much government regulation involving social responsibility issues? Should there be less?

Case 2 案例 2：全食超市的全食交易保障

Inside Whole Trade at Whole Foods

Whole Foods Market, a natural supermarket chain, was founded in Austin, Texas, in 1980. At the time, the market for natural, unprocessed foods was small, but the company soon expanded to new cities as demand grew. Now, the grocer can be found in 500 locations across North America and the United Kingdom. Since the beginning, responsible sourcing has been a core component of Whole Foods' business. This stakeholder orientation focuses on the needs of its customers, its employees, its communities, and people at every level of its supply chain.

The Whole Trade Guarantee is Whole Foods' ethical trading program. It supports ethical trade, proper working conditions, and environmental protection in the production of the products it sells. Products with this label meet rigorous quality standards and come from certified farms that have a history of positive impacts on their employees, supply chain partners, communities, and the environment. Through the program, Whole Foods provides funds to the farms they work with to support various community initiatives such as community centers, medical services, and dental care. Programs such as Whole Trade support Whole Foods' mission to nourish both people and the planet.

Whole Foods has often been called "Whole Paycheck" because of the more expensive price tags on its products. However, Whole Foods believes that, as a responsible buyer, it has a duty to monitor its impact on the environment and individuals throughout the supply chain. Pressure from retailers to lower costs can lead to farm owners exploiting workers to deliver products cheaply. One of Whole Foods' goals is to provide its shoppers with affordable, sustainable food that also supports farmers and farmworkers.

Beyond creating win–win partnerships with its suppliers, Whole Foods ultimately views customers as its most important stakeholder. To differentiate itself from its competitors, Whole Foods emphasizes the quality of its products over price. The company has a variety of quality standards to ensure its customers get the best, including standards for its meat, eggs, seafood, supplements, beauty products, and household cleaners. In addition, Whole Foods bans more than 100 ingredients such as high-fructose corn syrup.

Employees at Whole Foods are another top priority. Full-time team members are offered comprehensive health insurance. The company also provides its team members with career and learning development, volunteer programs through the Whole Planet Foundation, and team member assistance plans. In addition to competitive pay, the company also offers 401(k) plans and health savings accounts, discounts, and paid time off.

All of these efforts combined help Whole Foods earn profits, which in turn creates value for its shareholders. Profits are essential for any business to survive, and Whole Foods believes it has a responsibility to its parent company, Amazon, to use its capital in the best way possible to achieve the best results possible. Not everyone was pleased when Amazon acquired Whole Foods in 2017 for $13.4 billion. Many employees noticed a change in working conditions such as heavier workloads and budget cuts. Amazon also sought to make Whole Foods' products more affordable by purchasing a greater number of products from national food distributors rather than local farms. Prices have since returned to pre-Amazon levels but other initiatives—such as discounts for Amazon Prime members—remain to provide customers with more value.

Whole Food's strong relationships with its supply chain partners are fostered by its Whole Trade program. This is a core strength that can be leveraged by both Whole Foods and Amazon to stand out. Though many criticized Amazon's acquisition of Whole Foods due to their cultural differences, Amazon's deep pockets and robust supply chain knowledge will surely benefit Whole Foods in the long run. By committing to ethical and sustainable trading practices, Whole Foods sets itself apart from traditional supermarkets.[47]

Questions

1. Why do you think Whole Foods wants to support the farmers and farmworkers in its supply chain?
2. Why are customers willing to pay a premium for goods at Whole Foods?
3. How does Whole Foods meet the needs of its customers?

Building Skills for Career Success 为成功的职业生涯培养技能

1. Social Media Exercise

Lego has been making children's toys since the 1930s and its iconic plastic building blocks since 1958. Company executives, wanting their products to have a lasting legacy, have launched several initiatives to leave the world a better place. Visit Lego's website to learn more about these initiatives and search for Lego on YouTube.

1. What responsibilities do you think Lego has to its customers—the children as well as their parents?

2. Are these initiatives consistent with the firm's mission and values?Why or why not?
3. Search YouTube and then describe how Lego's sustainability efforts compare with those of rivals like Mattel and Hasbro.

2. Building Team Skills

A firm's code of ethics outlines the kinds of behaviors expected within the organization and serves as a guideline for encouraging ethical behavior in the workplace. It reflects the rights of the firm's workers, shareholders, and consumers.

Assignment

1. Working in a team of four, find a code of ethics for a business firm. Start the search by asking firms in your community for a copy of their codes, by visiting the library, or by searching and downloading information from the internet.
2. Analyze the code of ethics you have chosen, and answer the following questions:
   a. What does the company's code of ethics say about the rights of its workers, shareholders, consumers, and suppliers? How does the code reflect the company's attitude toward competitors?
   b. How does this code of ethics resemble the information discussed in this chapter? How does it differ?
   c. As an employee of this company, how would you personally interpret the code of ethics? How might the code influence your behavior within the workplace? Give several examples.

3. Researching Different Careers

Business ethics has been at the heart of many discussions over the years and continues to trouble employees and shareholders. Stories about dishonesty and wrongful behavior in the workplace appear on a regular basis in newspapers and on the national news.

Assignment

Prepare a written report on the following:

1. Why can it be so difficult for people to do what is right?
2. What is your personal code of ethics? Prepare a code outlining what you believe is morally right. The document should include guidelines for your personal behavior.
3. How will your code of ethics affect your decisions about:
   a. The types of questions you should ask in a job interview?
   b. Selecting a company in which to work?

Chapter

3

Global Business

全球商务

Learning Objectives

Once you complete this chapter, you will be able to:

3-1 Explain the economic bases for and importance of international business.

3-2 Explore the methods by which a firm can organize for and enter into international markets.

3-3 Discuss the challenges businesses face when entering international markets, especially the restrictions nations place on international trade.

3-4 Identify the facilitators of international trade, including international trade agreements and international economic organizations working to foster trade.

3-5 Describe sources of export assistance.

3-6 Identify institutions that can help businesses and nations finance international business.

Why Should You Care?

Free trade—are you for or against it? Most economists support free-trade policies, but public support can be lukewarm, and certain groups are adamantly opposed, contending that "trade harms large segments of U.S. workers," "degrades the environment," and "exploits the poor."

Inside Business 商业透视：星巴克走向全球以实现增长

Starbucks Goes Global for Growth

Starbucks, the world's largest coffeehouse chain, has more stores internationally than it does in the United States as a result of putting global expansion at the center of its growth strategy. Domestically, Starbucks has slowed new store openings and closed locations deemed redundant in dense metro areas in order to put the company in a more profitable position. While Starbucks tackles changing consumer behavior in the United States, other countries present valuable growth opportunities.

An aggressive push into China, Starbucks' fastest-growing market, has been successful for the company. According to Starbucks China CEO and chairperson Belinda Wong, at one point in time, Starbucks opened a new store in China every 15 hours. The company announced plans to invest $150 million in a roasting plant in China, deepening its commitment to building the Starbucks brand throughout Asia. The company's only other non-U.S. roasting facility is in Amsterdam to support Europe.

To penetrate China's coffee market, the coffeehouse chain focused on rolling out innovation even faster than in the United States. For example, to appeal to local tastes, the menu in China includes a variety of tea-based beverages as well as exclusive drink categories. Additionally, Starbucks rolled out delivery in Beijing and Shanghai and 11 other cities in China before it expanded delivery in the United States. The Asia-Pacific market accounts for approximately half of Starbucks' global new store growth.[1]

Did you know?

Starbucks has 32,000 stores across more than 80 markets.

Like Starbucks, many companies, large and small, do business around the world. Did you know that only 31 percent of the Coca-Cola Company's sales come from North America? Asia-Pacific and Latin American markets generate 14 percent and 11 percent, respectively, of the revenues of the beverage giant.[2] Even small businesses can find great success in global markets. One such company is Combustion Associates of Corona, California, a small business founded by husband-and-wife immigrants from Bangladesh. The company designs, manufactures, and exports large power generators to developing countries.[3] Whether they buy or sell products across national borders, these companies are all contributing to the volume of international trade that is fueling the global economy.

Theoretically, international trade is every bit as logical and worthwhile as interstate trade between, say, California and Washington. Yet, nations tend to restrict the import of certain goods for a variety of reasons. For example, the United States restricted the import of Mexican fresh tomatoes because they were undercutting price levels of domestic fresh tomatoes. Despite such restrictions, international trade has increased almost steadily since World War II. Many of the industrialized nations have signed trade agreements intended to reduce problems in international business and to help less-developed nations participate in world trade. Individual firms around the world have seized the opportunity to compete in foreign markets by exporting products and increasing foreign production, as well as by other means.

In this chapter, we describe international trade in terms of modern specialization, whereby each country trades the surplus goods and services it produces most efficiently for products its citizens and organizations need. We also consider the importance and extent of international trade with the U.S. economy. Next, we explore several methods of entering international markets. We then examine the challenges business organizations face when engaging in trade across borders and identify organizations working to

创业成功：阿里巴巴通过提供指导助力企业家

Entrepreneurial Success

Alibaba Provides Guidance to Help Entrepreneurs

Alibaba, one of the world's largest e-commerce companies, invests in Hong Kong and Taiwan-based entrepreneurs through its not-for-profit arm, the Alibaba Entrepreneurs Fund. In addition to investment capital, Alibaba provides guidance to help individuals scale their businesses, making use of Alibaba's tools and resources. The e-commerce giant aims to build Hong Kong's start-up ecosystem by fueling entrepreneurship and innovation.

According to a survey conducted by Alibaba and KPMG, corporate executives benefit from collaborating with start-ups because it helps keep them up to date on the latest innovations. Entrepreneurs develop new ideas, find solutions that address society's needs, diversify the economy, and create upward mobility. Lynk, one of the businesses Alibaba has invested in, is the first-ever Software-as-a-Service platform built on an expert network. The service allows businesses to easily connect with a diverse set of 840,000 advisors rather than hiring experts in-house. The company has raised more than $30 million in capital.

By supporting the entrepreneurial landscape in China, Alibaba's marketplace and other platforms will benefit. The Alibaba Entrepreneurs Fund follows a venture capitalist model, except profits from the company's venture investments are returned to the fund for reinvestment, ensuring capital is always available. Independent professionals with start-up experience evaluate and select the entrepreneurs that will receive funding and strategic guidance from Alibaba's network of business leaders. The not-for-profit looks for innovative start-ups in the big data, cleantech, e-commerce, fintech, and logistics sectors, among others. Alibaba then leverages its resources to help the entrepreneurs grow their businesses.

Sources: Based on information in "Alibaba Hong Kong Entrepreneurs Fund Launches JUMPSTARTER 2021 Global Pitch Competition," *Business Wire*, July 28, 2020; Alibaba Entrepreneurs Fund, "Transforming Hong Kong Through Entrepreneurship"; Catherine Shu, "Lynk, a 'Knowledge -as-a-Service' Platform with More Than 840,000 Experts, Raises $24 Million," *TechCrunch*, January 27, 2021.

facilitate global trade. We also outline the various sources of export assistance available from the federal government. Finally, we identify some of the institutions that provide the complex financing necessary for modern international trade.

国际商务基础

3-1 The Basis for International Business

Learning Objective

3-1 Explain the economic bases for and importance of international business.

International business encompasses all business activities that involve exchanges across national boundaries. Thus, a firm is engaged in international business when it buys some portion of its input from, or sells some portion of its output to, an organization located in a foreign country. (A small retail store may sell goods produced in some other country. However, because it purchases these goods from American distributors, it is not engaged in international trade.)

绝对优势和比较优势

3-1a Absolute and Comparative Advantage

Some countries are better equipped than others to produce particular goods or services. The reason may be a country's natural resources, its labor supply, or even customs or a historical accident. In such cases, it would be advantageous for a country to specialize in the production of such products so that it can produce them most efficiently. The country could use what it needed of these products and then trade the surplus for products it could not produce efficiently on its own. Saudi Arabia thus has specialized in the production of crude oil and petroleum products; South Africa, in diamonds; and Australia, in wool. Each of these countries is said to have an absolute advantage with regard to a particular product. An **absolute advantage** is the ability to produce a specific product more efficiently than any other nation.

国际商务
international business all business activities that involve exchanges across national boundaries

绝对优势
absolute advantage the ability to produce a specific product more efficiently than any other nation

A U.S. absolute advantage. The United States has long specialized in the production of wheat. Because of its specific geography and climate, the United States enjoys an absolute advantage—the ability to produce wheat more efficiently than countries in other parts of the world.

One country may have an absolute advantage with regard to several products, whereas another country may have no absolute advantage at all. Yet it is still worthwhile for these two countries to specialize and trade with each other. To see why this is so, imagine that you are the president of a successful manufacturing firm and that you can accurately type 90 words per minute. Your assistant can type 80 words per minute but would run the business poorly. Thus, you have an absolute advantage over your assistant in both typing and managing. However, you cannot afford to type your own letters because your time is better spent in managing the business. That is, you have a comparative advantage in managing. A **comparative advantage** is the ability to produce a specific product more efficiently than any other product. Your assistant, on the other hand, has a comparative advantage in clerical duties because he or she can do that better than managing the business. Thus, you spend your time managing, and you leave the document preparation to your assistant. Overall, the business is run as efficiently as possible because you are each working in accordance with your own comparative advantage.

The same is true for nations. Goods and services are produced more efficiently when each country specializes in the products for which it has a comparative advantage. Moreover, by definition, every country has a comparative advantage in some product. The United States has many comparative advantages—in research and development, high-technology industries, and identifying new markets, for instance.

进出口

3-1b Exporting and Importing

Suppose that the United States specializes in producing corn. It then will produce a surplus of corn, but perhaps it will have a shortage of wine. France, on the other hand, specializes in producing wine but experiences a shortage of corn. To satisfy both needs—for corn and for wine—the two countries should trade with each other. The United States should export corn and import wine. France should export wine and import corn.

Exporting is selling and shipping raw materials or products to other nations. The Boeing Company, for example, exports its airplanes to a number of countries for use by their airlines. On a smaller scale, the Liriope Factory, a small Louisiana nursery, has expanded the customer base for its ground cover plants by exporting to European markets.[4] Figure 3-1 shows selected top merchandise-exporting states in the United States.

Importing is purchasing raw materials or products in other nations and bringing them into one's own country. Thus, buyers for Macy's department stores may purchase rugs in India or raincoats in England and have them shipped back to the United States for resale.

贸易差额

3-1c Balance of Trade

Importing and exporting are the principal activities in international trade. They give rise to an important concept called the *balance of trade*. A nation's **balance of trade** is the total value of its exports minus the total value of its imports over

比较优势
comparative advantage the ability to produce a specific product more efficiently than any other product

出口
exporting selling and shipping raw materials or products to other nations

进口
importing purchasing raw materials or products in other nations and bringing them into one's own country

贸易差额
balance of trade the total value of a nation's exports minus the total value of its imports over a specified period of time

Figure 3-1 Selected Top Exporting States

Texas and California account for about one-third of all U.S. exports.

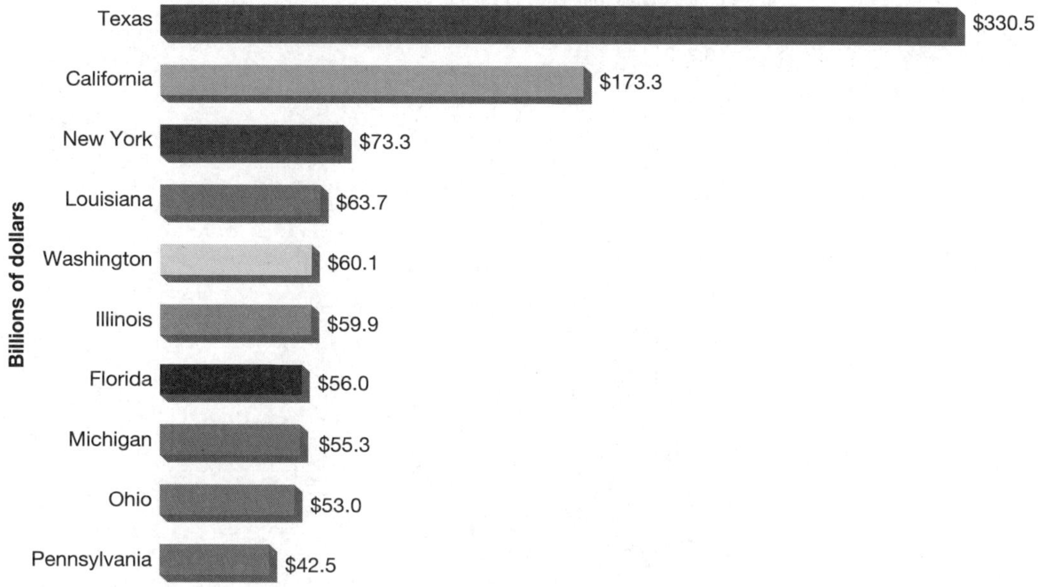

Source: Daniel Workman, "America's Top 20 Export States," *World's Top Exports*, March 2020.

a specified period of time. If a country imports more than it exports, its balance of trade is negative and is said to be *unfavorable*. On the other hand, when a country exports more than it imports, it is said to have a *favorable* balance of trade.

In 2020, the United States imported $2,810.6 billion worth of goods and services and exported $2,131.9 billion worth. It thus had a trade deficit of $678.7 billion.[5] A **trade deficit** is a negative balance of trade (refer to Figure 3-2). However, the United States has consistently enjoyed a large and rapidly growing surplus in services, such as computer and banking services. For example, in 2020, the United States imported $460.1 billion worth of services and exported $697.1 billion worth, thus creating a favorable balance of $237 billion.[6]

贸易逆差
trade deficit a negative balance of trade

U.S. exports. U.S. aircraft and spacecraft products represent the third largest U.S. exports.

Figure 3-2 U.S. International Trade in Goods and Services

If a country imports more goods than it exports, the balance of trade is negative, as it was in the United States from 2000 to 2020.

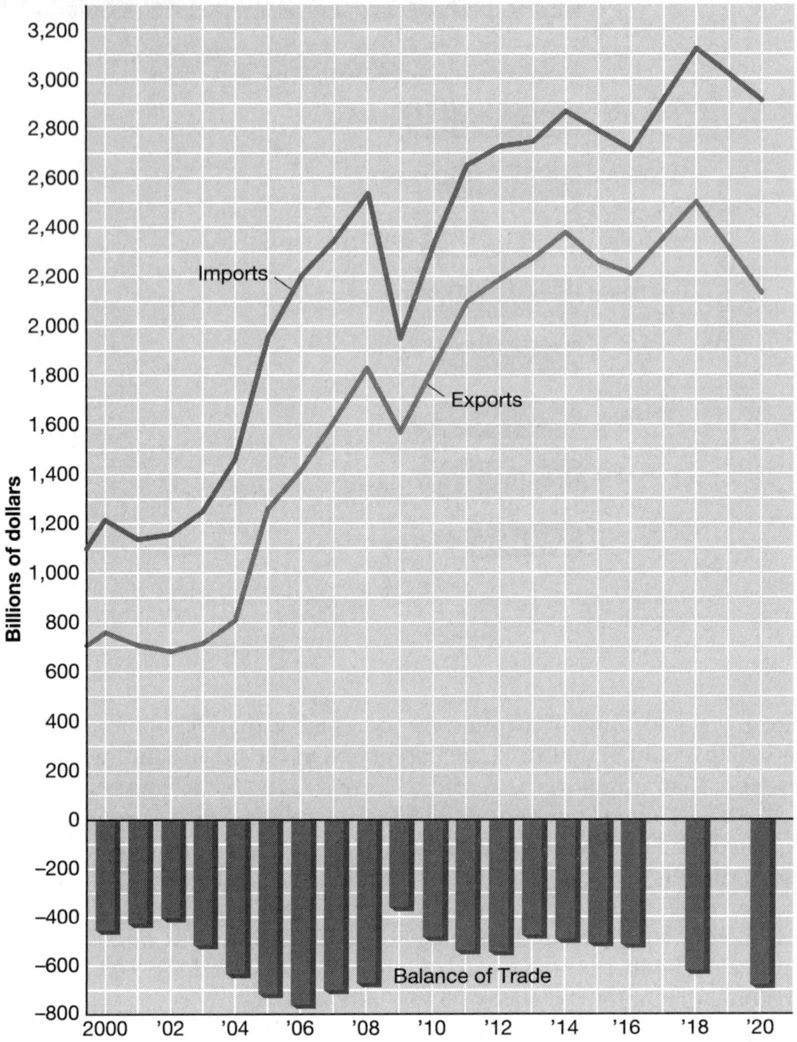

Sources: U.S. Department of Commerce, International Trade Administration; U.S. Bureau of Economic Analysis, "U.S. International Trade in Goods and Services, December 2020," February 5, 2021; U.S. Bureau of Economic Analysis, "U.S. International Trade in Goods and Services, December 2018," March 6, 2019.

Question: *Are trade deficits bad?*

Answer: It's complicated. A negative balance of trade is often viewed as unfavorable because the country must export money to pay for its excess imports. However, trade deficits also mean that consumers at home have the benefit of a wider variety of products at competitive prices. Consider the iPhone, which is manufactured in China. If it were to be made in the United States, it likely would retail for $2,000, but lower supply and labor costs overseas mean that Apple can sell most models for less than $1,000, or twice as many.[7] These lower prices also help stifle the threat of inflation. In the long run, though, trade deficits give rise to sending more jobs overseas where costs are often significantly lower, thereby resulting in less job creation at home. This is indeed what is happening in the United States.

A nation's **balance of payments** is the total flow of money into a country minus the total flow of money out of that country over a specified period of time. Balance of payments, therefore, is a much broader concept than balance of trade. It includes imports and exports, of course. However, it also includes investments, money spent by foreign tourists, payments by foreign governments, aid to foreign governments, and all other receipts and payments. A continual deficit in a nation's balance of payments (a negative balance) can cause other nations to lose confidence in that nation's economy. Alternatively, a persistent surplus may indicate that the country encourages exports but limits imports by imposing trade restrictions.

国际贸易的经济展望

3-1d The Economic Outlook for Trade

International trade is a major growth vehicle for the United States. More than 40 million full- and part-time jobs, or about one out of every five jobs in the United States, depend on international trade. The percentage of American jobs tied to global trade has doubled since 1992, growing from 10.4 percent to 20.2 percent.[8] In 2018, for the first time, the U.S. exports exceeded $2.5 trillion, up from $25 billion in 1960.[9] Many other countries have experienced similar growth. This dramatic increase in trade volume over the past 60 years has been one of the most important factors in the rise of living standards around the world. During this time, exports have become increasingly important to the U.S. economy. Exports as a percentage of U.S. GDP have increased steadily since 1970, except during recessions. Table 3-1 shows U.S. exports and imports for selected world areas in 2020, and Table 3-2 shows the value of U.S. merchandise exports to, and imports from, each of the nation's eight major trading partners. Note that Canada and Mexico are our best partners for our exports; China and Mexico, for imports.

Although the worldwide recessions of 1991, 2001–2002, and 2008–2009 slowed the rate of growth, and the global COVID-19 pandemic economic crisis caused the sharpest decline in more than 75 years, globalization is a reality of our time. In the United States, international trade now accounts for over one-fourth of gross domestic product (GDP). As trade barriers decrease, new competitors enter the global marketplace, creating more choices for consumers and new opportunities for job seekers. Looking ahead, the International Monetary Fund (IMF), an international bank with 190 member nations, expected global growth to continue, albeit more slowly as world economies recover from the pandemic and social unrest. The IMF

Table 3-1 U.S. Exports and Imports of Goods for Selected World Areas in 2020 in Billions of Dollars

Selected World Area*	Exports	Imports
North America	$468	$596
Europe	$332	$577
Euro Area	$213	$368
European Union	$232	$415
Pacific Rim	$376	$825
South/Central America	$130	$91
Africa	$22	$24
OPEC	$35	$19
Other Countries	$74	$209

*Countries may be included in more than one area grouping.

Source: U.S. Department of Commerce, Bureau of Economic Analysis, "Monthly U.S International Trade in Goods, December 2020".

国际收支

balance of payments the total flow of money into a country minus the total flow of money out of that country over a specified period of time

Table 3-2 Top Trading Partners: Value of U.S. Merchandise Exports and Imports of Goods, 2020

Rank	Country	Exports ($ billions)	Imports ($ billions)	Total Trade ($ billions)	Percent of Total Trade
1	China	124.6	435.4	560.1	14.9
2	Mexico	212.7	325.4	538.1	14.3
3	Canada	255.4	270.4	525.8	14.0
4	Japan	64.1	119.5	183.6	4.9
5	Germany	57.8	115.1	172.9	4.6
6	Korea, South	51.2	76.0	127.2	3.4
7	United Kingdom	59.0	50.2	109.2	2.9
8	Switzerland	18.0	74.8	92.8	2.5

Source: U.S. Department of Commerce, Census Bureau, "Top Trading Partners".

expected the world economic growth to be 5.5 percent and 4.2 percent in 2021 and 2022, respectively,[10] although the lingering economic effects of the COVID-19 pandemic may reduce that. Let's take a quick look at trade with some major nations and regions.

Canada and Western Europe Due in part to sharing a border and language, the economic relationship between the United States and Canada is one of the most efficient, most integrated, and most dynamic in the world. Together, the two nations generated 703.8 billion in bilateral trade in 2019—almost $2 billion a day, or $23,000 every second.[11] The nearly 450 million residents of the European Union make its member countries attractive trading partners, generating an estimated trade in goods of more than $658 billion in 2020.[12] Most other advanced economies, including Norway, Sweden, Switzerland, and the United Kingdom, are also major importers to and buyers of exports from the United States. Thanks in part to stability, similar per capita incomes, and growing economies, these relationships are likely to endure.

International expansion. Uber continues its globalization efforts by offering its services in more than 10,000 cities worldwide.

Mexico and Latin America Mexico, another leading trading partner, represents a tremendous opportunity for businesses looking for new markets. Latin America is home to 10 Free Trade Area countries and more than 650 million consumers. In addition to Mexico, these countries include Chile, Colombia, Peru, and the six countries of the Dominican Republic-Central America FTA or "CAFTA-DR" (Costa Rica, The Dominican Republic, El Salvador, Guatemala, Honduras, and Nicaragua). U.S. trade in goods with Central and South American nations added up to $221 billion a year in 2020[13] and is expected to grow as trade barriers among the nations ease.

Technology and Innovation

技术与创新：Spotify 谋求全球主导地位

Spotify Makes a Play for Global Dominance

Spotify, a Swedish digital music, podcast, and video streaming service, has more than 354 million users in 93 markets. Although the company controls about one-third of the global music-streaming market, it faces steep competition for consumer dollars against Pandora, Apple Music, YouTube Music, Tidal, and Amazon Music, among others. To grow its market share, Spotify is eyeing global expansion.

Spotify sees international growth as an opportunity to stay ahead of the streaming competition. Russia, one of Spotify's latest markets, is the fastest-growing market for music. In addition, Spotify expanded to Albania, Belarus, Bosnia and Herzegovina, Croatia, Kazakhstan, Kosovo, Moldavia, Montenegro, North Macedonia, Serbia, Slovenia, and Ukraine. In each market, Spotify works with local distributors and establishes local partnerships to offer a local experience on a global platform.

Spotify follows a freemium pricing strategy, meaning it offers free entry-level access, hoping to convert free users into premium subscribers. Its premium service eliminates advertisements and allows users to download music, skip an unlimited number of songs, and access Spotify's full library of music. This pricing strategy is not unique, however, as many of its competitors, including Pandora and Amazon Music, also offer free versions of their platforms.

To increase revenue, leadership at Spotify says it will increase subscription prices in mature markets where it offers more value than it did previously. The company has been busy developing and releasing original and exclusive content in 16 markets to differentiate the platform from competitors. Spotify's goal is to solidify its dominance in the audio streaming market while increasing earnings from active subscribers.

Sources: Based on information in Spotify, "Company Info"; David Trainer, "It Sounds Like Spotify Is In Trouble," *Forbes*, October 13, 2020; Kenneth Li, Supantha Mukherjee, "Spotify Expands to Russia and 12 Other Countries," *Reuters*, July 14, 2020; Sarah Perez, "Spotify CEO Says Company Will 'Further Expand Price Increases'," *TechCrunch*, October 29, 2020.

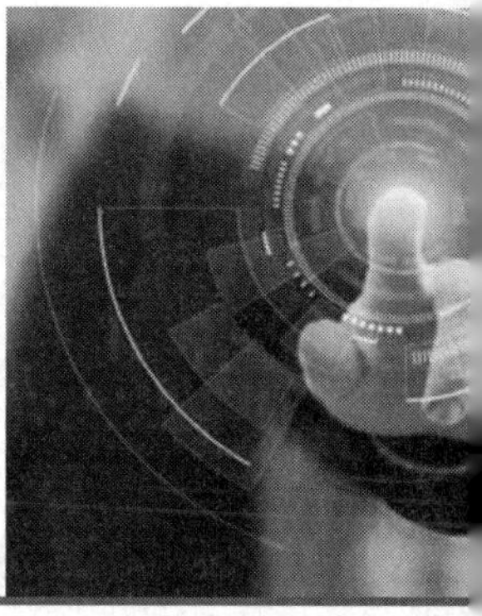

Asia Japan is the world's third largest economy and the United States' fourth largest trading partner. China's emergence as a global economic power has been among the most dramatic economic developments of recent decades. Indeed, China has grown to be the world's second largest economy, and the United States shares more than half a trillion dollars in annual bilateral trade. Also, as the emerging middle class in India, buys U.S. products, it means jobs and income for the U.S. middle class. With a market of over 1.35 billion of the world's consumers and per capita incomes expected to grow, India's vast market promises U.S. companies continued strong demand for goods and services.

Africa Sub-Saharan Africa is home to 1.1 billion people in 46 countries with immense natural resources that offer great trade potential. U.S. trade to and from Africa has tripled over the past decade, and U.S. exports of goods to this region now exceed $22 billion.[14] Although some of these nations have experienced conflict and stagnating economies, Ghana, Rwanda, Ethiopia, and others have experienced dramatic economic growth in recent years. Companies are increasingly looking for opportunities in these growing economies, whose residents are younger than average and have growing disposable incomes.

Middle East/North Africa Some of the countries of the Middle East and North Africa (MENA)—particularly Egypt and Saudi Arabia—have become important trading partners to the United States. Although political instability in the region has been a challenge to developing long-term relationships, the vast natural resources and growing per capita incomes make the region desirable to companies.

✓ Concept Check

- Why do firms engage in international trade?
- What is the difference between an absolute advantage and a comparative advantage?
- What is the difference between balance of trade and balance of payments?
- Which nations are the principal trading partners of the United States?

进入国际商务的方式

3-2 Methods of Entering International Business

Learning Objective

3-2 Explore the methods by which a firm can organize for and enter into international markets.

A firm that has decided to enter international markets can do so in several ways. These different approaches require varying degrees of involvement, investment, and risk. Typically, a firm begins its international operations at the simplest level. Then, depending on its goals, it may progress to higher levels of involvement. Table 3-3 describes the steps in entering international markets.

出口

3-2a Exporting

Exporting can be a relatively low-risk method of expanding operations by entering foreign markets. As an example, the Canadian firm LED Roadway Lighting Ltd. manufactures energy-efficient road lighting products that can help cities and utilities meet their goals to cut costs and reduce their climate footprint. To expand its business beyond Canada, the company began exporting its products to customers

Table 3-3 Steps in Entering International Markets

Step	Activity	Marketing Tasks
1	Identify exportable products	Identify key selling features Identify needs that they satisfy Identify the selling constraints that are imposed
2	Identify key foreign markets for the products	Determine who the customers are Pinpoint what and when they will buy Do market research Establish priority, or "target," countries
3	Analyze how to sell in each priority market (methods will be affected by product characteristics and unique features of country/market)	Locate available government and private-sector resources Determine service and backup sales requirements
4	Set export prices and payment terms, methods, and techniques	Establish methods of export pricing Establish sales terms, quotations, invoices, and conditions of sale Determine methods of international payments, secured and unsecured
5	Estimate resource requirements and returns	Estimate financial requirements Estimate human resources requirements (full- or part-time export department or operation) Estimate plant production capacity Determine necessary product adaptations
6	Establish overseas distribution network	Determine distribution agreement and other key marketing decisions (price, repair policies, returns, territory, performance, and termination). Know your customer (use U.S. Department of Commerce international marketing services)
7	Determine shipping, traffic, and documentation procedures and requirements	Determine methods of shipment (air or ocean freight, truck, rail) Finalize containerization Obtain validated export license Follow export-administration documentation procedures
8	Promote, sell, and be paid	Use international media, communications, advertising, trade shows, and exhibitions Determine the need for overseas travel (when, where, and how often?) Initiate customer follow-up procedures
9	Continuously analyze current marketing, economic, and political situations	Recognize changing factors influencing marketing strategies Constantly reevaluate

Source: U.S. Department of Commerce, International Trade Administration, Washington, DC.

in Caribbean nations, where high power rates allow customers to quickly realize savings from using LED lighting products. LED Roadway Lighting continues to look for new export opportunities such as the United Kingdom.[15] Exporting opens up several levels of involvement to exporting firms.

At the most basic level, the exporting firm may sell its products outright to an *export-import merchant,* which is a type of wholesaler specializing in international trade. This merchant assumes all the risks of product ownership, distribution, and sale. It may even purchase the goods in the producer's home country and assume responsibility for exporting the goods. An important and practical issue for domestic firms dealing with foreign customers is securing payment. Figure 3-3 depicts a simplified version of the process. This is a two-sided issue that reflects the mutual concern rightly felt by both parties to the trade deal: The exporter would like to be paid before shipping the merchandise, whereas the importer obviously would prefer to know that it has received the shipment before releasing any funds. Neither side wants to take the risk of fulfilling its part of the deal only to discover later that the other side has not. The result would lead to legal costs and complex, lengthy dealings that would waste everyone's resources. This mutual level of mistrust, in fact, makes good business sense and has been around since the beginning of trade centuries ago. The solution then was the same as it still is today—for both parties to use a mutually trusted go-between who can ensure that the payment is held until the merchandise is in fact delivered according to the terms of the trade contract. The go-between representatives employed by the importer and exporter are still, as they were in the past, the local domestic banks involved in international business.

Alternatively, the exporting firm may ship its products to an *export-import agent,* which arranges the sale of the products to foreign intermediaries for a commission or fee. The agent is an independent firm—like other agents—that sells and may perform other marketing functions for the exporter. The exporter, however, retains title to the products during shipment and until they are sold.

An exporting firm also may establish its own *sales offices,* or *branches,* in foreign countries. These installations are international extensions of the firm's distribution system. They represent a deeper involvement in international business than the other exporting techniques we have discussed—and thus they carry a greater risk. The exporting firm maintains control over sales, and it gains both experience in and knowledge of foreign markets. Eventually, the firm also may develop its own sales force to operate in conjunction with foreign sales offices.

Figure 3-3 Exporting to International Markets

After signing contracts, the importer will ask its local bank to issue a *letter of credit* for the funds needed to pay for the merchandise. The transporter of the merchandise provides the exporter evidence of the shipment via a *bill of lading*. The exporter signs over title to the merchandise and issues a *draft* from its bank, which orders the importer's bank to pay for the merchandise.

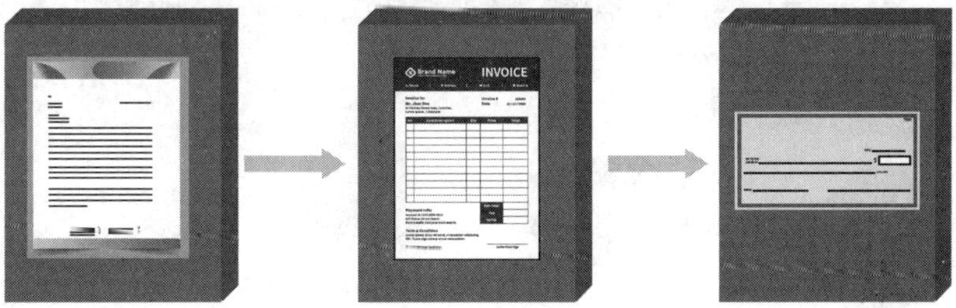

Another option is via a **trading company**, which provides a link between buyers and sellers in different countries. A trading company, as its name implies, is not involved in manufacturing or owning assets related to manufacturing. It buys products in one country at the lowest price consistent with quality and sells to buyers in another country. An important function of trading companies is taking title to products and performing all the activities necessary to move the products from the domestic country to a foreign country. For example, large grain-trading companies operating out of home offices both in the United States and overseas control a major portion of the world's trade in basic food commodities. These trading companies sell homogeneous agricultural commodities that can be stored and moved rapidly in response to market conditions.

In the early 1990s, many developing nations had major restrictions on converting domestic currency into foreign currency. Therefore, companies that wanted to export had to resort to barter agreements with importers. **Countertrade** is essentially an international barter transaction in which goods and services are exchanged for different goods and services. As an example, Iran has purchased rice and other imports from India with payment in crude oil.[16] Countertrade is still used today, particularly for trade with countries that have difficult relations with the home nation.

许可和特许经营
3-2b Licensing and Franchising

Licensing and franchising represent slightly more complex arrangements for international trade. **Licensing** is a contractual agreement in which one firm permits another to produce and market its product and to use its brand name in return for a royalty or other compensation. For example, Yoplait yogurt is a French yogurt licensed for production in the United States. The Yoplait brand maintains an appealing French image, and in return, the U.S. producer pays the French firm a percentage of its income from sales of the product.

Licensing is especially advantageous for small manufacturers wanting to launch a well-known domestic brand internationally. For example, Swedish-owned Electrolux licenses many of its products to firms in India, China, and many other countries. Licensing thus provides a simple method for expanding into a foreign market with virtually no investment. On the other hand, if the licensee does not maintain the licensor's product standards, the product's reputation may be damaged.

贸易公司
trading company provides a link between buyers and sellers in different countries

对等贸易
countertrade an international barter transaction

许可
licensing a contractual agreement in which one firm permits another to produce and market its product and to use its brand name in return for a royalty or other compensation

Another possible disadvantage is that a licensing arrangement may not provide the original producer with any foreign marketing experience.

Franchising is similar to licensing in that it is a contractual arrangement for an individual or organization to operate facilities, typically stores, on behalf of another. A franchisor allows a franchisee to use the franchisor's brand name and methods of doing business in its own stores in exchange for fees and royalties. This arrangement can enable a popular brand to expand into overseas markets with relatively little investment. Consider that consumers around the world can get donuts, muffins, bagels, and coffee at 3,200 Dunkin' restaurants in 36 countries, in addition to 8,500 restaurants in the United States.[17]

合同制造
3-2c Contract Manufacturing

Companies that want a little more control over their products and are willing to take on a greater degree of risk may engage in contract manufacturing. **Contract manufacturing** occurs when one firm employs another business—often in another country—to manufacture its products or product components to the domestic firm's specifications. The resulting product typically carries the domestic firm's name. In fact, many U.S. companies use contract manufacturing to take advantage of lower labor costs in other countries, which can help lower the prices of their products to consumers. Contract manufacturing is used far more often than you might guess, and it is common in the electronics, automotive, and fashion industries, among others. Consider Swedish fast-fashion retailer H&M, which contracts with hundreds of different companies in 40 countries to produce its trendy clothing. Recently, the firm has begun identifying the company, country, and even factory producing each item of clothing for interested consumers and stakeholders.[18]

Indeed, **outsourcing**, the contracting of manufacturing and/or other activities to overseas companies that specialize in those activities and can offer them at a lower cost, has become very common in recent years. Many companies have achieved significant cost savings from outsourcing manufacturing to countries such as India, Bangladesh, Vietnam, and the Philippines, where labor costs and taxes are significantly lower than in the United States. In most cases, these savings are passed on to shareholders and to consumers in the form of lower prices. However, outsourcing is controversial because it has resulted in the loss of American manufacturing jobs and higher unemployment in manufacturing sectors.

合同制造
contract manufacturing an arrangement in which one firm contracts with another business, often in another country, to manufacture products or product components to its specifications

外包
outsourcing an arrangement in which one firm contracts manufacturing or other activities to a firm in another country that specializes in those activities and can offer them at a lower cost than domestic firms

战略联盟
strategic alliance a partnership formed to create competitive advantage on a worldwide basis

合资企业和联盟
3-2d Joint Ventures and Alliances

A *joint venture* is a partnership formed to achieve a specific goal or to operate for a specific period of time. A joint venture with an established firm in a foreign country provides immediate market knowledge and access, reduced risk, and control over product attributes. However, joint-venture agreements established across national borders can become extremely complex. As a result, joint-venture agreements generally require a very high level of commitment from all the parties involved. A joint venture may be used to produce and market an existing product in a foreign nation or to develop an entirely new product. For example, New York-based Pfizer, one of the world's leading pharmaceutical companies, entered into a joint venture with BioNTech, a German biotechnology company, to create and distribute a vaccine for the COVID-19 virus.[19]

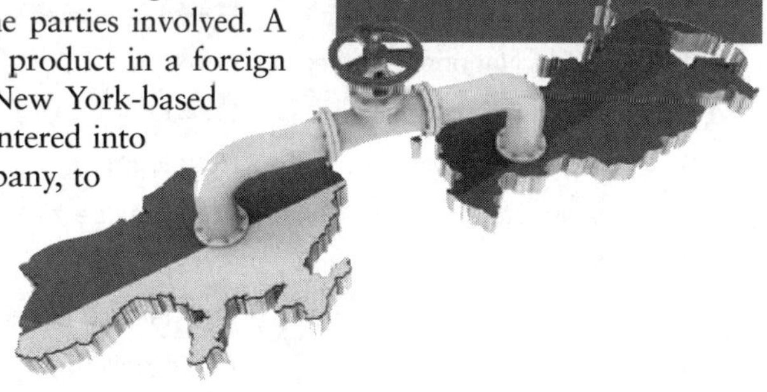

Joint venture. Large pipelines can involve multiple countries. They can be organized based on the use of joint ventures.

A **strategic alliance**, a more recent form of international business structure, is a partnership formed to create competitive advantage on a worldwide basis. Strategic alliances are very similar to joint ventures. The number of strategic alliances is growing at an estimated rate of about 20 percent per year. In fact, in the automobile and computer industries, strategic alliances are becoming the predominant means of competing. International competition is so fierce and the costs of competing on a global basis are so high that few firms have all the resources needed to do it alone. Thus, individual firms that lack the internal resources essential for international success may seek to collaborate with other companies. An example of such an alliance is the agreement between Honda and General Motors to collaborate to make electric vehicles using technologies from both firms.[20]

直接投资

3-2e Direct Investment

At a still deeper level of involvement in international business, a firm may invest directly in its own facilities, that is, its own production and marketing facilities in one or more foreign nations. This *direct investment* provides complete control over operations, but it carries a greater risk than the joint venture. The firm is really establishing a subsidiary in a foreign country. Most firms do so only after they have engaged in simpler levels of international trade and acquired some knowledge of the host country's markets.

Direct investment may take either of two forms. In the first, the company builds or purchases manufacturing and other facilities in a foreign country. It uses these facilities to produce its own established products and to market them in that country and perhaps in neighboring countries. Firms such as General Motors, Dow Chemical, and Colgate-Palmolive are multinational companies with worldwide manufacturing facilities.

A second form of direct investment in international business is the purchase of an existing firm in a foreign country under an arrangement that allows it to operate independently of the parent company. When Sony Corporation (a Japanese firm) decided to enter the motion picture business in the United States, it chose to purchase Columbia Pictures Entertainment, Inc., rather than start a new motion picture studio from scratch.

跨国公司

3-2f Multinational Firms

A **multinational corporation** is a firm that operates on a worldwide scale without ties to any specific nation or region. The multinational firm represents the highest level of involvement in international business. It is equally "at home" in most countries of the world. In fact, as far as the operations of the multinational enterprise are concerned, national boundaries exist only on maps. It is, however, organized under the laws of its home country. Table 3-4 shows the ten largest foreign and U.S. public multinational companies; the ranking is based on a composite score reflecting each company's best three out of four rankings for sales, profits, assets, and market value.

✓ Concept Check

- List the most common methods of entering international business.
- Two methods of engaging in international business may be categorized as either direct or indirect. How would you classify each of the methods described in this chapter? Why?
- In what ways is a multinational corporation different from a large corporation that does business in several countries?

跨国公司

multinational corporation a firm that operates on a worldwide scale without ties to any specific nation or region

Table 3-4 The Ten Largest Foreign and U.S. Multinational Corporations

Rank	Company	Business	Country	Revenue ($ millions)
1	Walmart	General Merchandise	United States	523,964
2	Sinopec	Energy	China	407,009
3	State Grid	Power Grids	China	383,906
4	China National Petroleum	Energy	China	379,130
5	Royal Dutch Shell	Energy	Netherlands	352,106
6	Saudi Aramco	Petroleum	Saudi Arabia	329,784
7	Volkswagen	Automobiles	Germany	282,760
8	BP	Energy	United Kingdom	282,616
9	Amazon	Internet and Retail	United States	280,522
10	Toyota	Automobiles	Japan	275,288

Source: "Global 500," *Fortune*.

Sustaining the Planet 保护地球：宜家开设第一家二手店

IKEA Opens Its First Second-Hand Store

IKEA, a ready-to-assemble furniture retailer, has a reputation for sustainability. The company's goal is to become 100 percent circular. The term *circular economy* refers to an economic system that eliminates waste and keeps products in use. For IKEA, this translates to creating products with renewable or recycled materials, helping customers extend the life of their products, and developing circular capabilities in its supply chain. One way IKEA is achieving this is through its secondhand store concept.

IKEA opened its first secondhand store in Sweden, its home country. Consumers donate their furniture at municipal recycling centers. The furniture is repaired or repurposed in IKEA's repair shop and then sold below the item's initial price. IKEA's goal is to be circular by 2030. By then, the company also aims to reduce more greenhouse gas emissions than emitted by its value chain. Helping customers get more use out of their products is key to achieving both goals.

The store is located in ReTuna Shopping Centre, a mall where all products sold are either reused or recycled. IKEA hopes to learn more about second-hand retail, including how to attract shoppers and what causes customers to donate products. To incentivize individuals to return old IKEA furniture, the company offered local customers vouchers. If IKEA's secondhand store is successful, it will roll out the concept in additional markets.

Sources: Based on information in Anna Ringstrom, "IKEA Opens Pilot Second-Hand Store in Sweden," *World Economic Forum*, October 30, 2020; IKEA, "Why the Future of Furniture Is Circular".

国际商务挑战

3-3 International Business Challenges

Learning Objective

3-3 Discuss the challenges businesses face when entering international markets, especially the restrictions nations place on international trade.

Specialization and international trade can result in the efficient production of want-satisfying goods and services on a worldwide basis. As we have noted, international business generally is increasing. Yet the nations of the world continue to erect barriers to free trade. They do so for reasons ranging from internal political and economic pressures to simple mistrust of other nations. In this section, we examine the types of trade restrictions that nations may apply, the arguments for and against trade restrictions, and additional challenges to international trade.

贸易限制

3-3a Trade Restrictions

Nations generally are eager to export their products. They want to provide markets for their industries and to develop a favorable balance of trade. Hence, most trade restrictions are applied to imports from other nations.

Tariffs Perhaps the most commonly applied trade restriction is the tariff, also known as a customs or import duty. A **tariff** is a tax levied on a particular foreign product entering a country. For example, the United States imposed a 2.2 percent import duty on fresh Chilean tomatoes, an 8.7 percent duty if tomatoes are dried and packaged, and nearly 12 percent if tomatoes are made into ketchup or salsa. Two types of tariffs are revenue tariffs and protective tariffs; both have the effect of raising the price of the product in the importing nations, but for different reasons. *Revenue tariffs* are imposed solely to generate income for the government. *Protective tariffs,* on the other hand, are imposed to protect a domestic industry from competition by keeping the price of competing imports level with or higher than the price of similar domestic products. Because fewer units of the product will be sold at the increased price, fewer units will be imported. The French and Japanese agricultural sectors would both shrink drastically if their nations abolished the protective tariffs that

关税
tariff a tax levied on a particular foreign product entering a country

keep the price of imported farm products high. In recent years, the United States has imposed significantly greater tariffs on imports of products from around the world, ranging from Scotch whiskey to Chinese electronics, ostensibly to protect domestic industries from foreign competition. However, when countries alter their trade policies to include more tariffs, other countries are likely to respond in kind, which can lead to a *trade war* that oftentimes harms producers in all involved countries.

Some countries rationalize their protectionist policies as a way of offsetting an international trade practice called *dumping*. **Dumping** is the exportation of large quantities of a product at a price lower than that of the same product in the home market. Thus, dumping drives down the price of the domestic item. Recently, the Foil Trade Enforcement Working Group of the Aluminum Association, which represents U.S. aluminum manufacturers, claimed that low-priced aluminum foil from Armenia, Brazil, Oman, Russia, and Turkey was being sold in the United States at less than fair value prices. The producers contend that the dumped foil is harming the domestic industry, and they therefore asked to obtain an antidumping duty through the government to offset the advantage of the foreign product.[21]

Nontariff Barriers A **nontariff barrier** is a nontax measure imposed by a government to favor domestic over foreign suppliers. Nontariff barriers create obstacles to the marketing of foreign goods in a country and increase costs for exporters. The following are a few examples of government-imposed nontariff barriers:

- An **import quota** is a limit on the amount of a particular good that may be imported into a country during a given period of time. The limit may be set in terms of either quantity (so many pounds of beef) or value (so many dollars' worth of shoes). Quotas also may be set on individual products imported from specific countries. Once an import quota has been reached, imports are halted until the specified time has elapsed.
- An **embargo** is a complete halt to trading with a particular nation or of a particular product. The embargo is used most often as a political weapon. At present, the United States has import embargoes against Iran and DPRK—both the result of extremely poor political relations.
- An **exchange control** is a restriction on the amount of a particular foreign currency that can be purchased or sold. By limiting the amount of foreign currency importers can obtain, a government limits the amount of goods importers can purchase with that currency. This has the effect of limiting imports from the country whose foreign exchange is being controlled.
- A nation can increase or decrease the value of its money relative to the currency of other nations. **Currency devaluation** is the reduction of the value of a nation's currency relative to the currencies of other countries.

Devaluation increases the cost of foreign goods, whereas it decreases the cost of domestic goods to foreign firms. For example, suppose that the British pound is worth $2. In this case, an American-made $2,000 computer can be purchased for £1,000. However, if the United Kingdom devalues the pound so that it is worth only $1, that same computer will cost £2,000. The increased cost, in pounds, will reduce the import of American computers—and all foreign goods—into England. On the other hand, before devaluation, a £500 set of English bone china will cost an American $1,000. After the devaluation, the set of china will cost only $500. The decreased cost will make the china—and all English goods—much more attractive to U.S. purchasers.

Bureaucratic red tape is more subtle than the other forms of nontariff barriers. Yet it can be the most frustrating trade barrier of all. A few examples are the restrictive application of standards and complex requirements related to product testing, labeling, and certification.

倾销
dumping exportation of large quantities of a product at a price lower than that of the same product in the home market

非关税壁垒
nontariff barrier a nontax measure imposed by a government to favor domestic over foreign suppliers

进口配额
import quota a limit on the amount of a particular good that may be imported into a country during a given period of time

禁运
embargo a complete halt to trading with a particular nation or of a particular product

外汇管制
exchange control a restriction on the amount of a particular foreign currency that can be purchased or sold

货币贬值
currency devaluation the reduction of the value of a nation's currency relative to the currencies of other countries

Reasons for and against Trade Restrictions Various reasons are given for trade restrictions either on the import of specific products or on trade with particular countries. We have noted that political considerations usually are involved in trade embargoes. Other frequently cited reasons for restricting trade include the following:

- *To equalize a nation's balance of payments.* This may be considered necessary to restore confidence in the country's monetary system and in its ability to repay its debts.
- *To protect new or weak industries.* A new, or infant, industry may not be strong enough to withstand foreign competition. Temporary trade restrictions may be used to give it a chance to grow and become self-sufficient. Of course, once an industry is protected from foreign competition, it may not want to give up the protections, and these "temporary" trade restrictions may become permanent.
- *To protect national security.* Restrictions in this category generally apply to technological products that must be kept out of the hands of potential enemies. For example, strategic and defense-related goods cannot be exported to unfriendly nations.
- *To protect the health of citizens.* Products may be embargoed because they are dangerous or unhealthy (e.g., farm products contaminated with insecticides).
- *To retaliate for another nation's trade restrictions.* A country whose exports are taxed by another country may respond by imposing tariffs on imports from that country.
- *To protect domestic jobs.* By restricting imports, a nation can protect jobs in domestic industries. However, while protectionist policies can have positive effects in the short run, they can be harmful in the long term.

Trade restrictions have immediate and long-term economic consequences—both within the restricting nation and in world trade patterns. These include the following:

- *Higher prices for consumers.* Higher prices may result from the imposition of tariffs or the elimination of foreign competition, as described earlier. For example, imposing quota restrictions and import protections adds $25 billion annually to U.S. consumers' apparel costs by directly increasing costs for imported apparel.
- *Restriction of consumers' choices.* Again, this is a direct result of the elimination of some foreign products from the marketplace and of the artificially high prices that importers must charge for products that are still imported.
- *Misallocation of international resources.* The protection of weak industries results in the inefficient use of limited resources. The economies of both the restricting nation and other nations eventually suffer because of this waste.
- *Loss of jobs.* The restriction of imports by one nation must lead to cutbacks—and the loss of jobs—in the export-oriented industries of other nations. Furthermore, trade protection has a significant effect on the composition of employment. U.S. trade restrictions—whether on textiles, apparel, steel, or automobiles—benefit only a few industries while harming many others. The gains in employment

accrue to the protected industries and their primary suppliers, and the losses are spread across all other industries. A few states gain employment, but many other states lose employment.

Consider that former President Donald Trump's protectionist policies—intended to slash the nation's trade deficit with China and stem job losses in American manufacturing—ultimately did neither. Instead, Trump's trade policy, which relied heavily on tariffs, resulted in a trade war with China which ultimately raised the prices of important Chinese imports while reducing American exports to China, at a cost of American jobs in affected industries. While jobs did grow in a few industries, so did the trade deficit with China.[22]

经济挑战

3-3b Economic Challenges

Businesspeople desiring to engage in international trade must also recognize that there are likely to be differences in countries' standards of living, individual income and buying power, national resources, and infrastructure. Among the world's nations, the United States has the highest GDP, which we defined in Chapter 1 as the value of all products produced by all people within a nation in a specified time period. While GDP can provide an estimate of the size of a national economy, businesspeople are often more interested in per capita GDP (a nation's GDP divided by its population) as this gives more insight into a nation's standard of living and market potential. Consider that the GDP per capita of the United States is $63,051, yet a number of countries have higher rates of GDP per capita, including Switzerland, Norway, and Luxembourg.[23] Businesspeople can also find tremendous opportunities in countries with far less incomes. The countries of Brazil, Russia, India, China, and South Africa (BRICS) have in recent years experienced rapid economic expansion and growing middle classes, making them very attractive markets for companies looking to develop their brands.

Another economic challenge is that in most cases nations use different currencies. The value of the American dollar, European euro, and the Japanese yen has a significant impact on product prices in most countries. Many countries allow the value of their currencies to float, or fluctuate according to supply and demand on the foreign exchange market. In recent times, the value of the U.S. dollar has been strong relative to other currencies. This means that U.S. exports cost more when purchased using euros in Europe or renminbi in China. Because the value of a nation's currency can change from day to day, the change in value can also affect how much profit (or loss) a firm may realize on an international transaction.

Another factor that can affect the attractiveness of and opportunities within another country is its level of *infrastructure*—the transportation, energy transmission, communication networks, and other systems that facilitate the functions of civilization. Developing countries may have less reliable infrastructure systems, which may create challenges when introducing certain types of products. On the other hand, a lack of communications and utility infrastructure in some countries spurred entrepreneurs to invest in wireless and alternative energy technologies and solutions at a faster rate than in the United States. As an example, in many developing countries, a significant percentage of the population lacks reliable access to banking services. Safaricom, a large Kenyan telecom provider, partnered with banks, nonprofit organizations, and microcredit organizations to launch M-Pesa, a payment platform. M-Pesa functions as a digital wallet allowing users to send and receive payments via an app and to save and withdraw funds from Safaricom retail stores throughout Kenya. As M-Pesa grew and competing apps from other telecoms proliferated, these services have boosted the percentage of Kenyans using financial services from 26 percent to 75 percent in just a decade.[24]

Ethics and Social Responsibility

商业伦理与社会责任：打开数字支付的大门

Opening the Gates to Digital Payments

It may be surprising to learn that digital payment services have been established in developing countries for more than a decade. M-Pesa, a mobile phone-based money transfer and financing service, serves millions in Kenya who previously were limited to cash and informal networks, lifting nearly 200,000 individuals out of poverty. Now, a coalition of nonprofits and tech companies, including the Bill and Melinda Gates Foundation and Google, want to build on the digital payment revolution M-Pesa started.

The coalition, called Mojaloop Foundation, will facilitate the development of real-time digital payment systems through an open-source platform. Open-source software includes the source code so developers can alter and distribute it. One major goal is to digitally connect the fragmented financial service offerings currently available such as M-Pesa. M-Pesa and its imitators are mostly privately owned and operated, often resulting in high transaction fees between systems. Mojaloop Foundation aims to reduce friction.

Bridging the gap between these banking and payment systems could add value to each service rather than pitting them against each other as competitors. Another of Mojaloop's goals is to boost the global economy. Studies show that when affordable digital finance tools are available in developing nations, economies grow by 6 percent. But providing the software is only one piece of the puzzle. Mojaloop will also connect experts with countries to tackle problems and influence government policies.

Sources: Based on information in David Z. Morris, "Google and Gates Foundation to Help Spread Digital Payments in Developing Countries," *Fortune*, May 6, 2020; Mojaloop Foundation, "Mission".

法律和政治环境

3-3c **Legal and Political Climate**

Beyond infrastructure and economic issues, the laws, regulatory agencies, political systems, and special-interest groups within a country all have a great impact on international business. In the United States, as in many countries, the political, legal, and regulatory forces of the environment are closely interconnected. Even when different countries seem similar, differences in legal, political, or regulatory conditions in their home countries can shape trade. We have already mentioned some of the challenges that businesses may face when they engage in international trade: trade restrictions such as tariffs and import quotas often are the result of the political will within the country.

Additionally, rules that Americans take for granted may differ in other nations. Privacy rules in Europe, for example, are considerably stricter than within the United States, as are rules related to advertising to children. On the other hand, U.S. law prohibits direct involvement in payoffs and bribes by American businesspersons and companies. The Foreign Corrupt Practices Act (FCPA) of 1977 also makes it illegal for U.S. firms to attempt to make large payments or bribes to influence policy decisions of foreign governments. These laws can make it challenging for U.S. companies to compete with foreign firms that do engage in these practices.

社会和文化障碍

3-3d **Social and Cultural Barriers**

One of the most significant barriers to international trade relates to social and cultural issues. Differences due to religious institutions, values, customs, social systems, and language can affect communications, negotiations, and perceptions of products and companies. Obviously, language can be problematic when translating advertising and other communications into other languages. On more than one occasion, such efforts led to comical yet potentially disastrous situations. For example, KFC's long-running slogan "Finger lickin' good" was translated in China as "Eat your fingers off," while Schweppes'

✓ Concept Check

- List and briefly describe the principal restrictions that may be applied to a nation's imports.
- What reasons are generally given for imposing trade restrictions?
- What are some economic challenges that businesspeople need to consider in international trade?
- How can the political and legal climate of a nation affect trade?
- Describe some social and cultural factors that can influence product acceptance in another country.

carbonated water was translated in Italy as "toilet water."[25] Even when language is shared, words may still mean different things. Consider that "football" is a leading sport outside the United States—but the term refers to what Americans call soccer.

Cultural barriers can impede acceptance of products in foreign countries. For example, illustrations of feet are regarded as offensive in Thailand. Even so simple a thing as the color of a product or its package can present a problem. In Japan, black and white are the colors of mourning, so they should not be used in packaging. In Brazil, purple is the color of death. And in Egypt, green is never used on a package because it is the national color. Many retailers on the internet have yet to come to grips with the task of designing an online shopping site that is attractive and functional for all global customers. When customers are unfamiliar with particular products from another country, their general perceptions of the country itself affect their attitude toward the product and help to determine whether they will buy it.

国际贸易促进者

3-4 Facilitators of International Trade

Learning Objective

3-4 Identify the facilitators of international trade, including international trade agreements and international economic organizations working to foster trade.

Although the previous pages may make international trade seem daunting, there are many organizations and agreements that facilitate trade across national borders, including the World Trade Organization (WTO) and numerous free trade agreements.

关税与贸易总协定和世界贸易组织

3-4a The General Agreement on Tariffs and Trade and the World Trade Organization

At the end of World War II, the United States and 22 other nations organized the body that came to be known as GATT. The **General Agreement on Tariffs and Trade (GATT)** was an international organization of 164 nations dedicated to reducing or eliminating tariffs and other barriers to world trade. Headquartered in Geneva, Switzerland, GATT provided a forum for tariff negotiations and a means for settling international trade disputes and problems. It also conferred "most-favored-nation status (MFN)," meaning that each GATT member nation was to be treated equally by all contracting nations. Therefore, MFN ensured that any tariff reductions or other trade concessions were extended automatically to all GATT members.

From 1947 to 1994, the body sponsored eight rounds of negotiations to reduce trade restrictions. Three were especially constructive. The *Kennedy Round,* which began in 1964, was successful in reducing tariffs and other barriers to trade in industrial and agricultural products by an average of more than 35 percent. The *Tokyo Round,* which was completed in 1979, negotiated phased tariff cuts of 30 to 35 percent and removed or eased nontariff barriers such as import quotas, unrealistic quality standards for imports, and unnecessary red tape in customs procedures. In 1986, the *Uruguay Round* was able to lower tariffs by greater than one-third, reform trade in agricultural goods, write new rules of trade for intellectual property and services, and strengthen the dispute-settlement process. Arguably the most significant result of the Uruguay Round was the creation of the World Trade Organization (WTO) on January 1, 1995. The **World Trade Organization (WTO)** is an international forum that facilitates world trade among member nations by mediating disputes and fostering continued efforts to reduce trade barriers. Membership in the WTO obliges 164 member nations to observe GATT rules.

关税与贸易总协定（关贸总协定）
General Agreement on Tariffs and Trade (GATT) an international organization of nations dedicated to reducing or eliminating tariffs and other barriers to world trade

世界贸易组织
World Trade Organization (WTO) powerful successor to GATT that facilitates world trade among member nations by mediating disputes and fostering efforts to reduce trade barriers

经济共同体
economic community an organization of nations formed to promote the free movement of resources and products among its members and to create common economic policies

国际贸易协定和联盟

3-4b International Trade Agreements and Alliances

The primary objective of the WTO is to remove barriers to trade on a worldwide basis. On a smaller scale, an **economic community** is an organization of nations formed to promote the free movement of resources and products among its members and to create common economic policies. A number of economic communities now exist.

The United States-Mexico-Canada Agreement (USMCA) The *United States-Mexico-Canada Agreement (USMCA)* joined the United States with its first- and second-largest export trading partners, Canada and Mexico, in 2020. USMCA replaced an earlier accord, the *North American Free Trade Agreement (NAFTA)*, which went into effect in 1994. NAFTA gradually eliminated tariffs on goods produced and traded among the three nations and created a free trade area of more than 503 million people. After 25 years, NAFTA succeeded in its core goals of expanding trade and investment between the United States, Canada, and Mexico. For example, from 1993 to 2017, trade among the NAFTA nations increased nearly four-fold to $1.3 trillion, significantly more than U.S. trade with other countries.[26] Companies in all three nations experienced growth in exports, while consumers gained better prices and selection.

USMCA. The United States-Mexico-Canada Agreement has unlocked opportunities for millions of Americans by supporting Made-in-America jobs and exports. Many American small business exporters' first customers are in Canada or Mexico.

However, NAFTA critics maintained that it resulted in the loss of American jobs to Mexico, harmed workers by eroding labor standards, undermined national sovereignty, and did nothing to help the environment. Moreover, the original accord was unable to address technological changes that had occurred since its implementation, particularly with regard to intellectual property rights. Some critics felt that Mexico and Canada got more out of the deal than the United States. In 2018, the three nations began renegotiating the agreement that ultimately became the United States-Mexico-Canada Agreement.

USMCA retains a number of NAFTA's provisions but updates it in significant ways:

- The agreement will be formally reviewed at least every six years to ensure that it remains beneficial to all three nations.
- It has significant dispute resolution systems, which the prior agreement lacked.
- It strengthens labor laws and provides for greater enforcement of them, creating a more equitable situation for U.S. workers.
- It includes provisions related to digital technology and intellectual property.
- It includes funds to address environmental issues stemming from trade between the three nations.[27]

The European Union Operating as a single market with 27 countries, the European Union (EU), also known as the European Economic Community and the Common Market, was formed in 1957 by six countries—France, the Federal Republic of Germany, Italy, Belgium, the Netherlands, and Luxembourg. Its objective was freely conducted commerce among these nations and others that might later join. Many more nations have joined the EU since then. The citizens of the United Kingdom voted in 2016 to exit the European Union; however, "Brexit" did not actually go into effect until January 2020. The EU, with a population of 450 million, is now an economic force to be recognized by even the most advanced economies such as of the United States and Japan.

Since 2002, 19 member nations of the EU have been participating in a common currency, the euro, which facilitates trade by removing the need to convert different

currencies used in transactions across borders. The euro, used by over 341 million Europeans, is the single currency of the European Monetary Union nations. However, the remaining eight EU members still maintain their own currencies.

The Dominican Republic-Central America Free Trade Agreement (CAFTA-DR) The Central American Free Trade Agreement (CAFTA) was created in 2003 by the United States and four Central American countries—El Salvador, Guatemala, Honduras, and Nicaragua. The CAFTA became CAFTA-DR when the Dominican Republic joined the group in 2007. Costa Rica joined CAFTA-DR as the sixth member in 2009. CAFTA-DR creates the third-largest U.S. export market in Latin America, behind only Mexico and Brazil.

The Association of Southeast Asian Nations (ASEAN) The Association of Southeast Asian Nations, with headquarters in Jakarta, Indonesia, was established in 1967 to promote political, economic, and social cooperation among its seven member countries: Indonesia, Malaysia, the Philippines, Singapore, Thailand, Brunei, and Vietnam. With three new members, Cambodia, Laos, and Myanmar, this region of more than 667 million people, and GDP of $3.3 trillion, is already our fifth-largest trading partner.

The Commonwealth of Independent States The Commonwealth of Independent States was established in December 1991 as a free trade association of 11 republics of the former Soviet Union. Today, its members include Armenia, Azerbaijan, Belarus, Kazakhstan, Kyrgyzstan, Moldova, Russia, Tajikistan, and Uzbekistan. Ukraine and Georgia no longer participate.

Comprehensive and Progressive Agreement for Trans-Pacific Partnership (CPTPP) In 2011, the leaders of twelve countries—Australia, Brunei Darussalam, Canada, Chile, Japan, Malaysia, Mexico, New Zealand, Peru, Singapore, Vietnam, and the United States—agreed to form the Trans-Pacific Partnership, which would have been the world's largest free trade agreement. However, the United States withdrew from the agreement in 2017, and the remaining members renegotiated the treaty, which then became known as the *Comprehensive and Progressive Agreement for Trans-Pacific Partnership*. This partnership will boost the economies of the member countries, lower barriers to trade and investment, increase exports, and create more jobs. There is speculation that the United States may rejoin the free trade agreement after the election of President Joseph R. Biden.

The Common Market of the Southern Cone (MERCOSUR) Headquartered in Montevideo, Uruguay, the *Common Market of the Southern Cone (MERCOSUR)* was established in 1991 under the Treaty of Asuncion to unite Argentina, Brazil, Paraguay, and Uruguay as a free-trade alliance; Venezuela became a member later. In more recent times, Colombia, Ecuador, Peru, Bolivia, Chile, Guyana, and Surinam have enrolled as associate members.

✓ Concept Check

- Define and describe the major objectives of the World Trade Organization (WTO) and the international economic communities.
- What is the U.S.-Mexico-Canada Agreement (USMCA)? What is its importance for the United States, Canada, and Mexico?

出口援助的来源

3-5 Sources of Export Assistance

Learning Objective

3-5 Describe sources of export assistance.

There are a number of federal and state agencies that can assist U.S. firms interested in developing export-promotion programs. The services and programs of these agencies can help American firms to compete in foreign markets and create new jobs in the United States. As an example, the state of Texas, one of the leading exporting states, offers several programs, resources, and even grants for small and medium-sized Texas companies looking to export their products. The state's Export Assistance Program can also facilitate the participation of delegations of small businesses in export-oriented trade shows and missions around the world.[28] Table 3-5 provides an overview of selected U.S. government export assistance programs.

These and other sources of export information enhance the business opportunities of U.S. firms seeking to enter expanding foreign markets. Another vital energy factor is financing.

✓ Concept Check

- List some key sources of export assistance. How can these sources be useful to small business firms?

Table 3-5 U.S. Government Export Assistance Programs

International Trade Administration	Promotes trade and investment and enforces U.S. trade laws and agreements
U.S. Commercial Service	Part of the International Trade Administration; offers assistance and information to exporters through its domestic and overseas commercial offices
Advocacy Center	Part of the International Trade Administration; assists U.S. firms competing for major projects with foreign governments
Small Business Administration U.S. Export Assistance Centers	Provide assistance in export marketing and trade finance
Small Business Administration, Office of International Trade	Publishes many helpful guides to assist small and medium-sized companies

国际商务融资

3-6 Financing International Business

Learning Objective

3-6 Identify institutions that can help businesses and nations finance international business.

International trade compounds the concerns of financial managers. Currency exchange rates, tariffs and foreign exchange controls, and the tax structures of host nations all affect international operations and the flow of cash. In addition, financial managers must be concerned both with the financing of their international operations and with the means available to their customers to finance purchases.

Fortunately, along with business in general, a number of large banks have become international in scope. Many banks have established branches in major cities around the world. Citi, for example, provides banking and finance services to both consumer and business customers in offices in 96 countries.[29] Thus, like firms in other industries, they can provide services to their customers where and when they are needed. In addition, financial assistance is available from U.S. government and international sources.

One such source is the U.S. Small Business Administration, which provides up to $5 million in short-term loans to U.S. small business exporters. The agency also provides up to $500,000 in export development financing to buy, produce goods, or provide services for exports to small businesses that have exporting potential but need funds to cover the initial costs of entering an export market. Several of today's international financial organizations were founded many years ago to facilitate free trade and the exchange of currencies among nations. Some, such as the Inter-American Development Bank, are supported internationally and focus on developing countries. Others, such as the Export-Import Bank, are operated by one country but provide international financing.

美国进出口银行

3-6a The Export-Import Bank of the United States

美国进出口银行
Export-Import Bank of the United States an independent agency of the U.S. government whose function is to assist in financing the exports of American firms

The **Export-Import Bank of the United States**, created in 1934, is an independent agency of the U.S. government whose function is to assist in financing the exports of American firms. *Ex-Im Bank,* as it is commonly called, extends and guarantees credit to overseas buyers of American goods and services and guarantees short-term financing for exports. It also cooperates with commercial banks in helping American exporters to offer credit to their overseas customers. In the last decade, Ex-Im Bank

Mission possible. The Export-Import Bank of the United States (Ex-Im Bank), with 87 years of experience, is the official export credit agency of the United States. Ex-Im Bank's mission is to assist in financing the export of U.S. goods and services to international markets. Its goal is to end extreme poverty by 2030, promote shared prosperity, and support the global sustainable development agenda.

has supported more than 1.44 million jobs in the United States. In 2019, nearly 90 percent of the Bank's transactions—nearly 2,100—directly supported American small businesses.[30]

世界银行
3-6b The World Bank

A **multilateral development bank (MDB)** is an internationally supported bank that provides loans to developing countries to help them grow. The most familiar is the **World Bank**, a cooperative of 189 member countries, which operates worldwide. Established in 1944 and headquartered in Washington, DC, the bank provides low-interest loans, interest-free credits, and grants to developing countries. The loans and grants help these countries to:

- supply safe drinking water
- build schools and train teachers
- increase agricultural productivity
- expand citizens' access to markets, jobs, and housing
- improve healthcare and access to water and sanitation
- manage forests and other natural resources
- build and maintain roads, railways, and ports, and
- reduce air pollution and protect the environment.[31]

In addition to the World Bank, four other MDBs operate primarily in Central and South America, Asia, Africa, and Eastern and Central Europe. All are supported by the industrialized nations, including the United States.

The Inter-American Development Bank The *Inter-American Development Bank (IDB),* the oldest and largest regional bank, was created in 1959 by 19 Latin American countries and the United States. The bank, which is headquartered in Washington, DC, makes loans and provides technical advice and assistance to countries. Today, the IDB is owned by 48 member nations.

The Asian Development Bank With 68 member nations, the *Asian Development Bank (ADB),* created in 1966 and headquartered in the Philippines, promotes economic and social progress in Asian and Pacific regions. The U.S. government is the second-largest contributor to the ADB's capital, after Japan.

The African Development Bank The African Development Bank (AFDB), also known as *Banque Africaines de Development,* was established in 1964 with headquarters in Abidjan, Ivory Coast. Its members include 54 African and 27 non-African countries from the Americas, Europe, and Asia. The AFDB's goal is to foster the economic and social development of its African members. The bank pursues this goal through loans, research, technical assistance, and the development of trade programs.

European Bank for Reconstruction and Development Established in 1991 to encourage reconstruction and development in Eastern and Central European countries, the London-based *European Bank for Reconstruction and Development* is owned by 69 countries and two intergovernmental institutions (the European Union and the European Investment Bank). Its loans are geared toward developing market-oriented economies and promoting private enterprise.

国际货币基金组织
3-6c The International Monetary Fund

The **International Monetary Fund (IMF)** is an international bank with 190 member nations that makes short-term loans to developing countries experiencing balance-of-payment deficits. This financing is contributed by member nations, and it must be

多边开发银行
multilateral development bank (MDB) an internationally supported bank that provides loans to developing countries to help them grow

世界银行
World Bank a cooperative banking institution with 189 member countries

国际货币基金组织
International Monetary Fund (IMF) an international bank that makes short-term loans to developing countries experiencing balance-of-payment deficits

✓ Concept Check

- What is the Export-Import Bank of the United States? How does it assist U.S. exporters?
- What is a multilateral development bank (MDB)? Who supports these banks?
- What is the International Monetary Fund? What types of loans does the IMF provide?

repaid with interest. Loans are provided primarily to fund international trade. Created in 1945 and headquartered in Washington, DC, the bank's main goals are to:

- promote international monetary cooperation
- facilitate the expansion and balanced growth of international trade
- promote exchange rate stability
- assist in establishing a multilateral system of payments, and
- make resources available to members experiencing balance-of-payment difficulties.

Summary 小 结

3-1 Explain the economic bases for and importance of international business.

International business encompasses all business activities that involve exchanges across national boundaries. International trade is based on specialization, whereby each country produces the goods and services that it can produce more efficiently than any other goods and services. A nation is said to have an absolute or comparative advantage relative to these goods. International trade develops when each nation trades its surplus products for those in short supply.

International trade involves selling and shipping raw materials or products to other nations (exporting) and/or purchasing raw materials or products in other nations and bringing them into one's own country (importing). A nation's balance of trade is the difference between the value of its exports and the value of its imports. Its balance of payments is the difference between the flow of money into and out of the nation. Generally, a negative balance of trade is considered unfavorable. The United States has largely positive and growing trade relationships with most countries around the world.

3-2 Explore the methods by which a firm can organize for and enter into international markets.

A firm can enter international markets in several ways that require varying degrees of involvement, investment, and risk. It may export its products and sell them through foreign intermediaries or its own sales organization abroad, or it may sell its exports outright to an export-import merchant. It may license or franchise a foreign firm to produce and market its products. It may outsource or contract an overseas firm to manufacture its products, or it may enter into a joint venture or strategic alliance with a foreign firm. It may establish its own foreign subsidiaries, or it may develop into a multinational corporation.

Generally, each of these methods represents an increasingly deeper level of involvement in international business, with exporting being the simplest and the development of a multinational corporation the most involved.

3-3 Discuss the challenges businesses face when entering international markets, especially the restrictions nations place on international trade.

Despite the benefits of world trade, nations tend to use tariffs and nontariff barriers (import quotas, embargoes, and other restrictions) to limit trade. Tariffs—taxes levied on products entering a country—may be imposed to generate revenue or to protect domestic industries from foreign competition. These restrictions typically are justified as being needed to protect a nation's economy, industries, citizens, or security. They can result in the loss of jobs, higher prices, fewer choices in the marketplace, and the misallocation of resources. Businesspeople must recognize that there are differences in countries' standards of living, individual income and buying power, national resources, and infrastructure. The laws, regulatory agencies, political systems, and special-interest groups within a country all have a great impact on international business. Differences due to religious institutions, values, customs, social systems, and language can affect communications, negotiations, and perceptions of products and companies.

3-4 Identify the facilitators of international trade, including international trade agreements and international economic organizations working to foster trade.

The General Agreement on Tariffs and Trade (GATT) was formed to dismantle trade barriers and provide an environment in which international business can grow. Today, the World Trade Organization (WTO) and various economic communities carry on this mission. Among the most significant of these world economic communities are the European Union, the United States-Mexico-Canada Agreement, the Dominican Republic-Central America Free Trade Agreement, the Association of Southeast Asian Nations, the Commonwealth of Independent States, Comprehensive and Progressive Agreement for Trans-Pacific Partnership, and the Common Market of the Southern Cone.

3-5 Describe sources of export assistance.

Many government and international agencies provide export assistance to U.S. and foreign firms. Some of the most important sources of export assistance include the International Trade Administration, the Small Business Administration, and other governmental and international agencies.

3-6 Identify institutions that can help businesses and nations finance international business.

The financing of international trade is more complex than that of domestic trade. Institutions such as the Ex-Im Bank and the International Monetary Fund have been established to provide financing and ultimately to increase world trade for American and international firms.

Key Terms 关键术语

You should now be able to define and give an example relevant to each of the following terms:

international business
absolute advantage
comparative advantage
exporting
importing
balance of trade
trade deficit
balance of payments
trading company
countertrade
licensing
contract manufacturing
outsourcing
strategic alliance
multinational corporation
tariff
dumping
nontariff barrier
import quota
embargo
exchange control
currency devaluation
General Agreement on Tariffs and Trade (GATT)
World Trade Organization (WTO)
economic community
Export-Import Bank of the United States
multilateral development bank (MDB)
World Bank
International Monetary Fund (IMF)

Discussion Questions 讨论题

1. When should a firm consider expanding from strictly domestic trade to international trade? When should it consider becoming further involved in international trade? What factors might affect the firm's decisions in each case?
2. Some politicians think tariffs will reduce their countries' trade deficits. Are they correct?
3. What effects might the devaluation of a nation's currency have on its business firms, its consumers, and the debts it owes to other nations?
4. Should imports to the United States be curtailed, by 20 percent or so, to eliminate our trade deficit? What might happen if this were done?
5. When the U.S. dollar is strong relative to other nations' currencies, what is the effect on imports and exports?
6. How can another country's cultural and political climate influence a firm's efforts to export there?
7. The United States restricts imports but, at the same time, supports the WTO and international banks whose objective is to enhance world trade. As a member of Congress, how would you justify this contradiction to your constituents?
8. How can a firm obtain the expertise needed to produce and market its products in another part of the world, for example, the EU?

Case 3 案例 3：本田的战略就是电动化且令人振奋

Honda's Strategy Is Electrifying

Honda Motor Company, a Japan-based multinational motorcycle manufacturer, was founded by Soichiro Honda in 1937. Honda, a Japanese engineer and innovator, built Honda Motor Company from the ground up. The automotive manufacturer, which started with 12 employees retrofitting bicycles with engines, has grown to more than 218,000 employees producing 19 million motorcycles, nearly 5 million automobiles, and more than 5 million power products every year. Today, Honda continues to innovate as the automotive market accelerates its transition to electric and hybrid technology.

Soichiro Honda always had an interest in vehicles. He founded Tokai Seiki (Eastern Sea Precision Machine Company) to make piston rings. Though he won a contract with Toyota, he lost the contract when it became evident that quality was lacking. He visited Toyota factories across Japan to learn more about quality control and perfect his product. Eventually, he created acceptable pistons using an automated process that could employ unskilled war-time laborers. At the start of World War II, Tokai Seiki was placed under the control of the Ministry of Commerce and Industry, and Honda was demoted at his own company. After the war, Honda sold what remained of Tokai Seiki to Toyota and used the profits to open the Honda Technical Research Institute.

With just a dozen employees in 1946, the company built and sold motorized bicycles using the former Imperial Army's generator engines. Demand was high, and the Honda Technical Research Institute soon ran out of stock. The company set out to make its own engine. Honda liquidated his business and used the money to incorporate Honda Motor Company. Its first complete motorcycle, the Honda 1949 D-Type, was just the start. The company grew to become the largest manufacturer of motorcycles by 1964.

In 1959, Honda Motor Company expanded into North America, opening its first overseas subsidiary in Los Angeles. Around this time, Honda opened Honda R&D Co., Ltd. to independently focus on research and development. Over the next several decades, Honda Motor Company continued to expand its product lines as well as operations and exports, opening its first overseas production facility in Belgium and becoming the first Japanese car manufacturer to open a production facility in the United States. Honda is now a household name with a reputation for producing quality cars and motorcycles.

Though Honda Motor Company is the world's largest manufacturer of internal combustion engines, it has had its sights set on new mobility for decades. In 2002, the company offered customers in the United States and Japan the Honda FCX, a fuel-cell powered car. Regulatory change and shifting consumer behavior in Europe have accelerated Honda's long-term electrification plans for the region, a strategy the company calls "Electric Vision." These changes have pushed Honda to introduce electrified powertrains for all of its European mainstream models several years ahead of schedule. Additionally, the company's advanced two-motor hybrid technology seen in the Honda Jazz hatchback and CR-V Hybrid has been met with acclaim across Europe. In a traditional hybrid model, an electric motor assists the car's engine, but in the Jazz hybrid electric vehicle, an electric engine assists the motor.

In the United States, on the other hand, Honda has a long road ahead to an electric future. Honda phased out the Clarity EV, its only all-electric car in the U.S. market at the time, leaving its fuel-cell and plug-in hybrid models. Buyers were unimpressed with its 89-mile driving range. In contrast, both the Chevy Bolt EV and Tesla Model 3 travel around 240 miles. To focus on the next generation of products, Honda partnered with rival General Motors (GM) to create two new all-electric vehicles using GM's proprietary Ultium battery and hands-free driver-assist technology wrapped in Honda's design. Strategic alliances such as this allow companies to pool resources, combine scale and manufacturing efficiencies, and create a competitive advantage.

By 2030, the majority of Honda's cars will be electric, zero-emission vehicles. Though there is still much progress to be made in the United States, Honda is quickly bringing its Electric Vision strategy to life in Europe. Additionally, Honda stands to greatly benefit from its strategic partnership with GM. Honda Motor Company's long history and its reputation for quality show that Honda is a company that knows how to innovate and adapt.[32]

Questions

1. How did Honda Motor Company build its reputation for producing quality cars and motorcycles?
2. What are the advantages of Honda's strategic alliance with GM?
3. How is Honda adapting to regulatory change and shifting consumer behavior in Europe?

Building Skills for Career Success 为成功的职业生涯培养技能

1. Social Media Exercise

Although Nike was founded in the Pacific Northwest and still has its corporate headquarters near Beaverton, Oregon, the company has become a multinational enterprise. The firm employs more than 75,000 people across six continents and is now a global marketer of footwear, apparel, and athletic equipment.

Because it operates in more than 170 countries around the globe and manufactures products in more than 500 factories in 39 different countries, sustainability is a big initiative for Nike. Today, Nike uses the YouTube social media site to share its sustainability message with consumers, employees, investors, politicians, and other interested stakeholders. To learn about the company's efforts to sustain the planet, follow these steps:

- Go to YouTube website.
- Enter the words "Nike" and "Sustainability" in the search window and click the search button.

1. View at least three different YouTube videos about Nike's sustainability efforts.
2. Based on the information in the videos you watched, do you believe that Nike is a good corporate citizen because of its efforts to sustain the planet? Why or why not?
3. Prepare a one- to two-page report that describes how Nike is taking steps to reduce waste, improve the environment, and reduce its carbon footprint while manufacturing products around the globe.

2. Building Team Skills

The United States-Mexico-Canada Agreement (USMCA), which replaced the North American Free Trade Agreement (NAFTA), went into effect in 2020. It has made a difference in trade among the countries and has affected the lives of many people.

Assignment

1. Working in teams and using the resources of your library, investigate USMCA. Answer the following questions:
   a. What are USMCA's objectives?
   b. What are its benefits?
   c. What impact have NAFTA and USMCA had on trade, jobs, and travel?
   d. Some Americans were opposed to the implementation of NAFTA. What were their objections? Were any of these objections justified?
   e. Have NAFTA and USMCA influenced your life? How?
2. Summarize your answers in a written report. Your team also should be prepared to give a class presentation.

3. Researching Different Careers

Today, firms around the world need employees with special skills. In some countries, such employees are not always available, and firms then must search abroad for qualified applicants. One way they can do this is through global workforce databases. As business and trade operations continue to grow globally, you may one day find yourself working in a foreign country, perhaps for an American company doing business there or for a foreign company. In what foreign country would you like to work? What problems might you face?

Assignment

1. Choose a country in which you might like to work.
2. Research the country. The CIA's World Fact Book and the International Trade Administration are good places to start. Find answers to the following questions:
   a. What language is spoken in this country? Are you proficient in it? What would you need to do if you are not proficient?
   b. What are the economic, social, and legal systems like in this nation?
   c. What is its history?
   d. What are its culture and social traditions like? How might they affect your work or your living arrangements?
3. Describe what you have found out about this country in a written report. Include an assessment of whether you would want to work there and the problems you might face if you did.

我们去买个 Graeter's 冰淇淋吧

Let's Go Get a Graeter's!

Only a tiny fraction of family-owned businesses are still growing four generations and more than 150 years after their founding, but happily for lovers of premium-quality ice cream, Graeter's is one of them.

Now a nearly $125 million firm with national distribution, Graeter's was founded in Cincinnati in 1870 by Louis Charles Graeter and his wife, Regina Graeter. The young couple made ice cream and chocolate candies in the back room of their shop, sold them in the front room, and lived upstairs. Ice cream was a special treat in this era before refrigeration, and the Graeters started from scratch every day to make theirs from the freshest, finest ingredients. Even after freezers were invented, the Graeters continued to make ice cream in small batches to preserve the quality, texture, and rich flavor.

After her husband's death, Regina's entrepreneurial leadership became the driving force behind Graeter's expansion from 1920 until well into the 1950s. At a time when few women owned or operated a business, Regina opened 20 new Graeter's stores in the Cincinnati area and added manufacturing capacity to support this ambitious—and successful— growth strategy. Her sons and grandchildren followed her into the business and continued to open ice-cream shops all around Ohio and beyond. Today, three of Regina's great-grandsons run Graeter's with the same attention to quality that made the firm famous. In her honor, the street in front of the company's ultramodern Cincinnati factory is named Regina Graeter Way.

The Scoop on Graeter's Success

Graeter's fourth-generation owners are Richard Graeter II (CEO), Robert (Bob) Graeter (vice president of operations), and Chip Graeter (vice president of retail operations). They grew up in the business, learning through hands-on experience how to do everything from packing a pint of ice cream to locking up the store at night. They also absorbed the family's dedication to product quality, a key reason for the company's enduring success. "Our family has always been contented to make a little less profit in order to ensure our long-term survival," explains the CEO.

Throughout its history, Graeter's has used a unique, time-consuming manufacturing process to produce its signature ice creams in small batches. "Our competition is making thousands and thousands of gallons a day," says Chip Graeter. "We are making hundreds of gallons a day at the most. All of our ice cream is packed by hand, so it's a very laborious process." Graeter's "French pot" manufacturing method ensures that very little air gets into the product. As a result, the company's ice cream is dense and creamy, not light and fluffy—so dense, in fact, that each pint weighs nearly a pound.

Another success factor is the use of simple, fresh ingredients like high-grade chocolate, choice seasonal fruits, and farm-fresh cream. Graeter's imports some ingredients, such as vanilla from Madagascar, and buys other ingredients from U.S. producers known for their quality. "We use a really great grade of chocolate," says Bob Graeter. "We don't cut corners on that . . . Specially selected great black raspberries, strawberries, blueberries, and cherries go into our ice cream because we feel that we want to provide flavor not from artificial or unnatural ingredients but from really quality, ripe, rich fruits." Instead of tiny chocolate chips, Graeter's products contain giant chunks formed when liquid chocolate is poured into the ice-cream base just before the mixture is frozen and packed into pints.

Maintaining the Core of Success

Graeter's "fanatical devotion to product quality" and its time-tested recipes have not changed over the years. The current generation of owners is maintaining this core of the company's success while mixing in a generous dash of innovation. "If you just preserve the core," Bob Graeter says, "ultimately you stagnate. And if you are constantly stimulating progress and looking for new ideas, well, then you risk losing what was important. . . . Part of your secret to long-term success is knowing what your core is and holding to that. Once you know what you're really all about and what is most important to you, you can change everything else."

One of those "important" things is giving back to the community and its families via local charities and other initiatives. "Community involvement is just part of being a good corporate citizen," observes Richard Graeter. When Graeter's celebrated a recent new store opening, for example, it made a cash donation to the neighborhood public library. It is also a major sponsor of The Cure Starts Now Foundation, a research foundation seeking a cure for pediatric brain cancer. In line with its focus on natural goodness, Graeter's has been doing its part to preserve the environment by recycling and by boosting production efficiency to conserve water, energy, and other resources.

Graeter's Looks to the Future

Even though Graeter's recipes reflect its 19th-century heritage, the company is clearly a 21st-century operation. It has more than 200,000 Facebook "likes," connects with brand fans on Twitter and Instagram, and invites customers to subscribe to its email newsletter. The company sells its products online, shipping orders via United Parcel Service to ice-cream lovers across the continental United States. Its newly opened production facility uses state-of-the-art refrigeration, storage, and sanitation—yet the ice cream is still mixed by hand rather than by automated equipment. With an eye toward future growth, Graeter's is refining its information system to provide managers with all the details they need to make timely decisions in today's fast-paced business environment.

Graeter's competition ranges from small, local businesses to international giants such as Unilever, which owns Ben & Jerry's, and Froneri, which owns Haagen-Dazs. Throughout the economic ups and downs of recent years, Graeter's has continued to expand, and its ice creams are now distributed through 4,000 stores in 46 states. Oprah Winfrey and other celebrities have praised its products in public. But the owners are just as proud of their hometown success. "Graeter's in Cincinnati is synonymous with ice cream," says Bob Graeter. "People will say, 'Let's go get a Graeter's.'"[34]

Questions

1. How have Graeter's owners used the four factors of production to build the business over time?
2. Which of Graeter's stakeholders are most affected by the family's decision to take a long-term view of the business rather than aiming for short-term profit? Explain your answer.
3. Knowing that Graeter's competes with multinational corporations as well as small businesses, would you recommend that Graeter's expand by licensing its brand to a company in another country? Why or why not?

Building a Business Plan 制订商业计划

A *business plan* is a carefully constructed guide for a person starting a business. The purpose of a well-prepared business plan is to show how practical and attainable the entrepreneur's goals are. It also serves as a concise document that potential investors can examine to see if they would like to invest or assist in financing a new venture. A business plan should include the following 12 components:

- Introduction
- Executive summary
- Benefits to the community
- Company and industry
- Management team
- Manufacturing and operations plan
- Labor force
- Marketing plan
- Financial plan
- Exit strategy
- Critical risks and assumptions
- Appendix

The goal of these exercises in this textbook is to help you work through the preceding components to create your own business plan. In the exercise for this part, you will make decisions and complete the research that will help you develop the intro-duction for your business plan and the benefits to the com-munity that your business will provide. In the exercises for Parts 2 through 6, you will add more components to your plan and eventually build a plan that actually could be used to start a business. The flowchart shown in Figure 3-4 gives an overview of the steps you will be taking to prepare your business plan.

The First Step: Choosing Your Business

One of the first steps for starting your own business is to decide what type of business you want to start. Take some time to think about this decision. Before proceeding, answer the following questions:

- Why did you choose this type of business?
- Why do you think this business will be successful?
- Would you enjoy owning and operating this type of business?

Warning: Do not rush this step. This step often requires much thought, but it is well worth the time and effort. As an added bonus, you are more likely to develop a quality business plan if you really want to open this type of business.

Now that you have decided on a specific type of business, it is time to begin the planning process. The goal for this part is to complete the introduction and benefits-to-the-community components of your business plan.

Figure 3-4 Business Plan

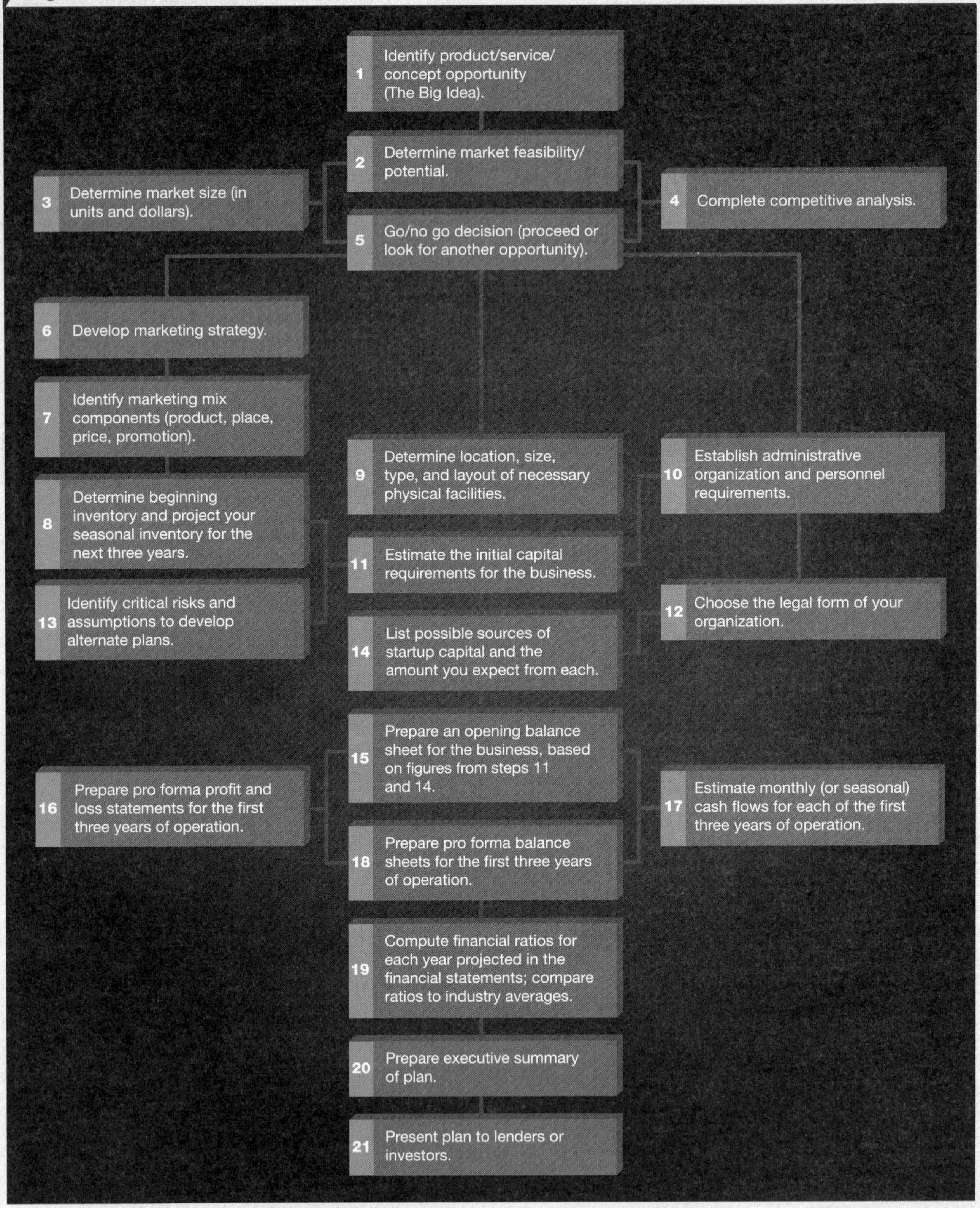

Source: Hatten, Timothy, *Small Business Management*, Fifth Edition. Copyright 2012 Cengage Learning.

Before you begin, it is important to note that the business plan is not a document that is written and then set aside. It is a living document that an entrepreneur should refer to continuously in order to ensure that plans are being carried through appropriately. As entrepreneurs begin to execute the plan, they should monitor the business environment continuously and make changes to the plan to address any challenges or opportunities that were not foreseen originally.

Throughout this course, you will, of course, be building your knowledge about business. Therefore, it will be appropriate for you to continually revisit parts of the plan that you have already written in order to refine them based on your more comprehensive knowledge. You will find that writing your plan is not a simple matter of starting at the beginning and moving chronologically through to the end. Instead, you probably will find yourself jumping around the various components, making refinements as you go. In fact, the second component—the executive summary—should be written last, but because of its comprehensive nature and its importance to potential investors, it appears after the introduction in the final business plan. By the end of this course, you should be able to put the finishing touches on your plan, making sure that all the parts create a comprehensive and sound whole so that you can present it for evaluation.

The Introduction Component

1.1. Start with the cover page. Provide the business name, street address, telephone number, Web address (if any), name(s) of owner(s) of the business, and the date the plan is issued.

1.2. Next, provide background information on the company and include the general nature of the business: retailing, manufacturing, or service; what your product or service is; what is unique about it; and why you believe that your business will be successful.

1.3. Then include a summary statement of the business's financial needs, if any. You probably will need to revise your financial needs summary after you complete a detailed financial plan.

1.4. Finally, include a statement of confidentiality to keep important information away from potential competitors.

The Benefits-to-the-Community Component

In this section, describe the potential benefits to the community that your business could provide. Chapter 2 in your textbook, "Ethics and Social Responsibility in Business," can help you in answering some of these questions. At the very least, address the following issues:

1.5. Describe the number of skilled and nonskilled jobs the business will create, and indicate how purchases of supplies and other materials can help local businesses.

1.6. Next, describe how providing needed goods or services will improve the community and its standard of living.

1.7. Finally, state how your business can offer attractive wages; develop new technical, management, or leadership skills; and provide other types of individual growth.

Review of Business Plan Activities

Read over the information that you have gathered. Because the Building a Business Plan exercises at the end of Parts 2 through 6 are built on the work you do in Part 1, make sure that any weaknesses or problem areas are resolved before continuing. Finally, write a brief statement that summarizes all the information for this part of the business plan.

Exploring Social Media and e-Business
探索社交媒体和电子商业

Learning Objectives

Once you complete this chapter, you will be able to:

4-1 Examine why it is important for a business to use social media.

4-2 Discuss how businesses use social media tools.

4-3 Explain the business objectives for using social media.

4-4 Describe how businesses develop a social media plan.

4-5 Explain the meaning of e-business.

4-6 Define the fundamental models of e-business.

4-7 Identify the factors that will affect the future of the internet, social media, and e-business.

Why Should You Care?

Question: How important are social media and e-business for a business today? Answer: Today, more and more businesses are using social media and e-business to reach new customers and increase sales and profits.

Inside Business 商业透视：Netflix 在客户保留率方面领先于竞争对手

Netflix Tops the Competition in Customer Retention

Netflix, the world's largest subscription-based streaming service, is deep in the trenches of the streaming war. Although it may have been the first successful entertainment company to stream programming, Netflix's advantage is quickly fading because of new competitors, including Amazon Prime Video, Hulu, Disney+, HBO Max, Apple TV+, and Peacock. In order to maintain its standing as the largest streaming service, Netflix must continue to build its content library, provide exceptional customer service, create original programming, retain existing customers, and add new subscribers to stay ahead of competitors.

While Netflix faces stiff competition, one measurement—churn rate—indicates that Netflix is likely to remain the leader in streaming services. Churn rate refers to the percentage of subscribers who do not renew their subscriptions during a given time frame. As competition heats up, one would expect Netflix's churn rate to increase because subscribers have more choices, but that hasn't been the case. The company's churn rate is between 2 and 3 percent, which is below the same measurement for all of its rivals. Competitors like HBO and Showtime often see a temporary increase in subscribers because viewers want to watch a new series that has been heavily marketed to build subscriber interest. Once subscribers see the series finale, streaming companies often experience a churn rate spike because they don't have additional content subscribers want. On the other hand, Netflix is able to retain customers because of its extensive content library that enables subscribers to always find something interesting that they want to watch.

Netflix also adds value to its service through personalization, an area where other streaming competitors lag behind. By considering the viewer's previous content choices and investing in search site algorithms, text analytics, and filtering to power its search function, Netflix is able to improve the subscriber's browsing experience and help viewers choose the content they will enjoy.

Is Netflix winning the war for subscribers? With 200 million subscribers worldwide and year-over-year subscriber growth rates in the double digits, it is beating the competition—for now. Still, Netflix knows the war is far from over. To maintain its number one position, Netflix knows it must retain existing customers and find ways to reach new customers. It must also continue to innovate and to build on the business and marketing practices that enabled it to become the leader in the subscription-based streaming service market.[1]

Did You Know?

Netflix has more than 200 million subscribers.

Take a moment to think about how social media and e-business affect your own life. In just a few short years, it has changed the way we communicate with each other, it has changed the way we meet people, and it has changed the way we shop. It has also changed the way we watch television. Netflix, the company profiled in the Inside Business feature for this chapter, is the leader in subscription streaming services. And yet, Netflix has big-name competitors that want a share of this market. The fact there are so many companies competing for a share of a large global market is evidence of how important streaming services (and e-business) have become. In this chapter, we explore how these trends affect both individuals and businesses.

We begin this chapter by examining why social media is important for both individuals and business firms. Next, we discuss how companies can use social media to build relationships with customers, the objectives for social media, the steps to build a social media plan, and ways to measure the effectiveness of a firm's social media activities. In the last part of this chapter, we take a close look at how firms use e-business and technology to conduct business using computers and the internet and what growth opportunities and challenges affect both social media and e-businesses.

为什么社交媒体很重要

4-1 Why Is Social Media Important?

Next time you go to lunch at your favorite restaurant or go to a ball game or the shopping mall, take a look at the number of people using their smartphones or even a tablet *and* social media to communicate with friends and relatives. In fact, if you are under the age of 40, you know exactly what social media is because you have grown up with computers and technology and are comfortable sharing information about yourself. If you are anyone else, social media seems like a strange (but exciting) phenomenon where millions of people freely share, create, vote, and connect with other people effortlessly using internet-based technologies.

Learning Objective

4-1 Examine why it is important for a business to use social media.

什么是社交媒体，它有多受欢迎

4-1a What Is Social Media and How Popular Is It?

Today, there are many definitions of social media because it is still developing and continually changing. For our purposes, **social media** represents the online interactions that allow people and businesses to communicate and share ideas, personal information, and information about products and services. Simply put, social media is about people. It is about a culture of participation, meaning that people can now discuss, vote, create, connect, and advocate much easier than ever before. For example, you can post your plans for a weekend trip on Facebook. Then you can share a travel itinerary and chronicle your trip through videos, photos, and ratings on Facebook, Snapchat, Pinterest, Twitter*, and other social media sites. While it's hard to imagine, many popular social media sites like Facebook and Google were only created in the past 25 years (refer to Figure 4-1). Because early social media sites were so successful, more sites were developed. For example, TikTok was launched in 2016 and had more than 675 million monthly users at the beginning of 2021.

So, how popular are social media sites? A recent Pew Internet Research study found that 70 percent of Facebook users visit the site each day as part of their daily routine. Other sites including Instagram (59 percent), Snapchat (59 percent), YouTube (54 percent), and Twitter (46 percent) also have a large percentage of users that visit each site every day.[2] Among the most popular worldwide social media sites are Facebook, which has approximately 2.7 billion users, YouTube, which has more than 2 billion users, and Instagram, which has more than 1 billion users.[3] These numbers increase daily as people log onto social media from home, from work, and from smartphones to stay in touch with family and friends, reconnect with old friends or classmates, share photos and videos, and obtain information available on the internet.

社交媒体
social media the online interactions that allow people and businesses to communicate and share ideas, personal information, and information about products and services

企业为什么要使用社交媒体

4-1b Why Businesses Use Social Media

Social media has completely changed the business environment. Just the sheer number of people using social media makes using social media a top priority for many business firms. Today, a business can use social media to:

- Connect with its customers and stakeholders;
- Provide information that is valuable to customers; and
- Provide another means of customer service.

Now many companies, large and small, are using social media to learn about customers' likes and dislikes, seek public input about products and marketing, and promote specific products. Macy's, for example, is active on Facebook, Twitter, Pinterest, YouTube, and a blog designed

The leader! When it comes to social media, Facebook is the most popular site in the world and has more than 2.7 billion users. For many people, Facebook is the go-to site to keep up with friends and relatives or reconnect with people they haven't talked to in years. Other people just want to see what's happening in someone else's life.

* 编者注：Twitter 于 2023 年 7 月更名为 X。

Figure 4-1 Timeline for Many Popular Social Media Sites

Ever wonder when your favorite social media site was created? To answer that question, look at the timeline below.

SOCIAL MEDIA BREAKTHROUGH	
1998	• Google
2003	• LinkedIn
2004	• Facebook, Yelp
2005	• YouTube, Mashable
2006	• Twitter
2007	• Tumblr
2010	• Pinterest, Instagram
2011	• Snapchat, Twitch
2012	• Tinder
2013	• Vine, Telegram
2014	• Periscope
2016	• TikTok
The Future	• Who knows what the next generation of social media will mean for both individuals and business?

Note: Although there have been fewer internet and social media startups since 2016, they are usually small and when successful are often acquired by larger companies—many of the same companies listed in this figure.

to be read on mobile screens. The company uses its Facebook site, for example, to provide fashion tips and news about new products and special events to communicate with its 14.6 million-plus Facebook fans. Often it uses the Twitter hashtag #Macys to highlight special in-store events and announce discounts and clearance sales. A **hashtag** is either a word or a short phrase, preceded by the pound sign (#), to identify different topics. On Pinterest, Macy's lets pictures do the talking with "pinned" images of the latest in beauty products, fashions, bridal registry items, and home decor. Its YouTube channel includes Macy's commercials, coverage of the annual Thanksgiving Day Parade, behind-the-scenes designer interviews, and videos about fashion trends.

The fact that so many people are actively sharing information about themselves and their likes and dislikes online for all to see was a driving force for many companies to develop a social media presence. Unlike social media, traditional marketing and advertising messages were top-down because companies used television, newspapers, and magazine ads to promote their product to a large audience without any opportunity for feedback. With social media, customers can and do provide feedback. If people have bad experiences with a product or service, they tend to let the world know by writing about it on a blog, mentioning it on Facebook, or tweeting about it. A recent survey by Customer Care Measurement and Consulting found that 66 percent of households experienced a problem with a product or service in the last 12 months, and many of the survey respondents used social media to complain. In addition, the survey also discovered that 55 percent of the respondents expect a response to a complaint posted on social media and nearly half of the same respondents got no response. Seventeen percent of customers who experience poor customer service tell their friends and neighbors to raise public awareness of their experience.[4] While companies no longer have much

话题标签
hashtag a word or a short phrase, preceded by the pound sign (#), to identify different topics

Figure 4-2 The Six Most Important Benefits for a Business That Uses Social Media

While there are many reasons a business uses social media, the number one reason is that social media generates increased exposure for a business.

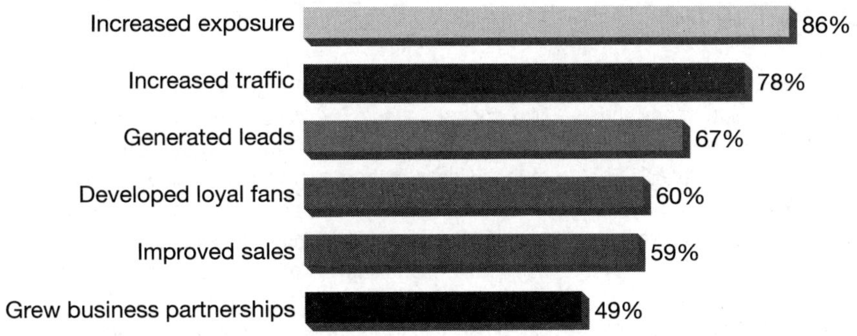

Source: Michael A. Stelzner, "2020 Social Media Marketing Industry Report," The Social Media Examiner.

control over what is said about their products or services, many still respond to negative comments about the company and its products or services made by their customers. Even if the company's response doesn't completely resolve the issue, customers appreciate the company's effort to improve customer service.

In addition to complaints, companies often use social media to respond to questions and positive customer feedback to provide additional information and build customer goodwill. The bottom line: If businesses aren't using social media to see what customers are saying about their products or services, they are missing an opportunity to increase sales and profits. For more information about why businesses use social media (and the benefits for a business), refer to Figure 4-2.

✓ Concept Check

- According to material in this section, what are the reasons why people use social media?
- How has social media changed the environment for business firms?

商用社交媒体工具

4-2 Social Media Tools for Business Use

Learning Objective

4-2 Discuss how businesses use social media tools.

For a business, part of what makes social media so challenging is the sheer number of ways to interact with other businesses and existing and potential customers. For example, companies can use **social content sites** to create and share information about their products. Commercials, for example, can go viral on social media, especially when linked to major sporting events like the Super Bowl or the World Cup. Jeep, Doritos, and Facebook used social media to generate millions of online views for their Super Bowl commercials both before and after the game.[5] For businesses selling to other businesses, social content sites can also include webinars and online promotional materials. In addition to social content sites, businesses can use blogs, photos, videos, podcasts, and social media ratings to increase customer awareness of their products and services.

博客的商业用途

4-2a Business Use of Blogs

A **blog** is a website that allows a company to share information to increase customers' knowledge about its products and services, as well as to build trust. Once a story or information is posted, customers can provide feedback through comments, which is one of the most important ways of creating a conversation with customers, not just as existing or potential customers, but as people.

Blogs are effective at developing better relationships with customers, attracting new customers, telling stories about the company's products or services, and providing an active forum for testing new ideas. For example, the Brooklyn-based online crafts marketplace Etsy uses its blogs to communicate with both buyers and

社交内容网站
social content sites websites which allow companies to create and share information about their products and services

博客
blog a website that allows a company to share information to increase the customer's knowledge about its products and services, and to build trust

Exploring Careers

职业探索：HBO Max实习生玩转抖音

HBO Max Interns Rock TikTok

Social media is an ever-changing landscape, making it challenging for companies to keep up with emerging trends and platforms. To bring in a fresh perspective, HBO Max hired five interns, Ashley Xu, Gray Fagan, Preeti Singh, Conor Driscoll, and Paravi Das, to create TikTok videos to promote the HBO Max subscription video on demand service. While each video was tied to HBO Max and its entertainment content, they were also created to entertain and make viewers laugh and at the same time increase HBO Max's TikTok following. The move paid off. Because of the videos created by the interns, HBO Max's TikTok following increased from 29,000 to more than 728,000 followers at the time of publication of your text.

TikTok is a short-form mobile video platform known for viral memes, dancing, educational content, challenges, and comedic sketches. The key for businesses like HBO Max to succeed on TikTok is to create content that feels in line with the app's culture and target viewers. While there are exceptions, the majority of TikTok viewers are Gen Z (people born after 1997) and Millennials (people born between 1981 and 1996). To reach the target audience, the five interns began by creating a makeup challenge video to promote the HBO Max show *Euphoria*. The video went viral, receiving more than 3 million views. Their first video was topped by another of their videos that got more than 32 million views.

HBO Max's competitive paid internship program is immersive and hands-on. While someone doesn't need a degree in business or marketing to work in social media, a wide variety of skills are valuable in this arena. For example, Fagan was a film production major, Driscoll was a business administration major, and Singh was a public relations and advertising major. The interns pooled their knowledge of public relations, advertising, business, film production, and, of course, social media to produce 60-second TikTok skits to engage users on the platform. Their creativity and ability to tell stories made them an asset to the company. Though their internship was set to end, the students successfully pitched a proposal to HBO Max leadership to extend their stay. And, in typical fashion, the five made a TikTok video to go along with their proposal. End result: Their internship was extended for another three months.

Sources: Based on information in Sarah Whitten, "HBO Max Activations Double to 17.2 Million in Fourth Quarter," *CNBC*, January 27, 2021; Kelsey Sutton, "HBO Max's Secret to Viral TikToks: Letting Their Interns Run the Account," *Adweek*, October 12, 2020; Michelle Anguka, "Savvy Storytelling, TikTok Skills Lead Chapman Film Students to HBO Max Internships," *Chapman University Newsroom*, October 7, 2020.

媒体共享网站
media sharing sites websites which allow users to upload photos, videos, and podcasts

sellers. Its blog posts, some written by artisans and some by Etsy personnel, profile online shops, highlight new fashion trends, teach do-it-yourself craft techniques, and showcase unusual and unique items for sale. Etsy also maintains a "Seller Handbook" blog to help sellers succeed on Etsy.

照片、视频和播客

4-2b Photos, Videos, and Podcasts

In addition to blogs, another tool for social content is **media sharing sites**, which allow users to upload photos, videos, and podcasts. Before creating a media sharing site, managers and employees should consider the following three factors:

- Who will create the photos, videos, and podcasts that will be used?
- How will the content be distributed to interested businesses and consumers?
- How much will it cost to create and distribute the material?

One increasingly popular form of media is photo sharing. Today, photo sharing provides a method for a company to tell a compelling story about its products or services through postings on either the company's website or a social media site. Target, Gap, and many other retailers, for example, post photos of clothing available in their stores or online on their Pinterest sites.

Videos have also gained popularity because of their ability to tell stories. Companies know that YouTube and other sites are useful because they are already recognized by other businesses and consumers as a source of both entertainment and information. For example, entertainment companies, like Disney and MGM, use YouTube to showcase movie trailers. Home Depot and Lowe's have also posted great do-it-yourself videos on their YouTube channels. For example, Martha Stewart has teamed up with Home Depot to create livestream videos that describe how you can create home décor. Other uses of livestream videos include online classes, interviews, and question and answer sessions with a social media influencer. An **influencer** is a person known on social media who has an influence over a large number of followers.

Podcasts are digital audio or video files that people listen to or watch online on tablets, computers, smartphones, or other mobile devices. Think of podcasts as programs that are distributed through various means and not linked to scheduled time periods. The great thing about podcasts is that they are available for download at any time. Shopify—an e-commerce site that provides e-commerce software and other management tools to help business start-ups and existing businesses—uses a series of podcasts to provide entrepreneurs with information that can be used to grow their businesses.

How do you find the best restaurant in town? Answer: Read the ratings social media users post on Yelp. While known for its restaurant reviews, the Yelp site also has ratings for shopping, automotive repairs, home services, and even nightlife. More than 175 million people visit the Yelp website each month to find out what other people think about local businesses.

社交媒体评级

4-2c Social Media Ratings

Social media enables shoppers to access ratings, reviews, opinions, recommendations, and referrals from others who have bought a product or service. Sites for reviews and ratings are based on the idea that consumers trust the opinions of others when it comes to purchasing products and services. According to a recent survey by BrightLocal, a marketing research company with locations in the United States and three other countries, 93 percent of consumers used the internet to find a local business in the last year.[6] Based on the early work of Amazon, eBay, Google, and Yelp, consumers can rate local businesses or compare products and services. In addition, individual businesses that range from retailers like Home Depot and Target to travel services like Priceline and Trip Advisor provide a way for consumers to share information about products and services.

According to consumers, the most important review factors are the overall star rating, if the review seems to be legitimate, if the reviews are current, and the number of reviews.[7] Consumer reviews are especially influential in certain purchase situations. For example, retailers, restaurants, medical services, repair services, and travel are types of businesses where ratings make a difference in consumer buying decisions. Knowing this, Wyndham Hotel Group puts the ratings of consumers who use TripAdvisor directly on its websites so travelers can see what others say about each individual hotel. By examining the reviews, Wyndham can get a good sense of its online reputation and identify specific areas for improvement.[8]

大咖
influencer a person known on social media who has an influence over a large number of followers

播客
podcasts digital audio or video files that people listen to or watch online on tablets, computers, smartphones, or other mobile devices

✓ Concept Check

- What is a blog? How can a business use a blog to develop relationships with customers?
- What types of content can be used on a media sharing site? What factors should be considered when developing content for a media sharing site?
- How important are social media ratings for consumers? For businesses?

通过社交媒体实现商业目标

4-3 Achieving Business Objectives Through Social Media

Learning Objective

4-3 Explain the business objectives for using social media.

Although social media is a recent phenomenon, many businesses are already using it to achieve important objectives. Some of these goals are long term— such as building brand awareness and brand reputation—while others are more short term—such as increasing website traffic or generating sales leads. Regardless of how social media is used, there are a lot of business opportunities. In this section, we explore a few ways that companies have used social media effectively to achieve business objectives.

社交媒体社区

4-3a Social Media Communities

Social media communities are groups of people who share common interests and who want to use technology and the internet to connect with people with similar interests. People who are part of the communities can share information and even develop profiles. Individuals in a community can be called friends, fans, followers, or connections. Popular social networking sites include Facebook (the largest), LinkedIn (for professionals), Twitter, YouTube, Pinterest, and many others. To see how many businesses use the top six social media community sites, refer to Figure 4-3.

There are social communities for every interest, ethnic group, and lifestyle. Different types of social communities include forums and wikis. A **forum** is an interactive version of a community bulletin board that focuses on threaded discussions. These are particularly popular with people who share a common interest such as animal protection, health issues, or the latest movies. One of the most popular internet forums is Reddit, which is a massive collection of forums where people can share news and content and comment on other people's posts. Reddit is further broken down into subreddits, which are forums dedicated to specific topics. For example, there are subreddit communities for gaming, sports, television, travel, health and fitness, fashion, and many others. In reality, there are thousands of subreddits, and the number of subreddits continues to increase as more people with special interests interact on the Reddit site.

Another community based on social media is a wiki. A **wiki** is a collaborative online working space that enables members to contribute content that can be shared with other people. With wikis, members of the community are the editors and gatekeepers ensuring that the content is correct and updated. Wikipedia—the free online encyclopedia—is the best example of a wiki.

Figure 4-3 The Top Six Social Media Networking Sites Used by Businesses

For businesses using social media, the most popular social networking sites are Facebook and Instagram.

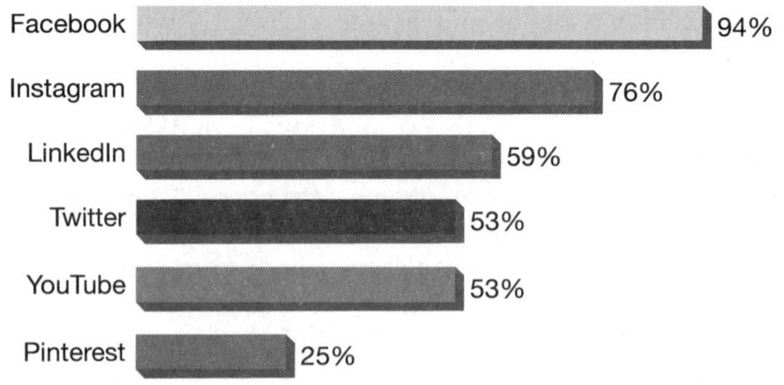

Source: Michael A. Stelzner, "2020 Social Media Marketing Industry Report," The Social Media Examiner.

社交媒体社区
social media communities groups of people who share common interests and who want to use technology and the internet to connect with people with similar interests

论坛
forum an interactive version of a community bulletin board that focuses on threaded discussions

维基
wiki a collaborative online working space that enables members to contribute content that can be shared with other people

Today, many companies and nonprofit organizations are using social media to build communities to achieve important objectives. For a business, developing social media communities is a way to interact with customers. Coca-Cola uses many different types of social media to build a community for people who want more information about Coca-Cola products and stories about Coke's involvement in the community. Because companies like Coca-Cola recognize the value of this type of social media, the largest companies now have a team of professionals to develop and monitor their social media activities led by a social media community manager. A **social media community manager** is a high-level executive who is responsible for all of a company's social media activities. Nonprofit organizations also use social media to promote and fund their programs. The nonprofit organization Kiva has helped build communities around the globe by matching lenders and struggling would-be entrepreneurs. Using Kiva to identify potential borrowers, anyone who can lend $25 (or more) can loan money to people who need a bit of cash to go into business or keep a business running. To date, there are 1.9 million Kiva lenders that have funded loans of more than $1.6 billion to people in 77 different countries.[9]

危机与声誉管理

4-3b Crisis and Reputation Management

One of the most important reasons for listening to stakeholders is to determine whether there is a crisis brewing. Crises happen more often than most managers, employees, and customers realize. A recent survey by accounting firm PricewaterhouseCoopers (PWC) found that almost 70 percent of corporate managers have experienced a crisis in the last five years.[10] For example, consider the effect of the COVID-19 pandemic on businesses throughout the world. The pandemic quickly made its way to regions including Europe, South America, and North America. Businesses in the United States were especially hit hard when non-essential businesses were in lockdown during spring 2020. Then the virus made a resurgence toward the end of the year. In many cases, social media was used to let customers know if businesses were open and what precautions they were using to keep both customers and employees safe during the pandemic. For example:

- Many businesses, including Home Depot, Lowe's, and Ace Hardware, were open, but strict requirements for masks, social distancing, and reduced operating hours were announced on their social media sites.
- Restaurants including Saltgrass Steakhouses, the Olive Garden, Red Lobster, and other national chains used social media to inform people of their operating hours and if they were open for food pick-up, delivery, or if dine-in was an option at some of their locations.
- Many manufacturers used social media to communicate with their customers—wholesalers, distributors, and retailers—about plant closures, product availability, and expected delivery dates.

Although the previous examples highlight how companies used social media to inform customers, employees, and stakeholders of the steps they were taking to fight a pandemic, often they will use social media to respond to negative reviews about the company's products or services. The following illustrates how Jet Blue Airlines handled a negative Twitter post.[11]

Customer – *My view during all the flight (4 hours). No movies, no TV. First complaint to one of my favorite airlines. [Followed by an image of a blank TV screen]*
Jet Blue Response – *Oh no! That's not what we like to hear! Were all the TVs out on the plane or is it just yours?*
Customer – *Just my TV. The ones I saw next to me, everything was working.*
Jet Blue Response – *We always hate it when that happens. Send us a direct message with your confirmation code to get you a credit for the non-working TV.*

社交媒体社区经理
social media community manager a high-level executive who is responsible for all of a company's social media activities

The Jet Blue Twitter team did a great job responding to this customer's complaint. First, they quickly acknowledged the problem, and then they asked for more information. Finally, they apologized and offered a credit for the non-working TV.

Although most companies spend more time responding to negative reviews, they also respond to positive complements about their product or service. In either case, the goal is to build customer goodwill, increase customer retention, and ultimately increase sales. Even though businesses can't anticipate when and what type of crisis will occur or when they will receive negative reviews, planning should begin before a problem situation develops. Employees should already be trained in social media etiquette and be monitoring social media sites to see what is said about the company and its products. During a crisis, companies can use social media to answer questions with carefully worded posts, reassure the public, and present positive information to help rebuild their reputations.

听取利益相关者的意见

4-3c Listening to Stakeholders

Listening to people, whether they are customers or not, is always an important aspect of a company's social media plan. Indeed, listening is often the first step when developing a social media strategy. By monitoring Facebook, Twitter, or other social media sites, companies can determine what customers think about their products or services. If a company receives negative comments, it's important to respond

Technology and Innovation

技术与创新：大众在愚人节的恶作剧适得其反

VW's April Fools' Day Prank Backfires

While social media is a valuable tool to help brands recover in the wake of a reputational crisis, it can also be a threat to an organization's reputation. If a crisis is handled poorly, social media can amplify damage rather than restoring faith in the brand. Additionally, because of the viral nature of social media, news can quickly spread, putting a company in the global spotlight before a company even has time to respond to negative comments. Consider what happened with an April Fool's Day prank orchestrated by automaker Volkswagen.

April Fool's Day pranks often cause a stir on social media. VW discovered that's not always a good thing. The company leaked a phony press release saying it would change its name to Voltswagen to bring attention to its $86 billion push into the electric vehicle market. The company tweeted, "We know, 66 is an unusual age to change your name, but we've always been young at heart. Introducing Voltswagen. Similar to Volkswagen, but with a renewed focus on electric driving."

Unfortunately, many people, including reporters, did not realize it was a joke because it seemed authentic and was posted days ahead of April Fool's Day. The announcement was shared as a real news story on *USA Today*, *The Associated Press*, the *BBC*, *The Verge*, and dozens of other outlets. Social media users speculated about the press release for days before VW finally declared the announcement was a prank.

"What began as an April Fool's effort got the whole world buzzing," VW tweeted. "Turns out people are as passionate about our heritage as they are about our electric future. So, whether it's Voltswagen or Volkswagen, people talking about electric driving and our ID.4 can only be a good thing." (Note: ID.4 is VW's new electric SUV.) Consumers and the media did not agree, and the stunt was widely slammed.

The automaker, which was at the center of a previous emissions scandal where it lied to the public and regulators in 2015, has worked for years to repair its reputation. The April Fool's misstep dredged up memories of its unethical past. In fact, many media experts believe Volkswagen undermined its own efforts to move on from the emission scandal and eroded the company's trust and credibility.

Sources: Based on information in Aaron Gold, "How Volkswagen's 'Voltswagen' April Fools' Prank Backfired," *Motortrend*, April 5, 2021; Sean O'Kane, "Volkswagen of America Lied about Rebranding to 'Voltswagen'," *The Verge*, March 30, 2021; Volkswagen [@VW], *Twitter*, March 31, 2021; @RationalEtienne, *Twitter*, March 31, 2021.

quickly. A personal response either on social media or a personal contact often will help resolve a complaint and at the same time restore customer goodwill. It also helps if the customer feels that the company will take action to correct the problem. For example, many companies encourage customers to complete quick surveys about products or services. Brinker International—parent company of Chili's and Maggiano's restaurants—provides customers with a link to a short survey on the bottom of their receipt. Customers are free to provide both positive and negative comments about their dining experience. Those comments are then used to fine-tune restaurant operations. In some cases, when negative reviews are justified, customers receive a personal note, a phone call, or an email reply that may be accompanied with a gift card to encourage customers to become return customers.

目标客户
4-3d Targeting Customers

Many companies are using social media to increase awareness and build their brand among customers. It is especially valuable to target people based on their age. Common population age groups are often referred to as generations. For example, Generation Z (people born after 1997) is America's largest generation and accounts for 27 percent of the U.S. population.[12] Other generations in the U.S. population include:

- Millennials—people born between 1981 to 1996 and represent 25 percent;
- Generation X—people born between 1965 to 1980 and represent 20 percent;
- Baby Boomers—people born between 1946 to 1964 and represent 21 percent;
- The Silent Generation—people born between 1928 to 1945 and represent 7 percent; and
- The Greatest Generation—people born before 1928 and represent less than 1 percent.

To reach people who are included in each generation, it helps to identify who the customer is and what characteristics make the customer unique. For example, many people in Generation Z are now teenagers and represent younger consumers compared to people in the other generations. People in Generation Z grew up with technology, the internet, and social media. Facebook, Instagram, Snapchat, and YouTube are popular social media sites for people in this age group. In fact, Generation Z is quickly surpassing Millennials as a key target group of customers for retailers and manufacturers. For example, Nike—one of the most well-known brands in the world—recognizes Generation Z as one of the most important groups to reach on social media. In fact, Nike uses Instagram, Facebook, Twitter, YouTube, and Pinterest to reach out to people in each generation.[13] Each of these social media sites is used to promote Nike athletic footwear, clothing, and other items with many posts, photos, and social media activities directed to specific age groups in different generations. As a result of social media and other promotion activities, the Nike swoosh and its marketing phrase "Just Do It" are known throughout the world. And yet, the real story is that the brand isn't using social media to just sell a specific product; Nike is selling the benefits and image of its products that literally become part of a person's lifestyle.[14] For the company, the investment in social media has increased brand awareness, but more importantly increased sales and profits.

社交媒体营销
social media marketing the utilization of software, computer technology, and the internet to provide information about a firm's products and services, increase sales revenues, and improve customer service

面向消费者的社交媒体营销
4-3e Social Media Marketing for Consumers

Social media marketing is the utilization of software, computer technology, and the internet to provide information about a firm's products and services, increase sales revenues, and improve customer service.

As companies become more comfortable with social media, we can expect even more companies to use social media to market products and services to their customers. Already, research indicates that companies are shifting their advertising money from traditional marketing (like television and magazines) to digital marketing (like internet search engines and social media). Experts now predict that companies will shift more marketing dollars to digital marketing over the next few years. And by 2024, some experts expect that spending on digital marketing will account for more than 50 percent of the marketing budget for many firms.[15] The primary reason is simple: People are spending more time on social media sites. Often the first step for a business that wants to use social media is to go to Facebook, Twitter, Snapchat, YouTube, LinkedIn, or some other popular social media site. As you can see from the information in Figure 4-4, companies like Snapchat make using their technology as easy as possible to connect with potential or existing customers.

其他业务的社交媒体营销

4-3f Social Media Marketing for Other Businesses

集客式营销
inbound marketing a marketing term that describes new ways of gaining attention, and ultimately customers, by creating content on a website that pulls customers in

Today, many companies have been quite successful using social media marketing not only to develop customer awareness, but also to obtain sales leads and increase actual sales to other businesses. HubSpot, for example, is a software company that helps companies develop inbound marketing programs. **Inbound marketing** is a marketing term that describes new ways of gaining attention, and ultimately customers, by

Figure 4-4 Snapchat's Marketing Solutions for Businesses

Like many social media sites, Snap's marketing tools help businesses connect with customers all over the globe. By using Snapchat, Domino's Pizza strengthened its brand awareness and surpassed both the company's and Snapchat's "success" benchmarks after a recent promotional campaign in Norway.

Source: Snapchat, https://forbusiness.snapchat.com/inspiration/dominos-strengthened-their-appeal-through-successful-campaign-on-snapchat, March 24, 2021.

creating content on a website that pulls customers in. Tools used for inbound marketing programs include search engine optimization, emails, blogging, videos, and social media. In order to market its software products, HubSpot shunned traditional advertising and began to practice what it preached. First, the company developed its own inbound marketing program by creating valuable content and marketing information that was then distributed through social media and search engine websites. Companies interested in HubSpot's software were required to enter contact information (name, phone number, and email address) in order to view the information because they believed the company's software could help them improve their marketing activities. As a result of HubSpot's inbound marketing program, the cost of generating new sales leads was reduced, the number of customers increased, and sales increased.

Companies also use social media marketing to sell goods and services, invite customer feedback, and reinforce a positive brand image. For General Electric (GE), social media marketing sets the stage for global sales of turbines, jet engines, and medical devices, among other products. GE is a social media innovator with award-winning videos, striking Instagram and Pinterest photos of its industrial products, followers on Facebook and Twitter, and a popular YouTube channel.

As important as social media marketing is, it is only one aspect of digital marketing. Indeed, digital marketing (sometimes referred to as online marketing) is comprised of several areas and also includes:

- *Search engine optimization*—using keywords in a company's website in order to rank higher in search engine results;
- *Search engine marketing*—buying advertising on sites like Google Ads to increase traffic to a company's website;
- *Display advertising*—buying banner ads; and
- *Email marketing*—targeting customers through opt-in email campaigns.

众包
crowdsourcing outsourcing tasks to a group of people in order to tap into the ideas of the crowd

From an ethical perspective, all company employees should identify themselves during social media interactions with customers and be transparent about their role in digital marketing. For example, Intel, which makes computer chips, is one of many businesses that require disclosure of ties to the company when employees participate in different types of digital marketing.

产生新产品创意

4-3g Generating New Product Ideas

Companies can use social media to conduct much of their consumer-based research. Using insight gained from Facebook or Twitter, for example, allows a company to modify existing products and services and develop new ones. Another method, **crowdsourcing** involves outsourcing tasks to a group of people in order to tap into the ideas of the crowd. In some cases, valuable information can be obtained by crowd voting. Frito-Lay, for example, has used crowd voting to determine which television commercials to advertise its popular Doritos brand. The company has also used crowdsourcing for product development. And in 2020, Frito-Lay used crowdsourcing to honor ordinary people who do extraordinary things to create joy in their communities. Family and friends were able to nominate someone who goes to great lengths to inspire joy. Once the crowd—a national sample of 5,000 adults—chose the winners, Frito-Lay then redesigned its famous potato chip bags to feature the smiles of the winners.[16]

The power of the crowd. LEGO—the Danish toymaker—uses crowdsourcing to generate new product ideas. Here's how it works. Customers can post and vote on ideas at https://ideas.lego.com. Ideas that get at least 10,000 votes are submitted to the company's review board. Then LEGO makes a final selection of promising ideas that begin the production process. For LEGO, the benefits include a new way to generate new product ideas and to build customer loyalty.

Companies can even build communities for specific brands in order to obtain information and new ideas from consumers. The Danish toymaker LEGO has created an online site called LEGO Ideas (https://ideas.lego.com) where brand enthusiasts can post and vote on new product ideas. LEGO benefits from its customers' creativity and the goodwill generated by seeking the community's input. Just as important, the creators receive credit for their ideas plus a small royalty from product sales.[17]

Concept Check

- In your own words, describe how social media can help businesses to connect with other businesses and consumers.
- For a business, why are crisis and reputation management, listening to stakeholders, and targeting specific types of customers important activities?
- How can social media be used to market a firm's products or services to consumers and other businesses?
- How can social media help a firm generate new product ideas and recruit employees?

招聘员工

4-3h Recruiting Employees

For years, companies have used current employees to recruit new employees based on the theory that "birds of a feather flock together." The concept is simple: Current employees' friends and family may prove to be good job candidates. Social media takes that concept to a whole new level. LinkedIn, the largest social network for professionals, has been used quite effectively by large corporations, small businesses, nonprofit organizations, and government agencies that want to recruit new employees. Because LinkedIn hosts more than 750 million registered members, employers using the site can save time, reduce their recruiting costs, and see more information about individual candidates.[18] Companies like 3M, Coca-Cola, Four Seasons Hotels and Resorts, Hewlett Packard, IBM, Microsoft, Procter & Gamble, and many others have all had recruiting success with LinkedIn. Many other social media sites, including Glassdoor, Facebook, Instagram, and YouTube, can also be used for networking and to learn about a company where you might want to work.

制订社交媒体计划

4-4 Developing a Social Media Plan

Learning Objective

4-4 Describe how businesses develop a social media plan.

Before developing a plan to use social media, it is important to determine how social media can improve the organization's overall performance and how it "fits" with a company's objectives and other promotional activities. For example, if a social media plan attempts to improve customer service, it needs to link to the company's other efforts to improve customer service.

制订社交媒体计划的步骤

4-4a Steps to Build a Social Media Plan

Once it is determined how social media links to the company's other activities, there are several steps that should be considered.

Step 1: Listen to Determine Opportunities As pointed out earlier in this chapter, social media is often used to "listen" to what customers like and don't like about a company's products or services. For example, reading comments on social media sites can yield some insight into how consumers are reacting to a price increase for an existing product or service. Monitoring social media sites also allows managers and employees to not only listen but also to enter the conversation and tell the company's side of the story. In addition, companies can monitor social media sites to gather information about competitors as well as what is being said about the industry.

Step 2: Establish Social Media Objectives After listening to customers and analyzing the information obtained from social media sites, it is important to use that information to develop specific objectives. For social media, an objective is a statement about what a social media plan should accomplish. Each objective should be specific, measurable, achievable, realistic, and oriented toward the future. In addition, all objectives need to be linked to specific actions that can be used to accomplish each objective.

For most companies, the most popular objectives are:[19]

- Improving customer service
- Increasing brand awareness

- Building brand presence
- Acquiring new customers
- Developing loyalty programs

Other objectives that are often important for many firms include introducing new products, improving search engine ranking, and increasing the number of people who visit the company's social media sites.

Step 3: Segment and Target the Social Media Customer Ideally, a company will have developed a customer profile that describes a typical customer in terms of age, income, gender, ethnicity, etc. When segmenting or targeting customers, it also helps to know how they think, how they spend their time, how much they buy, and how often they buy. Additionally, it is important to really understand how customers use social media.

- Do they create content like photos, videos, blog posts, etc.?
- Do they use social media for information, ratings, and reviews?
- Do they spend a lot of time using social media?

More information about potential customers will help you develop a social media plan to achieve a company's objectives. Lack of information about customers can lead to wasted time and money and the inability to successfully achieve the firm's social media objectives. For example, most companies feel that they must use Facebook, Instagram, and Twitter. But if their core customer does not use these social media sites, then it does not make sense to use them. Some of the information that can help you target just the "right" social media customer is illustrated in Figure 4-5.

Figure 4-5 Types of Information That Can Help Target Different Social Media Customers

The more information you have about customers, the easier it is to develop a social media plan that targets the "right" customer.

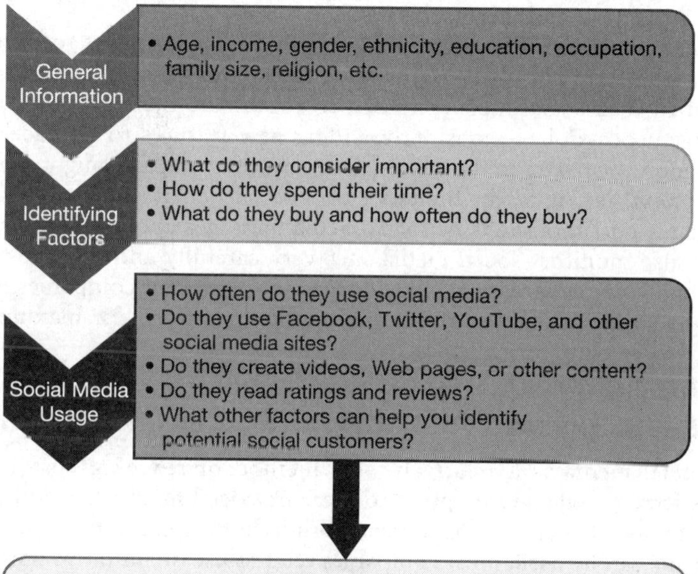

Step 4: Select Social Media Tools The search for the right social media tool(s) usually begins with the company's social media objectives, outlined in Step 2. It also helps to review the target customer or segment of the market the company is trying to reach (Step 3). With this information, the next step is to choose the right social media tools to reach the right customers. A company can use social media content sites, blogs, photos, videos, podcasts, or crowdsourcing to reach potential or existing customers. For example, if the goal is to recruit college graduates for sales positions for a large pharmaceutical company, LinkedIn may be a good choice. Remember, it is not necessary (or even advisable) to use all of the above tools. It is also possible for a business to build a social media community—especially when the objective is to fund business start-ups. Often money for worthwhile projects is obtained through crowdfunding. **Crowdfunding** is a method of raising money to fund a project for a business, a nonprofit organization, or an individual. The money raised can be an investment, a loan, or a donation. For example, a young startup company, Oculus VR, used Kickstarter—a crowdfunding site to raise $250,000. The money (along with later funding from venture capitalists) was used to build a virtual-reality headset, Oculus Rift, that puts players into their favorite games. Oculus VR was so successful that later Facebook bought the company for $2 billion.[20]

Step 5: Implement and Integrate the Plan Once social media tools have been identified, a company can implement and integrate the social media plan. Because a social media plan doesn't necessarily have a start and stop date, it is different from traditional advertising campaigns. Some social media activities continue and have a life of their own. For example, Zappos, a very successful online retailer, is a company that is always "on" in terms of its social media. Indeed, they do very little traditional advertising and instead rely on the company's website and social media to promote products, monitor customer service, and enhance the company's reputation. If a customer uses social media to complain, their customer service representatives will often contact the customer and try to resolve any problems the customer has experienced. This customer-focused approach often leads to increased customer satisfaction and increased sales.

Some companies, on the other hand, feel that it is important to have a mix of short- and long-term social media promotion. In this case, it's important to key the content to each social media site and to coordinate the timing of promotions. For example, Coca-Cola is constantly adding new features to its Facebook page, which has more than 105 million likes. One day, the company might post its latest video. The next day, it might invite visitors to participate in a survey. Knowing that customers post thousands of social media messages about its brand every day, Coca-Cola also monitors social media sites very carefully and responds quickly to questions and comments. Finally, like a growing number of companies, Coca-Cola integrates its social media and traditional marketing efforts for maximum impact and to get "more bang for the buck."

衡量和调整社交媒体计划

4-4b Measuring and Adapting a Social Media Plan

Because social media is a relatively new method of reaching customers, many companies struggle when attempting to measure social media. Generally, there are two types of social media measurement. While both quantitative and qualitative measurements can be used, most companies tend to use quantitative measurements.

Quantitative Social Media Measurement **Quantitative social media measurement** consists of using numerical measurements, such as counting the number of website visitors, number of fans and followers, number of leads generated, and the number of new customers. Table 4-1 shows a few popular quantitative ways to measure social media. A company like Macy's counts not

众筹

crowdfunding a method of raising money to fund a project for a business, a nonprofit organization, or an individual

量化社交媒体测量

quantitative social media measurement using numerical measurements, such as counting the number of website visitors, number of fans and followers, number of leads generated, and the number of new customers

Table 4-1 Quantitative Measurements for Selected Social Media Websites

Type of Social Media	Typical Measurements
Blogs	• Unique visitors • Number of views • Ratio of visitors to posted comments
Twitter	• Number of followers • Number of tweets and retweets • Click through rate (CTR) of tweeted links • Visits to website from tweeted links
Facebook	• Number of likes • Number of comments and responses • Visits to websites from Facebook links
YouTube	• Number of videos • Number of visitors • Ratio of comments to the number of videos • Watch time

关键绩效指标
key performance indicators (KPIs) measurements that define and measure the progress of an organization toward achieving its objectives

定性社交媒体测量
qualitative social media measurement the process of accessing the opinions and beliefs about a brand

情感分析
sentiment analysis a measurement that uses technology to detect the mood, attitudes, or emotions of people who experience a social media activity

only the number of social media likes and followers but also the number of times the company is mentioned each day. Although such measures help the company gauge brand awareness, determining how social media affects actual purchases of consumer products, like clothing and jewelry, can be difficult. Business-to-business marketers frequently set additional goals to track how social media activities lead to sales contacts and then to purchases. SAP North America, which markets software and technology services to corporations, uses social media to generate leads and facilitate the sales process. For example, SAP sponsors special events, workshops, and presentations that showcase the firm's software products. Both current and prospective customers often find out about these programs by accessing the firm's social media sites. To attend many of these events, people must register and provide basic contact information. Later, the person's contact information is used to initiate future sales calls.[21] By tracking such contacts, SAP can determine the effect of its programs on the company's sales revenues.

A number of companies are also using key performance indicators to measure their social media activities. **Key performance indicators (KPIs)** are measurements that define and measure the progress of an organization toward achieving its objectives. Generally, KPIs are *quantitative* (based on numbers like the number of YouTube views).

If measuring the success or failure of social media activities with KPIs, the first step is to connect KPIs with objectives. The second step is to set a benchmark—a number that shows what success should look like. Assume Mercedes-Benz sets a benchmark of 750,000 views for a new YouTube video that introduces a new S-Class model automobile. If at the end of a specified time period, 840,000 people have viewed the video, it would indicate the company's video campaign was successful.

Quantitative or qualitative measurements—Which one is best? That's a hard question to answer. Both methods can be used to measure the effectiveness of a company's social media plan. Quantitative measurements are numerical, like the number of visitors to a site. Qualitative measurements analyze a customer's sentiments, like what people think about a company's customer service. Sometimes just asking customers to check a box if they like a product or service or not is all it takes.

Qualitative Social Media Measurement **Qualitative social media measurement** is the process of accessing the opinions and beliefs about a brand. This process primarily uses sentiment analysis to categorize what is being said about a company. **Sentiment analysis** is a measurement that uses technology to detect the mood, attitudes, or emotions of people who experience a social media activity. Other measurements for determining customer sentiment include:

- *Customer satisfaction score*—the relative satisfaction of customers;
- *Issue resolution rate*—the percentage of customer service inquiries resolved satisfactorily using social media; and
- *Resolution time*—the amount of time taken to resolve customer service issues.

When compared to quantitative measurement, it should be noted that many of these qualitative social media measurements are more subjective in nature.

维护社交媒体计划的成本
4-4c The Cost of Maintaining a Social Media Plan

Basic assumption: Social media is not free and can be quite expensive. Because social media costs both time and money, it is important to measure the success of a social media plan and make adjustments and changes if needed. Based on quantitative and qualitative measurements, the company may also try to determine if it is getting a positive return on its investment in social media.

After reviewing results for social media activities against pre-established benchmarks, it may be necessary to make changes and update the plan to increase the effectiveness of the social media plan. A social media plan, for example, must provide current and up-to-date information in order to keep customers coming back to see what's new. Without updates, customers lose interest and the number of returning customers can drop dramatically. After all, one of the major objectives of social media activities is to provide customers and stakeholders with current and useful information about the company and its products or services. Once it is determined that updates and changes are needed, many of the same steps described in this section may be used to improve a firm's social media plan. It is also important to create future social media plans based on what worked and what didn't work in previous plans.

Social media is particularly important to businesses that use computers and the internet to sell their products and services online. In the next section, we take a close look at how e-business firms are organized, satisfy needs online, and earn profits.

✓ Concept Check

- What are the steps required to develop a social media plan?
- What is the difference between quantitative and qualitative measurements? Which type of measurement do you think is the most reliable when measuring the effectiveness of a company's social media plan?

电子商业的定义
4-5 Defining e-Business

Learning Objective

4-5 Explain the meaning of e-business.

In Chapter 1, we define *business* as the organized effort of individuals to produce and sell, for a profit, the goods and services that satisfy society's needs. Working from this original definition, then, **e-business (or electronic business)**, can be defined as the organized effort of individuals to produce and sell, for a profit, the goods and services that satisfy society's needs *through the facilities available on the internet.* Sometimes people use the term *e-commerce* instead of *e-business.* In a strict sense, e-business is used when you're talking about all business activities and practices conducted on the internet by an individual firm or industry. On the other hand, **e-commerce** is a part of e-business and usually refers only to buying and selling activities conducted online. Although actual statistics vary depending on the source, U.S. e-commerce retail sales already account for approximately $432 billion a year and are expected to increase to $563 billion by 2025.[22]

With the popularity of smartphones and tablet computers, many companies are also using **mobile marketing** to communicate with and sell to customers through mobile devices. Mobile marketing covers a range of activities, from optimizing websites for viewing on smartphones and tablets to delivering promotional messages and discounts via mobile devices. Because mobile devices are used in over 40 percent of online transactions, many businesses are investing more heavily in mobile marketing.[23] A growing number of companies have *apps* to make mobile

电子商业
e-business (or **electronic business)** the organized effort of individuals to produce and sell, for a profit, the goods and services that satisfy society's needs through the facilities available on the internet

电子商务
e-commerce a part of e-business and usually refers only to buying and selling activities conducted online

移动营销
mobile marketing communicating with and selling to customers through mobile devices

transactions faster and more convenient for customers. For example, Starbucks offers an easy-to-use app for customers to pay for their lattes or espressos directly from a smartphone or tablet.

组织电子商业资源

4-5a Organizing e-Business Resources

As noted in Chapter 1, to be organized, a business must combine *human, material, informational,* and *financial resources.* This is true of e-business, too (refer to Figure 4-6), but in this case, the resources may be more specialized than in a typical business. For example, people who can design, create, and maintain websites are only a fraction of the specialized human resources required by e-businesses. Material resources often include customized computers and high-speed internet connections. Computer software programs that track the number of visitors who view a firm's website and customers who make online purchases are generally among the specialized informational resources required. Financial resources, the money required to start and maintain the firm and allow it to grow, usually reflect greater participation by individual entrepreneurs, venture capitalists, and investors willing to invest in a high-tech firm instead of conventional financial sources such as banks.

In an effort to reduce the cost of specialized resources that are used in e-business, many firms have turned to outsourcing. **Outsourcing** is the process of finding outside vendors and suppliers that provide professional help, parts, or materials at a lower cost. For example, a firm that needs computer programmers and specialized software to complete a project may turn to an outside firm located in another part of the United States, India, or an Eastern European country.

满足线上需求

4-5b Satisfying Needs Online

The internet has created some new customer needs that did not exist before its creation. Consider what happened during the second quarter (April, May, and June) of 2020. e-Commerce sales grew an average of 45 percent when compared to the same period the previous year.[24] The growth was the result of the COVID-19 pandemic. Because of a shutdown of non-essential businesses and fear for the health of not only themselves but also their families, customers turned to online shopping to obtain the products they needed. For the remainder of the year, the growth rate for e-commerce continued to rise to record levels. For example, 44 percent more

Figure 4-6 Combining e-Business Resources

While all businesses use four resources (human, material, informational, and financial), these resources are typically more specialized when used in an e-business.

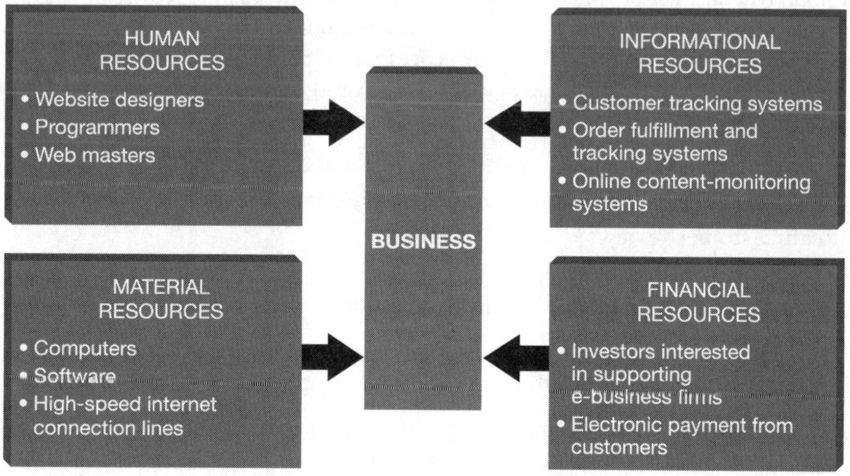

外包
outsourcing the process of finding outside vendors and suppliers that provide professional help, parts, or materials at a lower cost

Entrepreneurial Success

创业成功：为什么小企业喜欢 Shopify

Why Small Businesses Like Shopify

In 2004, Tobias Lütke, Daniel Weinand, and Scott Lake came up with the idea for Shopify, a Canadian e-commerce platform, while opening a small online business for snowboarding equipment called Snowdevil. The three entrepreneurs were dissatisfied with existing e-commerce sites, so Lütke, a computer programmer, decided to build his own. Two years later, the platform hosting Snowdevil was launched as Shopify.

Now, more than 1 million businesses in 175 countries use Shopify to sell merchandise. One of the keys to Shopify's success is that instead of positioning itself as a traditional e-commerce platform, it markets itself as a one-stop-shop for business owners to start, run, and grow their businesses. Small business owners that use Shopify typically use a variety of services, including email marketing, website hosting, logistics management, and point-of-sale software. This all-in-one approach is attractive for small business owners who have limited time, resources, and technical expertise because it eliminates the need to deal with third parties to get the tools that they need to operate their businesses. For example, its customizable themes and drag-and-drop store builder tool eliminate the need for design skills. Another attractive feature allows Shopify users to sync online and in-store sales using its point-of-sales software. According to many users, Shopify offers solutions, tools, and services that were previously unavailable for many small business owners for a relatively small monthly fee.

Shopify was already growing steadily when the COVID-19 pandemic struck. With lockdown restrictions in place for many nonessential businesses and an increasing number of customers shopping online, many small business owners scrambled to get their businesses online. Shopify enticed new users by extending its 14-day free trial to 90 days for a limited time on select plans. Extending the free trial gave customers more time to determine if Shopify was the right e-commerce platform for them. As a result, Shopify experienced rapid growth.

Small business owners aren't the only ones enjoying everything Shopify has to offer. Major brands such as Pepsi, Heinz, and Staples also use the Shopify e-commerce platform. While it faces a variety of e-commerce competitors, including Adobe's Commerce, BigCommerce, WooCommerce, Wix, and even Amazon, Shopify stands out from the competition because of its ability to meet the needs of its small-business customers.

Sources: Based on information in Lauren Debter, "During Pandemic, Shopify Woos A Wave Of Small Businesses Eager To Get Online," *Forbes*, May 8, 2020; Matt Grossman and Kimberly Chin, "Shopify's Revenue Nearly Doubles as Covid-19 Pushes Shopping Online," *The Wall Street Journal*, July 30, 2020; Laura Forman, "Shopify's Business Sells Itself, for Now," *The Wall Street Journal*, July 29, 2020.

people made purchases online during the Thanksgiving to Cyber Monday period in 2020 when compared to the previous year.[25] This increase was caused by people avoiding crowded stores that are typical of this holiday season. Now even as people return to more normal times, many experts predict online sales will continue to increase and sales in brick-and-mortar stores will decline in the future. While there are many reasons for the increase in e-commerce and online shopping, major reasons include the ability to:

- Save time when compared to shopping at the mall or store;
- Compare prices for the same product on different websites;
- Read customer reviews;
- Avoid checkout lines; and
- Have products delivered without leaving home.

In addition to purchasing products, the internet can be used by both individuals and business firms to obtain information. For example:

- Internet users can access newspapers, magazines, radio, and television programming at a time and place convenient to them.

- The internet provides the opportunity for two-way interaction between an internet firm and the customer. For example, many new-car dealers have a "chat" option on their websites for customers who can ask specific questions or want more information about their automobiles or service.
- Finally, the internet allows customers to choose the content they are offered. For the advertiser, knowing that its advertisements are being directed to the most likely customers represents a better way to spend advertising dollars.

Who is the largest retailer in the world? Walmart is number one when you measure total sales from brick-and-mortar stores *and* e-commerce. And yet, if you *measure just e-commerce sales*, Amazon is larger. One of the reasons why Amazon is the leader in online retailing is that it is easy to purchase just about anything you want and have it delivered in a few days or even the same day in some locations. Now that's fast.

创造电子商业利润

4-5c Creating e-Business Profit

Business firms can increase profits either by increasing sales revenue or by reducing expenses through a variety of e-business activities.

Increasing Sales Revenue Each source of sales revenue flowing into a firm is referred to as a **revenue stream**. Today, there are many different ways to use the internet and technology to increase sales revenue. Because the opportunity to shop on the internet is virtually unrestricted, traditional retailers like Target (www.target.com) and Walmart (www.walmart.com) can obtain additional revenue by selling to a global customer base 24 hours a day, seven days a week. However, shifting revenues earned from customers inside a real store to revenues earned from these same customers online does not create any real new revenue for a firm. The goal is to find *new customers* that shop online and generate *new sales* so that *total revenues are increased.*

Intelligent information systems also can help to generate sales revenue for internet firms such as Amazon (www.amazon.com). Such systems store information about each customer's purchases, along with a variety of other information about the buyer's preferences. Using this information, the system can assist customers the next time they visit the website. For example, if the customer has bought a Carrie Underwood CD in the past, the system might suggest CDs by similar artists who have won awards from the Academy of Country Music.

Many internet firms generate revenue from commissions earned from sellers of products linked to their internet sites. For example, both Amazon and eBay earn revenue by providing a website where vendors can sell merchandise to buyers who may be located any place in the world.

Although some customers may not make a purchase online, the existence of the firm's website and the services and information it provides may lead to increased sales in the firm's physical stores. For example, Honda's website (www.honda.com) can provide basic comparative information for shoppers so that they are better prepared for their visit to an automobile showroom.

In addition to selling products or services online, e-business revenue streams are created by advertising placed on web pages and by subscription fees charged for access to online services and information. For example, Dun & Bradstreet (www.dnb.com/), a comprehensive source for company and industry information, makes some of its online content free for anyone who visits the site, but more detailed information is available only by paid subscription.

Reducing Expenses Reducing expenses is the second major way in which e-businesses can help to increase profitability. Providing online access to information

收入流
revenue stream a source of revenue flowing into a firm

✓ Concept Check

- What are the four major factors contained in the definition of e-business?
- How does e-business satisfy needs online?
- How do e-businesses generate revenue streams, reduce expenses, and earn a profit?

that customers want can reduce the cost of dealing with customers. T-Mobile, for instance, is just one company that maintains an extensive website where potential customers can learn more about products and services, and where current customers can access personal account information, send questions to customer service, and purchase additional products or services. With such extensive online services, T-Mobile does not have to maintain as many physical store locations as it would without these online services. We examine more examples of how e-business contributes to profitability throughout this chapter, especially as we focus on some of the business models for activity on the internet.

电子商业的基本模式

4-6 Fundamental Models of e-Business

Learning Objective

4-6 Define the fundamental models of e-business.

A **business model** represents a group of common characteristics and methods of doing business to generate sales revenues and reduce expenses. Each of the models discussed in the following text represents a primary e-business model. Regardless of the type of business model, planning often depends on if the e-business is a new firm or an existing firm adding an online presence—refer to Figure 4-7. It also helps to keep in mind that in order to generate sales revenues and profits, a business—especially an e-business—must meet the needs of its customers.

企业对企业（B2B）模式

4-6a Business-to-Business (B2B) Model

Some firms use the internet mainly to conduct business with other businesses. These firms are generally referred to as having a **business-to-business (or B2B) model.**

Figure 4-7 Planning for a New Internet Business or Building an Online Presence for an Existing Business

The approach taken to creating an e-business plan will depend on whether you are establishing a new Internet business or adding an online component to an existing business.

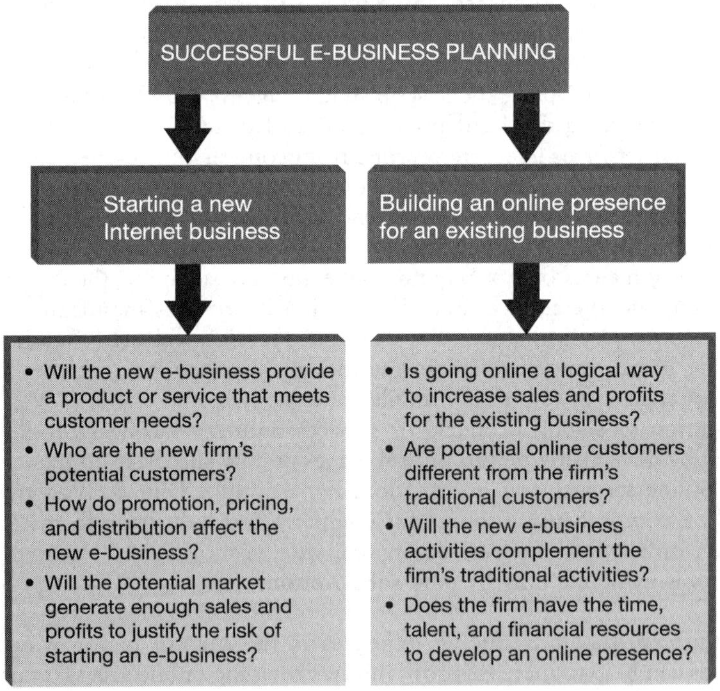

商业模式
business model a model that represents a group of common characteristics and methods of doing business to generate sales revenues and reduce expenses

企业对企业（或 B2B）模式
business-to-business (or B2B) model a model used by firms that conduct business with other businesses

When examining B2B firms, two clear types emerge. In the first type, the focus is facilitating sales transactions between businesses. For example, Dell manufactures computers to specifications that customers enter on the Dell website (www.dell.com). A large portion of Dell's online orders are from corporate clients who are well informed about the products they need and are looking for fairly priced, high-quality computer products that will be delivered quickly. By dealing directly with Dell, customers eliminate costs associated with wholesalers and retailers, thereby helping to reduce the price they pay for equipment.

A second, more complex type of B2B model involves a company and its suppliers. Today, suppliers use the internet to bid on products and services they wish to sell to a business customer and learn about the customer's rules and procedures that must be followed. For example, Ford, General Motors, and Chrysler have developed a B2B model to link thousands of suppliers that sell the automobile makers parts, supplies, and raw materials worth millions of dollars each year. Although the B2B site is expensive to start and maintain, there are significant savings for all three automakers. Given the potential savings, it is no wonder that many other manufacturers and their suppliers are beginning to use the same kind of B2B systems that are used by the automakers.

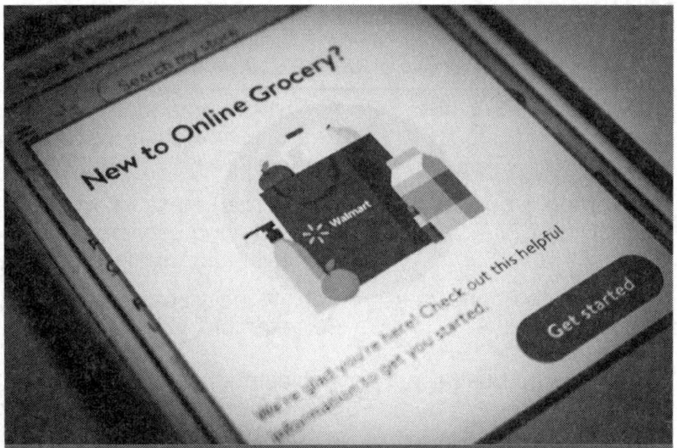

KOSHIRO K/SHUTTERSTOCK.COM

Tired of standing in the checkout line at the grocery store? Then shop online. Many supermarket chains are experiencing an uptick in the number of consumers who are using their e-commerce sites to buy groceries. For consumers, the process is simple: Order your merchandise online, pay online, and then either pick up your groceries at the store's customer pickup location or have your purchases delivered to your home.

企业对消费者（B2C）模式

4-6b Business-to-Consumer (B2C) Model

In contrast with the B2B model, firms such as Amazon (www.amazon.com), Walmart (www.walmart.com), and Dick's Sporting Goods clearly are focused on individual consumers. These companies are referred to as having a **business-to-consumer (or B2C) model**. In a B2C situation, understanding how consumers behave online is critical to a firm's success. Typically, a business firm that uses a B2C model must answer the following questions:

- What sorts of products and services are best suited for online consumer shopping?
- Will consumers use websites to simplify and speed up comparison shopping?
- Will consumers purchase services and products online or end up buying at a traditional retail store?
- Are consumers willing to wait for purchases to be delivered, will they pay for next-day delivery, or will they collect online purchases from a convenient pickup site?

In addition to providing round-the-clock global access to all kinds of products and services, B2C firms often attempt to build long-term relationships with their customers. Often, firms will make a special effort to make sure that the customer is satisfied and that problems, if any, are solved quickly. Most B2C firms, for example, have liberal return policies and often pay for returning merchandise that the customer does not like. Specialized software can also help build good customer relationships. Tracking the decisions and buying preferences when customers shop online, for instance, helps a B2C business provide suggestions for additional merchandise or services the customer may want to consider. In essence, this is Orbitz's (www.orbitz.com) online selling

企业对消费者（或 B2C）模式
business-to-consumer (or B2C) model a model used by firms that focus on conducting business with individual consumers

Table 4-2 Other Business Models That Perform Specialized e-Business Activities

Although modified versions of B2B or B2C, these business models perform specialized e-business activities to generate revenues.

Advertising e-business model	Advertisements that are displayed on a firm's website in return for a fee. Examples include pop-up and banner advertisements on search engines and other popular internet and social media sites.
Brokerage e-business model	Online marketplaces where buyers and sellers are brought together to facilitate an exchange of goods and services. One example is 1stDIBS (www.1stdibs.com), which provides a site for buying and selling furniture, lighting, home décor, antiques, jewelry, and fashion items.
Consumer-to-consumer model	Peer-to-peer software that allows individuals to share information over the internet. For example, Craigslist is a site where users can buy and sell all kinds of items.
Consumer to business model	Social media influencers, bloggers, or paid reviewers create content that promotes a company's products or services. In turn, the business pays either a predetermined dollar amount or a percentage of revenue for the promotion or information provided.
Subscription and pay-per-view e-business models	While some information may be free, detailed content is available only to users who pay a fee to gain access to a website. Examples include investment information provided by Morningstar (www.morningstar.com) and business research provided by Forrester Research, Inc. (www.forrester.com).

✓ Concept Check

- What are the two-fundamental e-business models?
- Assume that you are the owner of a small company that produces outdoor-living furniture. Describe how you could use the B2C business model to sell your products to consumers.

approach. By tracking and analyzing customer data, the online travel company can provide individualized service to its customers. Although a "little special attention" may increase the cost of doing business for a B2C firm, the customer's repeated purchases will repay the investment many times over.

Today, B2B and B2C models are the most popular business models for e-business. And yet, there are other business models that perform specialized e-business activities to generate revenues. Most of the business models described in Table 4-2 are modified versions of the B2B and B2C models.

互联网、社交媒体和电子商业的未来

4-7 The Future of the Internet, Social Media, and e-Business

Learning Objective

4-7 Identify the factors that will affect the future of the internet, social media, and e-business.

Since the beginning of commercial activity on the internet, developments in computer technology, social media, and e-business have been rapid, with spectacular successes such as Facebook, Amazon, Google, eBay, and Pinterest. However, success is not guaranteed just because it is a "technology" firm. Even firms with a promising idea must develop a business plan to turn the idea into a reality—and a successful business. Today, most firms involved in the internet, social media, and e-business use a very intelligent approach to the initial start-up phase and expansion and development. The long-term view held by the vast majority of analysts is that the internet, social media, and e-business will continue to expand to meet the needs of businesses and consumers.

互联网的增长潜力

4-7a Internet Growth Potential

To date, only about 65 percent of the global population uses the internet. In late 2020, estimates suggest that about 5.1 billion of the 7.9 billion people in the world use the internet.[26] In the United States, 297 million, or about 90 percent of the nation's population use the internet. With approximately 90 percent of the U.S. population already using the internet, potential growth in the United States is limited.[27] On the other hand, the number of internet users in the world's developing countries is expected to increase dramatically.

Although the number of global internet users is expected to increase, that's only part of the story. Perhaps the more important question is why people are using the internet. Primary reasons for using the internet include the ability to connect with other people, to obtain information, or to purchase a firm's products or services. Of particular interest to business firms is the growth of social media. For example, Facebook now has approximately 2.7 billion users worldwide. And because only about 34 percent of the world population currently uses Facebook, the number of Facebook users is expected to continue to increase for years to come.[28] In fact, the number of users for other social media sites, like TikTok, YouTube, Twitter, Instagram, and Pinterest, is also expected to increase.

Experts also predict that the number of companies using e-business to increase sales and reduce expenses will continue to increase. Firms that adapt existing business models to an online environment will continue to dominate development. Although products or services will continue to be sold in the traditional way, more and more products will be sold online.

Even small businesses can sell merchandise online. While big retailers like Macy's, Walgreens, and Home Depot are increasing sales revenue from online sales, small businesses can also sell merchandise online. In fact, if a small business doesn't have a website, it's missing an opportunity to sell its products and services—especially unique or one-of-a-kind items.

伦理和法律问题

4-7b Ethical and Legal Concerns

The social and legal concerns for the internet, social media, and e-business extend beyond those shared by all businesses. Essentially, the internet is a new "frontier" without borders and with little control by governments or other organizations.

Ethics and Social Responsibility Socially responsible and ethical behavior by individuals and businesses on the internet are major concerns. For example, an ethically questionable practice in cyberspace is the unauthorized use of information discovered through computerized tracking of users once they are connected to the internet. Essentially, a user may visit a website and unknowingly receive a small piece of software code called a **cookie**. This cookie can track where the user goes on the internet and measure how long the user stays at any particular website. Although this type of software may produce valuable customer information, it also can be viewed as an invasion of privacy, especially since users may not even be aware that their movements are being monitored. AT&T, Verizon, and other cell phone service providers use cookies to track an individual's browsing on mobile devices for advertising purposes. Shoppers with smartphones and a retailer's app on their smartphones may even be tracked when they enter a store. Once the store knows your location in the store, it can send texts or posts about discounts and merchandise that is on sale. Unlike the situation with cookies, however, shoppers must download the app to be tracked—but in exchange, they benefit by receiving personalized discounts.

Some firms also practice data mining. **Data mining** refers to the practice of searching through data records looking for useful information. Customer registration forms typically require a variety of information before a user is given access to a site. Based on an individual's information, data mining analysis can then provide what might be considered private and confidential information about individuals. For instance, assume an individual frequents a website that provides information about a life-threatening disease. If this information is sent to an insurance company, the

网络跟踪软件
cookie a small piece of software sent by a website that tracks an individual's internet use

数据挖掘
data mining the practice of searching through data records looking for useful information

The hackers are coming! Today it's hard to turn on your computer or read an email without worrying if you will get a computer virus that will enable hackers to steal your personal and financial information and then use it for their own personal gain. In fact, identity and computer security is such a big problem that it has created a whole new industry—the software security industry.

company might refuse to insure this individual, thinking that there is a higher risk associated with someone who wants more information about this disease.

Besides the unauthorized use of cookies and tracking your location and your online behavior, there are several other threats to users' privacy and confidentiality. Monitoring an employee's computer usage may be intended to help employers police unauthorized internet use on company time. However, the same records can also give a firm the opportunity to observe what otherwise might be considered private and confidential information. A recent survey of over 300 employers by the American Management Association and the ePolicy Institute found that two thirds of employers monitor employee usage.[29] Today, legal experts suggest that, at the very least, employers need to disclose the level of surveillance to their employees and consider the corporate motivation for monitoring employees' behavior.

Ethics and Social Responsibility

商业伦理与社会责任：加州加大隐私保护力度

California Ups the Ante on Privacy Protection

Data privacy is a major legal and ethical issue. In fact, 85 percent of U.S. internet users are concerned about how much information advertisers have collected about them. Even so, there is no comprehensive federal law that governs data privacy in the United States. Personal information, such as postal addresses, credit card numbers, email addresses, and browsing history, is a valuable marketing tool for companies, but the same information can open the door for identity thieves if it is not handled properly.

California took matters into its own hands with the California Consumer Privacy Act (CCPA). The act gave consumers more control over how their data is collected and used by businesses. The CCPA secured privacy rights for Californians, including the right to know what data is being collected and how it is used and shared, the right to have companies delete personal information (with some exceptions), the right to opt-out of having their personal information sold by one company to another, and the right to non-discrimination for exercising their CCPA rights.

California voters have also amended CCPA with the California Privacy Rights Act (CPRA). The CPRA amendment raised the privacy bar even higher. The original provisions put the burden on individuals to become aware of and protect their data instead of changing the way businesses collect, store, and use the data. The CPRA amendment created new requirements for businesses, such as limiting data retention, protecting data security, and minimizing data collection. It also strengthens accountability measures by requiring companies to conduct privacy risk assessments and cybersecurity audits.

Although the law was enacted in California, the importance of these laws goes beyond the state's boundaries because of the number of businesses that do business with California consumers. Also, the laws impact how marketers and ad publishers such as Facebook and Google personalize digital advertising. Finally, compliance will affect businesses financially when they hire data protection officers, implement new policies and procedures, train employees, modify processes, and monitor compliance.

Experts predict that California's privacy laws could become the national standard for data privacy, whether a federal law is created or not. Even if Congress enacts a national privacy law, it could face stiff opposition from Californians if the federal law does not meet or exceed the protections provided by the existing California law. The bottom line: Companies will need to find ways to help prevent identity theft and improve data protection now more than ever.

Sources: Based on information in Cameron F. Kerry and Caitlin Chin, "By Passing Proposition 24, California Voters up the Ante on Federal Privacy Law," *Brookings*, November 17, 2020; Yory Wurmser, "Election Impact: Why the Passing of California's Prop 24 Matters for Marketers and What to Expect in 2021," Business Insider, November 4, 2020; State of California Department of Justice, "California Consumer Privacy Act (CCPA)".

Internet Crime Because the internet is often regarded as an unregulated frontier, both individuals and business users must be particularly aware of online risks and dangers. For example, a general term that describes software designed to infiltrate a computer system without the user's consent is **malware**. Malware is often based on the creator's criminal or malicious intent and can include computer viruses, spyware, deceptive adware, and other software capable of criminal activities. According to TechJury, more than 30,000 websites are hacked each day.[30] In fact, the increase in internet crime and the devastating effects of both malware and computer viruses have given rise to a software security industry.

In addition to the risk of computer viruses and hackers, identity theft is one of the most common computer crimes that impacts both individuals and business users. A recent report by the United States Federal Trade Commission (FTC) determined that more than 1.4 million Americans reported identity theft in one year.[31] In recent years, major government entities including the United States government and many businesses such as Microsoft, MGM Resorts, Walgreens, T-Mobile, and many others have been hacked by thieves who stole sensitive data from tens of millions of people.[32]

Most consumers are also concerned about fraud. Because the internet allows easy creation of websites, access from anywhere in the world, and anonymity for the creator, it is almost impossible to know with certainty that the website, organization, or individuals that you believe you are interacting with are what they seem. As always, caveat emptor ("let the buyer beware") is a good suggestion to follow whether on the internet or not.

计算机技术、社交媒体和电子商业的未来挑战
4-7c Future Challenges for Computer Technology, Social Media, and e-Business

Today, more information and technology is available than ever before. Although individuals and business users may think we are at the point of information overload, the amount of information will only increase in the future. In order to obtain more information in the future, both business users and individuals must consider the cost of obtaining additional information and computer technology. In an effort to reduce expenses and improve accessibility, some companies and individuals are now using cloud computing. **Cloud computing** is a type of computer usage in which services stored on the internet are provided to users on a temporary basis. When cloud computing is used, a third party makes processing power, software applications, databases, and storage available for on demand use from anywhere. Instead of running software and storing data on their employer's computer network or their individual computers, employees log onto the third party's system and use (and pay for) only the applications and data storage they actually need. Amazon Web Services (AWS), Microsoft, Google, IBM, Oracle, and many other firms in the technology industry offer cloud services. In addition to just cost, there are a number of external and internal factors that a business must consider.

Although the demands for a business are complex, it is useful to think of them as either *internal* or *external* forces that affect how a business uses computer technology. Internal forces are those that are closely associated with the actions and decisions taking place within a firm. As shown in Figure 4-8, typical internal forces include a firm's planning activities, organizational structure, human resources, management decisions, information database, and available financing. A shortage of skilled employees needed for a specialized project, for instance, can undermine a firm's ability to sell its services to clients. Unlike the external environmental forces affecting the firm, internal forces, such as this one, are more likely to be under the direct control of management. In this case, management can either hire the needed staff or choose to pass over a prospective project or outsource some of the work that is needed. In addition to the obvious internal factors that affect how a company operates, a growing number of firms are concerned about how their use of technology affects the environment. The term **green IT** is now used to describe all of a firm's activities to support a healthy environment

恶意软件
malware software designed to infiltrate a computer system without the user's consent

云计算
cloud computing a type of computer usage in which services stored on the internet are provided to users on a temporary basis

绿色 IT
green IT a term used to describe all of a firm's activities to support a healthy environment and sustain the planet

Figure 4-8 Internal and External Forces That Affect an e-Business

Today, managers and employees of an e-business must respond to internal forces within the organization and external forces outside the organization.

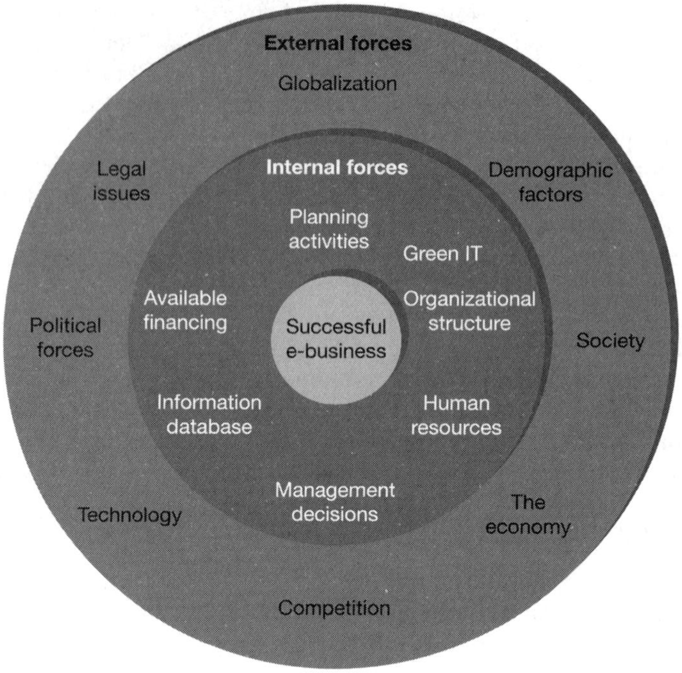

✓ Concept Check

- Experts predict that the internet will continue to expand along with related technologies. What effect will this expansion have on society, business, and individuals in the future?
- Give an example of an unethical use of computer technology by a business.
- What is the difference between internal and external forces that affect an e-business?

and sustain the planet. Many offices, for example, are reducing the amount of paper they use by storing data and information on computers.

In contrast, external forces affect a company's use of technology and originate outside the organization. These forces are unlikely to be controllable by a company. Instead, managers and employees of a company generally will react to these forces, attempting to shield the organization from any negative effects and finding ways to take advantage of opportunities in an ever-changing technology environment. The primary external forces affecting a company's use of technology include globalization, demographic, societal, economic, competitive, technological, and political and legal forces.

In this chapter, we have explored how both individuals and businesses use social media. We also examined how e-business and e-commerce are changing the way that firms do business. In Chapter 5, we examine a business firm's need for information and why accounting is a major source of information for business.

Summary 小 结

4-1 Examine why it is important for a business to use social media.

Millions of people of all ages use social media to interact with people and share ideas, personal information, and information about products and services. The primary reason for using social media is to stay in touch with family and friends. Other reasons include sharing photos or videos and obtaining information available on the internet. Just the sheer numbers of people using social media make using social media a top priority for business. Even though companies have used social media to share information about their products and services and improve customer service, many are still uncomfortable with this new method of communicating with customers because they do not have much control over what is said about their products or services.

4-2 Discuss how businesses use social media tools.

Companies use social media to connect with customers and stakeholders, provide customer service, provide information to customers, and engage customers in product development. To share social content (information about products and services), companies can use blogs, photos, videos, and podcasts. Before creating a media sharing site, managers and employees should consider who will create the photos, videos, and podcasts, how the content will be distributed, and how much it will cost. In addition, social media also enables shoppers to access opinions, recommendations, and referrals from others within and outside their own social circle. Rating and review sites are based on the idea that people trust the opinions of others when it comes to purchasing products and services.

4-3 Explain the business objectives for using social media.

Although its popularity is a recent phenomenon, many businesses are already using social media to achieve important goals and objectives. In fact, there are many ways for businesses to use social media to take advantage of business opportunities to build connections with other businesses and consumers. For example, businesses can use social media to build a community. Social media communities are social networks based on the relationships among people. Today, there are social communities for every interest, ethnic group, and lifestyle. Different types of communities include both forums and wikis. Other reasons for using social media include crisis and reputation management, listening to stakeholders, targeting customers, social media marketing, generating new product ideas, and recruiting employees.

4-4 Describe how businesses develop a social media plan.

Before developing a plan to use social media, it is important to determine how social media can improve the organization's overall performance and how the plan "fits" with a company's objectives and other promotional activities. Once it is determined how social media links to the company's other activities, the first step is to listen to what customers like and don't like about a company's products or services. Typically, the second step is to establish social media objectives that are specific, measurable, achievable, realistic, and oriented toward the future. After listening and establishing objectives, the third step is to identify the customer or market segment a business is trying to reach with a social media promotion. The fourth step is to select the social media tools that will be used to reach customers. While it is not necessary (or even advisable) to use all of the available tools, a company can use social media communities, blogs, photos, videos, and podcasts to reach potential or existing customers. Once social media tools have been identified, a company can implement and integrate the social media plan.

Both quantitative and qualitative measurements can be used to determine the effectiveness of a social media plan. Quantitative social media measurement consists of using numerical measurements. Key performance indicators (KPIs), for example, are generally quantitative measurements. Qualitative measurement is the process of accessing the opinions and beliefs about a brand and primarily uses sentiment analysis to categorize what is being said about a company. Because social media costs both time and money, it is important to maintain, update, and measure the success of a social media plan and make adjustments and changes if needed.

4-5 Explain the meaning of e-business.

e-Business, or electronic business, can be defined as the organized effort of individuals to produce and sell, for a profit, the goods and services that satisfy society's needs *through the facilities available on the internet*. e-Commerce is a part of e-business and usually refers only to buying and selling activities conducted online. The human, material, information, and financial resources that any business requires are highly specialized for e-business. In an effort to reduce the cost of e-business resources, many firms have turned to outsourcing. It is also possible to use mobile marketing to increase sales and profits.

Using e-business activities, it is possible to satisfy new customer needs created by the internet as well as traditional ones in unique ways. Meeting customer needs is especially important when an e-business is trying to earn profits by increasing sales. Each source of revenue flowing into the firm is referred to as a revenue stream. It is also possible to reduce expenses by using e-business activities.

4-6 Define the fundamental models of e-business.

e-Business models focus attention on the identity of a firm's customers. Firms that use the internet mainly to conduct business with other businesses generally are referred to as having a business-to-business, or B2B, model. When examining B2B firms, two clear types emerge. In the first type of B2B, the focus is simply on facilitating sales transactions between businesses. A second, more complex type of the B2B model involves a company and its suppliers. In contrast to the focus of the B2B model, firms such as Macy's, Walgreens, or Dick's Sporting Goods are focused on individual buyers and are thus referred to as having a business-to-consumer, or B2C, model. In a B2C situation, understanding how consumers behave online is critical to the firm's success. Successful B2C firms often make a special effort to build long-term relationships with their customers. While B2B and B2C models are the most popular e-business models, there are other models that perform specialized e-business activities to generate revenues (refer to Table 4-2).

4-7 Identify the factors that will affect the future of the internet, social media, and e-business.

Since the beginning of commercial activity on the internet, developments in computer technology, social media, and e-business have been rapid. Today firms with a promising idea must develop a business plan to turn an idea into a reality—and a successful business. The long-term view held by the vast majority of analysts is that use of the internet will continue to expand along with related technologies. Because approximately 90 percent of Americans now have access to the internet, potential growth is limited in the United States. On the other hand, only 5.1 billion of the 7.9 billion people in the world use the internet. Clearly, the number of internet users in the world's developing countries is expected to increase dramatically.

The future of computer technology and the internet will be influenced by advances in technology, the increasing popularity of social media, and the increasing use of e-business. Other factors, including ethics, social responsibility, and internet crime, will all impact the way that businesses and consumers use the internet. Although the environmental forces at work are complex, it is useful to think of them as either internal or external forces that affect how businesses use computer technology. Internal forces are those that are closely associated with the actions and decisions taking place within a firm. In contrast, external forces are those factors affecting an e-business originating outside an organization.

Key Terms 关键术语

You should now be able to define and give an example relevant to each of the following terms:

social media
hashtag
social content sites
blog
media sharing sites
influencer
podcasts
social media communities
forum
wiki
social media community manager
social media marketing
inbound marketing
crowdsourcing
crowdfunding
quantitative social media measurement
key performance indicators (KPIs)
qualitative social media measurement
sentiment analysis
e-business (or electronic business)
e-commerce
mobile marketing
outsourcing
revenue stream
business model
business-to-business (or B2B) model
business-to-consumer (or B2C) model
cookie
data mining
malware
cloud computing
green IT

Discussion Questions 讨论题

1. Given the fast pace of everyday life, most people often feel there is not enough time to do everything that needs to be done. Yet, people do find time to post text messages and personal information, photos, etc., on Facebook, Twitter, blogs, and other social media sites. Why do you think people are so fascinated with social media?
2. How can a small cosmetics wholesaler located in Jacksonville, Florida, use social media and e-business to increase its customer base, increase revenues, and reduce expenses?
3. Is outsourcing good for an e-business firm? The firm's employees? Explain your answers.
4. What distinguishes a B2B from a B2C e-business model?
5. Experts predict that the internet, social media, and e-business will continue to expand along with related computer technologies. What effect will this expansion have on how businesses (1) market and sell merchandise, (2) get paid for merchandise, and (3) deliver merchandise to customers?

Case 4 案例 4：Target 在数字领域的大赌注

Target's Big Bet on Digital

When Target's CEO Brian Cornell announced the company would spend $7 billion for capital improvements and $1 billion more per year for operating costs to modernize operations for the digital age, investors weren't sold. "I had people shaking their heads," Cornell said. "You could see it." Target's stock price plummeted the day the announcement was made. Looking back now, Cornell knows the company made the right decision.

Target, one of the largest retailers in the United States, has spent billions on its stores and technology infrastructure.

The company reimagined its stores, built new, smaller stores in urban areas, and invested in technology and fulfillment capabilities. According to the CEO, the investment is paying off. All of these elements have worked together to drive growth, increase market share, and boost in-store and online traffic.

One of the most important initiatives was focused on remodeling existing stores and opening new small-format stores. In Target's smaller stores, the company reduced the amount of inventory and adopted a just-in-time approach to inventory management. The goal was simple: Deliver what the stores need, when they need it.

Target also invested in its supply chain in order to meet the needs of the "new" Target. For example, the company now utilizes artificial intelligence and robotics to support its warehouse teams. And, Target invested in creating backroom shipping and packaging centers in retail stores that act as distribution centers for online orders. Using its own retail stores as distribution centers gives it a significant advantage over Amazon. In-store and curbside pickup, for example, cost 90 percent less on average than fulfilling orders from a warehouse and then delivering the merchandise.

Target's $550 million acquisition of Shipt has also paid off. Shipt—a company known for offering same-day and next-day delivery—enables Target to go head-to-head against Amazon and other e-commerce retailers. It also acquired technology assets from Deliv—a same day delivery startup in California. Target is even testing the use of sort centers in areas with high delivery volume. The centers will be smaller and less expensive than Target's usual retail footprint and will be closer to customers. Target hopes that the use of sort centers will eliminate the need to sort packages at the store level and reduce its overall shipping costs.

These and other improvements have helped Target support in-store pickup, curbside delivery, and home delivery of online orders. In fact, it is now possible for "guests," as Target often calls its customers, throughout the United States and other countries to shop for all major product categories available from Target 24 hours a day, seven days a week. As an added bonus, technology has reduced the number of out-of-stock items and ultimately improved the customer's overall shopping experience.

Target's investments were well-timed. As a result of the COVID-19 pandemic and stay-at home mandates, Target's online business surged as shoppers turned to e-commerce to make purchases. In the first quarter of 2020, Target fulfilled more curbside deliveries than it did in the entire year of 2019. The company has also found that when customers shop online and use more of its delivery options, they ultimately spend more both online and in-store.

By investing in these new distribution strategies, Target is now able to compete against some big e-commerce companies. Although Target is now one of the top ten e-commerce businesses in the United States, the company has a long way to go to capture more market share. Amazon controls nearly 40 percent of U.S. retail e-commerce sales. Target, which has 1.2 percent market share, lags behind not only Amazon, but also Walmart, eBay, Apple, Home Depot, Wayfair, and Best Buy. While Target has taken some giant steps to increase sales online and in its brick-and-mortar stores, there's still room for growth as more and more customers shop online. Looking forward, Target executives will need to remember the old phrase—Where there's a will, there's a way.[33]

Questions

1. Why do you think Target's plan to spend $7 billion for capital improvements and an additional $1 billion more per year for operating costs initially worried investors? What do you believe investors think now?
2. Although many people think of Target as a big discount store that competes with Walmart, it has opened new, smaller stores that carry less inventory. What do you think is the driving force behind Target's smaller store concept?
3. Much of the information in this case describes Target's efforts to improve its supply chain. In your own words describe what the term "supply chain" means. How important is a firm's supply chain for a retailer like Target that has both in-store and online sales?

Building Skills for Career Success 为成功的职业生涯培养技能

1. Social Media Exercise

The purpose of the first part of this chapter is to introduce you to social media and its importance to business. After reading the chapter, choose a business that you either know something about, you want to start, or is the company you already work for.

Assignment

1. Develop a social media plan for that business using what you learned in this chapter.
2. What are the objectives of your social media plan?
3. What social media tools would you choose and why? How would you measure success?
4. Prepare a report that describes how this exercise has helped you understand the material in this chapter.

2. Building Team Skills

After graduating from college with a degree in marketing, your first job was working in the marketing department for a fast-food chain located in the southwestern part of the United States. After three years, you were promoted and became director of the chain's social media program. While monitoring posts about the company on Facebook and Twitter, you notice the following post from one of the firm's former employees.

> "Got fired today, but I was tired of serving low-quality food with expired expiration dates. Don't eat there or any of the chain's restaurants unless you want to get deathly ill."

To make matters worse, a couple of other employees who had recently been fired chimed in and made posts of a similar nature.

Assignment

1. Working in small teams, create a response that can be used to convince consumers that your company is committed to food freshness and quality and that these posts were made by employees who had been terminated.
2. Choose a spokesperson who will read your response to the rest of the class.
3. As a class, discuss the pros and cons of each response developed by each team.
4. Ask all members of the class to vote on the best response.
5. Finally, each team should prepare a report for the company's management that describes what happened and the response that was made to tell the company's side of this issue and restore consumer confidence in the firm's food products.

3. Researching Different Careers

Today, there are a wide assortment of career opportunities in companies that are involved in technology, social media, and e-business. In many cases, these firms want people with a fresh outlook on how technology, social media, and e-business companies can differentiate their products or services from those of other companies in the same industry. They often prefer individuals with new ideas and employees without preconceived notions about how to proceed. Website managers, designers, creative artists, and content specialists are just a few of the positions available. Many large online job sites, such as Indeed, LinkedIn, Monster.com, Glassdoor, and others, can help you to find out about employment opportunities and the special skills required for various jobs.

Assignment

1. Identify a website that provides information about careers in technology, social media, or e-business.
2. Summarize at least three positions that appear to be in high demand.
3. What are some of the special skills required to fill these jobs?
4. What salaries and benefits typically are associated with these positions?
5. Which job seems most appealing to you personally? Why?

Chapter

5

Using Management and Accounting Information

利用管理和会计信息

Learning Objectives

Once you complete this chapter, you will be able to:

5-1 Examine how information can reduce risk when making a decision.

5-2 Discuss management's information requirements.

5-3 Outline the five functions of an information system.

5-4 Explain why accurate accounting information and audited financial statements are important.

5-5 Interpret a balance sheet.

5-6 Interpret an income statement.

5-7 Describe business activities that affect a firm's cash flow.

5-8 Summarize how managers evaluate the financial health of a business.

Why Should You Care?

Question: How important is management and accounting information for a successful business?

Answer: It would be extremely difficult to manage even a small business without management and accounting information.

Inside Business 商业透视：在四大会计师事务所工作是什么体验

What It's Like to Work for the Big Four

The four largest accounting firms in the world, referred to as the "Big Four," are Deloitte, Ernst & Young (EY), PricewaterhouseCoopers (PwC), and Klynveld Peat Marwick Goerdeler (KPMG). These organizations audit most of the companies in the S&P 500, a stock market index of 500 large companies in the United States. In addition to auditing services, the Big Four offer legal, tax, advisory, and consulting services, among others. They each earn billions in revenue each year and offer significant employment opportunities for accountants.

Working for a Big Four accounting firm can be an attractive career option. Employees must be prepared for the demands of a high-performance work culture to excel at a Big Four firm. Even landing a job at a Big Four accounting firm is competitive because these prestigious firms provide individuals with above average salaries, a variety of work experiences, education and training programs, and leadership development opportunities. KPMG International, for example, has several programs to help employees with professional development such as global short-term assignments, office relocations, and job rotation. The Big Four also offer competitive benefits packages, including generous parental leave policies, good health care, and gym reimbursement. At PwC, for example, employees can accrue between three weeks and one month of vacation time each year in addition to 15 paid holidays. Some firms even offer flexible schedules to support better work-life balance.

There are also drawbacks for employees at the Big Four accounting firms. For instance, tax season, which runs from January to April, can be demanding, with some individuals reporting 80-hour workweeks. Other tax filing deadlines throughout the year can also lead to working overtime. According to a survey by Vault, a career advice and company review website, Big Four employees often say firms are understaffed and compensation could be better, which can both lead to burnout and low morale. For these firms, long work hours, heavy workloads, and high stress can lead to high employee turnover.[1]

Did You Know?

Collectively, the Big Four firms employ more than 1 million people worldwide.

Information and accounting—that's what this chapter is all about! We begin this chapter with information about how employees in each of the Big Four accounting firms help clients obtain the information they need to operate a business and improve management decisions. Because employees at a Big Four firm are responsible for generating and reporting the information and accounting reports their clients need, working conditions are sometimes stressful and hours may be long. On the other hand, employees at the Big Four are paid above average salaries and enjoy competitive benefits packages. Working for a Big Four accounting firm is just one option in the information and accounting industries. There are other career options where employees can help businesses, nonprofit organizations, and government entities use information and accounting to improve decision making.

In this chapter, we begin by describing why employees need information. The first three major sections in this chapter answer the following questions:

- How can information reduce risk when making a decision?
- What is a management information system?
- How do employees use a management information system?

Next, we look at why accounting information is important and careers in the accounting industry. Then we examine the basic accounting equation and the three most important financial statements: the balance sheet, the income statement, and the statement of cash flows. Finally, we take a look at how managers evaluate the firm's financial health.

信息如何降低决策风险

5-1 How Can Information Reduce Risk When Making a Decision?

Learning Objective

5-1 Examine how information can reduce risk when making a decision.

Think back for a moment about the COVID-19 pandemic. For most people, one of the frustrations they faced was the inability to get information from reliable sources. While some information was based on facts, other information was based on opinions and conjecture without valid research to back up the statements some "experts" and politicians were making. Unfortunately, the lack of reliable information just added to the uncertainty of the pandemic and increased the risk of making poor decisions for both individuals and businesses.

As we know, information is one of the four major resources (along with material, human, and financial resources) managers must have to operate a business. Although a successful business uses all four resources efficiently, it is information that helps managers reduce risk when making a decision.

信息和风险

5-1a Information and Risk

To improve the decision-making process, the information used by individuals and business firms must be relevant. Using relevant information results in better decisions.

Relevant information → Better intelligence and knowledge → Better decisions

For businesses, better intelligence and knowledge that lead to better decisions are especially important because they can provide a *competitive edge* over competitors and improve a firm's *profits*.

Theoretically, with accurate and complete information, there is no risk whatsoever. On the other hand, a decision made without any information is a gamble. These two extreme situations are rare in business. For the most part, business decision makers see themselves located someplace between the extremes. As illustrated in Figure 5-1, when the amount of available information is high, there is less risk; when the amount of available information is low, there is more risk.

Think for a moment about Tesla's plan to produce a new all-electric sports car called the Model R. To make very important decisions, executives at Tesla relied on information. Without any information, Tesla executives might as well have made the decision by flipping a coin—heads we make the new Model R or tails we don't. For a decision this important that could impact both sales and profits for the entire company, executives began by gathering information from customers. Simply put: Did customers think a new all-electric, high performance roadster was a good idea? Customers also provided Tesla with additional information about the price that they were willing to pay for the car and about features and options they would like on a new vehicle. Information was also obtained from Tesla's own product engineers, production employees, marketing employees, and key executives. Only after all of the information was obtained and analyzed did Tesla make the decision to produce and market the Model R. Thus, information, when understood properly, produces knowledge and empowers managers and employees to make better decisions while also reducing the risk of making bad decisions.

Figure 5-1 The Relationship Between Information and Risk

When the amount of available information is high, managers tend to make better decisions. On the other hand, when the amount of information is low, there is a high risk of making a poor decision.

信息规则

5-1b Information Rules

Marketing research continues to show that discounts influence people when buying consumer products. Simply put, if manufacturers and retailers lower prices on their products or services, their sales will increase. For example, if Best Buy lowers its price for a new Vizio 75-inch LED television from $1,699 to $1,499, the retailer will sell more televisions. This relationship between buyer behavior and price can be thought of as an information rule that will usually guide the marketing manager correctly. An information rule emerges when research confirms the same results each time that it studies the same or a similar set of circumstances.

Because of the volume of information they receive each day and their need to make decisions on a daily basis, businesspeople try to accumulate information rules to shorten the time they spend analyzing choices. Information rules are the "great simplifiers" for all decision makers. Managers and employees are continuously looking for new rules that can be put to good use and looking to discredit old ones that are no longer valid. This ongoing process is necessary because business conditions rarely stay the same for very long.

数据和信息的区别

5-1c The Difference Between Data and Information

Many people use the terms *data* and *information* interchangeably, but the two differ in important ways. **Data** are numerical or verbal descriptions that usually result from some sort of measurement. Your current wage level, the amount of last year's after-tax profit for Google, and the current retail prices of Dell computers are all data. Most people think of data as being numerical only, but they can be nonnumerical as well. A description of an individual as a "tall, athletic person with short, dark hair" certainly would qualify as data.

数据
data numerical or verbal descriptions that usually result from some sort of measurement

信息
information data presented in a form that is useful for a specific purpose

Information is data presented in a form that is useful for a specific purpose. For example, Apple has earned a reputation as one of the best employers in the nation based on employee satisfaction, employee diversity and company culture, and its efforts to promote equal pay when female and male employees perform the same duties in the workplace. To verify that all employees receive the same pay for the same job, Apple has analyzed the salaries and bonuses that employees received over the last few years. To complete the analysis, human resources managers begin with data reported in computer printouts listing each worker employed by the firm, job classification, and each worker's current wages. Such printouts consist of data rather than information.

Numbers and charts and more numbers and charts. In today's business world, there's so much data available that many managers and employees often believe they are looking for a needle in a haystack. To find just the right information, they often must dig deeper and use computers and graphics programs to process large amounts of data into the information they need to make informed decisions.

Now suppose that the manager uses a computer to graph the average wages paid to men and to women for each job classification. The result is information because the manager can use it to compare wages paid to women with those paid to men. If a gap exists, based on the information presented in the graph, management can address the problem. For a manager, information presented in a practical, useful form, such as a graph, simplifies the decision-making process.

知识管理

5-1d Knowledge Management

The average company maintains a great deal of data that can be transformed into information. Typical data include records pertaining to personnel, inventory, sales, expenses, manufacturing, and accounting. Often each type of data is stored in individual departments within

Technology and Innovation

技术与创新：美国国税局利用人工智能和技术来改善税收

The IRS Uses Artificial Intelligence and Technology to Improve Tax Collection

Data scientists at the IRS are using artificial intelligence (often referred to as AI) and increased technology to detect tax evasion, accounting fraud, and more. By translating tax regulations into source code and software, a group of computer scientists from the Massachusetts Institute of Technology was able to demonstrate how algorithms can detect tax evasion. Tax evasion occurs when an individual or business does not report income, takes more deductions than they are entitled, or are not paying taxes on income.

With a tight budget, the IRS has been slow to update its technology over the years. However, investing in AI and technology to fight tax evasion and accounting fraud may pay off since taxes are the primary source of income for the federal and state governments. As a result of the renewed interest in AI and technology, there are a number of ways the IRS is increasing the amount of taxes collected from tax cheaters. For example, the IRS is creating a tool for auditors that will spot questionable activities when auditing suspicious tax returns. Technology is also used to analyze internal and external data to identify people and businesses that are not filing tax returns. AI is even used to analyze the methods—letters, formal notices, or audits—that are most likely to convince taxpayers to pay back taxes and penalties.

AI is not without risks. Algorithmic "bias" in AI systems can exist when inaccurate data and information are used to build the algorithm. For example, an AI-powered auditing tool could provide inaccurate recommendations for auditing specific returns based on race, gender, or geographic location. It is also limited in that tax laws often have gray areas that are open to human interpretation, which could be challenging for machine intelligence to handle. Finally, U.S. taxpayers often find dealing with the IRS becomes even more impersonal when AI and technology are used.

At the same time the IRS is using AI and technology to fight tax fraud, tax preparers and accounting firms are using the same technology to boost tax refunds and minimize tax bills. In fact, all of the Big Four accounting firms (Deloitte, EY, PwC, and KPMG) use artificial intelligence tools for advising clients. The bottom line: AI and technology are already changing how taxes are collected and how individuals and businesses do tax planning.

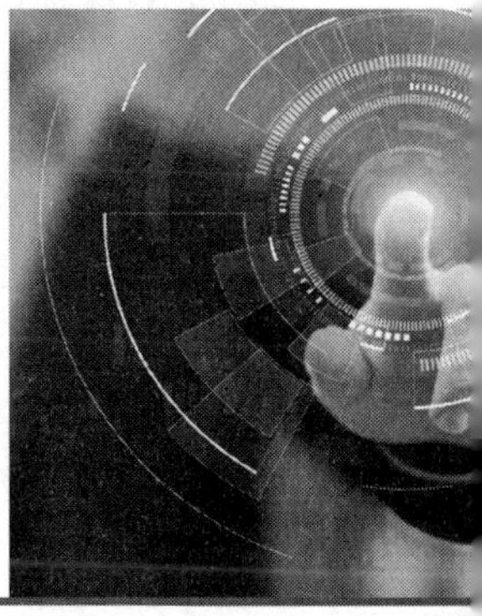

Sources: Based on information in Richard Rubin, "AI Comes to the Tax Code," *The Wall Street Journal*, February 26, 2020; Naveen Joshi, "How AI And Robotics Can Change Taxation," *Forbes*, January 9, 2020; Lynnley Browning, "Computer Scientists Wield Artificial Intelligence to Battle Tax Evasion," *The New York Times*, October 9, 2015.

an organization. However, the data can be used more effectively when they are organized into a database. A **database** is a single collection of data and information stored in one place that can be used by people throughout an organization to make decisions. Although databases are important, the way the data and information are used is even more important—and more valuable to the firm. As a result, management information experts now use the term **knowledge management (KM)** to describe a firm's procedures for generating, using, and sharing important data and information.

数据库
database a single collection of data and information stored in one place that can be used by people throughout an organization to make decisions

知识管理
knowledge management (KM) a firm's procedures for generating, using, and sharing important data and information

决策支持系统
decision-support system (DSS) a type of software program that provides relevant data and information to help a firm's employees make decisions

Making Smart Decisions How do managers and employees sort out relevant and useful information from spam, junk mail, and useless data? Today, different software applications can actually help to improve and speed the decision-making process for people at different levels within an organization. For example, a **decision-support system (DSS)** is a type of software program that provides relevant data and information to help a firm's employees make decisions. It also can be used to determine the effect of changing different variables and answer "what if"-type questions. For example, managers at D.R. Horton, one of the largest home builders

Table 5-1 Current Business Application Software Used to Improve Productivity

Word processing	Users can prepare and edit written documents and store them in the computer or on a memory device.
Desktop publishing	Users can combine text and graphics in professional reports, newsletters, and pamphlets.
Accounting	Users can record routine financial transactions and prepare financial reports at the end of the accounting period.
Database management	Users can electronically store large amounts of data and transform the data into information.
Graphics	Users can display and print pictures, drawings, charts, and diagrams.
Spreadsheets	Users can organize numerical data into a grid of rows and columns.

✓ Concept Check

- In your own words, describe how information reduces risk when you make a personal or work-related decision.
- What are information rules? How do they simplify the process of making decisions?
- What is the difference between data and information? Give an example of accounting data and accounting information.
- Describe how decision support systems, expert systems, and business application software can help improve employee productivity.

in the United States, can use a DSS to determine prices for new homes built in an upscale, luxury subdivision. By entering the number of homes that will be built along with different costs associated with land, labor, building materials, building permits, promotional costs, and all other costs, a DSS can help determine a base price for each new home. When a DSS is used, it is also possible to revise home prices if building costs change. For example, if the cost of materials or labor increases, a DSS can determine new home prices for each set of assumptions.

Another type of software program is an expert system that uses computers, software, data, and information to mimic the thinking of employees. Simply put, an **expert system** is a type of computer program that uses artificial intelligence to imitate a human's ability to think. Using a set of rules determined by employees, an expert system can analyze available data and information about a particular activity or problem. Based on the information supplied, the expert system then provides recommendations or suggests specific actions in order to help make decisions. Expert systems, for example, have been used to schedule manufacturing tasks, diagnose illnesses, determine credit limits for credit card customers, evaluate loan applications, and develop electronic games.

专家系统
expert system a type of computer program that uses artificial intelligence to imitate a human's ability to think

管理信息系统
management information system (MIS) a system that provides managers and employees with the information they need to perform their jobs as effectively as possible

Business Application Software In addition to decision support and expert systems, a number of business software applications can improve both employee decision making and productivity. Early business application software typically performed a single function. Today, however, *integrated* software combines many functions in a single package. Integrated packages allow for the easy linking of text, numerical data, graphs, photographs, and even audiovisual clips. A business report prepared using the Microsoft Office package, for instance, can include all these components. From a career standpoint, you should realize that employers will assume that you possess, or will possess after training, a high degree of working comfort with several of the software applications described in Table 5-1.

Typically, data, information, databases, knowledge management, and computer software all become important parts of a firm's management information system.

什么是管理信息系统

5-2 What Is a Management Information System?

Learning Objective

5-2 Discuss management's information requirements.

A **management information system (MIS)** is a system that provides managers and employees with the information they need to perform their jobs as effectively as possible. The purpose of an MIS (sometimes referred to as an information technology system or simply an IT system) is to distribute timely and useful information from both internal and external sources to the managers and employees who need it.

Figure 5-2 Management Information System (MIS)

After an MIS is installed, employees and managers can get information directly from the MIS without having to go through other people in the organization.

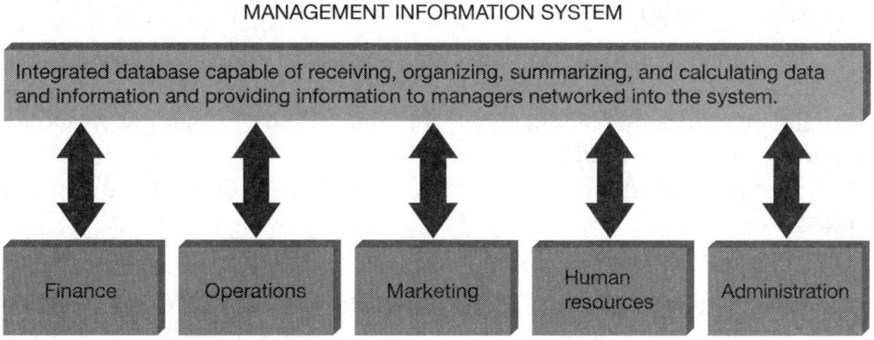

企业的信息需求

5-2a A Firm's Information Requirements

Employees and managers have to plan for the future, implement their plans in the present, and evaluate results against what has been accomplished in the past. Of course, the specific types of information they need depend on their work area and on their level within the firm.

Today, many firms are organized into five areas of management: *finance, operations, marketing, human resources,* and *administration.* Managers in each of these areas need specific information in order to make decisions (refer to Figure 5-2).

- *Financial managers* are obviously most concerned with a firm's finances. They must ensure that the firm's managers and employees, lenders and suppliers, stockholders and potential investors, and government agencies have the information they need to measure the financial health of the firm.
- *Operations managers* are concerned with present and future sales levels; current inventory levels of resources, work in process, and finished goods; and the availability and cost of the resources required to produce goods and services.
- *Marketing managers* need to have detailed information about a firm's products and services and those offered by competitors. Such information includes sales projections, promotion and pricing strategies, products that competitors are test marketing, information concerning the firm's customers, and new and pending product legislation that may impact future sales.
- *Human resources managers* must be aware of anything that pertains to a firm's employees. Key examples include current wage levels and benefits packages both within the firm and in firms that compete for valuable employees and current legislation and court decisions that affect employment practices.
- *Administrative managers* are responsible for the overall management of the organization. Thus, they are concerned with the coordination of information—just as they are concerned with the coordination of material, human, and financial resources.

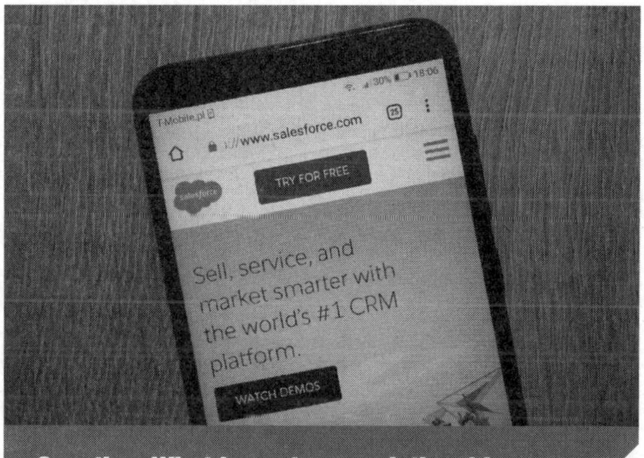

Question: What is customer relationship management (CRM) software? The quick answer is that customer relationship management software is designed to enable a company and its salesforce to use data and information to track all interactions with potential and existing customers to increase sales and profits. While there are many companies that can provide CRM software, the world's leading source for help improving customer satisfaction and building customer loyalty is Salesforce.com located in San Francisco, California.

Administrative managers must ensure information is used in a consistent manner throughout the firm. For example, in 2018, Airbus began constructing a new $300 million plant in Mobile, Alabama, to produce A220 passenger airplanes. In the initial planning stages, Airbus' administrative managers and employees wanted answers to many questions:

- Was the capacity of the plant consistent with marketing plans based on sales projections?
- Would human resources managers be able to recruit employees with the appropriate skills to staff the plant?
- Did sales projections indicate enough income to cover the expected cost of the plant?
- How long would it take before the plant could start building planes?

After much planning and construction, the production facility was completed, workers were hired, and the assembly process could begin. Eventually, new A220 aircraft were sold to Delta, JetBlue, Air Canada, and other airlines.

Also, administrative managers must make sure all managers and employees are able to use the information technology that is available. Certainly, this requires that all employees receive the skills training required to access the information. Finally, administrative managers must commit to the costs of updating the firm's MIS and providing additional training when necessary.

管理信息系统的成本和限制

5-2b Costs and Limits of the System

Can employees, managers, and executives have too much information? The answer is yes. The truth is that each group needs relevant information that helps them make better decisions. And yet, too much information can lead to information overload. Another problem is the amount of worthless information, junk emails, and advertising that contribute to information overload. Unfortunately, there are many misuses of information technology that do nothing but rob employees of time that could be devoted to more productive activities.

In addition to lower employee productivity, the cost of computers, software, and related equipment can be staggering. One of the main goals of a firm's information technology officer (or IT department) is to make sure that a firm has the equipment necessary to provide information the employees need to make effective decisions—*at a reasonable cost.*

In reality, an MIS must be tailored to the needs of the organization it serves. In some firms, a tendency to save on initial costs may result in a system that is too small or overly simple. Such a system generally ends up serving only one or two management levels or a single department. Managers in other departments "give up" on the system as soon as they find that it cannot process their data, is unreliable, or is too slow to meet their information needs.

Almost as bad is an MIS that is too large or too complex for the organization. Unused capacity and complexity do nothing but increase the cost of owning and operating the system. In addition, a system that is difficult to use probably will not be used at all.

✓ Concept Check

- How do the information requirements of managers differ by management area?
- What happens if a business has a management information system that is too large?
- What happens if a business has a management information system that is too small?

员工如何使用管理信息系统

5-3 How Do Employees Use a Management Information System?

Learning Objective

5-3 Outline the five functions of an information system.

To provide information, an MIS must perform five specific functions. It must (1) collect data, (2) store the data, (3) update the data, (4) process the data into information, and (5) present the information to users (refer to Figure 5-3).

步骤 1：收集数据

5-3a Step 1: Collecting Data

A firm's employees, with the help of an MIS system, must gather the data and information needed to establish the firm's *database*. The database should include all past and current data that may be useful in managing the firm. Clearly, the data entered into the system must be *relevant* to the needs of the firm's employees. And perhaps most important, the data must be *accurate*. Irrelevant data are simply useless; inaccurate data can be disastrous. There are two data sources: *internal* and *external*.

Typically, most of the data gathered for an MIS come from internal sources. The most common internal sources of information are managers and employees, company records and reports, accounting data, and minutes of meetings.

External sources of data include customers, suppliers, banks, trade and business publications, industry conferences, online computer services, lawyers, government sources, and firms that specialize in gathering marketing research for organizations.

Whether the source of the data is internal or external, always remember the following two cautions:

1. The cost of obtaining data from some external sources, such as marketing research firms, can be quite high.
2. Although computers generally do not make mistakes, the people who use them can make or cause errors. When data (or information) and your judgment disagree, always check the data.

Figure 5-3 Five Management Information System Functions

Every MIS must be tailored to the organization it serves and must perform the following five functions.

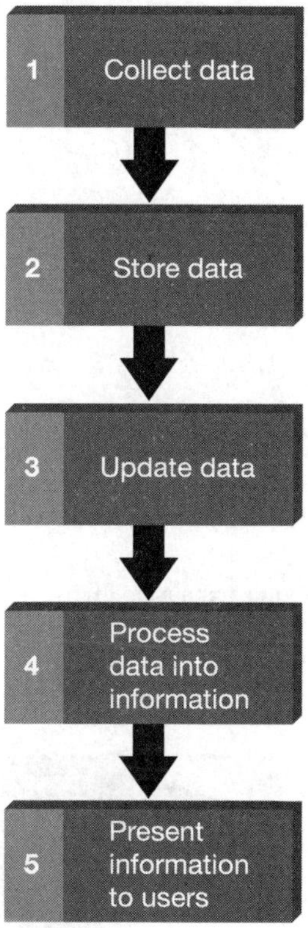

步骤 2：存储数据

5-3b Step 2: Storing Data

An MIS must be capable of storing data until they are needed. Typically, the method chosen to store data depends on the size and needs of the organization. Small businesses may enter data and then store them directly on an employee's computer. Generally, medium-sized to large businesses store data in a larger computer system and provide access to employees through a management information system.

步骤 3：更新数据

5-3c Step 3: Updating Data

Today, an MIS must be able to update stored data regularly to ensure that the information presented to managers and employees is accurate, complete, and up-to-date. The frequency with which the data are updated depends on how fast they change and how often they are used. When it is vital to have current data, updating may occur as soon as the new data are available. For example, Macy's, a national retailer that sells a wide range of merchandise including apparel, cosmetics, home furnishings, and other consumer goods, has cash registers that automatically transmit data on each item sold in each store and online to a central computer. The computer adjusts the store's inventory records accordingly. In addition to maintaining accurate inventory records, sales representatives can tell customers where they can obtain merchandise if the store where they are shopping is out of the merchandise they want or if the merchandise can be purchased online. Data may also be entered into a firm's data bank at certain intervals—every 24 hours, weekly, or monthly.

步骤 4：处理数据

5-3d **Step 4: Processing Data**

Some data are used in the form in which they are stored, whereas other data require processing to extract, highlight, or summarize the information they contain. **Data processing** is the transformation of data into a form that is useful for a specific purpose.

For verbal data, this processing consists mainly of extracting the pertinent material from storage and combining it into a report. Most financial data, however, are in the form of numbers—large groups of numbers, such as daily sales totals or production costs for a specific product. Fortunately, computer software can process large volumes of numbers quickly, and their contents can be summarized through the use of statistics. A **statistic** is a measure that summarizes a particular characteristic of an entire group of numbers.

步骤 5：信息呈现

5-3e **Step 5: Presenting Information**

An MIS must be capable of presenting information in a usable form. That is, the method of presentation—reports, graphs, charts, or tables, for example—must be appropriate for the information itself and for its intended use.

数据处理
data processing the transformation of data into a form that is useful for a specific purpose

统计
statistic a measure that summarizes a particular characteristic of an entire group of numbers

Business Reports Verbal information may be presented in list or paragraph form. Employees often are asked to prepare formal business reports. A typical business report includes:

- An introduction
- The body of the report
- The conclusions
- The recommendations

The *introduction,* which sets the stage for the remainder of the report, describes the problem to be studied in the report, identifies the research techniques that were used, and previews the material that will be presented in the report. The *body* of the report should objectively describe the facts that were discovered in the process of completing the report. The *conclusions* are statements of fact that describe the findings contained in the report. The *recommendations* section presents suggestions on how the problem might be solved. Like the conclusions, the recommendations should be specific, practical, and based on the evidence contained in the report.

With the right information and a computer, preparing a report may be easier than you think! The decision makers in a successful business need information that is relevant, accurate, up-to-date, *and* accessible. To make information more accessible, employees are often asked to prepare a report that summarizes information in a more concise form. This same information may even be easier to understand if the report contains graphs, charts, or tables—all features that are easily created using computer software.

Visual Displays and Tables A visual display can also be used to present information and may be a diagram that represents several items of information in a manner that makes comparison easier. Figure 5-4 illustrates examples of visual displays including graphs, bar charts, and pie charts generated by a computer.

A tabular display is used to present verbal or numerical information in columns and rows. It is most useful in presenting information about two or more related variables. A table, for example, can be used to illustrate the number of salespeople in each region of the country, sales for different types of products, and total sales for all products

Figure 5-4 Typical Visual Displays Used in Business Presentations

Visual displays help businesspeople present information in a form that can be understood easily.

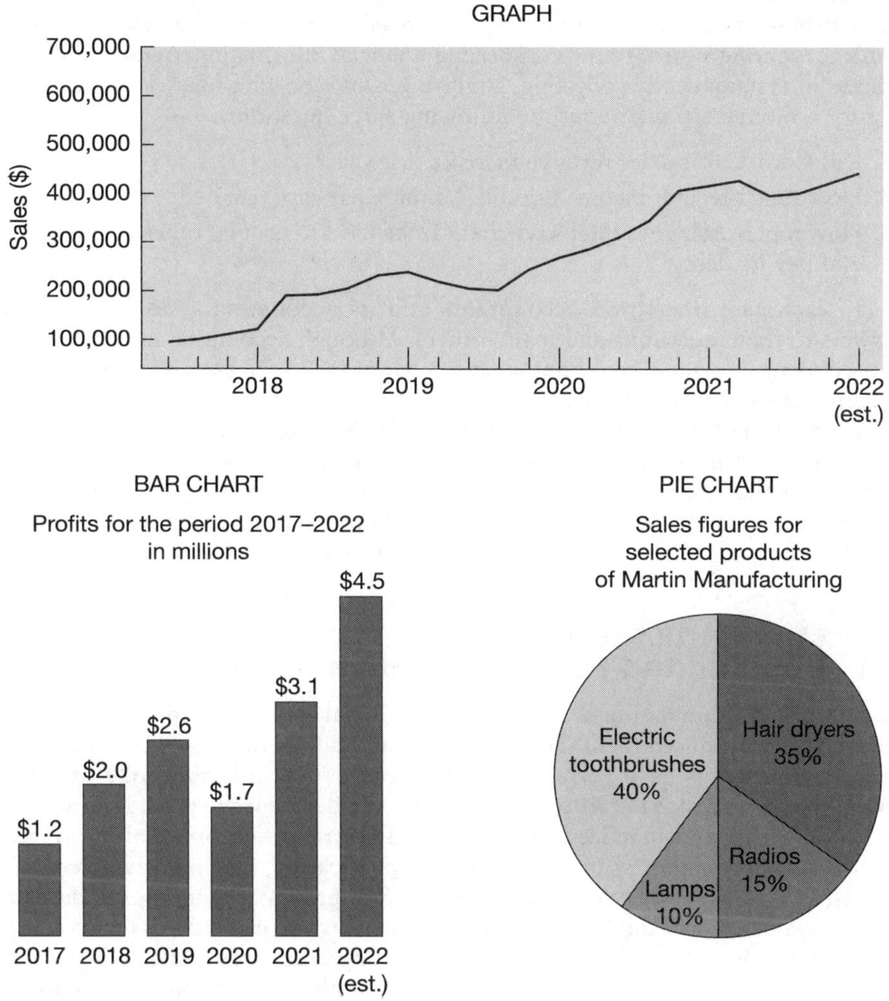

(refer to Table 5-2). Tabular displays generally have less impact than visual displays. However, displaying the information that could be contained in a multicolumn table such as the one shown in Table 5-2 would require several bar or pie charts.

Table 5-2 Typical Four-Column Table Used in Business Presentations

Tables are most useful for displaying information about two or more variables. All-Star Technology Projected Sales

Section of the Country	Number of Salespeople	Consumer Electronic Products ($)	Industrial Electronic Components ($)
Eastern territory	15	1,500,000	3,500,000
Midwestern territory	20	2,000,000	5,000,000
Western territory	10	1,000,000	4,000,000
TOTAL	45	4,500,000	12,500,000

✓ Concept Check

- List the five functions of an MIS.
- What are the components of a typical business report?
- What types of information could be illustrated in a visual display? In a tabular display?

为什么会计信息很重要
5-4 Why Accounting Information Is Important

Learning Objective

5-4 Explain why accurate accounting information and audited financial statements are important.

In order to obtain needed information, firms use an MIS like the one described in the first part of this chapter. Executives, managers, and employees also rely on the firm's accounting system to provide needed financial information. **Accounting** is the process of systematically collecting, analyzing, and reporting financial information. Just for a moment, think about the following three questions:

1. Did Coca-Cola's sales revenue increase last year?
2. How much federal income tax did Walmart pay last year?
3. How much cash does Intel have that can be used to acquire other business firms and pay its debts?

In each case, the firm's accountants and its accounting system provide the answers to these questions and many others. Although accounting information can be used to answer questions about what has happened in the past, it can also be used to help make decisions about the future.

Because the information provided by a firm's accountants and its accounting system is so important, managers and employees, investors, financial analysts, lenders, suppliers, government agencies, and other interested groups must be able to "trust the numbers." To improve the accuracy of a firm's accounting information and its financial statements, businesses rely on audits conducted by accountants employed by public accounting firms.

为什么审计过的财务报表很重要
5-4a Why Audited Financial Statements Are Important

An **audit** is an examination of a company's financial statements and the accounting practices that produced them. The purpose of an audit is to make sure that a firm's financial statements have been prepared in accordance with **generally accepted accounting principles (GAAPs)**. GAAPs have been developed to provide an accepted set of guidelines and practices for U.S. companies reporting financial information and the accounting profession. At the time of publication, the Financial Accounting Standards Board (FASB), which establishes and improves accounting standards for U.S. companies, is working toward establishing a new set of standards that combines GAAPs with the International Financial Reporting Standards (IFRS) to create one set of accounting standards that can be used by both U.S. and multinational firms. For multinational firms like Johnson & Johnson, Royal Dutch Shell, ExxonMobil, Walmart, and Toyota, the benefits of global accounting standards are huge because preparing financial statements and accounting records that meet global standards saves both time and money.

If accountants determine that a firm's financial statements present financial information fairly and conform to GAAPs, then they will issue the following statement:

> *In our opinion, the financial statements ... present fairly, in all material respects the financial position of the company ... in conformity with generally accepted accounting principles.*

Although an audit and the resulting report do not *guarantee* that a company has not "cooked" the books, it does imply that, on the whole, the company has followed GAAPs. Also, it should be noted that without the audit function and GAAPs, there would be very little oversight or supervision. The reliability of a firm's financial statements and its accounting records would drop quickly, and firms would find it difficult to obtain debt financing, use credit to purchase goods and services from suppliers, find investor financing, or prepare documents requested by government agencies.

会计
accounting the process of systematically collecting, analyzing, and reporting financial information

审计
audit an examination of a company's financial statements and the accounting practices that produced them

一般公认会计原则
generally accepted accounting principles (GAAPs) an accepted set of guidelines and practices for U.S. companies reporting financial information and for the accounting profession

Ethics and Social Responsibility

商业伦理与社会责任：毕马威深陷欺诈丑闻

KPMG Caught in Widespread Cheating Scandal

KPMG, one of the Big Four accounting firms, was caught engaging in a series of unethical behaviors. First, KPMG stole regulatory information to cheat on audit inspections. The company, which employs more than 219,000 individuals worldwide and earns more than $29 billion annually, improperly received inspection information from the Public Company Accounting Oversight Board (PCAOB). Allegedly, KPMG obtained information about which of its audits the PCAOB would review from a former PCAOB staff member it hired. This behavior continued as other PCAOB staffers sought employment at KPMG. This resulted in $50 million in fines.

Then, during the Securities and Exchange Commission (SEC) investigation of this scandal, it was uncovered that KPMG auditors, including some senior partners responsible for public company audits, engaged in sharing questions and answers for internal exams related to mandatory ethics, integrity, and compliance training. As part of a settlement with the SEC, three former KPMG audit partners were suspended from accounting activities, including financial reporting and auditing for public companies. As a result of the cheating scandal, KPMG took steps to strengthen its governance and compliance program.

Ethics and compliance programs alone are not enough to ensure misconduct will not occur. Employee training, behavior monitoring, and ongoing reevaluation of the ethics program and business practices are also required. Additionally, management is responsible for setting the tone at the top of the organization and creating an ethical atmosphere. The fact that executives and senior partners were involved in these scandals suggests KPMG could have a more widespread culture problem on its hands.

Sources: Based on information in KPMG, "KPMG Fast Facts," March 18, 2021; Francine McKenna, "The KPMG Cheating Scandal Was Much More Widespread Than Originally Thought," *Market Watch*, June 18, 2019; Aaron Nicodemus, "KPMG Audit Partners Settle Test Cheating Allegations," *Compliance Week*, May 19, 2020.

会计欺诈、伦理行为和改革

5-4b Accounting Fraud, Ethical Behavior, and Reform

Question: Why did Celadon, one of the largest trucking companies in the United States, file for bankruptcy?

Answer: While there are other factors, accounting fraud was a major factor behind the bankruptcy filing.[2]

Celadon's problems began when the company used a complex accounting scheme to inflate the values for older trucking equipment. The Securities and Exchange Commission (SEC) charged Celadon, the president and chief operating officer, and the chief financial officer with violating various antifraud provisions of the federal securities laws, lying to auditors, and "cooking" the books to inflate the amounts reported for income and earnings per share. Eventually, Celadon agreed to pay a $42.2 million fine to settle the SEC case. Because of the accounting problems, the SEC lawsuit, and a downturn in the trucking industry, the company eventually filed bankruptcy in December 2019. On March 31, 2021—15 months after the initial bankruptcy filing—the Celadon case was finally closed.

Unfortunately, the ones hurt when companies (and their executives and accountants) report inaccurate or misleading accounting information often are not the high-paid corporate executives. In many cases, it's the employees who lose their jobs, as well as the money they invested in the company's retirement program, if the company files for bankruptcy. In addition, investors, lenders, and suppliers who relied on fraudulent accounting information in order to make a decision to invest in or lend money to the company also usually experience a loss.

Today, much of the pressure on corporate executives to "cook" the books is driven by the desire to look good to Wall Street analysts and investors. Recently, the SEC charged Illinois-based Power Solutions, and its former CEO and two other

Ouch—an audit! The word audit only contains five letters, but this word often provokes a deep fear in most people including business executives and employees. The audit process for a business is to make sure the company has followed generally accepted accounting principles (GAAPs) when it prepared its financial statements and accounting information. While an audit does not guarantee a company hasn't "cooked" the books, it does provide assurance it has used GAAPs to report financial information.

former executives with inflating financial results by almost $25 million. All three executives were charged with securities fraud by the SEC and the Department of Justice. The company agreed to pay $1.7 million to settle the SEC charges. The motivation behind the accounting fraud was to meet sales and revenue projections.[3] If a company reports sales and profit figures that are higher than expected, the company's stock value can increase dramatically. On the other hand, if a company, like Power Solutions, reports sales and revenue that are lower than expected, its stock can drop. Greed—especially when executive salaries and bonuses are tied to a company's stock value—is another factor that can lead some corporate executives to use unethical accounting methods to inflate a firm's sales revenues and profit amount.

To help ensure that corporate financial information is accurate and to prevent the type of accounting scandals that have occurred in the past, Congress enacted the Sarbanes-Oxley Act. Key components include the following:[4]

- The SEC is required to establish a full-time five-member public company accounting oversight board.
- Executive and financial officers are responsible for accuracy, documentation, and submission of financial reports and are liable for intentional violations of securities reporting requirements.
- Accounting firms are prohibited from providing many types of non-audit and consulting services to the companies they audit.
- Auditors or accountants must maintain financial documents and audit work papers. The time period is usually five to seven years depending on the type of document.
- Auditors, accountants, and employees can be imprisoned for up to 20 years and subject to fines for destroying financial documents and for willful violations of the securities laws.
- A public corporation must change its lead auditing firm every five years.
- There is added protection for whistle-blowers who report violations of the Sarbanes-Oxley Act.

Although most people welcome the Sarbanes-Oxley Act, complex rules make compliance more expensive and time-consuming for corporate management and more difficult for accounting firms. Yet, most people agree that the cost of compliance is justified.

会计的不同类型

5-4c Different Types of Accounting

Although many people think that all accountants do the same tasks, there are special areas of expertise within the accounting industry. In fact, accounting is usually broken down into two broad categories: managerial and financial.

管理会计

managerial accounting provides managers and employees with the information needed to make decisions about a firm's financing, investing, marketing, and operating activities

Managerial accounting provides managers and employees within the organization with the information needed to make decisions about a firm's financing, investing, marketing, and operating activities. By using managerial accounting information, both managers and employees can evaluate how well they have done in the past and what they can expect in the future.

Financial accounting, on the other hand, generates financial statements and reports for interested people outside of an organization. Typically, investors, financial analysts, bankers, lenders, suppliers, government agencies, and other interested groups use the information provided by financial accounting to determine how well a business firm has achieved its goals. In addition to managerial and financial accounting, additional special areas of accounting include the following:

- *Cost accounting*—determining the cost of producing specific products or services
- *Tax accounting*—planning tax strategy and preparing tax returns for firms or individuals
- *Government accounting*—providing basic accounting services to ensure that tax revenues are collected and used to meet the goals of state, local, and federal agencies
- *Not-for-profit accounting*—helping not-for-profit organizations to account for all donations and expenditures

Ever wonder what an accountant does during a typical workday? While activities vary, there is a good chance an accountant is preparing information about the items listed in this photo that can be reported to the people who need it—employees, managers, business owners, and individuals—to improve their financial decisions.

会计职业

5-4d Careers in Accounting

Accounting can be an exciting and rewarding career. To be successful in the accounting industry, employees must:

- be responsible, honest, and ethical;
- have a strong background in financial management;
- know how to use a computer and software to process data into accounting information; and
- be able to communicate with people who need accounting information.

According to the *Occupational Outlook Handbook,* published by the Department of Labor, job opportunities for accountants, as well as auditors in the accounting area, are expected to experience a 4 percent increase by the year 2029.[5] And more good news: Salaries for employees in the accounting industry are often higher than the salaries for other industries.

What is the typical day like for accountants? While each day may be different than the next and depending on if they are self-employed, work for a business, or work for an accounting firm, accountants typically:

- assist employees, managers, and owners to improve financial decisions;
- suggest ways to reduce costs, increase revenues, and improve profits;
- ensure the business is using generally accepted accounting procedures;
- prepare financial statements at the end of an accounting period;
- calculate the amount of taxes owed, prepare tax returns, and ensure that taxes are paid properly and on time; and
- organize and maintain financial records and make sure the firm's bills are paid on time.

Today, accountants generally are classified as either private accountants or public accountants. A *private accountant* is employed by a specific organization. On the other hand, a *public accountant* works on a fee basis for clients and may be self-employed or be the employee of an accounting firm. Accounting firms range

财务会计
financial accounting generates financial statements and reports for interested people outside an organization

Exploring Careers

职业探索：法务会计正在兴起

Forensic Accounting Is on the Rise

Why do people become forensic accountants? The answer: It is an exciting career path that is growing and combines accounting, auditing, and investigative skills to analyze financial documents in search of fraudulent activities and financial misconduct. Simply put, forensic accountants function as detectives. Their findings and analysis are often used in legal proceedings to prosecute people guilty of accounting fraud or even criminal activities. The origins of forensic accounting date back to the 1930s with the publishing of *Principles of Criminology*, which described the so-called fraud triangle. The triangle outlines how opportunity, incentive, and rationalization contribute to the risk of fraud.

Today, the demand for forensic accounting is on the rise. To comply with current auditing standards and laws such as the Sarbanes-Oxley Act, many accounting and auditing firms are expanding their fraud-detection services. Additionally, several federal government agencies use forensic accountants to tackle complex investigative work related to corporate fraud, healthcare fraud, securities fraud, and more.

The analysis provided by forensic accountants can even be applied to areas such as cybercrime, public corruption, and counterterrorism. For example, the Federal Bureau of Investigation (FBI) hires forensic accountants to follow money trails of criminal activity and national security threats by acquiring, organizing, analyzing, and reporting financial data.

The duties of a forensic accountant can include gathering evidence, investigating financial documents, examining business records, working alongside law enforcement, and testifying in court. These duties require strong analytical and reasoning skills, the ability to effectively communicate, and a skeptical mind. The Association of Certified Fraud Examiners (ACFE), which is the world's largest anti-fraud organization, certifies accounting professionals as certified fraud examiners (CFEs). ACFE has grown to more than 90,000 members with the goal of reducing business fraud around the world and improving public confidence within the profession of accounting.

Sources: Based on information in Association of Certified Fraud Examiners, "About ACFE," March 16, 2021; FBI Jobs, "Forensic Accountants," March 15, 2021; Yigal Rechtman, "The Past, Present, and Future of Forensic Accounting," *The CPA Journal*, April 2020.

---

in size from one-person operations to huge international firms with hundreds of accounting partners and thousands of employees.

Typically, public accounting firms include on their staffs at least one **certified public accountant (CPA)**, an individual who has met state requirements for accounting education and experience and has passed a rigorous accounting examination. More information about general requirements and the CPA profession can be obtained by contacting the American Institute of CPAs (AICPA) at www.aicpa.org. Be sure and click on the tab "Career Guidance" for information about how to become a CPA.

✓ Concept Check

- What purpose do audits and GAAPs serve in today's business world?
- How do the major provisions of the Sarbanes-Oxley Act affect a public company's audit procedures?
- Based on the information in this section, would you choose accounting as a career?

会计恒等式和资产负债表

5-5 The Accounting Equation and the Balance Sheet

Learning Objective

5-5 Interpret a balance sheet.

At the beginning of this chapter, *information* was defined as data presented in a form that is useful for a specific purpose. Now, we examine how financial *data* are transformed into financial *information* and reported on three very important financial statements—the balance sheet, income statement, and statement of cash flows. We begin by describing why the fundamental accounting equation is the basis for a firm's balance sheet.

会计恒等式
5-5a The Accounting Equation

The accounting equation is a simple statement that forms the basis for the accounting process. This equation shows the relationship between a firm's assets, liabilities, and owners' equity.

- **Assets** are the resources a business owns—cash, inventory, equipment, and real estate.
- **Liabilities** are the firm's debts—borrowed money it owes to others that must be repaid.
- **Owners' equity** is the difference between total assets and total liabilities—what would be left for the owners if the firm's assets were sold and the money used to pay off its liabilities.

The relationship between assets, liabilities, and owners' equity is shown by the following **accounting equation**:

Assets = Liabilities + Owners' equity

Whether a business is a small corner grocery store or a global giant like Procter & Gamble or Amazon, the total dollar amount for assets must equal the sum of its liabilities and owners' equity. To use this equation, a firm's accountants must record raw data—that is, the firm's day-to-day financial transactions—using the double-entry system of bookkeeping. The **double-entry bookkeeping system** is a system in which each financial transaction is recorded as two separate accounting entries to maintain the balance shown in the accounting equation. At the end of a specific accounting period, all of the financial transactions can now be summarized in the firm's financial statements. The form of the financial statements is pretty much the same for all businesses, from a neighborhood video store or small dry cleaner to giant corporations such as Home Depot, Boeing, and FedEx. A firm's financial statements are prepared at least once a year and included in the firm's annual report. An **annual report** is a report distributed to stockholders and other interested parties that describes a firm's operating activities and its financial condition. Because the information contained in financial statements can help executives and employees manage a business and plan for the future, most firms also have financial statements prepared semiannually, quarterly, or monthly.

注册会计师
certified public accountant (CPA) an individual who has met state requirements for accounting education and experience and has passed a rigorous accounting examination

资产
assets the resources that a business owns

负债
liabilities a firm's debts and obligations

所有者权益
owners' equity the difference between a firm's assets and its liabilities

会计恒等式
accounting equation the basis for the accounting process: *Assets = Liabilities + Owners' equity*

复式簿记系统
double-entry bookkeeping system a system in which each financial transaction is recorded as two separate accounting entries to maintain the balance shown in the accounting equation

年度报告
annual report a report distributed to stockholders and other interested parties that describes the firm's operating activities and its financial condition

资产负债表（或财务状况表）
balance sheet (or statement of financial position) a summary of the dollar amounts of a firm's assets, liabilities, and owners' equity accounts at the end of a specific accounting period

资产负债表
5-5b The Balance Sheet

Question: *Where could you find the total amount of assets, liabilities, and owners' equity for The Hershey Company?*

Answer: The firm's balance sheet.

A **balance sheet** (sometimes referred to as a **statement of financial position**) is a summary of the dollar amounts of a firm's assets, liabilities, and owners' equity accounts at the end of a specific accounting period. The balance sheet must demonstrate that assets are equal to liabilities plus owners' equity, and the accounting equation is still in balance. Most people think of a balance sheet as a statement that reports the financial condition of a business firm such as The Hershey Company, but balance sheets apply to individuals, too. For example, Marty Campbell graduated from college three years ago and now is employed as a sales representative for a medical supply firm. After going to work, he established a checking and savings account and purchased an automobile, stereo, television, and furniture for his apartment. Marty paid cash for some purchases, but he had to borrow money to pay for the larger ones. Figure 5-5 shows Marty's current personal balance sheet. Marty Campbell's assets total $26,500, and his liabilities amount to $10,000. Although the difference between total assets and total liabilities is referred to as *owners' equity* or

Figure 5-5 Personal Balance Sheet

Often, individuals determine their net worth by subtracting the value of their liabilities from the value of their assets.

Marty Campbell
Personal Balance Sheet
December 31, 20XX

ASSETS			LIABILITIES		
Cash	$ 2,500		Automobile loan	$ 9,500	
Savings account	5,000		Credit card balance	500	
Automobile	15,000		TOTAL LIABILITIES		$10,000
Stereo	1,000				
Television	500				
Furniture	2,500		NET WORTH (Owners' Equity)		16,500
TOTAL ASSETS		$26,500	TOTAL LIABILITIES AND NET WORTH		$26,500

stockholders' equity for a business, it is normally called *net worth* for an individual. As reported on Marty's personal balance sheet, net worth is $16,500. The total assets ($26,500) and the total liabilities *plus* net worth ($26,500) are equal. Thus, the accounting equation (Assets = Liabilities + Owners' equity) is still in balance.

Figure 5-6 shows the balance sheet for Northeast Art Supply, a small wholesale business that sells picture frames, paints, canvases, and other artists' supplies

Figure 5-6 Business Balance Sheet

A balance sheet (sometimes referred to as a statement of financial position) summarizes a firm's assets, liabilities, and owners' equity. Note that assets ($340,000) equal liabilities plus owners' equity ($340,000) and the accounting equation is still in balance.

NORTHEAST ART SUPPLY, INC.

Balance Sheet
December 31, 20XX

ASSETS

Current assets			
Cash		$ 59,000	
Marketable securities		10,000	
Accounts receivable	$ 40,000		
Less allowance for doubtful accounts	2,000	38,000	
Notes receivable		32,000	
Merchandise inventory		41,000	
Prepaid expenses		2,000	
Total current assets			$182,000
Fixed assets			
Delivery equipment	$110,000		
Less accumulated depreciation	20,000	$ 90,000	
Furniture and store equipment	$62,000		
Less accumulated depreciation	15,000	47,000	
Total fixed assets			137,000
Intangible assets			
Patents		$ 21,000	
Total intangible assets			21,000
TOTAL ASSETS			$340,000

LIABILITIES AND STOCKHOLDERS' EQUITY

Current liabilities			
Accounts payable	$ 35,000		
Notes payable	25,675		
Salaries payable	4,000		
Taxes payable	5,325		
Total current liabilities		$ 70,000	
Long-term liabilities			
Mortgage payable on store equipment	$ 40,000		
Total long-term liabilities		$ 40,000	
TOTAL LIABILITIES			$110,000
Stockholders' equity			
Common stock (25,000×$6)		$ 150,000	
Retained earnings		80,000	
TOTAL OWNERS' EQUITY			230,000
TOTAL LIABILITIES AND OWNERS' EQUITY			$340,000

to retailers in New England. Let's work through the different accounts in Figure 5-6.

资产

5-5c Assets

On a balance sheet, assets are listed in order from the *most liquid* to the *least liquid*. The **liquidity** of an asset is the ease with which it can be converted into cash.

Current Assets **Current assets** are assets that can be converted quickly into cash or that will be used in one year or less. Because cash is the most liquid asset, it is listed first. Next are *marketable securities*—stocks, bonds, and other investments—that can be converted into cash in a matter of days.

Next are the firm's receivables. Its *accounts receivable,* which result from allowing customers to make credit purchases, generally are paid within 30 to 60 days. However, the firm expects that some of these debts will not be collected. Thus, it has reduced its accounts receivables by a 5 percent *allowance for doubtful accounts.* The firm's *notes receivable* are receivables for which customers have signed promissory notes. They generally are repaid over a longer period of time than the firm's accounts receivable.

Northeast's *merchandise inventory* represents the value of goods on hand for sale to customers. Since Northeast Art Supply is a wholesale business, the inventory listed in Figure 5-6 represents finished goods ready for sale to retailers. For a manufacturing firm, inventory also may represent raw materials or work that has been partially completed but requires further processing.

Northeast Art's last current asset is *prepaid expenses,* which are assets that have been paid for in advance but have not yet been used. An example is insurance premiums. They are usually paid at the beginning of the policy year. The unused portion (say, for the last four months of the time period covered by the policy) is a prepaid expense. For Northeast Art, all current assets total $182,000.

This Caterpillar bulldozer is no toy. While the child is wondering if he could drive this monster, this bulldozer is a necessary piece of equipment that costs thousands of dollars for a construction company. Like all other assets, the value of this bulldozer and other heavy construction equipment would be listed as a fixed asset on the construction firm's balance sheet.

Fixed Assets **Fixed assets** are assets that will be held or used for a period longer than one year. They generally include land, buildings, and equipment used in the continuing operation of the business. Although Northeast Art owns no land or buildings, it does own delivery equipment that originally cost $110,000. It also owns furniture and store equipment that originally cost $62,000.

Note that the values of both fixed assets are decreased by their *accumulated depreciation.* **Depreciation** is the process of apportioning the cost of a fixed asset over the period during which it will be used. The depreciation amount allotted to each year is an expense for that year, and the value of the asset must be reduced by the amount of depreciation expense. For example, $20,000 of Northeast's delivery equipment value has been depreciated since it was purchased. Its value at this time is $110,000 less $20,000, or $90,000. For Northeast Art, all fixed assets total $137,000.

流动性
liquidity the ease with which an asset can be converted into cash

流动资产
current assets assets that can be converted quickly into cash or that will be used in one year or less

固定资产
fixed assets assets that will be held or used for a period longer than one year

折旧
depreciation the process of apportioning the cost of a fixed asset over the period during which it will be used

Intangible Assets **Intangible assets** are assets that do not exist physically but that have a value based on the rights or privileges they confer on a firm. They include patents, copyrights, trademarks and brands, and goodwill. By their nature, intangible assets are long-term assets—they are of value to the firm for a number of years.

Northeast Art Supply lists a *patent* for a special oil paint that the company purchased from the inventor. The firm's accountants estimate that the patent has a current market value of $21,000. The firm's intangible assets total $21,000. Now it is possible to add the total amounts for current assets ($182,000), fixed assets ($137,000), and intangible assets ($21,000) to calculate total assets for Northeast Art. As shown in Figure 5-6, total assets are $340,000.

负债和所有者权益
5-5d Liabilities and Owners' Equity

The liabilities and the owners' equity accounts complete the balance sheet. The firm's liabilities are separated into two categories—current and long-term liabilities.

Current Liabilities A firm's **current liabilities** are debts that will be repaid in one year or less. Northeast Art Supply purchased merchandise from its suppliers on credit. Thus, its balance sheet includes an entry for accounts payable. *Accounts payable* are short-term obligations that arise as a result of a firm making credit purchases.

Notes payable are obligations that have been secured with promissory notes. They are usually short-term obligations, but they may extend beyond one year. Only those that must be paid within the year are listed under current liabilities.

Northeast Art also lists *salaries payable* and *taxes payable* as current liabilities. These are both expenses that have been incurred during the current accounting period but will be paid in the next accounting period. For Northeast Art, current liabilities total $70,000.

Long-Term Liabilities **Long-term liabilities** are debts that need not be repaid for at least one year. Northeast Art lists only one long-term liability—a $40,000 *mortgage payable* for store equipment. As you can see in Figure 5-6, Northeast Art's current and long-term liabilities total $110,000.

Owners' or Stockholders' Equity For a sole proprietorship or partnership, the owners' equity is shown as the difference between assets and liabilities. In a partnership, each partner's share of the ownership is reported separately in each owner's name. For a corporation, the owners' equity usually is referred to as *stockholders' equity.* The dollar amount reported on the balance sheet is the total value of stock plus retained earnings that have accumulated to date. **Retained earnings** are the portion of a business's profits not distributed to stockholders.

The original investment by the owners of Northeast Art Supply was $150,000 and was obtained by selling 25,000 shares at $6 per share. In addition, $80,000 of Northeast Art's earnings have been reinvested in the business since it was founded. Thus, owners' equity totals $230,000. Now it is possible to add the total for liabilities ($110,000) and owners' equity ($230,000) to calculate the total for liabilities and owners' equity. As shown in Figure 5-6, the sum of total liabilities and owners' equity is $340,000.

As the two grand totals in Figure 5-6 show, Northeast Art's assets and the sum of its liabilities and owners' equity are equal—at $340,000. The accounting equation (Assets = Liabilities + Owners' equity) is still in balance.

无形资产
intangible assets assets that do not exist physically but that have a value based on the rights or privileges they confer on a firm

流动负债
current liabilities debts that will be repaid in one year or less

长期负债
long-term liabilities debts that need not be repaid for at least one year

留存收益
retained earnings the portion of a business's profits not distributed to stockholders

✓ Concept Check

- How are current assets distinguished from fixed assets?
- Why are fixed assets depreciated on a firm's balance sheet?
- How do you determine the dollar amount of owners' equity for a sole proprietorship, a partnership, or a corporation?
- If a business firm has assets worth $170,000 and liabilities that total $40,000, what is the value of the owners' equity?

Sustaining the Planet

保护地球：会计师越来越关注社会和环境问题

Accountants Grow Concerned About Social and Environmental Issues

To measure the effect a business has on society and the environment, many businesses use social accounting to take a look at the bigger picture. This type of accounting considers how the organization creates value for various stakeholders and attempts to demonstrate how organizations are providing not only economic value, but also how businesses impact society and the environment. Even though many companies issue annual social responsibility audits and sustainability reports along with their financial reports, they are often separate, which makes it difficult to make connections between financial performance and the impact a firm has on society.

According to a survey by the Association of Chartered Certified Accountants (ACCA), accountants are worried about environmental and social issues. In fact, 90 percent of those surveyed believe businesses can make a more positive impact on society and the environment. Ninety-five percent of the accountants surveyed also agreed that accountants and finance managers have a role to play in building a more socially inclusive and environmentally protected world in the future. Already, accountants in many businesses are beginning to track the results and costs of a firm's social impact and sustainability activities. However, experts are quick to point out that an organization's social responsibility and environmental initiatives should not be judged solely on the financial cost.

Conclusion: Even though more and more accountants recognize the need for businesses to better address social inequalities and environmental issues, there are still some barriers that discourage more robust social accounting activities. Potential costs, lack of buy-in from upper management, and misaligned financial priorities can hinder efforts to improve the current situation. Still, it is important to effectively measure an organization's social and environmental impact to prove that these activities provide value. And combining financial data with social and environmental data can strengthen the case for businesses to invest further in these types of initiatives.

Sources: Based on information in Carleton Centre for Community Innovation, "Accounting for Social Impact," March 10, 2021; Michael Cohn, "Accountants Worried About Environmental and Social Issues," *Accounting Today*, October 13, 2020; George Spencer, "5 Steps for Reliable ESG Reporting Amid Growing Demand," *Journal of Accountancy*, February 5, 2021.

损益表

5-6 The Income Statement

Learning Objective

5-6 Interpret an income statement.

Question: *Where can you find the profit amount for Apple, Inc.?*

Answer: The firm's income statement.

An **income statement** is a summary of a firm's revenues and expenses during a specified accounting period—one month, three months, six months, or a year. The income statement is sometimes called the *earnings statement* or *the statement of income and expenses*. Let's begin our discussion by constructing a personal income statement for Marty Campbell. Having worked as a sales representative for a medical supply firm for the past three years, Marty now earns $45,000 a year, or $3,750 a month. After deductions, his take-home pay is $2,625 a month. As illustrated in Figure 5-7, Marty's typical monthly expenses include payments for an automobile loan, credit card payments, apartment rent, utilities, food, clothing, and recreation and entertainment.

损益表
income statement a summary of a firm's revenues and expenses during a specified accounting period

Although the difference between income and expenses is referred to as *profit* or *loss* for a business, it is normally referred to as a *cash surplus* or *cash deficit* for

Figure 5-7 Personal Income Statement

By subtracting expenses from income, you can construct a personal income statement and determine if you have a surplus or deficit at the end of each month.

Marty Campbell
Personal Income Statement
For the month ended December 31, 20XX

INCOME (Take-home pay)		$2,625
LESS MONTHLY EXPENSES		
Automobile loan	$ 350	
Credit card payment	100	
Apartment rent	900	
Utilities	200	
Food	325	
Clothing	100	
Recreation & entertainment	250	
TOTAL MONTHLY EXPENSES		2,225
CASH SURPLUS (or profit)		$ 400

an individual. Fortunately for Marty, he has a surplus of $400 at the end of each month. He can use this surplus for savings, investing, or paying off debts. It is also possible to use the information from a personal income statement to construct a personal budget. A *personal budget* is a specific plan for spending your income—over the next month or a specified time period.

Figure 5-8 shows the income statement for Northeast Art Supply. For a business,

Revenues *less* → Cost of goods sold *less* → Operating expenses equals → Net income

收入

5-6a Revenues

Revenues are the dollar amounts earned by a firm from selling goods, providing services, or performing business activities. Like most businesses, Northeast Art Supply obtains its revenues solely from the sale of its products or services. The revenues section of its income statement begins with gross sales. **Gross sales** are the total dollar amount of all goods and services sold during the accounting period. Deductions made from this amount are:

- *sales returns*—merchandise returned to the firm by its customers;
- *sales allowances*—price reductions offered to customers who accept slightly damaged or soiled merchandise; and
- *sales discounts*—price reductions offered to customers who pay their bills promptly.

The remainder is the firm's net sales. **Net sales** are the actual dollar amounts received by the firm for the goods and services it has sold after adjustment for returns, allowances, and discounts. For Northeast Art, net sales are $451,000.

收入
revenues the dollar amounts earned by a firm from selling goods, providing services, or performing business activities

销售总额
gross sales the total dollar amount of all goods and services sold during the accounting period

净销售收入
net sales the actual dollar amounts received by a firm for the goods and services it has sold after adjustment for returns, allowances, and discounts

Figure 5-8 Business Income Statement

An income statement summarizes a firm's revenues and expenses during a specified accounting period. For Northeast Art Supply, net income after taxes is $28,045.

NORTHEAST ART SUPPLY, INC.

Income Statement
for the Year Ended
December 31, 20XX

Revenues			
Gross sales		$465,000	
Less sales returns and allowances	$ 9,500		
Less sales discounts	4,500	14,000	
Net sales			$451,000
Cost of goods sold			
Beginning inventory, January 1, 20XX		$ 40,000	
Purchases	$346,000		
Less purchase discounts	11,000		
Net purchases		335,000	
Cost of goods available for sale		$375,000	
Less ending inventory December 31, 20XX		41,000	
Cost of goods sold			334,000
Gross profit			$117,000
Operating expenses			
Selling expenses			
Sales salaries	$ 22,000		
Advertising	4,000		
Sales promotion	2,500		
Depreciation—store equipment	3,000		
Depreciation—delivery equipment	4,000		
Miscellaneous selling expenses	1,500		
Total selling expenses		$ 37,000	
General expenses			
Office salaries	$ 28,500		
Rent	8,500		
Depreciation—furniture	1,500		
Utilities expense	2,500		
Insurance expense	1,000		
Miscellaneous expense	500		
Total general expense		42,500	
Total operating expenses			79,500
Net income from operations			$ 37,500
Less interest expense			2,000
NET INCOME BEFORE TAXES			$ 35,500
Less federal income taxes			7,455
NET INCOME AFTER TAXES			$ 28,045

销货成本

5-6b Cost of Goods Sold

The standard method of determining the **cost of goods sold** by a retailing or a wholesaling firm can be summarized as follows:

Cost of goods sold = Beginning inventory + Net purchases – Ending inventory

According to Figure 5-8, Northeast Art Supply began its accounting period on January 1 with a merchandise inventory that cost $40,000. During the next 12 months, the firm purchased merchandise valued at $346,000. After deducting *purchase discounts,* however, it paid only $335,000 for this merchandise. Thus, during the year, Northeast had total *goods available for sale* valued at beginning inventory ($40,000) plus net purchases ($335,000), for a total of cost of goods available for sale ($375,000).

Twelve months later, at the end of the accounting period on December 31, Northeast still had inventory valued at $41,000. For Northeast, the cost of goods available for sale ($375,000) less ending inventory ($41,000) equals the firm's total of cost of goods sold ($334,000). It is now possible to calculate gross profit.

销货成本
cost of goods sold the dollar amount equal to beginning inventory *plus* net purchases *less* ending inventory

The firm's **gross profit** is net sales ($451,000) *less* cost of goods sold ($334,000), for a $117,000 gross profit.

营业费用

5-6c Operating Expenses

A firm's **operating expenses** are all business costs other than the cost of goods sold. Total operating expenses generally are divided into two categories: selling expenses and general expenses.

Selling expenses are costs related to the firm's marketing activities. For Northeast Art Supply, selling expenses total $37,000. *General expenses* are costs incurred in operating a business, in this case, a total of $42,500. Now it is possible to total both selling and general expenses. As Figure 5-8 shows, total operating expenses for the accounting period are $79,500.

净收益

5-6d Net Income

When revenues exceed expenses, the difference is called **net income**. When expenses exceed revenues, the difference is called **net loss**.

Profit or Loss = Revenues − Expenses

As Figure 5-8 shows, Northeast Art's *net income from operations* is computed as gross profit ($117,000) less total operating expenses ($79,500). For Northeast Art, net income from operations is $37,500. From this amount, *interest expense* of $2,000 is deducted to obtain a *net income before taxes* of $35,500. The interest expense is deducted in this section of the income statement because it is not an operating expense. Rather, it is an expense that results from financing the business.

Northeast Art's *federal income taxes* are $7,455. Although these taxes may or may not be payable immediately, they are definitely an expense that must be deducted from income. This leaves Northeast Art with a *net income after taxes* of $28,045. This amount may be used to pay a dividend to stockholders, it may be retained or reinvested in the firm, it may be used to reduce the firm's debts, or all three.

If you want to know if a company is profitable or not, look at its income statement. An income statement is the "go-to" source for executives, managers, employees, and investors who want to know if a firm is earning a profit or operating at a loss. This same statement also contains information about its costs of goods sold, operating expenses, finance costs, and the amount of taxes it must pay.

✓ Concept Check

- What is the difference between a balance sheet and an income statement?
- Explain how a retailing firm would determine the cost of goods sold during an accounting period.
- If a retailer has revenues of $700,000, cost of goods sold that total $270,000, and operating expenses that total $200,000, what is its net income before taxes?

现金流量表

5-7 The Statement of Cash Flows

Learning Objective

5-7 Describe business activities that affect a firm's cash flow.

Cash is vital to any business. Both the Securities and Exchange Commission and the Financial Accounting Standards Board require all publicly traded companies to include a statement of cash flows, along with their balance sheet and income statement, in their annual report. The **statement of cash flows** illustrates how the company's operating, investing, and financing activities affect cash during an accounting period. While a firm's balance sheet reports dollar values for assets, liabilities, and owners' equity and an income statement reports the firm's dollar amount of profit or loss, the statement of cash flows focuses on how much cash is on hand to pay the firm's bills. Also, the information on the statement of cash flows can be used to evaluate decisions related to a firm's future investments and financing needs. Investors, lenders, and suppliers are also interested in a firm's statement of cash flows. Investors want to know if a firm can pay dividends. Before extending credit to a firm, lenders and suppliers often use the information on the statement of cash flows to evaluate the firm's ability to repay its debts.

毛利润
gross profit a firm's net sales *less* the cost of goods sold

营业费用
operating expenses all business costs other than the cost of goods sold

净收益
net income occurs when revenues exceed expenses

净亏损
net loss occurs when expenses exceed revenues

A statement of cash flows for Northeast Art Supply is illustrated in Figure 5-9. It provides information concerning the company's cash receipts and cash payments and is organized around three different activities: operating, investing, and financing.

- *Cash flows from operating activities.* This is the first section of a statement of cash flows. It addresses the firm's primary revenue source—providing goods and services. Typical adjustments include adding the amount of depreciation to a firm's net income. Other adjustments that increase or decrease the amounts for accounts receivable, inventory, accounts payable, and income taxes payable are also required to reflect a true picture of cash flows from operating activities.
- *Cash flows from investing activities.* The second section of the statement is concerned with cash flow from investments. This includes the purchase and sale of equipment, land, and other assets and investments.
- *Cash flows from financing activities.* The third and final section deals with the cash flow from all financing activities. It reports changes in debt obligation and owners' equity accounts. This includes loans and repayments, the sale and repurchase of the company's own stock, and cash dividends.

现金流量表
statement of cash flows a statement that illustrates how the company's operating, investing, and financing activities affect cash during an accounting period

The totals of all three activities are added to the beginning cash balance to determine the ending cash balance. For Northeast Art Supply, the ending cash

Figure 5-9 Statement of Cash Flows

A statement of cash flows summarizes how a firm's operating, investing, and financing activities affect its cash during a specified accounting period. For Northeast Art Supply, the amount of cash at the end of the year reported on the statement of cash flows is $59,000—the same amount reported for the cash account on the firm's balance sheet.

NORTHEAST ART SUPPLY, INC.

Statement of Cash Flows
for the Year Ended
December 31, 20XX

Cash flows from operating activities		
Net Income		$28,045
Adjustments to reconcile net income to net cash flows		
Depreciation	$ 8,500	
Decrease in accounts receivable	1,000	
Increase in inventory	(5,000)	
Increase in accounts payable	6,000	
Increase in income taxes payable	3,000	13,500
Net cash provided by operating activities		$41,545
Cash flows from investing activities		
Purchase of equipment	$ (2,000)	
Purchase of investments	(10,000)	
Sale of investments	20,000	
Net cash provided by investing activities		8,000
Cash flows from financing activities		
Payments on debt	$(23,000)	
Payment of dividends	(5,000)	
Net cash provided by financing activities		(28,000)
NET INCREASE IN CASH		$21,545
Cash at beginning of year		37,455
CASH AT END OF YEAR		$59,000

✓ Concept Check

- What is the purpose of the statement of cash flows?
- In a statement of cash flows, what is included in the operating activities section? In the investing activities section? In the financial activities section?

balance is $59,000. Note that this is the same amount reported for the cash account on the firm's balance sheet. Together, the statement of cash flows, balance sheet, and income statement illustrate the results of past business decisions and reflect the firm's ability to pay debts and dividends and to finance new growth.

评估财务报表
5-8 Evaluating Financial Statements

Learning Objective
5-8 Summarize how managers evaluate the financial health of a business.

All three financial statements—the balance sheet, the income statement, and the statement of cash flows—can provide answers to a variety of questions about a firm's ability to do business and stay in business, its profitability, and its value as an investment. Even more information about a firm's financial health can be obtained by comparing its financial information with the same information for competing firms, with industry averages, and with its financial information over recent accounting periods.

比较财务数据
5-8a Comparing Financial Data

Comparisons of a firm's financial and accounting information are possible as long as accountants follow GAAPs to prepare the firm's financial statements. Except for minor differences in format and terms, a balance sheet, income statement, and statement of cash flows for Lowe's, for example, will be similar to the financial statements for Home Depot because both companies are in the home improvement industry. Comparisons among firms give executives, managers, and employees a general idea of a firm's standing within the industry. Competitors' financial information can be obtained from their annual reports, information filed with the SEC, and investment sites like Bloomberg and Yahoo! Finance—if they are public corporations. Industry averages are published by reporting services such as Dun & Bradstreet (D&B) and BizMiner, as well as by some industry trade associations.

Today, most corporations include in their annual reports comparisons of the important elements of their financial statements for recent years. For example, Figure 5-10 shows comparisons—of revenue, research and development (R&D) costs, operating income, and sales and marketing expenses—for Microsoft Corporation, a world leader in the computer software industry. By examining this information, a manager in the research and development division can tell whether R&D expenditures have been increasing or decreasing over the past three years. The vice president of marketing can determine if the total amount of sales and marketing expenses is changing. Stockholders and potential investors, on the other hand, may be more concerned with increases or decreases in Microsoft's revenues and operating income over the same time period. Still another type of analysis of a firm's financial health involves computation of financial ratios.

财务比率
5-8b Financial Ratios

A **financial ratio** is a number that shows the relationship between two elements of a firm's financial statements. While it is possible to calculate many different financial ratios, we'll only discuss three different ratios that are used to measure a firm's profitability, its ability to pay its debts, and how often it sells its inventory. Like the individual elements in financial statements, these ratios can be compared with those of competitors, with industry averages, and with the firm's past ratios from previous accounting periods. The information required

财务比率
financial ratio a number that shows the relationship between two elements of a firm's financial statements

Figure 5-10 Comparisons of Present and Past Financial Statements for Microsoft Corporation

Most corporations include in their annual reports comparisons of the important elements of their financial statements for recent years.

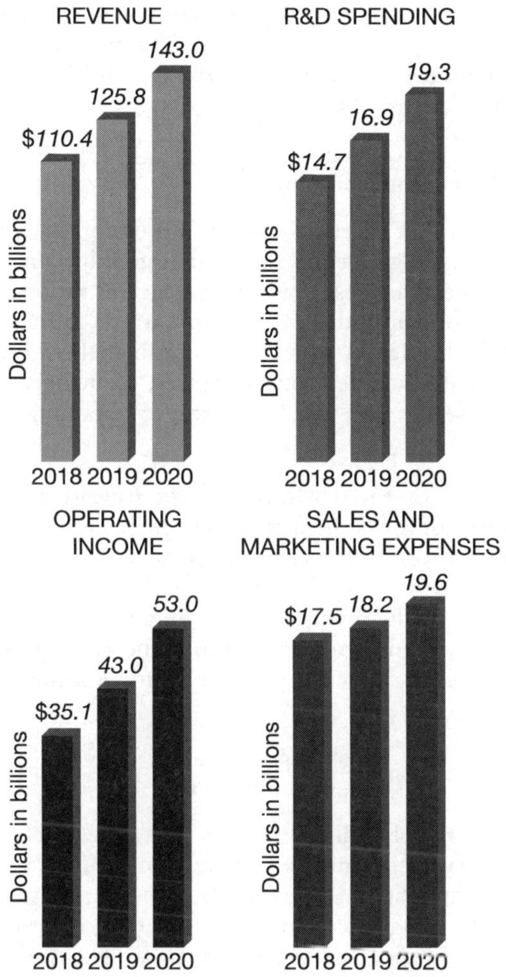

Source: Adapted from the Microsoft Corporation 2020 Annual Report.

to form these ratios is found in a firm's balance sheet, income statement, and statement of cash flows.

Measuring a Firm's Ability to Earn Profits A firm's net income after taxes indicates whether the firm is profitable. It does not, however, indicate how effectively the firm's resources are being used. For this latter purpose, a net profit margin can be computed. **Net profit margin** (sometimes called **return on sales**) is a financial ratio calculated by dividing net income after taxes by net sales. For Starbucks—a company known for world class coffee—its net profit margin is 4.8 as calculated below.

$$\text{Net profit margin} = \frac{\text{Net income after taxes}}{\text{Net sales}} = \frac{\$\ 928 \text{ million}}{\$\ 19{,}165 \text{ million}}$$

$$= 0.048 = 4.8 \text{ percent}$$

净利润率（或销售利润率）
net profit margin (or **return on sales)** a financial ratio calculated by dividing net income after taxes by net sales

A higher return on sales is better than a low one. Today, the average net profit margin for all business firms is between 4 and 5 percent. With a return on sales of 4.8 percent, Starbucks is toward the high end of the average. A low return on sales can be increased by reducing expenses and increasing sales.

Measuring a Firm's Ability to Pay Its Debts A current ratio can be used to evaluate a firm's ability to pay its current liabilities. A firm's **current ratio** is computed by dividing current assets by current liabilities. The current ratio for Starbucks is 1.06 as calculated below.

$$\textbf{Current ratio} = \frac{\text{Current assets}}{\text{Current liabilities}} = \frac{\$7{,}806 \text{ million}}{\$7{,}347 \text{ million}} = 1.06$$

This ratio indicates that Starbucks has $1.06 of current assets for every $1 of current liabilities. The average for this ratio varies greatly from industry to industry, but many financial experts suggest that a firm's current ratio should range between 1.2 and 2 depending on the industry. A high current ratio indicates that a firm can pay its current liabilities. A low current ratio (below 1.2) can be improved by repaying current liabilities, reducing expenses, reducing dividend payments to stockholders to increase the firm's cash balance, or obtaining additional cash from investors.

Measuring How Well a Firm Manages Its Inventory A firm's **inventory turnover** is the number of times the firm sells its merchandise inventory in one year. It is approximated by dividing the cost of goods sold in one year by the average value of the inventory.

The average value of the inventory for one accounting period can be found by adding the beginning inventory value and the ending inventory value and dividing the sum by 2. The inventory turnover for Starbucks is 5 as calculated below.

$$\textbf{Inventory turnover} = \frac{\text{Cost of goods sold}}{\text{Average inventory}} = \frac{\$7{,}695 \text{ million}}{\$1{,}540 \text{ million}} = 5$$

Starbucks sells its merchandise inventory five times each year, or about once every 73 days. The average inventory turnover for all firms ranges between 5 and 10 depending on the industry. For example, supermarkets may have inventory turnover rates of 20 or higher, whereas inventory turnover rates for furniture stores are generally well below the national average. The quickest way to improve inventory turnover is to order merchandise in smaller quantities at more frequent intervals.

Like the three ratios described in this section, the calculations for other financial ratios, including return on owners' equity, earnings per share, working capital, and debt-to-equity, are based on the information contained in a firm's balance sheet, income statement, and statement of cash flows. For more detailed information on ratio analysis, you may want to read more on the topic in an accounting or finance textbook or use an internet search engine.

In this chapter we have discussed the importance of information and accounting information. In Chapter 6, we examine how information can help improve a firm's financial planning. We also examine why firms need financing, how they obtain it, and how they ensure that funds are used effectively in keeping with the organization's goals.

流动比率
current ratio a financial ratio computed by dividing current assets by current liabilities

存货周转率
inventory turnover a financial ratio calculated by dividing the cost of goods sold in one year by the average value of the inventory

✓ Concept Check

- What are the benefits of comparing a firm's current financial information with information for previous accounting periods, with industry averages, and with financial information for competitors?
- Explain the calculation procedures for and significance of each of the following:
  a. Net profit margin
  b. Current ratio
  c. Inventory turnover

Summary 小 结

5-1 Examine how information can reduce risk when making a decision.

Information produces knowledge and empowers managers and employees to make better decisions. Because of the volume of information they receive each day and their need to make decisions on a daily basis, businesspeople use information rules to shorten the time spent analyzing choices. Although many people use the terms *data* and *information* interchangeably, there is a difference. Data are numerical or verbal descriptions that usually result from some sort of measurement. Information is data presented in a form that is useful for a specific purpose. A database is a single collection of data and information stored in one place that can be used by people throughout an organization to make decisions. Management information experts now use the term knowledge management (KM) to describe a firm's procedures for generating, using, and sharing data and information. To aid the decision-making process, managers and employees can use a decision-support system (DSS), expert system, and business application software to make decisions and to report data and information.

5-2 Discuss management's information requirements.

A management information system (MIS) is a means of providing managers with the information they need to perform their jobs as effectively as possible. The purpose of an MIS (sometimes referred to as an information technology system or simply an IT system) is to distribute timely and useful information to the decision makers who need it. The specific types of information managers need depend on their area of management and level within the firm. The size and complexity of an MIS must be tailored to the information needs of the organization it serves.

5-3 Outline the five functions of an information system.

The five functions performed by an MIS system are collecting data, storing data, updating data, processing data into information, and presenting information. Data may be collected from internal sources and external sources. An MIS must be able to store data until they are needed and to update them regularly to ensure that the information presented to managers and employees is accurate, complete, and timely. Data processing is the MIS function that transforms stored data into a form useful for a specific purpose. Finally, the processed data (which now can be called information) must be presented in a form that is useful. Verbal information generally is presented in the form of a report. Numerical information is often displayed in graphs, charts, or tables.

5-4 Explain why accurate accounting information and audited financial statements are important.

Accounting is the process of systematically collecting, analyzing, and reporting financial information. It can be used to answer questions about what has happened in the past; it also can be used to help make decisions about the future. The purpose of an audit is to make sure that a firm's financial statements and accounting information have been prepared in accordance with generally accepted accounting principles (GAAPs). To help ensure that corporate financial information is accurate and in response to accounting scandals, the Sarbanes-Oxley Act was signed into law. Although many people think all accountants do the same thing, typical areas of expertise include managerial, financial, cost, tax, government, and not-for-profit. A private accountant is employed by a private firm. A public accountant performs accounting work for various individuals or firms on a fee basis. Most accounting firms include on their staffs at least one CPA.

5-5 Interpret a balance sheet.

A balance sheet (sometimes referred to as a statement of financial position) is a summary of a firm's assets, liabilities, and owners' equity accounts at the end of an accounting period. This statement must demonstrate that the accounting equation is in balance. On the balance sheet, assets are categorized as current, fixed, or intangible. Liabilities can also be classified as current liabilities and long-term liabilities. For a sole proprietorship or partnership, owners' equity is shown as the difference between assets and liabilities. For corporations, the owners' equity is the total value of stock when issued plus retained earnings that have accumulated to date.

5-6 Interpret an income statement.

An income statement is a summary of a firm's revenues and expenses during the specified accounting period. On the income statement, the company's gross profit is computed by subtracting the cost of goods sold from net sales. Operating expenses and interest expenses then are deducted to compute net income before taxes. Finally, income taxes are deducted to obtain the firm's net income after taxes.

5-7 Describe business activities that affect a firm's cash flow.

Both the Securities and Exchange Commission (SEC) and the Financial Accounting Standards Board (FASB) require all publicly traded companies to include a statement of cash flows in their annual reports. This statement illustrates how the company's operating, investing, and financing activities affect cash during an accounting period. The information in this statement helps employees, investors, and other interested people to evaluate the financial health of a business.

5-8 Summarize how managers evaluate the financial health of a business.

The firm's financial statements and its accounting information become more meaningful when compared with the company's corresponding information for competitors, for the industry in which the firm operates, and the firm's own information from previous accounting periods. Such comparisons permit managers, employees, lenders, investors, and other interested people to pick out trends in growth, borrowing, income, and other business variables and to determine whether the firm is on the way to accomplishing its long-term goals. A number of financial ratios can be computed from the information in a firm's financial statements. These ratios provide a picture of a firm's profitability, its ability to pay its debts, and how often it sells its inventory. Like the information on the firm's financial statements, these ratios can and should be compared with corresponding information for previous years, for competitors, and for the industry in which the firm operates.

Key Terms 关键术语

You should now be able to define and give an example relevant to each of the following terms:

data
information
database
knowledge management (KM)
decision-support system (DSS)
expert system
management information system (MIS)
data processing
statistic
accounting
audit
generally accepted accounting principles (GAAPs)
managerial accounting
financial accounting
certified public accountant (CPA)
assets
liabilities
owners' equity
accounting equation
double-entry bookkeeping system
annual report
balance sheet (or statement of financial position)
liquidity
current assets
fixed assets
depreciation
intangible assets
current liabilities
long-term liabilities
retained earnings
income statement
revenues
gross sales
net sales
cost of goods sold
gross profit
operating expenses
net income
net loss
statement of cash flows
financial ratio
net profit margin (or return on sales)
current ratio
inventory turnover

Discussion Questions 讨论题

1. Do managers really need all the kinds of information discussed in this chapter? If not, which kinds can they do without?
2. How can confidential data and information (such as the wages of individual employees) be kept confidential and yet still be available to managers who need them?
3. Bankers usually insist that prospective business borrowers submit audited financial statements along with a loan application. Why should financial statements be audited by a CPA?
4. Do the balance sheet, income statement, and statement of cash flows contain all the information you might want as a potential lender or investor? What other information would you like to examine?
5. Of the three financial ratios discussed in this chapter, which do you think is the most important financial ratio? Why?

Case 5 案例5：拉里·埃里森和甲骨文公司计划如何赢得云计算战争

How Larry Ellison and Oracle Plan to Win the Cloud Wars

Larry Ellison is an American businessperson and is one of the wealthiest people in the world. He is chairperson, chief technology officer, and co-founder of Oracle, an integrated cloud applications and platform services company based in Austin, Texas. The company sells cloud-based tools to store and analyze data and information as well as software, hardware, and other technology applications. The company was founded in 1977 after Ellison discovered there was a growing need for database management systems. Just two years later, the company introduced its own database management system, finally answering the question of how technology could help companies manage large amounts of data and information.

Oracle has always had a reputation for introducing new products before competitors. It developed the first client-server database, the first media server to support video on demand, and the first internet development suite, among others. The company's goal has always been to help its business customers collect, store, update, process, and present data—the five management information system functions described in this chapter. Now, according to Ellison, Oracle's databases manage most of the world's data with more than 430,000 customers in 175 countries. "We are the dominant database supplier on the planet Earth," Ellison said on a recent earning's call. He went on to say, "we're bigger than IBM and Microsoft combined" when it comes to total database revenues.

Oracle competes with companies such as technology giants IBM, Microsoft, and Amazon Web Service (AWS), which offer similar cloud databases and other cloud-based services. Though Oracle admittedly took longer than its competitors to take its database to the cloud, Ellison believes its systems are now more secure and more affordable than other available systems. In fact, Ellison plans to win the cloud wars by competing on price, quality, and security.

Lower pricing for Oracle's products that are recognized for quality helps Oracle win new customers. According to Oracle, its cloud infrastructure, for example, is consistently less expensive than Amazon Web Services. The method used to price some products also helps Oracle win new customers. Customers who use Oracle's FastConnect infrastructure, which transfers information from customer data centers to the cloud through private connections, pay fixed monthly charges. The fixed charge means that their customers have a predictable monthly bill compared to AWS customers who are billed based on data transfer activity.

To keep a leg up on the competition, Oracle invests heavily in research and development (R&D), which generates world-class technologies. The company has spent $56 billion on R&D since 2012 and an additional $80 billion on acquisitions of companies that had promising ideas or products that fit with Oracle's product mix. Its R&D activities are constantly finding ways to introduce new or improve existing products that can satisfy customer needs. For instance, Oracle created the world's first autonomous database. The product, Oracle Autonomous Linux, serves to reduce maintenance and downtime and at the same time increase security. Before Oracle's new product was introduced, companies that attempted to take their large workloads to the cloud experienced high costs and security concerns. When Oracle Autonomous Linux was introduced, the company had thousands of customers waiting in the wings for the product to be deployed in addition to thousands more who signed up for product demonstrations.

The company has also made significant investments in security all the way down to the chip level to reduce concerns of advanced and persistent threats that use sophisticated hacking techniques to steal data. Its products have layered security defenses and controls such as security zones, data encryption, and firewalls. This security-first approach builds trust among Oracle customers. One of the major selling points of its autonomous database is that it eliminates human error while improving cybersecurity.

A culture of innovation has fueled Oracle since day one. Ellison is competitive by nature and will do what it takes to build the best cloud management system and technology products possible. Introducing new and innovative products that are recognized for their quality, pricing its products competitively, and taking a security-first approach make Oracle a leader in cloud computing.[6]

Discussion Questions

1. While Oracle is a recognized giant in the technology world, it competes with other successful companies including IBM, Microsoft, and Amazon Web Services. Describe the three factors that Larry Ellison plans to use to win the technology wars.
2. Although Oracle is successful, it continues to invest in research and development and acquire other companies that have promising ideas or products that complement Oracle's product mix. Explain why you think continued research and development and acquisitions are important for Oracle's future growth.
3. How important is protection from hackers and computer security for a technology company like Oracle? What steps is Oracle taking to protect information stored in its cloud-based database and technology products?

Building Skills for Career Success 为成功的职业生涯培养技能

1. Social Media Exercise

All of the Big Four accounting firms are active on Twitter, as well as posting messages, content, and photos on Facebook, listing job openings on LinkedIn, and posting videos on YouTube. The idea is to connect with potential job candidates, interact with clients and potential clients, engage employees, showcase the firm's expertise, and polish their reputations.

Assignment

1. Choose one of the Big Four accounting firms (Deloitte, PricewaterhouseCoopers, Ernst & Young, or KPMG) and take a look at the information it posts on Twitter, Facebook, LinkedIn, or YouTube.
2. How does the accounting firm you chose use social media? Are they trying to reach potential job candidates, existing clients and potential clients, or employees?
3. Do you think that social media is an effective way for an accounting firm to reach its target audience?

2. Building Team Skills

This has been a bad year for Park Avenue Furniture. The firm increased sales revenues to $1,400,000, but total expenses ballooned to $1,750,000. Although management realized that some of the firm's expenses were out of control, including cost of goods sold ($700,000), salaries ($450,000), and advertising costs ($140,000), it could not contain expenses. As a result, the furniture retailer lost $350,000. To make matters worse, the retailer applied for a $350,000 loan at Fidelity International Bank and was turned down. The bank officer, Mike Nettles, said the firm had a net loss for the last 12 months and that the firm already had too much debt. At that time, liabilities totaled $420,000 and owners' equity was $600,000.

Assignment

1. In groups of three or four, analyze the financial condition of Park Avenue Furniture.
2. Discuss why you think the bank officer turned down Park Avenue's loan request.
3. Prepare a detailed plan of action to improve the financial health of Park Avenue Furniture over the next 12 months.

3. Researching Different Careers

To improve productivity, employers expect employees to use computers and computer software. Typical business applications include email, word processing, accounting, graphics, spreadsheets, and other business application software programs. By improving your skills in these areas, you can increase your chances not only of being employed but also of being promoted once you are employed.

Assignment

1. Assess your computer skills by placing a check in the appropriate column in the following table:

	Skill Level			
Software	**None**	**Low**	**Average**	**High**
Email				
Word processing				
Desktop publishing				
Accounting				
Database management				
Graphics				
Spreadsheet				
Internet research				

2. Describe your self-assessment in a written report. Specify the skills in which you need to become more proficient, and outline a plan for improvement.

Chapter 6

Mastering Financial Management
掌握财务管理

Learning Objectives

Once you complete this chapter, you will be able to:

6-1 Explain why financial management is important in today's competitive economy.

6-2 Identify a firm's short- and long-term financial needs.

6-3 Summarize the process of planning for financial management.

6-4 Identify the services provided by banks and financial institutions for their business customers.

6-5 Describe the advantages and disadvantages of different methods of short-term debt financing.

6-6 Evaluate the advantages and disadvantages of equity financing.

6-7 Evaluate the advantages and disadvantages of long-term debt financing.

Why Should You Care?

The old saying goes, "Money makes the world go around." For business firms, this is true. It's hard to operate a business without money. In this chapter, we discuss how financial management is used to obtain money and ensure that it is used effectively.

Inside Business 商业透视：疫情期间西南航空公司的财务管理

Southwest Navigates Financial Management During Pandemic

Southwest Airlines, the world's largest low-cost airline, carries more than 130 million passengers each year, earning more than $2.3 billion in income. *Until the COVID-19 pandemic, that is.* The pandemic, which was responsible for travel restrictions, flight cancellations, and limited seating capacity, left the company with a $3.5 billion annual loss in 2020, its first annual loss since 1972. While many airlines tried to minimize short-term losses during the pandemic, Southwest was able to focus on expanding its long-term competitive advantage because of aggressive financial management and its healthy balance sheet. These same factors enabled the air carrier to continue to operate during the pandemic and manage the economic problems caused by the downturn in air travel.

At one point during the pandemic, Southwest was able to fill only 8 percent of available seats with paying customers. Eventually the number of ticket sales began to increase, but recovery for most airlines was slow because of travel restrictions, and travelers were afraid to leave their homes and travel for business or pleasure. However, Southwest experienced a quicker recovery than many of its competitors. Unlike other major airlines that reduced flight schedules and eliminated less popular travel destinations, Southwest kept providing service to established destinations and was able to accommodate the customers that needed to travel in the initial stages of recovery. In fact, Southwest even launched service to six new destinations in 2020 with plans to begin service to at least eight more the following year. To further encourage passengers to choose Southwest, it left middle seats open for the majority of 2020 to allow for greater social distancing in addition to implementing other health and safety protocols.

Southwest's management team also had to consider the effect of the pandemic on employees and developed a plan with different options for employees who didn't feel that it was safe to work during the pandemic. In addition to implementing other health and safety protocols described above, Southwest offered its workforce a variety of voluntary severance packages rather than laying off or furloughing employees. Options included early retirement or extended leave of up to 18 months at half of their base pay. About 27 percent of Southwest's employees took one of these options. Though it cost the company $1.7 billion, these options helped increase employee loyalty and at the same time let employees know it was concerned about both their customers *and* their employees.

No one can argue that the travel and tourism industries were greatly impacted by the global pandemic. The financial management decisions that Southwest's executives made during the pandemic were "make or break" decisions and cost millions of dollars. And yet, these decisions enabled the airline to not only survive the pandemic but even build for the future.[1]

Did you know?

Southwest flies to 101 destinations across the United States and 10 additional countries.

A company like Southwest Airlines can't survive without money! Even though Southwest lost $3.5 billion during the COVID-19 pandemic, its financial management team was able to guide the company to recovery. Financial managers were also able to fund expansion and provide service to new destinations because Southwest had built a strong balance sheet and substantial cash reserves just in case of a downturn in air travel for any reason, including a pandemic.

Without money, employees don't get paychecks, creditors and lenders can't be paid, and the business may close its doors and cease to exist. On the other hand, when a company—like Southwest Airlines, Facebook, Citibank, or a small neighborhood business—manages its finances it can not only pay its bills and employees, but can also meet the needs of its customers and society and even grow and expand.

In this chapter we examine why financial management is important. Then, we discuss how firms find the financing required to start a business and keep it going and then how they manage that money effectively. We also look at how firms develop financial plans and evaluate financial performance. Finally, we examine typical banking services and compare various methods of obtaining short- and long-term financing.

为什么要进行财务管理

6-1 Why Financial Management?

Learning Objective

6-1 Explain why financial management is important in today's competitive economy.

Many businesses realized how planning coupled with effective financial management could increase their ability to meet the needs of customers, increase sales, and keep the doors open during the COVID-19 pandemic. For example, financial managers for each of the firms listed below had to compare the cost of each action with the potential increase in sales revenue before making a recommendation to implement the following changes:

- Red Roof Hotels offered special rates for rooms to provide a quiet, private space for workers who couldn't work at the office or home.
- Best Buy increased its focus on virtual support, technology repair, and promoted its e-commerce site as a way for customers to purchase computers and electronic gear without leaving their home.
- Kroger turned some locations into fulfillment centers designed to speed delivery of merchandise to an increasing number of customers who ordered online.
- Walgreens began offering delivery of personal care products and food items to customers.[2]

While the goals of each of these companies were to meet the needs of customers and increase sales, each action required executives and managers to make important financial decisions to turn the ideas into a reality.

Managers and employees must find the money needed to keep a business operating and fund all the goals and objectives that a successful business wants to achieve. A business that cannot pay its bills may have to close its doors and even be forced to file for bankruptcy protection. As shown in Figure 6-1, the number of business firms filing for bankruptcy varies from one year to the next. However, financial experts agree that the number of business bankruptcies increases or decreases depending on the stage of the business cycle the nation's economy may be in at a specific time. A nation's business cycle was compared to a roller coaster ride with periods of prosperity or high points and troughs or low points. A pandemic, political unrest, world economic problems, terrorist threats and wars, interest rates, and other factors can also lead to an increase

Figure 6-1 Business Bankruptcies in the United States

The nation's economy and other factors can affect the number of businesses that file for bankruptcy. (Note: At the time of publication, 2020 was the most recent year for which complete statistics were available.)

Source: Based on the American Bankruptcy Institute website.

Poor financial management can lead to bankruptcy. While business owners don't plan to fail, sometimes poor financial management, low sales revenues, poor location, uncontrolled expenses, and a lot of other factors including the nation's economy can cause a business to fail. In thousands of cases each year, bankruptcy may be the only solution for a business that cannot pay its creditors.

in business bankruptcies. Despite the COVID-19 pandemic, the number of businesses filing for bankruptcy in 2020 actually decreased when compared to the number of bankruptcy cases for the previous four years.

财务管理的必要性
6-1a The Need for Financial Management

Financial management consists of all the activities concerned with obtaining money and using it effectively. To some extent, financial management can be viewed as a two-sided problem. On one side, the uses of funds often dictate the type or types of financing needed by a business. On the other side, the activities a business can undertake are determined by the types of financing available. Financial managers must ensure that funds are available when needed both now and in the future, that they are obtained at the lowest possible cost, and that they are used as efficiently as possible. In addition, proper financial management must also ensure that:

- Financing priorities are established in line with organizational goals and objectives;
- Spending is planned and controlled;
- A firm's credit customers pay their bills on time, and the number of past due accounts is reduced;
- Bills are paid promptly to protect the firm's credit rating and its ability to borrow money;
- The funds required for paying the firm's taxes are available when needed to meet tax deadlines; and
- Excess cash is invested in certificates of deposit (CDs), government securities, or conservative, marketable securities.

To encourage more responsible financial management, political leaders, the Securities and Exchange Commission (SEC), self-regulatory organizations like the Financial Industry Regulatory Authority (FINRA), and companies in the banking and financial industry often enact regulations and create guidelines that encourage legal and ethical behavior. Many security laws date back to the 1930s and were enacted to curb the abuses and practices that led to the Great Depression in 1929. Through the years more laws have been passed to strengthen regulation of the banking and finance industry. One of the more important laws enacted is the Dodd-Frank Wall Street Reform and Consumer Protection Act, which was designed to create a sound economic foundation that would encourage job growth, rein in Wall Street and prohibit some speculative techniques, end financial bailouts, and prevent future financial crises. The Dodd-Frank Act also provided new regulations to protect American families from unfair and abusive financial and banking practices.

Even with the new regulations, some experts and politicians still argue current laws do not go far enough and there is a need for additional regulations and increased government oversight. For business firms, the impact of new laws could increase the time and cost of obtaining both short- and long-term financing.

财务管理
financial management all the activities concerned with obtaining money and using it effectively

Ethics and Social Responsibility

商业伦理与社会责任：高盛因海外贿赂被罚款数十亿美元

Goldman Sachs Fined Billions for Foreign Bribery

Goldman Sachs Group Inc., a leader in global investment banking, securities, and investment management, and its Malaysian subsidiary admitted to conspiring to violate the anti-bribery provisions of the Foreign Corrupt Practices Act (FCPA). It was discovered that over a period of five years the company engaged in bribery by offering financial incentives to influence high-level government officials. Goldman Sachs agreed to pay more than $2.9 billion in U.S. fines as well an additional $3.9 billion to settle with the Malaysian government.

Goldman Sachs engaged in a scheme to pay more than $1 billion in bribes to government officials in Malaysia in exchange for approval to sell bonds to raise $6.5 billion that had been earmarked to help the people of Malaysia. Government approval enabled Goldman Sachs to earn profits for selling the bonds, but most of the money from the sale of the bonds benefited the country's leaders and their associates.

Several current and former top executives were implicated in the scandal. These individuals were required to return more than $174 million in pay and bonuses from prior years. Repayments like this are often referred to as a clawback. Tim Leissner, Goldman Sachs' former Southeast Asia chairman, pleaded guilty to conspiracy to violate the FCPA and conspiracy to commit money laundering. Ng Chong Hwa (also known as Roger Ng), former head of investment banking for Goldman Sachs Malaysia, was also charged with conspiracy to violate the FCPA and conspiracy to commit money laundering. Ng was extradited from Malaysia to face trial in the United States.

The scandal negatively impacted not only Goldman Sachs' reputation but also the reputation of other American financial institutions operating abroad. Experts also point out that this type of unethical behavior, which involves high-level executives, suggests a culture problem exists and undermines public confidence in American business in the United States and abroad.

Sources: Based on information in United States Department of Justice, "Goldman Sachs Resolves Foreign Bribery Case And Agrees To Pay Over $2.9 Billion," October 22, 2020; "Goldman to Pay Nearly $3 Billion Fine Following Foreign Bribes Probe," *CBS News*, October 23, 2020; Matthew Goldstein and Emily Flitter, "Goldman Sachs Malaysia Arm Pleads Guilty in 1MDB Fraud," *The New York Times*, October 22, 2020.

金融职业

6-1b Careers in Finance

A career in finance can be rewarding. As an added bonus, the Bureau of Labor Statistics projects there will be a 15 percent increase in the number of jobs in the financial sector of the economy between now and 2029.[3] People in finance must have certain traits and skills. One of the most important priorities for someone interested in a finance career is honesty. Be warned: Investors, lenders, government regulators, and other corporate executives expect financial managers to be above reproach. In addition to honesty, managers and employees in the finance area must:

1. Have a strong background in finance, accounting, or mathematics.
2. Know how to use a computer to analyze data.
3. Be an expert at both written and oral communication.

Today, there are many different types of positions in finance. Typical job titles include chief financial officer, vice president of finance, bank officer, consumer credit officer, financial analyst, financial

Careers in the financial services industry are on the rise! Between now and 2029, jobs in finance are expected to increase 15 percent—that's much faster than the average growth for other industries. As an added bonus, employees enjoy higher salaries and increased benefits when compared to careers in other industries. You can find more information for this career and other options by exploring the information available in the Occupational Outlook Handbook.

planner, loan officer, insurance analyst, and investment account executive. Depending on qualifications, work experience, and education, salaries generally are higher in the financial industry when compared with careers in other industries. Many employees also have excellent benefits and other perks that make a career in financial management attractive.

✓ Concept Check

- For a business firm, what type of activities does financial management involve?
- To be successful, what traits and skills does an employee in the finance industry need?

融资需求

6-2 The Need for Financing

Learning Objective

6-2 Identify a firm's short- and long-term financial needs.

Money is needed both to start a business and to keep it going. The original investment of the owners, along with money they may have borrowed, should be enough to open the doors. After that, ideally sales revenues should be used to pay the firm's expenses and provide a profit as well.

This is exactly what happens in a successful firm—over the long run. However, income and expenses may vary from month to month or from year to year. Short-term financing may be needed when sales are low and expenses are high. For example, many businesses experienced lower sales during the COVID-19 pandemic, but still had expenses and bills that had to be paid. On the other hand, long-term financing may be needed to open new retail locations, to purchase equipment, or to build a new plant. For example, management at Cincinnati-based Graeter's Ice Cream—the company profiled in the end-of-part cases for this text—recognized they needed long-term financing to build a new plant and buy out an existing franchisee. To see how management financed both opportunities, read the case in the "Running a Business" section.

短期融资

6-2a Short-Term Financing

Short-term financing is money that will be used for one year or less. As illustrated in Table 6-1, there are many short-term financing needs, but three deserve special attention. First, certain business practices may affect a firm's cash flow and create a need for short-term financing. **Cash flow** is the movement of money into and out of an organization. The goal is to have sufficient money coming into the firm in any period to cover the firm's expenses during that period. This goal, however, is not always achieved. For example, California-based Callaway Golf offers credit to retailers that carry the firm's golf clubs, balls, clothing, and golf accessories. Credit purchases made by Callaway's retailers generally are not paid until 30 to 60 days (or more) after the transaction. Callaway therefore may need short-term financing to solve its cash flow problem and to pay its bills until its customers have paid theirs.

A second need for short-term financing is speculative production. **Speculative production** refers to the production of goods which is followed by a time lag before the actual sale of those goods. Consider what happens when a firm such as Connecticut-based Stanley Black & Decker begins to manufacture power and small hand tools for sale during the Christmas season. Manufacturing begins in March, April, and May, and the firm negotiates short-term financing to buy materials and

Table 6-1 Comparison of Short- and Long-Term Financing

Whether a business seeks short- or long-term financing depends on what the money will be used for.

Short-Term Financing Needs	Long-Term Financing Needs
Cash-flow problems	Business start-up costs
Speculative production	Mergers and acquisitions
Current inventory needs	New product development
Monthly expenses	Long-term marketing activities
Short-term promotional needs	Replacement of equipment
Unexpected emergencies	Expansion of facilities

短期融资
short-term financing money that will be used for one year or less

现金流
cash flow the movement of money into and out of an organization

投机性生产
speculative production the production of goods which is followed by a time lag before the actual sale of those goods

Figure 6-2 Cash Flow for a Manufacturing Business

Manufacturers such as Stanley Black & Decker often use short-term financing to pay expenses during the production process. Once goods are shipped to retailers and wholesalers and payment is received, sales revenues are used to repay short-term financing.

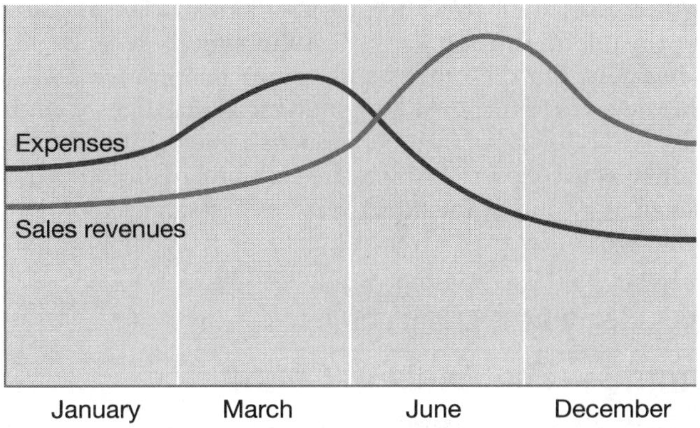

supplies, to pay wages and rent, and to cover inventory costs until its products eventually are sold to wholesalers and retailers later in the year. Take a look at Figure 6-2. Although Stanley Black & Decker manufactures and sells finished products all during the year, expenses peak during the first part of the year. During this same period, sales revenues are low. Once the firm's finished products are shipped to retailers and wholesalers and payment is received (usually within 30 to 60 days), sales revenues are used to repay short-term financing.

A third need for short-term financing is to increase inventory. Retailers that range in size from Walmart to the neighborhood drugstore need short-term financing to build up their inventories before peak selling periods. For example, Dallas-based Bruce Miller Nurseries must increase the number of shrubs, trees, and flowering plants that it makes available for sale during the spring and summer growing seasons. To enable Bruce Miller to obtain the merchandise inventory it needs, growers and wholesalers extend the repayment period. Then once the merchandise is sold, Bruce Miller repays the growers and wholesalers.

长期融资

6-2b Long-Term Financing

Long-term financing is money that will be used for longer than one year. Long-term financing obviously is needed to start a new business. As Table 6-1 shows, it is also needed for business mergers and acquisitions, new product development, long-term marketing activities, replacement of equipment that has become obsolete, and expansion of facilities.

长期融资
long-term financing money that will be used for longer than one year

The amounts of long-term financing needed by large firms can seem almost unreal. Intel—a leader in the technology industry with a long history of investing in research and development—spent over $13.5 billion in 2020 to develop new technology that is used to produce state-of-the art electronic devices.[4]

风险回报比率

6-2c The Risk–Return Ratio

According to financial experts, business firms will find it more difficult to raise both short- and long-term financing in the future for two reasons. First, financial reform and increased government regulations will lengthen the process required to obtain financing. Second, both investors and lenders are more cautious about who receives financing. As a result of these two factors, financial managers must develop a strong financial plan that describes how the money will be used and how it will be repaid. When developing a financial plan for a business, a financial manager must also consider the risk–return ratio when making decisions that affect the firm's finances. The **risk–return ratio** is based on the principle that a high-risk decision should generate higher financial returns for a business. On the other hand, more conservative decisions (with less risk) often generate lesser returns. Although financial managers want higher returns, they often must strive for a balance between risk and return. For example, Ohio-based American Electric Power is investing billions of dollars to fund research into renewable energy sources including wind and solar technology. Yet, financial managers (along with other executives and managers throughout the organization) must evaluate the potential return before committing to such a costly project.

✓ Concept Check

- How does short-term financing differ from long-term financing? Give two business uses for each type of financing.
- What is speculative production? How is it related to a firm's cash-flow problems?
- As an employee in the finance department of a large company, how would you explain the risk–return ratio to an investor?

计划——健全财务管理的基础

6-3 Planning—The Basis of Sound Financial Management

Learning Objective

6-3 Summarize the process of planning for financial management.

We defined a *plan* as an outline of the actions by which an organization intends to accomplish its goals and objectives. A **financial plan**, then, is a plan for obtaining and using the money needed to implement an organization's goals and objectives.

制订财务计划

6-3a Developing the Financial Plan

Financial planning (like all planning) begins with establishing a set of valid goals and objectives. Financial managers must then determine how much money is needed to accomplish each goal and objective. Finally, financial managers must identify available sources of financing and decide which to use. The three steps involved in financial planning are illustrated in Figure 6-3.

Figure 6-3 The Three Steps of Financial Planning

After a financial plan has been developed, it must be monitored continually to ensure that it actually fulfills the firm's goals and objectives.

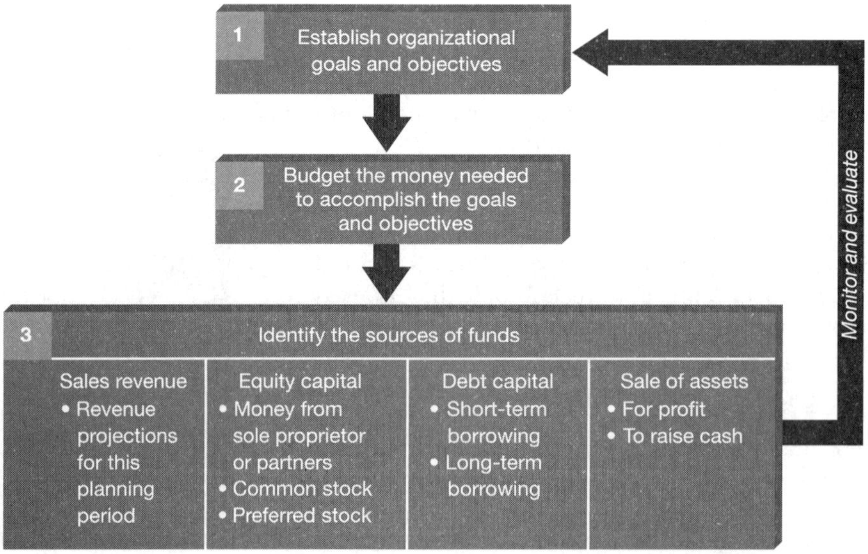

风险回报比率

risk–return ratio a ratio based on the principle that a high-risk decision should generate higher financial returns for a business and more conservative decisions often generate lower returns

财务计划

financial plan a plan for obtaining and using the money needed to implement an organization's goals and objectives

Establishing Organizational Goals and Objectives As we know, a *goal* is an end result that an organization expects to achieve over a one- to ten-year period. An *objective* was defined as a specific statement detailing what an organization intends to accomplish over a shorter period of time. If goals and objectives are not specific and measurable, they cannot be translated into dollar costs, and financial planning cannot proceed. For large corporations, both goals and objectives can be expensive. For example, have you ever wondered how much McDonald's spends on advertising? Well, to reach almost 70 million customers that it serves each day, the world's most famous fast-food restaurant chain spends over $600 million each year.[5]

Do you have a budget? After establishing goals and objectives, a successful business takes the next step and constructs a budget to project revenues, expenses, or both for a specified period of time. You, just like a business, can do the same thing and build a budget to help you manage your personal finances and achieve your short- and long-term goals.

Budgeting for Financial Needs Once planners know what the firm's goals and objectives are for a specific period—say, the next calendar year—they can construct a budget that projects the costs the firm will incur and the sales revenues it will receive. Specifically, a **budget** is a financial statement that projects income, expenditures, or both over a specified future period.

Usually, the budgeting process begins with the construction of departmental budgets for sales and various types of expenses. Financial managers can easily combine each department's budget for sales and expenses into a company-wide cash budget. A **cash budget** estimates cash receipts and cash expenditures over a specified period. Notice in the cash budget for Stars and Stripes Clothing, shown in Figure 6-4, cash sales and collections are listed at the top for each calendar quarter. Payments for purchases and routine expenses are listed in the middle section. Using this information, it is possible to calculate the anticipated cash gain or loss at the end of each quarter for this retail clothing store.

Most firms today use one of two approaches to budgeting. In the *traditional* approach, each new budget is based on the dollar amounts contained in the budget for the preceding year. These amounts are modified to reflect any revised goals,

预算
budget a financial statement that projects income, expenditures, or both over a specified future period

现金预算
cash budget a financial statement that estimates cash receipts and cash expenditures over a specified period

Figure 6-4 Cash Budget for Stars and Stripes Clothing

A company-wide cash budget projects cash sales, collections, purchases, and expenses over a specified period to anticipate cash gains and losses.

STARS AND STRIPES CLOTHING
Cash Budget — From January 1, 20xx to December 31, 20xx

	First Quarter ($)	Second Quarter ($)	Third Quarter ($)	Fourth Quarter ($)	Total ($)
Cash sales and collections	150,000	160,000	150,000	185,000	645,000
Less payments					
Purchases	110,000	80,000	90,000	60,000	340,000
Wages/salaries	25,000	20,000	25,000	30,000	100,000
Rent	10,000	10,000	12,000	12,000	44,000
Other expenses	4,000	4,000	5,000	6,000	19,000
Taxes	8,000	8,000	10,000	10,000	36,000
Total payments	157,000	122,000	142,000	118,000	539,000
Cash gain or (loss)	(7,000)	38,000	8,000	67,000	106,000

and managers are required to justify only new expenditures. The problem with this approach is that it leaves room for padding budget items to protect the (sometimes selfish) interests of managers or their department. This problem is essentially eliminated through zero-base budgeting. **Zero-base budgeting** is a budgeting approach in which every expense in every budget must be justified.

To develop a plan for long-term financing needs, managers often construct a capital budget. A **capital budget** estimates a firm's expenditures for major assets, including new product development, expansion of facilities, replacement of obsolete equipment, and mergers and acquisitions. For example, Uber—a company known for providing consumers with ride services and food delivery—acquired Postmates—a food delivery competitor. Uber constructed a capital budget to determine if it should pay cash or offer stock to pay for the smaller company. Uber chose to use the stock option and no cash outlay was required.[6]

零基预算
zero-base budgeting a budgeting approach in which every expense in every budget must be justified

资本预算
capital budget a financial statement that estimates a firm's expenditures for major assets and its long-term financing needs

Identifying Sources of Funds The four primary sources of funds, listed in Figure 6-3, are sales revenue, equity capital, debt capital, and proceeds from the sale of assets. Future sales revenue generally provides the greatest part of a firm's financing. Figure 6-4 shows that for Stars and Stripes Clothing, sales for the year are expected to cover all expenses and to provide a cash gain of $106,000. However, Stars and Stripes has a problem in the first quarter, when sales are expected to fall short of expenses by $7,000. In fact, one of the primary reasons for financial planning is to provide management with adequate lead time to solve this type of cash-flow problem.

Exploring Careers

职 业 探 索 ：如何成为首席财务官

How to Become a CFO

A chief financial officer (CFO) is a senior-level executive that manages a company's finances. As the overseer of the finance and accounting divisions, the CFO is responsible for planning how to finance the firm's activities, borrowing money when needed, managing cash flow, ensuring financial statements and tax returns are accurate, and even paying bills to protect the firm's credit rating. In addition to making important financial decisions, a CFO must help other high-level managers make decisions that could often make or break the business.

There is not just one route to becoming a CFO. Previous job titles often include senior financial controller, director of finance, or treasurer. To be successful, CFOs must have a working knowledge of accounting, financial analysis, risk management, regulatory compliance, investments, and budgeting. A broad understanding of business management, operations management, and retailing is also helpful.

For many CFOs, preparation begins with college courses in accounting or finance that eventually lead to a bachelor's or master's degree in business administration, accounting, or finance. A working knowledge of computers, software, and technology can also help process the data and information a CFO needs to make important decisions. In addition to these skills, the ability to communicate and work with people and to use critical thinking skills to solve problems are valuable skills for a CFO executive.

Following the CFO career path can be both rewarding and challenging. The average base salary for a CFO is more than $136,000, but salaries can be much higher in large corporations. Executives at this level also have excellent benefits and retirement packages. While this is a highly-paid position, it also comes with great responsibility. This important role is reserved for professionals with established track records, broad business experience, and a deep understanding of finance.

Sources: Based on information in "How to Become a CFO – 7 Steps to Guide Your Career Path," *Robert Half*, March 2020; Mitchell Grant, "Chief Financial Officer (CFO)," *Investopedia*, February 28, 2021; "Average Chief Financial Officer (CFO) Salary," *PayScale*, March 18, 2021.

A second type of funding is **equity capital**. For a sole proprietorship or partnership, equity capital is provided by the owner or owners of the business. For a corporation, equity capital is money obtained from the sale of shares of ownership in the business. Equity capital is used almost exclusively for long-term financing.

A third type of funding is **debt capital**, which is borrowed money. Debt capital may be borrowed for either short- or long-term use—and a short-term loan seems made to order for Stars and Stripes Clothing's shortfall problem. The firm probably would borrow the needed $7,000 (or perhaps a bit more) at some point during the first quarter and repay it from second-quarter sales revenue.

Proceeds from the sale of assets are the fourth type of funding. Selling assets is often a drastic step. However, it may be a reasonable last resort when sales revenues are declining, and equity capital or debt capital cannot be found. Assets also may be sold to increase a firm's cash balance or when they are no longer needed or do not "fit" with the company's core business. Berkshire Hathaway sold its newspaper holdings to Lee Enterprises for $140 million. Berkshire Hathaway—a corporate giant—can use the proceeds of the sale to acquire other companies with more potential.[7]

监督和评估财务绩效
6-3b Monitoring and Evaluating Financial Performance

It is important to ensure that financial plans are implemented properly and to catch potential problems before they become major ones. Despite efforts to raise additional financing, reduce expenses, and increase sales to become profitable, retailer JCPenney filed for bankruptcy in 2020 and closed over 150 stores or about 15 percent of its retail locations.[8] To prevent such problems, financial managers should establish a means of monitoring financial performance. Interim budgets (weekly, monthly, or quarterly) may be prepared for comparison purposes. These comparisons highlight areas that require additional or revised planning—or at least areas calling for a more careful investigation. Budget comparisons can also be used to improve the firm's future budgets.

✓ Concept Check

- What is the function of a cash budget? A capital budget?
- What is the difference between equity capital and debt capital?
- Describe the four sources of funds for a business.
- How does a financial manager monitor and evaluate a firm's financing?

银行和其他金融机构提供的金融服务
6-4 Financial Services Provided by Banks and Other Financial Institutions

Learning Objective

6-4 Identify the services provided by banks and financial institutions for their business customers.

For a business owner, it helps to know your banker. Banking services can be divided into three broad categories: traditional services, electronic banking services, and international services.

为商业客户提供的传统银行服务
6-4a Traditional Banking Services for Business Clients

Traditional services provided by banks and other financial institutions include savings and checking accounts, loans, processing credit card and debit card transactions, and providing professional advice.

Savings and Checking Accounts Savings accounts provide a safe place to store money a business doesn't immediately need. The usual *passbook savings account* earns between 0.05 and 0.25 percent in most financial institutions. A business with excess cash it is willing to leave on deposit with a bank for a set period of time can earn a higher rate of interest. To do so, the business firm buys a certificate of deposit. A **certificate of deposit (CD)** is a document stating that the bank will pay the depositor a guaranteed interest rate on money left on deposit for a specified period of time. At the time of publication, one-year CDs were paying between 0.25 and 1.10 percent. The rate can vary depending on the financial institution and the amount of time until maturity.

权益资本
equity capital money received from the owners or from the sale of shares of ownership in a business

债务资本
debt capital borrowed money obtained through loans of various types

存单
certificate of deposit (CD) a document stating that the bank will pay the depositor a guaranteed interest rate on money left on deposit for a specified period of time

For a business, a relationship with a banker can mean the difference between success and failure. Although JP Morgan Chase—often referred to as Chase—is the largest bank in the United States, it still must meet the needs of its customers. Like many competitors, Chase offers the services a business (or an individual) needs to manage their finances, including savings and checking accounts, short- and long-term loans, credit and debit card processing, and financial advice.

Business firms (and individuals) also deposit money in checking accounts so that they can write checks to pay for purchases. For businesses, monthly charges are based on the average daily balance in the checking account and/or the number of checks written.

Business Loans Banks, savings and loan associations, credit unions, and other financial institutions provide short- and long-term loans to businesses. *Short-term business loans* must be repaid within one year or less. To help ensure that short-term money will be available when needed, many firms establish a line of credit. A **line of credit** is a loan that is approved before the money is actually needed. Because all the necessary paperwork is already completed and the loan is preapproved, the business can obtain the money later without delay, as soon as it is required. Even with a line of credit, a firm may not be able to borrow money if the bank does not have sufficient funds available. For this reason, some firms prefer a **revolving credit agreement**, which is a guaranteed line of credit. Under this type of agreement, the bank guarantees that the money will be available when the borrower needs it. In return for the guarantee, the bank may charge a commitment fee. Typical commitment fees range from 0.25 to 1.0 percent of the *unused* portion of the revolving credit agreement. The usual interest rate is charged for the portion that *is* borrowed.

Long-term business loans are repaid over a period of years. The average length of a long-term business loan is generally 3 to 7 years but sometimes as long as 15 to 20 years. Loans to purchase real estate may even be as long as 30 years. Most lenders require some type of collateral for long-term loans. **Collateral** is real estate or property (e.g., stocks, bonds, equipment, or any other asset of value) pledged as security for a loan.

Repayment terms and interest rates for both short- and long-term loans are arranged between the lender and the borrower. For businesses, repayment terms may include monthly, quarterly, semiannual, or annual payments.

The Basics of Getting a Loan According to many financial experts, preparation is the key when applying for a business loan. To begin the process, you should get to know potential lenders before requesting a loan. Although there may be many potential lenders that can provide the money you need, the logical place to borrow money is where your business does its banking. Before applying for a loan, you may also want to check your firm's credit rating with a national credit bureau such as Dun & Bradstreet (sometimes referred to as D&B). Typically, business owners will be asked to fill out a loan application. In addition to the loan application, the lender will also want to see your current business plan. Be sure to explain how much funding you require to accomplish your goals and how the loan will be repaid. Most lenders insist that you submit current financial statements that have been prepared by an independent certified public accountant. Then compile a list of references that includes your suppliers, other lenders, or the professionals with whom you are associated. You may also be asked to discuss the loan request with a loan officer. Hopefully, your loan request will be approved. If not, try to determine why your loan request was rejected. Think back over the loan process and determine what you could do to improve your chances of getting a loan the next time you apply.

信用额度
line of credit a loan that is approved before the money is actually needed

循环信贷协议
revolving credit agreement a guaranteed line of credit

抵押品
collateral real estate or property pledged as security for a loan

Technology and Innovation

技术与创新：万事达卡推进其开放银行战略

Mastercard Advances Its Open Banking Strategy

Though Mastercard is often thought of as simply a credit card company, this multinational corporation is actually a technology company that specializes in financial services and global payment solutions. The company's consumer payment products include credit, debit, and prepaid cards. For businesses, Mastercard offers a variety of products and payment solutions such as secure payment systems that protect customers and merchants, co-branded cards, business-to-business (B2B) payment services, and more. It is also a leader in developing open banking.

The concept of open banking refers to sharing financial information electronically and securely with other businesses. To strengthen its open banking platform, Mastercard acquired Finicity for $825 million. Finicity is a company that has a history of helping consumers and organizations use financial data and technology to make better decisions. For Mastercard, the acquisition is another way to use a competitive edge over competitors like Visa, American Express, and Discover. At the same time, financial information gathered by Finicity will help connect consumers with companies—especially lenders—that need accurate, real time data to approve or reject credit applications. To illustrate how open banking can speed the loan approval process, consider the following example. A couple wants to buy a home, but they need financing. They apply for a loan from a lender like Rocket Mortgage. By accessing real-time data from Finicity, Rocket Mortgage obtains the financial data it needs to evaluate the couple's ability to repay the loan without having to go to multiple sources. Because of open banking, the time required to approve or reject a loan request can be reduced, which is an advantage for both the borrower and the lender.

Mastercard—the parent company of Finicity—believes that open banking platforms that use technology will become even more important as the financial industry continues to innovate and use technology to provide improved service to both consumers and merchants around the globe. Although open banking on a global scale can be challenging because every country has its own set of financial rules and regulations, Mastercard has already developed plans to expand its open banking solutions outside of the United States and Europe.

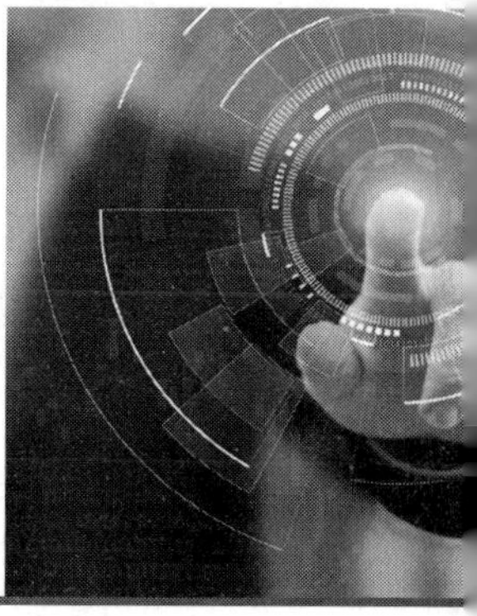

Sources: Based on information in Anna Hrushka, "Mastercard Deal Brings Finicity to Global Stage, CEO Says," *Banking Dive*, July 17, 2020; Mastercard, "Mastercard Extends Open Banking Efforts with Close of Finicity Acquisition," November 19, 2020; "DOJ Approves Mastercard's $825M Acquisition Of Finicity," *PYMNTS*, November 16, 2020.

借记卡交易、信用卡交易和移动支付

6-4b Debit and Credit Card Transactions and Mobile Pay

Today, customers have multiple ways to pay for merchandise and services. According to a recent Federal Reserve System survey that tracked payments made by more than 3,000 individuals over a three-day period, debit cards were used most often to pay for purchases followed by cash, credit cards, electronic payments, and checks—refer to Table 6-2.[9] Each of the payment options requires a business to set up procedures and work with banks and other financial institutions in order to process payments for merchandise and services. A **debit card** is a card that electronically subtracts the amount of the purchase from a customer's bank account at the moment the purchase is made. For example, when you use a debit card to pay for lunch at Olive Garden, the restaurant must use electronic equipment to process the debit card transaction before funds are deposited in the restaurant's account. Note: Don't confuse debit cards with credit cards. Although they may look alike, there are important differences. A debit card electronically subtracts the amount of a customer's purchase from a bank account at the moment the purchase is made. If you use a credit card to pay for your purchase, the credit card company extends short-term financing, and you do not make payment until you receive your next statement.

借记卡
debit card a card that electronically subtracts the amount of a purchase from a customer's bank account at the moment the purchase is made

Table 6-2 Consumer Payment Options

Although there are many ways to pay for merchandise and services, most people prefer using debit cards.

Payment Option	Percentage of People Who Prefer This Option
Debit cards	30 Percent
Cash	26 percent
Credit cards	24 percent
Electronic payments	11 percent
Checks	5 percent

Source: Laura Kim, Raynil Kumar, and Shaun O'Brien, "2020 Findings from the Diary of Consumer Payment Choice," Federal Reserve Bank of San Francisco.

Consumers also use credit cards to pay for everything from tickets on American Airlines to Zebco fishing gear. Recent statistics published by CardRates.com indicate that 61 percent of Americans have at least one credit card. And on average Americans have four cards. More importantly, 75 percent of consumers with credit cards carry an average balance of more than $6,200.[10] Still, merchants accept and even encourage customers to use credit cards to pay for their purchases. The reason is simple: Often consumers that don't have the cash to make a purchase will use a credit card to make the purchase. For example, many consumers used their credit cards to purchase everyday necessities in the spring of 2020 when the number of unemployed workers increased to record levels as a result of the temporary closure of nonessential businesses during the first phase of the COVID-19 pandemic.

By depositing credit transaction slips in a bank or other financial institution, the merchant can convert card sales into cash. In return for processing the merchant's card transactions, the financial institution charges a fee that generally ranges between 1 and 3.5 percent. The number of card transactions, the total dollar amount of debit and credit sales, and how well the merchant can negotiate the fees the financial institution charges determine actual fees. Typically, small, independent businesses pay more than larger stores or chain stores.

In addition to debit and credit cards, mobile payments are now accepted by many businesses. **Mobile payments** allow customers to use an electronic device or app to pay for a product or service. The most common electronic devices used to complete mobile payments are cell phones or tablets. Examples of mobile payment systems are Apple Pay, PayPal, and Google Pay. For merchants, processing a mobile payment is similar to processing debit card transactions. For customers, mobile pay is convenient and often safer than carrying plastic debit or credit cards. Most experts agree that mobile payments and other electronic payment methods will become even more popular in the future.

电子银行服务
6-4c Electronic Banking Services

An **electronic funds transfer (EFT) system** is a means of performing financial transactions through a computer terminal. The following four EFT applications are changing how banks and financial institutions help firms do business:

1. *Automated teller machines (ATMs)*. An ATM is an electronic bank teller—a machine that provides many of the same services a human teller can provide. Once the customer is properly identified, the machine dispenses cash from the customer's checking or savings account or makes a cash advance charged to a credit card. Customers have access to ATMs at all times of the day or night. There may be a fee for each transaction.
2. *Automated clearinghouses (ACHs)*. Designed to reduce the number of paper checks, automated clearinghouses process checks, direct deposits, recurring

移动支付
mobile payment payment for a product or service which is made using an electronic device or an app

电子资金转账系统
electronic funds transfer (EFT) system a means of performing financial transactions through a computer terminal

bill payments, Social Security benefits, and employee salaries. For example, large companies use the ACH network to transfer salaries directly into their employees' bank accounts, thus eliminating the need to make out individual paychecks.

3. *Point-of-sale (POS) terminals*. A POS terminal is a computerized cash register located in a retail store. Assume you want to pay for purchases at a Walmart Supercenter. You begin the process by pulling your credit or debit card through a magnetic card reader or inserting your card into the chip reader. A central processing center notifies a computer at your bank that you want to make a purchase. The bank's computer immediately adds the amount to your credit card account for a credit transaction. In a similar process, the bank's computer deducts the amount of the purchase from your bank checking account if you use a debit card. Finally, the amount of your purchase is added to the store's account. The Walmart store then is notified that the transaction is complete, and the cash register prints out your receipt. A POS system can also collect customer information for a marketing database and provide sales information for a firm's inventory system.
4. *Electronic check conversion (ECC)*. Electronic check conversion is a process used to convert information from a paper check into an electronic payment for merchandise, services, or bills. When you give your completed check to a store cashier at a Best Buy store, the check is processed through an electronic system that captures your banking information and the dollar amount of the check. Once the check is processed, the funds to pay for your transaction are transferred into the business firm's account. Finally, you are asked to sign a receipt, and you get a voided (canceled) check back for your records. ECC also can be used for checks you mail to pay for a purchase or to pay on an account.

EFTs are fast, and they eliminate the costly processing of paper checks. However, some customers are reluctant or afraid to use online banking or EFT systems because they fear the computer will garble their accounts. Others are afraid someone will steal their account information. Early on, Congress responded to such fears by passing the Fair Credit Billing Act and the Electronic Funds Transfer Act, which protect the customer in case the bank makes an error or the customer's credit or debit card is stolen.

国际银行服务

6-4d International Banking Services

For international businesses, banking services are extremely important. Depending on the needs of an international firm, a bank can help by providing a letter of credit or a banker's acceptance.

A **letter of credit** is a legal document issued by a bank or other financial institution guaranteeing to pay a seller a stated amount for a specified period of time if certain conditions or requirements are met. In most cases, a letter of credit is valid for 30 to 60 days. With a letter of credit, certain conditions or requirements, such as proof of shipment or delivery of the merchandise, may be specified before payment is made.

A **banker's acceptance** is a written order for a bank to pay a third party a stated amount of money on a specific date. With a banker's acceptance, no conditions or requirements are specified. It is simply an order to pay without any strings attached.

Both a letter of credit and a banker's acceptance are popular methods of paying for import and export transactions. Imagine that you are a business owner in the United States who wants to purchase some leather products from a small business in Florence, Italy. You offer to pay for the merchandise with your company's check drawn on an American bank, but the Italian business owner is worried about payment. To solve the problem, your bank can issue either a letter

信用证

letter of credit a legal document issued by a bank or other financial institution guaranteeing to pay a seller a stated amount for a specified period of time if certain conditions or requirements are met

银行承兑汇票

banker's acceptance a written order for a bank to pay a third party a stated amount of money on a specific date

✓ Concept Check

- Describe the traditional banking services provided by financial institutions.
- What are the major advantages of electronic banking services?
- How can a bank or other financial institution help American businesses to compete in the global marketplace?

Learning Objective

6-5 Describe the advantages and disadvantages of different methods of short-term debt financing.

of credit or a banker's acceptance to guarantee that payment will be made. In addition to a letter of credit and a banker's acceptance, banks also can use EFT technology to speed international banking transactions.

One other international banking service should be noted. Banks and other financial institutions provide for currency exchange. If you place an order with a Japanese manufacturer for merchandise valued at $50,000, how do you pay for the order? Do you use U.S. dollars or Japanese yen? To solve this problem, you can use the bank's currency-exchange service. To make payment, you can use either currency, and if necessary, the bank will exchange one currency for the other to complete your transaction.

短期债务融资来源

6-5 Sources of Short-Term Debt Financing

The decision to borrow money does not necessarily mean that a firm is in financial trouble. On the contrary, astute financial management often means regular, responsible borrowing of many different kinds to meet different needs. In this section, we examine the sources of *short-term debt financing* available to businesses. In the next two sections, we look at long-term financing options: equity capital and debt capital.

无担保短期融资来源

6-5a Sources of Unsecured Short-Term Financing

Short-term debt financing is usually easier to obtain than long-term debt financing for three reasons:

1. For the lender, the shorter repayment period means less risk of nonpayment.
2. The dollar amounts of short-term loans are usually smaller than those of long-term loans.
3. A close working relationship normally exists between the short-term borrower and the lender.

Most lenders do not require collateral for short-term financing. Remember in the last section that *collateral* was defined as real estate or property pledged as security for a loan. If they do require collateral, it is usually because they are concerned about the size of a particular loan, the borrowing firm's poor credit rating, or the general prospects of repayment.

Unsecured financing is financing that is not backed by collateral. A company seeking unsecured short-term financing has several options.

Trade Credit Manufacturers and wholesalers often provide financial aid to their customers by allowing them 30 to 60 days (or more) in which to pay for merchandise. This delayed payment, known as **trade credit**, is a type of short-term financing extended by a seller who does not require immediate payment after delivery of merchandise. It is the most popular form of short-term financing because most manufacturers and wholesalers do not charge interest for trade credit. In fact, from 70 to 90 percent of all transactions between businesses involve some trade credit.

Assume that Walmart receives a shipment of clothing from a manufacturer. Along with the merchandise, the manufacturer sends an invoice that states the terms of payment. Walmart now has two options for payment. First, it may pay the invoice promptly and take advantage of any cash discount the manufacturer offers. Cash-discount terms are specified on the invoice. For instance, "2/10, net 30" means that the customer—Walmart—may take a 2 percent discount if it pays the invoice within 10 days of the invoice date.

A second option is to wait until the end of the credit period before making payment. If payment is made between 11 and 30 days after the date of the invoice,

无担保融资
unsecured financing financing that is not backed by collateral

商业信用
trade credit a type of short-term financing extended by a seller who does not require immediate payment after delivery of merchandise

Walmart must pay the entire amount. As long as payment is made before the end of the credit period, the business maintains the ability to purchase additional merchandise from the seller using the trade-credit arrangement.

In 1950, Sam Walton opened a dime store called Walton's in Bentonville Arkansas. Then, in 1962, Mr. Walton opened the first Walmart Discount store in Rogers, Arkansas. Today, Walmart is the largest retailer in the world. A great deal of the retailer's success is built on its relationship with more than 2,800 suppliers that allow Walmart to use trade credit to purchase merchandise and then pay for it 30 to 60 days or more after the merchandise is sold in its stores.

Promissory Notes Issued to Suppliers A **promissory note** is a written pledge by a borrower to pay a certain sum of money to a creditor at a specified future date. Suppliers uneasy about extending trade credit may be less reluctant to offer credit to customers who sign promissory notes. Unlike trade credit, however, promissory notes usually require the borrower to pay interest. Although repayment periods may extend to one year, most short-term promissory notes are repaid in 60 to 180 days.

A promissory note offers two important advantages to the firm extending the credit.

1. A promissory note is legally binding and an enforceable contract.
2. A promissory note is a negotiable instrument.

Because a promissory note is negotiable, the manufacturer, wholesaler, or company extending credit may be able to discount, or sell, the note to its own bank (or another business). If the note is discounted, the dollar amount received by the company extending credit is slightly less than the maturity value because the bank charges a fee for the service. The company extending credit recoups most of its money immediately, and the bank collects the entire amount when the note matures.

Unsecured Bank Loans Banks and other financial institutions offer unsecured short-term loans to businesses at interest rates that vary with each borrower's credit rating. The **prime interest rate** is the lowest rate charged by a bank for a short-term loan. Figure 6-5 traces the fluctuations in the average prime rate

Figure 6-5 Average Prime Interest Rate Paid by U.S. Businesses, 1990–March 2021

The prime rate is the interest rate charged by U.S. banks when businesses with the "best" credit ratings borrow money. All other businesses pay higher interest rates than the prime rate.

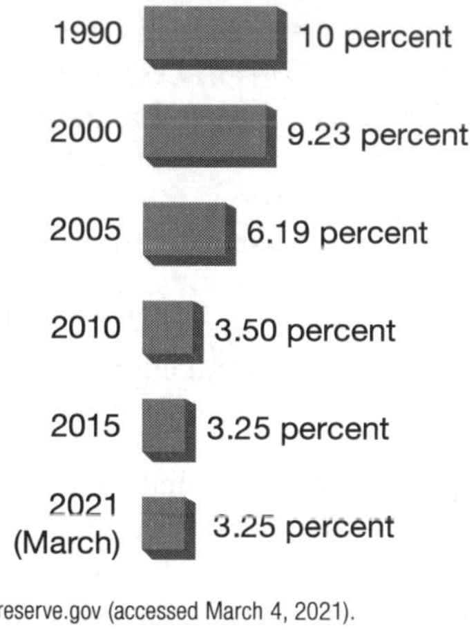

Source: Federal Reserve Bank, www.federalreserve.gov (accessed March 4, 2021).

期票
promissory note a written pledge by a borrower to pay a certain sum of money to a creditor at a specified future date

最优惠利率
prime interest rate the lowest rate charged by a bank for a short-term loan

charged by U.S. banks from 1990 to March 2021. This lowest rate generally is reserved for large corporations with excellent credit ratings. Organizations with good to high credit ratings may pay the prime rate plus 2 percent. Firms with questionable credit ratings may have to pay the prime rate plus 4 percent. Of course, if the banker believes that loan repayment may be a problem, the borrower's loan application may be rejected.

When a business obtains a short-term bank loan, interest rates and repayment terms may be negotiated. As a condition of the loan, a bank may require that a *compensating balance* be kept on deposit at the bank. Compensating balances, if required, are typically 10 to 20 percent of the borrowed funds. The bank may also require that every commercial borrower pay off its short-term loans at least once each year and not use short-term borrowing again for a period of 30 to 60 days.

Commercial Paper Large firms with excellent credit reputations like Microsoft, Procter & Gamble, and General Motors Acceptance Corporation can raise large sums of money quickly by issuing commercial paper. **Commercial paper** is a short-term promissory note issued by a large corporation. The maturity date for commercial paper is normally 270 days or less.

Commercial paper is secured only by the reputation of the issuing firm; no collateral is involved. The interest rate a corporation pays when it sells commercial paper is tied to its credit rating and its ability to repay the commercial paper. In most cases, corporations selling commercial paper pay interest rates below the interest rates charged by banks for short-term loans. Thus, selling commercial paper is cheaper than getting short-term financing from a bank.

Although it is possible to purchase commercial paper in smaller denominations, larger amounts—$100,000 or more—are quite common. Money obtained by selling commercial paper is most often used to purchase inventory, finance a firm's accounts receivables, pay salaries and other necessary expenses, and solve cash-flow problems.

有担保的短期融资来源
6-5b Sources of Secured Short-Term Financing

If a business cannot obtain enough money through unsecured financing, it must put up collateral to obtain additional short-term financing. Almost any asset can serve as collateral. However, *inventories* and *accounts receivable* are the assets most commonly pledged for short-term financing. Even when it is willing to pledge collateral to back up a loan, a firm that is financially weak may have difficulty obtaining short-term financing or its loan request may be rejected.

Loans Secured by Inventory Normally, manufacturers, wholesalers, and retailers have large amounts of money invested in finished goods. In addition, manufacturers carry raw materials and work-in-process inventories. All three types of inventory may be pledged as collateral for short-term loans. However, lenders prefer finished merchandise to raw materials or work-in-process inventories.

A lender may require that inventory used as collateral be stored in a public warehouse. Because of this requirement, this type of financing is sometimes referred to as warehouse financing. In this situation, the receipt issued by the warehouse is retained by the lender. Without this receipt, the public warehouse will not release the merchandise. The lender releases the warehouse receipt—and the merchandise—to the borrower when the borrowed money is repaid. In addition to paying the interest on the loan, the borrower must pay for storage in the public warehouse. As a result, this type of loan is more expensive than an unsecured short-term loan.

Loans Secured by Receivables As defined in Chapter 5, *accounts receivable* are amounts owed to a firm by its customers. A firm can pledge its accounts receivable as collateral to obtain short-term financing. A lender may advance 70 to 80 percent of the dollar amount of the receivables. First, however, it conducts

商业票据
commercial paper a short-term promissory note issued by a large corporation

Table 6-3 Comparison of Short-Term Financing Methods

Type of Financing	Cost	Repayment Period	Businesses That May Use It	Comments
Trade credit	Low, if any	30–60 days	All businesses with good credit	Usually no finance charge
Promissory note issued to suppliers	Moderate	One year or less	All businesses	Usually unsecured but requires legal document
Unsecured bank loan	Moderate	One year or less	All businesses	Promissory note is required and compensating balance may be required
Commercial paper	Moderate	270 days or less	Large corporations with high credit ratings	Usually available only to large firms
Secured loan	High	One year or less	Firms with questionable credit ratings	Inventory or accounts receivable often used as collateral
Factoring	High	None	Firms that have large numbers of credit customers	Accounts receivable sold to a factor

a thorough investigation to determine the *quality* of the receivables. (The quality of the receivables is the creditworthiness of the firm's customers, coupled with the customers' ability to repay their credit obligations when they are due.) If a favorable determination is made, the loan is approved. Like most business loans, the borrower and the lender negotiate interest rates and repayment terms.

应收账款保理

6-5c Factoring Accounts Receivable

Accounts receivable may be used in one other way to help raise short-term financing: They can be sold to a factoring company (or factor). A **factor** is a firm that specializes in buying other firms' accounts receivable. The factor buys the accounts receivable for less than their maturity value; however, it collects the full maturity value when each account matures. The factor's profit is the difference between the maturity value of the accounts receivable and the amount the factor has paid for them. Generally, the amount of profit the factor receives is based on the risk the factor assumes. Risk, in this case, is the probability that the accounts receivable will not be repaid when they mature.

Even though the firm selling its accounts receivable gets less than face value, it does receive needed cash immediately. Moreover, it has shifted both the task of collecting and the risk of nonpayment to the factor, which now owns the accounts receivable. Generally, customers whose accounts receivable have been factored are given instructions to make their payments directly to the factor.

成本比较

6-5d Cost Comparisons

Table 6-3 compares the various types of short-term financing. As you can see, trade credit is the least expensive. Secured loans and factoring of accounts receivable are typically the highest-cost methods shown.

股权融资来源

6-6 Sources of Equity Financing

Sources of long-term financing vary with the size and type of business. As mentioned earlier, a sole proprietorship or partnership acquires equity capital (sometimes referred to as *owners' equity*) when the owner or partners invest money in the business. For corporations, equity-financing options include the sale of stock and the use of profits not distributed to owners. All three types of businesses can also

✓ Concept Check

- How important is trade credit as a source of short-term financing?
- Why would a supplier require a customer to sign a promissory note?
- What is the prime rate? Who gets the prime rate?
- Explain how factoring works. Of what benefit is factoring to a firm that sells its receivables?

保理公司
factor a firm that specializes in buying other firms' accounts receivable

Learning Objective

6-6 Evaluate the advantages and disadvantages of equity financing.

obtain venture capital and use long-term debt capital (borrowed money) to meet their financial needs.

出售股票
6-6a Selling Stock

Some equity capital is used to start every business—sole proprietorship, partnership, or corporation. In the case of corporations, stockholders who buy shares in the company provide equity capital.

Initial Public Offering and the Primary Market An **initial public offering (IPO)** occurs when a corporation sells common stock to the general public for the first time. McAfee—a corporation known as a leader in protecting consumers, businesses, and governments from cyberattacks—used an IPO to raise $740 million in late 2020. At the time of publication of this text, there are more companies that plan to use IPOs to raise capital as the economy begins to stabilize after the COVID-19 pandemic. As illustrated in Figure 6-6, the largest IPOs for U.S. companies—Visa, Facebook, General Motors, AT&T Wireless, and Kraft Foods—involve companies from a number of different industries.

Established companies that plan to raise capital by selling subsidiaries to the public can also use IPOs. In 2020, global biotech giant GenScript completed an IPO valued at over $400 million by spinning off Legend BioTech—a company that engages in the discovery and development of drug therapies for different kinds of cancer treatments. Monies from the IPO will be used to increase the parent company's cash balance and provide funding for growth and expansion.[11] In addition to using an IPO to increase the cash balance for the parent company, corporations often sell shares in a subsidiary when shares can be sold at a profit or when the subsidiary no longer fits with its current business plan. Finally, some corporations will sell a subsidiary that is growing more slowly than the rest of the company's operating divisions.

When a corporation uses an IPO to raise capital, the stock is sold in the primary market. The **primary market** is a market in which an investor purchases financial securities (via an investment bank) directly from the issuer of the securities. An **investment banking firm** is an organization that assists corporations in raising funds, usually by helping to sell new issues of stocks, bonds, or other financial securities.

Although a corporation can have only one IPO, it can sell additional stock after the IPO, assuming that there is a market for the company's stock. Even though the cost of selling stock (often referred to as *flotation costs*) is high, the *ongoing* costs

首次公开募股
initial public offering (IPO) occurs when a corporation sells common stock to the general public for the first time

一级市场
primary market a market in which an investor purchases financial securities (via an investment bank) directly from the issuer of those securities

投资银行
investment banking firm an organization that assists corporations in raising funds, usually by helping to sell new issues of stocks, bonds, or other financial securities

Figure 6-6 The All-Time Largest Initial Public Offerings for U.S. Companies

These five U.S. corporations raised billions of dollars by selling stock. Visa—the record holder for companies in the United States—raised $17.9 billion when it sold stock for the first time in 2008.

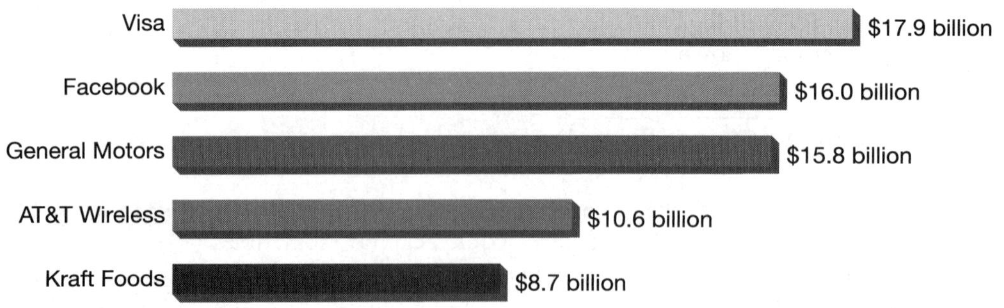

Source: "All-Time Largest U.S. IPOs," Renaissance Capital, Greenwich, CT.

associated with this type of equity financing are low for two reasons. First, the corporation does not have to repay money obtained from the sale of stock because the corporation is under no legal obligation to do so. If you purchase corporate stock and later decide to sell your stock, you may sell it to another investor—not the corporation.

A second advantage of selling stock is that a corporation is under no legal obligation to pay dividends to stockholders. As we know, a *dividend* is a distribution of earnings to the stockholders of a corporation. For any reason (e.g., if a company has a bad year), the board of directors can vote to omit dividend payments. Earnings then are retained for use in funding business operations. Of course, corporate management may hear from unhappy stockholders if expected dividends are omitted too frequently.

The Secondary Market Although a share of corporate stock is only sold one time in the primary market, the stock can be sold again and again in the secondary market. The **secondary market** is a market for existing financial securities that are traded between investors. Although a corporation does not receive money each time its stock is bought or sold in the secondary market, the ability to obtain cash by selling stock investments is one reason why investors purchase corporate stock. Without the secondary market, investors would not purchase stock in the primary market because there would be no way to sell shares to other investors. Usually, secondary-market transactions are completed through a securities exchange or the over-the-counter (OTC) market.

A **securities exchange** is a marketplace where member brokers meet to buy and sell securities. Generally, securities issued by larger corporations are traded at the New York Stock Exchange (NYSE) or at regional exchanges located in different parts of the country. The securities of very large corporations may be traded at more than one of these exchanges. Securities of firms also may be listed on foreign securities exchanges—in Tokyo or London, for example.

Stocks issued by several thousand companies are traded in the OTC market. The **over-the-counter (OTC) market** is a network of dealers who buy and sell the stocks of corporations that are not listed on a securities exchange. The term *over-the-counter* was coined more than 100 years ago when securities actually were sold "over the counter" in stores and banks. Many stocks are traded through an *electronic* exchange called the Nasdaq (pronounced "nazzdack"). The Nasdaq is now one of the largest securities markets in the world. Today, the Nasdaq is known for its forward-looking, innovative, growth companies, including Intel, Microsoft, Cisco Systems, and Apple Computer.

There are two types of stock: common and preferred. Each type has advantages and drawbacks as a means of long-term financing.

Common Stock A share of **common stock** represents the most basic form of corporate ownership. In return for the financing provided by selling common stock, management must make certain concessions to stockholders that may restrict or change corporate policies. For example, every corporation must hold an annual meeting, at which the holders of common stock may vote for the board of directors. Often, stockholders are also asked to approve or disapprove of major corporate actions.

二级市场
secondary market a market for existing financial securities that are traded between investors

证券交易所
securities exchange a marketplace where member brokers meet to buy and sell securities

场外交易市场
over-the-counter (OTC) market a network of dealers who buy and sell the stocks of corporations that are not listed on a securities exchange

普通股
common stock the most basic form of corporate ownership and whose owners may vote on corporate policies

The NYSE: The largest stock exchange in the world. Most investors think of the New York Stock Exchange—often referred to as the NYSE—as the securities exchange where stocks for well-established, stable companies are traded. On the other hand, Nasdaq—the second largest securities market in the world—is where stocks for many innovative and technology companies are traded. The bottom line: Both the NYSE and Nasdaq are necessary components that enable investors to buy and sell stocks.

Few investors will buy common stock unless they believe that their investment will increase in value. As already mentioned, stockholders may receive dividends if the corporation's board of directors approves a dividend distribution. Also, stockholders can profit from their investment if a corporate stock increases in value.

Preferred Stock As we know, the owners of *preferred stock* must receive their dividends before holders of common stock receive theirs. And, preferred stockholders know the dollar amount of their dividend because it is stated on the stock certificate. When compared to common stockholders, preferred stockholders also have first claim (after creditors) on assets if the corporation is dissolved or declares bankruptcy. Even so, as with common stock, the board of directors must approve dividends on preferred stock, and this type of financing does not represent a debt that must be legally repaid. In return for preferential treatment, preferred stockholders generally give up the right to vote at a corporation's annual meeting.

留存收益
6-6b Retained Earnings

Most large corporations distribute only a portion of their after-tax earnings to stockholders. The portion of a corporation's profits *not* distributed to stockholders is called **retained earnings**. Because they are undistributed profits, retained earnings are considered a form of equity financing.

The amount of retained earnings in any year is determined by corporate management and approved by the board of directors. Most small or growing corporations pay no cash dividend—or a very small dividend—to their stockholders. All or most earnings are reinvested in the business for research and development, expansion, or the funding of major projects. Reinvestment tends to increase the value of the firm's stock while it provides essentially cost-free financing for the business. More mature corporations may distribute 40 to 60 percent of their after-tax profits as dividends. Utility companies and other corporations with very stable earnings often pay out as much as 80 to 90 percent of what they earn. For a large corporation, retained earnings can amount to a hefty bit of financing. For example, as reported in its last annual report, the total amount of retained earnings for Procter & Gamble was over $100.2 billion.[12]

风险投资、天使投资人和私募
6-6c Venture Capital, Angel Investors, and Private Placements

To establish a new business or expand an existing one, an entrepreneur may try to obtain venture capital. We define *venture capital* as money invested in small (and sometimes struggling) firms that have the potential to become very successful. Most venture capital firms do not invest in the typical small business—a neighborhood convenience store or a local dry cleaner—but in firms that have the potential to become extremely profitable. For example, Google, Apple, Facebook, and Uber all received venture capital before they became large, successful companies.

Generally, a venture capital firm consists of a pool of investors, a partnership established by a wealthy family, or corporations with money to invest. In return for financing, these investors generally receive an equity or ownership position in the business and share in its profits. Although venture capital firms are willing to take chances, they have also become more selective about where they invest their money. Often, venture capitalists prefer to invest in companies that have passed the initial start-up phase and show potential for rapid growth, increased sales and profits, and expansion.

留存收益
retained earnings the portion of a corporation's profits not distributed to stockholders

Another source of capital for a start-up business is an angel investor. An **angel investor** is often a wealthy investor who provides financial backing for small business start-ups or entrepreneurs. Often, an angel investor may be an entrepreneur's family member or a friend that provides the financial support needed to start a business. Unlike venture capitalists, angel investors are often more focused on helping a business or an entrepreneur succeed rather than earning huge profits. Some angel investors even become more involved in the business and become mentors for entrepreneurs to help them grow and expand the business. Angel investors may provide more favorable financial terms when compared with venture capitalists, bankers, and other financial institutions. In return for providing needed financing, angel investors can become an owner with equity in the firm. In other cases, angel investors loan money to a small business much like a bank or other financial institution.

Another method of raising capital is through a private placement. A **private placement** occurs when stock and other corporate securities are sold directly to wealthy investors, banks and financial firms, insurance companies, pension funds, large institutional investors, or mutual funds. When compared with selling stocks and other corporate securities to the public, there are often fewer government regulations and the cost is generally less when the securities are sold through a private placement. Typically, terms between the buyer and seller are negotiated when a private placement is used to raise capital.

天使投资人
angel investor a wealthy investor who provides financial backing for small business start-ups or entrepreneurs

私募
private placement occurs when stock and other corporate securities are sold directly to wealthy investors, banks and financial firms, insurance companies, pension funds, large institutional investors, or mutual funds

✓ Concept Check

- What are the advantages of financing through the sale of stock?
- From a corporation's point of view, how does preferred stock differ from common stock?
- What is venture capital? An angel investor? A private placement?

Entrepreneurial Success 创业成功：小企业如何获得融资

How Can Small Businesses Secure Financing?

To start a small business and keep it running smoothly, owners must provide or obtain money, and there are a variety of financing options for small businesses. Selecting the right type of financing often depends on a variety of factors such as the business's financial needs, the business owner's financial resources, and the owner's willingness to share control of the business.

To start the search for financing, small business owners should determine what the money will be used for and how much money is needed. For example, money is often needed to purchase equipment; retail, manufacturing, or office space; inventory; marketing and advertising; computers and software; web services; and more. When small business owners do not have enough money to purchase the resources needed to open or grow their business, they must look to other sources to secure additional financing.

To retain control of the business, owners can apply for a loan. Applicants are expected to share their business plan, financial projections to demonstrate how much money is needed, how long it will take to repay the loan, and the type of collateral (if any) that will secure the loan. There are many types of loans small business owners can apply for, including business lines of credit, invoice financing available from suppliers, long-term loans, and loans from the Small Business Administration. It is even possible to apply for a microloan, which are offered by nonprofits and mission-based lenders to help small business owners start a business in disadvantaged communities. The most popular microloan source is Kiva (kiva.org).

To avoid involving investors and financial institutions, business owners can also use crowdfunding to raise small amounts of money from many individuals. The most popular sites for crowdfunding are Kickstarter, Indiegogo, and Patreon. Because people that contribute to crowdfunding projects do not receive a share of ownership in the companies they support, they are not considered investors or lenders.

One additional way business owners can secure funding is to seek venture capital. Venture capital is a form of private equity that provides businesses with money in exchange for an ownership share or an active role in the company. It is also considered a form of long-term financing. Venture capitalists typically focus on high-growth companies that have the potential to become extremely profitable. In return for higher returns, they are willing to accept the higher risk often associated with high-growth companies.

Sources: Based on information in U.S. Small Business Administration, "Fund Your Business," March 11, 2021; Steve Nicastro, "Types of Business Loans: Compare Your Financing Options," *Nerd Wallet*, December 23, 2020; Chloe Goodshore, "Best Small-Business Funding Options 2021," December 17, 2020.

长期债务融资来源

6-7 Sources of Long-Term Debt Financing

Learning Objective

6-7 Evaluate the advantages and disadvantages of long-term debt financing.

As pointed out earlier in this chapter, businesses borrow money on a short-term basis for many valid reasons other than desperation. There are equally valid reasons for long-term borrowing. In addition to using borrowed money to meet the long-term needs listed in Table 6-1, successful businesses often use the financial leverage it creates to improve their financial performance. **Financial leverage** is the use of borrowed funds to increase the return on owners' equity. To understand how financial leverage can increase a firm's return on owners' equity, study the information for Texas-based Cypress Springs Plastics presented in Table 6-4. Pete Johnston, the owner of the firm, is trying to decide how best to finance a $100,000 purchase of new high-tech manufacturing equipment.

- He could borrow $100,000 and pay 7 percent annual interest.
- He could invest an additional $100,000 in the firm.

Assuming that the firm earns $95,000 a year and that annual interest for this loan totals $7,000 ($100,000 × 0.07 = $7,000), the return on owners' equity for Cypress Springs Plastics would be higher if the firm borrowed the additional financing. Return on owners' equity is determined by dividing a firm's profit by the dollar amount of owners' equity. Based on the calculations illustrated in Table 6-4, Cypress Springs Plastics' return on owners' equity equals 17.6 percent if Johnston borrows the additional $100,000. The firm's return on owners' equity would decrease to 15.8 percent if Johnston invests an additional $100,000 in the business.

The most obvious danger when using financial leverage is that the firm's earnings may be lower than expected. If this situation occurs, the fixed interest charge actually works to reduce or eliminate the return on owners' equity. Of course, borrowed money eventually must be repaid.

For a small business, long-term debt financing is generally limited to loans. Large corporations have the additional option of issuing corporate bonds.

长期贷款

6-7a Long-Term Loans

Many businesses satisfy their long-term financing needs, such as those listed in Table 6-1, with loans from banks and other financial institutions. Manufacturers and suppliers of heavy machinery or equipment may also provide long-term debt financing.

财务杠杆
financial leverage the use of borrowed funds to increase the return on owners' equity

Table 6-4 Analysis of the Effect of Additional Capital from Debt or Equity

Additional Debt		Additional Equity	
Owners' equity	$500,000	Owners' equity	$500,000
Additional equity	+0	Additional equity	+100,000
Total owner's equity	$500,000	Total owner's equity	$600,000
Loan (@ 7%)	+100,000	No loan	+0
Total capital	$600,000	Total capital	$600,000
Year-End Earnings			
Gross profit	$95,000	Gross profit	$95,000
Less loan interest	−7,000	No interest	+0
Profit	$88,000	Profit	$95,000
Return on owners' equity	17.6%	Return on owners' equity	15.8%
($88,000 ÷ $500,000 = 17.6%)		($95,000 ÷ $600,000 = 15.8%)	

Term-Loan Agreements A **term-loan agreement** is a promissory note that requires a borrower to repay a loan in monthly, quarterly, semiannual, or annual installments. As discussed earlier in this chapter, repayment may be as long as 15 to 20 years, but long-term business loans normally are repaid in 3 to 7 years. Loans where real estate serves as collateral may be as long as 30 years.

Assume that Pete Johnston, the owner of Cypress Springs Plastics, decides to borrow $100,000 and take advantage of the principle of financial leverage illustrated in Table 6-4. Although the firm's return on owners' equity does increase, interest must be paid each year and, eventually, the loan must be repaid. To pay off a $100,000 loan over a three-year period with annual payments, Cypress Springs Plastics must pay $33,333 on the loan balance plus $7,000 annual interest, or a total of $40,333 the first year. Although the amount of interest decreases each year because of the previous year's payment on the loan balance, annual payments of this amount are still a large commitment for a small firm such as Cypress Springs Plastics.

The interest rate and repayment terms for term loans often are based on factors such as the reasons for borrowing, the borrowing firm's credit rating, and the value of collateral. Although long-term loans occasionally may be unsecured, the lender usually requires some type of collateral. Acceptable collateral includes real estate, stocks, bonds, equipment, or any asset with value. Lenders may also require that borrowers maintain a minimum amount of working capital.

Loan approval 101. Before you ask for a loan, you should get to know your banker (or lender). Make sure your banker understands your business, your future plans, and how the loan will be repaid. Then, you will be asked to complete a loan application and interview with a loan officer or even a loan committee before a decision to approve or reject a loan request is made.

公司债券

6-7b Corporate Bonds

In addition to loans, large corporations may choose to issue bonds in denominations of $1,000 to $50,000. Although the usual face value for corporate bonds is $1,000, the total face value of all the bonds in an issue usually amounts to millions of dollars. In fact, one of the reasons why corporations issue bonds is because they can sell bonds to a lot of different bondholders and raise larger amounts of money than could be borrowed from one lender. Also, the interest rate for corporate bonds is often lower than the interest rate for a long-term loan from a bank or other financial institution. A **corporate bond** is a corporation's written pledge that it will repay a specified amount of money with interest. Interest rates for corporate bonds vary with the financial health of the company issuing the bond. Specific factors that increase or decrease the interest rate that a corporation must pay when it issues bonds include:

- The corporation's ability to pay interest each year until maturity; and
- The corporation's ability to repay the bond at maturity.

For bond investors, the interest rate on corporate bonds is an example of the risk–return ratio discussed earlier in this chapter. Simply put: Investors expect a higher return when they purchase high-risk, speculative bond issues—refer to Figure 6-7.

Today, most corporate bonds are registered bonds. A **registered bond** is a bond registered in the owner's name by the issuing company. Many corporations do not issue actual bonds. Instead, the bonds are recorded electronically, and the specific details regarding the bond issue, along with the current owner's name and address, are maintained by computer. Computer entries are safer because they cannot be stolen, misplaced, or destroyed, and make it easier to transfer when a bond is sold.

定期贷款协议
term-loan agreement a promissory note that requires a borrower to repay a loan in monthly, quarterly, semiannual, or annual installments

公司债券
corporate bond a corporation's written pledge that it will repay a specified amount of money with interest

记名（公司）债券
registered bond a bond registered in the owner's name by the issuing company

Figure 6-7 The Risk–Return Ratio for Corporate Bond Investors

High-quality corporate bonds pay less interest when compared to bonds that are more speculative.

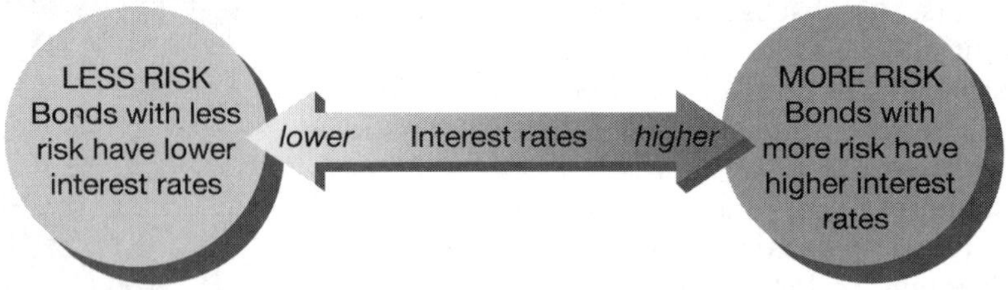

The **maturity date** is the date on which the corporation is to repay the borrowed money. Until a bond's maturity, a corporation pays interest to the bond owner at the stated rate. For example, owners of Dollar Tree bonds that mature in 2028 receive 4.20 percent interest per year for each bond they own. For each $1,000 bond issued, the corporation must pay bondholders $42 ($1,000 × 0.0420 = $42) each year. Because interest for corporate bonds is usually paid semiannually, the owner of a Dollar Tree bond will receive a $21 payment every six months for each bond they own. On the maturity date, a registered owner will receive cash equaling the face value of the bond.

Types of Bonds Corporate bonds are generally classified as debentures, mortgage bonds, or convertible bonds. Most corporate bonds are debenture bonds. A **debenture bond** is a bond backed only by the reputation of the issuing corporation. To make its bonds more appealing to investors, a corporation may issue mortgage bonds. A **mortgage bond** is a corporate bond secured by various assets of the issuing firm. The corporation can also issue convertible bonds. A **convertible bond** can be exchanged, at the owner's option, for a specified number of shares of the corporation's common stock. For example, Southwest Airlines—a passenger airline that provides scheduled flights in both the United States and nearby international locations—has issued convertible bonds that mature in 2025. Each bond can be converted to 25.9909 shares of Southwest Airlines common stock, which means investors could convert each $1,000 bond if the price of a share of the stock increases to $38.48 ($1,000 ÷ 25.9909 = $38.48) a share or higher. A corporation can gain in three ways by issuing convertible bonds. First, convertibles usually carry a lower interest rate than nonconvertible bonds. Second, the conversion feature attracts investors who are interested in the speculative gain that conversion to common stock may provide. Third, if the bondholder converts to common stock, the corporation no longer has to redeem the bond at maturity.

Repayment Provisions for Corporate Bonds Maturity dates for bonds generally range from one to 30 years after the date of issue. Some bonds are callable before the maturity date; that is, a corporation can buy back, or redeem, them. For these bonds, the corporation may pay the bond owner a call premium. The amount of the call premium, if any, is specified, along with other provisions, in the bond indenture. The **bond indenture** is a legal document that details all the conditions relating to a bond issue.

A corporation may use one of three methods to ensure that it has sufficient funds available to redeem a bond issue. First, it can issue the bonds as **serial bonds**, which are bonds of a single issue that mature on different dates. Second, the corporation can establish a sinking fund. A **sinking fund** is a sum of money to which deposits are made each year for the purpose of redeeming a bond issue. When Union Pacific Corporation sold a $275 million bond issue, the company agreed to contribute to a sinking fund until the bond's maturity in the year 2025. Third, a corporation can pay off an old bond issue by selling new bonds.

A corporation that issues bonds must also appoint a **trustee**, an individual or an independent firm that acts as the bond owners' representative. A trustee's duties

到期日
maturity date the date on which a corporation is to repay borrowed money

信用债券
debenture bond a bond backed only by the reputation of the issuing corporation

抵押债券
mortgage bond a corporate bond secured by various assets of the issuing firm

可转换债券
convertible bond a bond that can be exchanged, at the owner's option, for a specified number of shares of the corporation's common stock

债券契约
bond indenture a legal document that details all the conditions relating to a bond issue

分期偿还债券
serial bonds bonds of a single issue that mature on different dates

偿债基金
sinking fund a sum of money to which deposits are made each year for the purpose of redeeming a bond issue

受托人
trustee an individual or an independent firm that acts as the bond owners' representative

Table 6-5 Comparison of Long-Term Financing Methods

Type of Financing	Repayment	Repayment Period	Cost/Dividends/Interest	Businesses That May Use It
Equity				
Common stock	No	None	High initial cost; low ongoing costs because dividends not required	All corporations that sell stock to investors
Preferred stock	No	None	Dividends not required but must be paid before common stockholders receive any dividends	Large corporations that have an established investor base of common stockholders
Debt				
Long-term loan	Yes	Usually 3–7 years	Interest rates between 3 and 12 percent depending on economic conditions, the financial stability of the company requesting the loan, and the amount of the loan	All firms that can meet the lender's repayment and collateral requirements
Corporate bond	Yes	Usually 1–30 years	Interest rates between 1.25 and 8 percent depending on the financial stability of the company issuing the bonds and economic conditions	Large corporations that are financially healthy

are handled most often by a commercial bank or other large financial institution. The corporation must report to the trustee periodically regarding its ability to make interest payments and eventually redeem the bonds at maturity. In turn, the trustee transmits this information to the bond owners, along with its own evaluation of the corporation's ability to pay.

成本比较

6-7c Cost Comparisons

Table 6-5 compares some of the methods that can be used to obtain long-term equity *and* debt financing. Although the initial flotation cost of issuing stock is high, selling common stock is generally a popular option for most financial managers. Once the stock is sold and upfront, flotation costs are paid, the *ongoing* costs of using stock to finance a business are low. The type of long-term financing that generally has the highest *ongoing* costs is a long-term loan (debt).

To a great extent, businesses are financed through the investments of individuals—money that people have deposited in banks or have used to purchase stocks, mutual funds, and bonds.

✓ Concept Check

- Describe how financial leverage can increase return on owners' equity.
- For a corporation, what are the advantages of corporate bonds over long-term loans?
- What is a debenture? A mortgage bond? A convertible bond?
- Describe the three methods used to ensure that funds are available to redeem corporate bonds at maturity.

Summary 小结

6-1 Explain why financial management is important in today's competitive economy.

Financial management consists of all the activities concerned with obtaining money and using it effectively. For a business, the activities they can undertake are determined by the types of financing available. Financial managers must also ensure that funds are obtained at the lowest possible cost, and that they are used as efficiently as possible. The Dodd-Frank Wall Street Reform and Consumer Protection Act was signed into law to stabilize the economy, improve oversight of the financial industry, and protect consumers. And today, there is an ongoing debate if more regulations are needed. Still, there are a number of rewarding jobs in finance for qualified job applicants.

6-2 Identify a firm's short- and long-term financial needs.

Short-term financing is money that will be used for one year or less. There are many short-term needs, but cash flow, speculative production, and inventory are three for which financing is often required. Long-term financing is money that will be used for more than one year. Such financing may be required for a business start-up, for a merger or an acquisition, for new product development, for long-term marketing activities, for replacement of equipment, or for expansion of facilities. According to financial experts, business firms will find it more difficult to raise both short- and long-term financing in the future because of increased regulations and more cautious lenders. Financial managers must also consider the risk–return ratio when making financial decisions.

6-3 Summarize the process of planning for financial management.

A financial plan begins with an organization's goals and objectives. Next, a firm's goals and objectives are "translated" into departmental budgets that detail expected income and expenses. From these budgets, which may be combined into an overall cash budget, the financial manager determines what funding will be needed. The four principal sources of financing are sales revenues, equity capital, debt capital, and proceeds from the sale of assets. Whereas departmental and cash budgets emphasize short-term financing needs, a capital budget can be used to estimate a firm's expenditures for major assets and its long-term financing needs. Once the needed funds have been obtained, the financial manager is responsible for monitoring and evaluating the firm's financial activities.

6-4 Identify the services provided by banks and financial institutions for their business customers.

Banks and other financial institutions offer today's business customers an array of services. Among the most important banking services are savings accounts and certificates of deposit, checking accounts, short- and long-term loans, and debit card and credit card processing. Increased use of electronic funds transfer systems (automated teller machines, automated clearinghouse systems, point-of-sale terminals, and electronic check conversion) also will change the way that business firms bank and conduct typical business transactions. For firms in the global marketplace, a bank can provide letters of credit and banker's acceptances that will reduce the risk of nonpayment for sellers. Banks and financial institutions also can provide currency exchange to reduce payment problems for import or export transactions.

6-5 Describe the advantages and disadvantages of different methods of short-term debt financing.

Most short-term financing is unsecured; that is, no collateral is required. Sources of unsecured short-term financing include trade credit, promissory notes issued to suppliers, unsecured bank loans, and commercial paper. Sources of secured short-term financing include loans secured by inventory and accounts receivable. A firm may also sell its receivables to factors. Trade credit is the least expensive source of short-term financing. The cost of financing through other sources generally depends on the source and on the credit rating of the firm that requires the financing. Factoring is generally the most expensive approach.

6-6 Evaluate the advantages and disadvantages of equity financing.

The first time a corporation sells stock to the general public is referred to as an initial public offering (IPO). With an IPO, the stock is sold in the primary market. Once sold in the primary market, investors buy and sell stock in the secondary market. Usually, secondary market transactions are completed through a securities exchange or the over-the-counter market. Common stock is voting stock; holders of common stock elect the corporation's directors and often must approve major corporate actions. Holders of preferred stock must be paid dividends before holders of common stock are paid any dividends. Another source of equity funding is retained earnings, which is the portion of a business's profits *not* distributed to stockholders. Venture capital—money invested in small (and sometimes struggling) firms that have the potential to become very successful—is yet another source of equity funding. Angel investors can also provide the money needed to start or expand small businesses. Finally, a private placement can be used to sell stocks and other corporate securities.

6-7 Evaluate the advantages and disadvantages of long-term debt financing.

For a small business, debt financing is generally limited to loans. Large corporations have the additional option of issuing corporate bonds. Regardless of whether the business is small or large, it can take advantage of financial leverage. Financial leverage is the use of borrowed funds to increase the return on owners' equity. The rate of interest for long-term loans usually depends on the financial strength of the borrower, the reason for borrowing, and the kind of collateral pledged to back up the loan. Long-term business loans are normally repaid in 3 to 7 years. Money realized from the sale of corporate bonds must be repaid when the bonds mature. In addition, the corporation must pay interest from the time the bonds are issued until maturity. Maturity dates for bonds generally range from one to 30 years after the date of issue. Three types of bonds—debentures, mortgage bonds, and convertible bonds—are sold to raise debt capital. When comparing the cost of long-term financing, the ongoing costs of using stock (equity) to finance a business are low. The most expensive is a long-term loan (debt).

Key Terms 关键术语

You should now be able to define and give an example relevant to each of the following terms:

financial management
short-term financing
cash flow
speculative production
long-term financing
risk–return ratio
financial plan
budget
cash budget
zero-base budgeting
capital budget
equity capital
debt capital
certificate of deposit (CD)
line of credit
revolving credit agreement
collateral
debit card
mobile payment
electronic funds transfer (EFT) system
letter of credit
banker's acceptance
unsecured financing
trade credit
promissory note
prime interest rate
commercial paper
factor
initial public offering (IPO)
primary market
investment banking firm
secondary market
securities exchange
over-the-counter (OTC) market
common stock
retained earnings
angel investor
private placement
financial leverage
term-loan agreement
corporate bond
registered bond
maturity date
debenture bond
mortgage bond
convertible bond
bond indenture
serial bonds
sinking fund
trustee

Discussion Questions 讨论题

1. Many small business owners find it is difficult to obtain debt financing. What can small business owners do to improve their chances of getting a loan from a bank or other financial institutions?
2. If you were the financial manager of Stars and Stripes Clothing, what would you do with the excess cash that the firm expects in the second, third, and fourth quarters? (Refer to Figure 6-4.)
3. Develop a *personal* cash budget for the next six months. Explain what you would do if there are budget shortfalls or excess cash amounts at the end of any month during the six-month period.
4. Why would a lender offer unsecured short-term loans when it could demand collateral?
5. How can a business owner or corporate manager use financial leverage to improve the firm's profits and return on owners' equity? Is there a potential danger of using financial leverage?
6. In what circumstances might a large corporation sell stock rather than bonds to obtain long-term financing? In what circumstances would it sell bonds rather than stock?

Case 6 案例 6：DoorDash 完成了首次公开募股

DoorDash Delivers an IPO

After its initial public offering (IPO), DoorDash started trading publicly on the New York Stock Exchange (NYSE) in December 2020. An IPO occurs when a corporation sells stock to the general public for the first time. The DoorDash IPO raised over $3 billion when investors purchased its stock on the first day of trading. Notable investors in DoorDash include SoftBank and venture capital firms CRV and Kleiner Perkins. SoftBank, which is known for investing in ByteDance, Fanatics, and Slack, is now the largest shareholder in DoorDash with a 20 percent ownership share after the IPO. The money from this IPO could be used to pay down corporate debt, expansion of services, or any legal business expense.

DoorDash offered three different classes of stock. While all three classes of stock are the same as far as profit distributions are concerned, they have different voting rights. Class A has one vote per share, Class B has 20 votes, and Class C has no voting rights. Offering multiple classes of stock that give different voting rights to different groups of investors has become a common practice in Silicon Valley. As a result of a voting agreement between co-founders Tony Xu, Andy Fang, and Stanley Tang, Xu, who is the company's CEO, will have significant influence over actions requiring the approval of DoorDash's stockholders. These actions, for example, can include electing individuals to the board of directors, making changes to the corporate charter, and approving mergers or acquisitions.

Because of a potential increase in its user base and encouraging projections for future revenues and profits, investors were anxious to purchase shares in DoorDash's IPO. To understand the "why" behind the investor frenzy to get DoorDash stock, it helps to look at how the delivery company earns revenue. A substantial amount of its revenue comes from fees paid by customers and commissions and fees charged to merchants—usually restaurants and grocery stores—for orders completed through the DoorDash marketplace. In addition, the company's DashPass program, which costs a flat monthly delivery fee of $9.99, also generates revenue for DoorDash.

Another factor that encouraged investors was the effect of the COVID-19 pandemic on revenues for food delivery services. DoorDash, which is the leading food delivery app with a 50 percent market share and more than 18 million customers, benefited from an uptick in deliveries during the pandemic. Even after the temporary shelter-in-place orders were lifted, the surge in demand for food delivery continued. DoorDash quickly surpassed its competitors Uber Eats and Grubhub to become the number one food delivery service. To strengthen its position in the industry, DoorDash acquired on-demand food delivery and catering business Caviar in a deal worth $410 million. While these facts are good news for investors, DoorDash has warned that it may not be able to grow at the same pace that it did during the pandemic.

For investors, risk factors include DoorDash's ability to continue to grow and compete, avoid interruptions in services, and attract and retain dashers (delivery workers). In fact, many experts believe that DoorDash's success depends on the success of the restaurant industry. As a result of the pandemic, a significant percentage of restaurants have closed. At the same time, the availability of food delivery services like DoorDash has given rise to restaurateurs that don't have brick-and-mortar locations. Once food is prepared by the restaurateur in a "ghost kitchen," it is picked up by a food delivery service and is delivered to the consumer.

Over the long-term, DoorDash's growth may also slow as more individuals venture back into dine-in restaurants. Additionally, there is intense competition in the food delivery service. And to make matters worse, there is little differentiation between the big players in food delivery. It's very easy for consumers to switch between food delivery providers, and there is very little brand loyalty. In fact, most people have several food delivery apps downloaded to their phone and will compare prices, merchant selections, and promotions before placing their orders.

Another challenge DoorDash faces is keeping its dashers happy. Like the customers who use food delivery services, there is little loyalty among delivery workers. DoorDash operates in an industry where independent contractors (dashers) provide on-demand services for the company's clients. To maintain an adequate supply of dashers, DoorDash must provide its independent contractors with flexibility, compelling opportunities to earn money, and other incentive programs that meet or exceed those of its competitors.

Despite these challenges, DoorDash is confident that it can become a profitable company. The company continues to innovate and identify trends in the rapidly changing food delivery industry. For example, DoorDash has focused on growing its business in suburban areas, which typically have larger ticket totals and lower costs. So far, the company's strategies have paid off because it now controls a 58 percent market share in suburban areas.

Even though it currently is the recognized leader in the food delivery industry and is experiencing growth in both revenues and its user base, DoorDash will have to continue to innovate to maintain its healthy market share in order to earn a profit for its investors. Like many corporations that use an IPO to raise money, DoorDash can expect that the next few years will be interesting for both management and investors.[13]

Questions

1. For a company like DoorDash, what are the advantages and disadvantages of using an IPO to raise capital?
2. Why do you think DoorDash issued three different classes of stock with different voting rights for each class of stock? As an investor, how important is the right to vote on issues that affect the future of the corporation?
3. Although DoorDash currently has 50 percent of the market for food delivery services and more than 18 million users, it must continue to increase both its number of users and its revenues. What are the challenges and obstacles that could affect DoorDash's plans for future growth?

Building Skills for Career Success 为成功的职业生涯培养技能

1. Social Media Exercise

One of the best-known sites for help managing your finances is Mint. The main reasons people like Mint is that it provides an easy way to track spending, create budgets, and monitor cash flow. Another reason for Mint's popularity is the company's use of social media through its YouTube informative videos.

1. Examine the information on Mint's website at mint.com. Then view some of the videos provided by Mint on YouTube. Do you think Mint's videos on YouTube could help you make better financial decisions?
2. Although Mint is primarily designed for individuals, could the information on the Mint website and its videos on YouTube help small business owners improve their financial management?
3. Can you think of other companies that could use videos on a YouTube channel to share information that their customers could use?

2. Building Team Skills

Suppose that for the past three years you have been repairing lawn mowers in your garage. Your business has grown steadily and you recently hired two part-time workers. Your garage is no longer adequate for your business; it is also in violation of the city code, and you have already been fined for noncompliance. You have decided that it is time to find another location for your shop and that it also would be a good time to expand your business. If the business continues to grow in the new location, you plan to hire a full-time employee to repair small appliances. You are concerned, however, about how you will get the money to move your shop and get it established in a new location.

Assignment

1. With all class members participating, use brainstorming to identify the following:
   a. The funds you will need to accomplish your business goals
   b. The sources of short-term financing available to you
   c. Problems that might prevent you from getting a short-term loan
   d. How you will repay the money if you get a loan
2. Have a classmate write the ideas on the board.
3. Discuss how you can overcome any problems that might hamper your current chances of getting a loan and how your business can improve its chances of securing short-term loans in the future.
4. Summarize what you learned from participating in this exercise.

3. Researching Different Careers

Financial managers are responsible for determining the best way to raise funds at the lowest possible cost, for ensuring that the funds are used to accomplish their firm's goals and objectives, and for developing and implementing their firm's financial plan. Their decisions have a direct impact on the firm's level of success and if the firm is profitable or not.

Assignment

1. Investigate the job of financial manager by searching for information available in the library or on the internet or by interviewing a financial manager.
2. Find answers to the following questions:
   a. What skills do financial managers need?
   b. How much education is required?
   c. What is the starting salary? Top salary?
   d. What will the job of financial manager be like in the future?
   e. What opportunities are available?
   f. What types of firms are most likely to hire financial managers? What is the employment potential?
3. Prepare a report on your findings.

Graeter's 的增长秘诀：新系统、社交媒体和融资

Graeter's Recipe for Growth: New Systems, Social Media, and Financing

Graeter's still makes ice cream by hand, just like the founders did in 1870. But in every other respect, it's a very different business from the mom-and-pop firm founded by the great-grandparents of Richard, Robert, and Chip Graeter. For example, Graeter's now uses social media to stay in touch with customers and see what people say about its brand. Technology is also a factor in the new information systems Graeter's recently installed to keep the business running smoothly as it pursues fast-paced growth and expansion in new markets and in national supermarket chains across the United States. Just as important, the company has arranged financing to support its long-term plans for national expansion.

Graeter's Social Side

Even a small business can have a big presence in social media, including Facebook, Twitter, YouTube, and Pinterest. With more than 210,000 "likes," Graeter's provides information about the company, reviews from customers, schedules for special events, information about where its four food trucks will be located on specific dates, and more on its Facebook page. It also posts a new message or photo every few days, and reveals the names of mystery flavors on Facebook in advance of other publicity. As a result, fans return to its Facebook page often. In addition, Graeter's tweets frequently and periodically posts videos on its YouTube channel. There are even hundreds of photos of Graeter's ice cream and bakery products posted on the Pinterest site. Graeter's also monitors "mentions" of its brand on other social-media sites. As other people add their comments and click to "like," the conversation continues and the word of mouth builds buzz for Graeter's.

New Growth, New Systems

Paul Porcino, a consultant working with the Graeter family, observes that small, entrepreneurial firms often have only "a very small amount of information, and . . . it hasn't been pulled together in any meaningful way." The first step was to define what Graeter's executives needed to know to run the business. For example, they needed to be able to track unit sales online, in each store, and to each wholesale customer, and to measure both costs and profitability by product and distribution channel.

Despite some technical challenges during implementation, Graeter's has already experienced some of the benefits of collecting better information. When management noticed that overall bakery sales weren't up to par, "we had to adjust," comments Porcino. The remedy was surprising: "We actually reduced the number of products we were selling in the store. . . It wasn't very clear exactly how much we were selling, but at least [we had] the good-enough gut sense in terms of the ones that were not selling, and we . . . adjusted the total inventory line."

Counting on Accounting

Graeter's controller, David Blink, is responsible for preparing "all financial statements, all reports, payroll, [and] any ad hoc reports that any of the managers would need. I handle a lot of the reporting for the retail side as well as the manufacturing side," he says. With these reports in hand, the Graeter's team can make informed decisions about how many seasonal employees to hire, which products to keep, how much to invest in new equipment, and other issues that arise day by day. Although an outside payroll company actually prints the employees' checks, Blink's department collects and analyzes payroll data as input for management decisions. In addition, an outside accounting firm prepares financial statements and additional reports based on information supplied by Blink.

Money Matters

A number of years ago, the Graeter's team recognized they needed a new production facility. After examining what the business had done in the past and where it was going in the future, the three great-grandsons of Graeter's founders constructed a plan to obtain the financing needed to purchase the land and build an additional plant. After scouting possible locations, Graeter's signed a contract with Cincinnati, paying a token amount for land and borrowing $10 million from the city to pay for construction of a new 28,000-square-foot factory. The loan carried low interest rates and would be repaid over 20 years. In exchange, Graeter's committed to "stay and grow" in Cincinnati for at least 20 years, creating dozens of new jobs when the production facility opened and additional jobs as Graeter's growth continued. Now Graeter's has the right combination of ingredients for expanding from coast to coast and beyond.[14]

Questions

1. Suppose you were writing a social media plan for Graeter's, with two objectives: to improve brand awareness in new markets and to build e-commerce sales.
   a. What actions would be included in your plan?
   b. What quantitative and qualitative measurements would you use to evaluate the results of your plan?
2. Graeter's uses information to track cash, sales revenues, expenses, and inventory. How does this type of accounting and financial information facilitate effective decision making?
3. What kinds of questions do you think Cincinnati officials asked Graeter's owners before agreeing to loan the company $10 million? Why would Graeter's go with this financing arrangement rather than borrowing from a bank to pay for the new factory?

Building a Business Plan 制订商业计划

Now that you have a marketing plan, the next big and important step is to prepare an information and financial plan. One of the biggest mistakes an entrepreneur makes when faced with a need for financing is not being prepared. The information contained in Chapter 4 (Exploring Social Media and e-Business), Chapter 5 (Using Management and Accounting Information), and Chapter 6 (Mastering Financial Management) will help you prepare this section of the business plan and determine the amount of financing you need to start your business. With the help of information in the last three chapters of the text, the task may be easier than you think.

In this last section, you should also provide some information about your exit strategy, and discuss any potential trends, problems, or risks that you may encounter. Now is also the time to go back and prepare the executive summary, which should be placed at the beginning of the business plan.

The Information and Accounting Plan Component

Information and accounting systems are important if your business is to succeed. Your information and accounting plan should answer at least the following questions:

1.1. How will you gather information about competitors, their products, and the prices that they charge for their products and services?

1.2. Explain how you will develop a management information system to collect, store, update, process data, and present information.

1.3. Will your business have an e-commerce component? If so, explain how you sell your products or services online.

1.4. Are there ways that you can use social media to promote products and services and reach out to your customers?

1.5. Who will create and maintain the accounting system that you use to record routine business transactions for your business?

1.6. Will you hire an accountant to prepare financial statements and tax returns for your firm?

The Financial Plan Component

Your financial plan should answer at least the following questions about the investment needed, sales and cash-flow forecasts, breakeven analysis, and sources of funding:

1.7. What is the actual amount of money you need to open your business (start-up budget) and the amount needed to keep it open (operating budget)? Prepare a realistic budget.

1.8. How much money do you have, and can you obtain additional financing, if needed, from investors or lenders?

1.9. Prepare a projected income statement by month for the first year of operation and by quarter for the second and third years.

1.10. Prepare projected balance sheets for each of the first three years of operation.

1.11. Prepare a breakeven analysis. How many units of your products or service will have to be sold to cover your costs?

1.12. Reinforce your final projections by comparing them with industry averages for your chosen industry.

The Exit Strategy Component

Your exit strategy component should at least include answers to the following questions:

1.13. How do you intend to get yourself (and your money) out of the business?

1.14. Will your children take over the business, or do you intend to sell it later?

1.15. Do you intend to grow the business to the point of an IPO?

1.16. How will investors get their money back?

The Critical Risks and Assumptions Component

Your critical risks and assumptions component should answer at least the following questions:

1.17. What will you do if your market does not develop as quickly as you predicted? What if your market develops too quickly?

1.18. What will you do if your competitors underprice or make your product obsolete?

1.19. What will you do if there is an unfavorable industry-wide trend?

1.20. What will happen if trained workers are not available as predicted?

1.21. What will you do if there is an erratic supply of products or raw materials?

The Appendix Component

Supplemental information and documents often are included in an appendix. Here are a few examples of some documents that can be included:

- Résumés of owners and principal managers
- Advertising samples and brochures
- An organization chart
- Floor plans for your retail showroom, office, and storage areas

Review of Business Plan Activities

As you have discovered, writing a business plan involves a long series of interrelated steps. As with any project involving a number of complex steps and calculations, your business plan should be reviewed carefully and revised before you present it to potential investors.

Remember, there is one more component you need to prepare after your business plan is completed: The executive summary should be written last, but because of its importance, it appears after the introduction.

The Executive Summary Component

In the executive summary, give a one- to two-page overview of your entire business plan. This is the most important part of the business plan and is of special interest to busy bankers, investors, and other interested parties. Remember, this section is a summary; more detailed information is provided in the remainder of your business plan.

Make sure that the executive summary captures the reader's attention instantly in the first sentence by using a key selling point or benefit of the business.

Your executive summary should include answers to at least the following:

1.22. *Company information.* What product or service do you provide? What is your competitive advantage? When will the company be formed? What are your company objectives? What is the background of you and your management team?

1.23. *Market opportunity.* What is the expected size and growth rate of your market, your expected market share, and any relevant market trends?

Once again, review your answers to all the questions in the preceding parts to make sure that they are all consistent throughout the entire business plan.

Although many would-be entrepreneurs are excited about the prospects of opening their own business, remember that it takes a lot of hard work, time, and in most cases a substantial amount of money. While the business plan provides an enormous amount of information about your business, it is only the first step. Once it is completed, it is now your responsibility to implement the plan. Good luck in your business venture.

Endnotes 注释

Chapter 1

1. Based on information in "Tesla Overtakes Toyota to Become World's Most Valuable Carmaker," BBC, July 1, 2020; James Morris, "How Did Tesla Become the Most Valuable Car Company in the World?" *Forbes*, June 14, 2020; Karen Langley, "Tesla Is Now the Most Valuable U.S. Car Maker of All Time," *The Wall Street Journal*, January 7, 2020.
2. The Horatio Alger website.
3. Ibid.
4. Greg Kumparak, "A Brief History of Oculus," the Tech Crunch website.
5. Julie Stav, "How to Invest in the Stock Market," the YouTube website.
6. The General Mills website.
7. The Bureau of Economic Analysis website.
8. The Bureau of Economic Analysis website.
9. The Bureau of Labor Statistics website.
10. The Bureau of Economic Analysis website.
11. The U.S. Debt Clock website.
12. The National Bureau of Economic Research website.
13. "Distribution of the Workforce Across Economic Sectors in the United States from 2010 to 2020," The Statista website.
14. The Environmental Protection Agency website.
15. Based on information in Company Man, "Zoom - Why They're Successful," YouTube, June 17, 2020; Alex Konrad, "Zoom, Zoom, Zoom! The Exclusive Inside Story Of The New Billionaire Behind Tech's Hottest IPO," *Forbes*, April 19, 2019; Rich Karlgaard, "Why Zoom Is Booming," *Forbes*, September 16, 2020; Samantha Murphy Kelly, "Zoom's Massive 'Overnight Success' Actually Took Nine Years," *CNN*, March 27, 2020.

Chapter 2

1. Based on information in Sara Randazzo, "Purdue Pharma Reaches $8.34 Billion Settlement Over Opioid Probes," *The Wall Street Journal*, October 21, 2020; German Lopez, "Purdue Pharma Admits to Crimes for Its OxyContin Marketing. But No One Is Going to Prison," *Vox*, October 21, 2020; Austin Frakt, "Damage From OxyContin Continues to Be Revealed," *The New York Times*, April 13, 2020; Purdue Pharma, "Purpose Statement and Values".
2. Gwen Aviles, "Kendall Jenner to Pay $90,000 Settlement for Promoting Fyre Festival," *NBCNews*, May 21, 2020; Evan Comen and Thomas C. Frohlich, "The Biggest Corporate Scandals of the Decade," *247wallst.com*, December 20, 2019.
3. Ben Popken, "Chick-fil-A Sues Chicken Producers Alleging Price Fixing on Billions of Dollars of Poultry," *NBC News*, December 7, 2020.
4. "Marketers of Pain Relief Device Settle FTC False Advertising Complaint," press release, U.S. Federal Trade Commission, March 4, 2020.
5. Chris Isadore and Matt Egan, "Robinhood Agrees to Pay a $65 Million Fine for Deceiving Clients," *CNN*, December 17, 2020.
6. Shereen Siewart, "Wausau Woman Sentenced in $700k Embezzlement Case," *Wausau Pilot & Review*, July 29, 2020.
7. Chris Prentice, "Wels Fargo to Pay $3 Billion to U.S., Admits Pressuring Workers in Fake-Account Scandal," *Reuters*, February 21, 2020.
8. Ethics Compliance Initiative, "2020 Report: Global Business Ethics Survey," p. 6.
9. Jonathan Martin, "Plagiarism Costs Degree for Senator John Walsh," *The New York Times*, October 10, 2014.
10. Rob Golum, "Electronic Arts Investors Reject Executive Pay in Rare Rebuke," *Bloomberg News*, August 7, 2020; Stan Choe, "CEO Pay: When Investors Give Thumbs-Down to Soaring Compensation Packages," *Chicago Tribune*, May 24, 2019.
11. Marshall Cohen, "Financial Disclosures Reveal Postmaster General's Business Entanglements and Likely Conflicts of Interest, Experts Say," *CNN*, August 12, 2020, (accessed December 17, 2020); Allison Durkee, "Louis DeJoy Forced to Divest from Former Company that Contracts with Postal Service," *Forbes*, October 15, 2020.
12. Procter & Gamble Company, *Our Worldwide Business Conduct Manual*, p. 51.
13. "False Advertising Consumer Class Actions Related to Coffee Servings Continue with Suit Against Folgers," *The National Law Review*, December 4, 2020.

14. Jared Bryant, Amanda J. Beane, and Jason Howell, "$1 Million Settlement Announced in FTC's 'Made in USA' Enforcement Against Williams-Sonoma," *Consumer Protection Review*, April 24, 2020.
15. O. C. Ferrell and Larry Gresham, "A Contingency Framework for Understanding Ethical Decision Making in Marketing," *Journal of Marketing* 49 (Summer 1985), 89.
16. Starbucks, "Business Ethics and Compliance: Standards of Business Conduct".
17. "Kaiser Foundation Health Plan Will Pay $6.3 Million to Settle Medicare Advantage Fraud Allegations, Whistleblower Will Receive $1.5 Million," December 2, 2020.
18. Michael Josephson, "Can Corporate Ethics Programs Do Any Good," *Josephson Institute blog*, December 27, 2013.
19. "Google, Alphabet, Pledge $14.5 Million to Address Racial Inequity," *Philanthropy News Digest*, June 5, 2020.
20. Procter & Gamble, Tide's Loads of Hope, http://www.tide.com/en-us/about-tide/loads-of-hope/about-loads-of-hope (accessed December 18, 2020).
21. P. Terry's, https://pterrys.com/giving-back (accessed December 18, 2020).
22. Chris Kempczinski, "McDonald's CEO: How We Are Thinking Differently about Our Role in Society," *CNN*, November 25, 2020.
23. Lieff Cabraser, "11th Circuit Upholds $41 Million Individual Verdict Against RJ Reynolds and Philip Morris in Florida Tobacco Lawsuit," Lieff Cabraser Heimann & Bernstein, blog, March 24, 2020.
24. Isabella Kwai, "Consumer Groups Target Amazon Prime's Cancellation Process," *The New York Times*, January 14, 2021.
25. Larry Light, "Coca-Cola's Brand-Business Rationalization," *Forbes*, August 4, 2020; Toby Howell, "Coca-Cola Cuts 'Zombie Brands' From Its Portfolio," *Morning Brew*, October 8, 2020; "Brands," Coca-Cola Company.
26. Robert Glazer, "CVS Lost $2 Billion with 1 Decision—Here's Why They Were Right," *Forbes*, April 21, 2020.
27. Ryan Luckey, "This Pledge Day, Speak Up Against Distracted Driving," *AT&T*, press release, September 19, 2019.
28. Brittany Baumann, "Midas Hospitality and Boone Center, Inc. Create Hospitality Program," *HospitalityNet*, press release, January 31, 2020.
29. "The 2017 WBI U.S. Workplace Bullying Survey," Workplace Bullying Institute, 2017.
30. Lisa Evans, "Why the Office Bully Is Getting Promoted," *Fast Company*, October 23, 2014.
31. Robin Abcarian, "Just as We Thought: Richie Incognito Bullied Jonathan Martin," *Los Angeles Times*, February 14, 2014.
32. "Sexual Harassment," U.S. Equal Employment Opportunity Commission.
33. Sheryl Estrada, "McDonald's Hit with $500M Sexual Harassment Lawsuit," *HR Dive*, April 15, 2020.
34. "Sexual Harassment Payouts Hit All-Time High in 2019," Fisher Phillips law firm, blog, January 28, 2020.
35. Evans, "Why the Office Bully Is Getting Promoted."
36. United States Courts.
37. Food and Drug Administration, "Food Loss and Waste"; Jennifer Molidor, "Grocery Chains Need to Stop Buying into Food Waste," *Grocery Dive*, November 9, 2020; "Is 'Ugly Produce' the Key to Our Food Waste Problem?" *CBS News*, October 12, 2019.
38. "Company Fined for Ocean Pollution," *The (Kuau'i) Garden Island*, February 11, 2020.
39. Kie Relyea, "EPA Fines Company in Lynden $41,500 for Releasing Pollutants into Fishtrap Creek," *The Bellingham Herald*, June 25, 2020.
40. "Recycle Your Denim with Us," Madewell.
41. "Major Companies Using Green Energy in 2020," *SaveOnEnergy*, May 18, 2020.
42. Chipotle, "Cultivate a Better World: 2019 Sustainability Report Update," April 2020; Peter Adams, "Chipotle Lets Diners Track Environmental Impact of Burritos as Restaurants Prioritize Sustainability," *Marketing Dive*, October 26, 2020.
43. Monica J. Stover, "Environmental Marketing Claims and the FTC's 'Revised Green Guides'," *Michigan Environmental Law Journal*, 37 (Spring 2020).
44. "Environmental, Social and Governance Report, 2019," Citi, p. 114.
45. "Tae Yoo," Cisco.
46. "People Planet Play: Caesar's Entertainment 2019–2020 CSR Report," Caesar's Entertainment.
47. Whole Foods Market, "This Is Whole Trade | Whole Foods Market," *YouTube*, June 20, 2017; Whole Foods Market, "Your Guide to the Whole Trade Guarantee"; Whole Foods Market, "Whole Foods Market History"; Whole Foods Market, "Our Core Values"; Whole Foods Market, "Quality Standards"; Whole Foods Market, "Whole Benefits"; Cale Guthrie Weissman, "Whole Foods Is Becoming 'Whole Paycheck' Once Again," *Fast Company*, February 12, 2019; Andria Cheng, "Two Years After Amazon Deal, Whole Foods Is Still Working To Shed Its 'Whole Paycheck' Image," *Forbes*, August 28, 2019; Karen Weise, "Amazon Wants to Rule the Grocery Aisles, and Not Just at Whole Foods," *The New York Times*, July 28, 2019.

Chapter 3

1. Based on information in Heather Lalley, "International Starbucks Now Outnumber U.S. Units," *Restaurant Business Magazine*, January 11, 2019; Starbucks, "Starbucks Company Profile"; Starbucks, "Company Information"; Kristin Salaky, "Starbucks Will Close 100 Additional U.S. Locations As It Continues To Adapt To Changing Consumer Habits," *Delish*, November 2, 2020; Starbucks, "Starbucks Announces New Roasting Facility in China, Extending Its Global Roasting Network," March 12, 2020.
2. "About the Coca-Cola Company," Coca-Cola Company.

3. "Company Overview," Combustion Associates, Inc.
4. "Liriope Factory," Southern United States Trade Association.
5. U.S. Census Bureau, "U.S. International Trade in Goods and Services, December 2020," February 5, 2021.
6. Ibid.
7. Jefferson Graham, "An iPhone Made in America? Why Building Apple's Smartphone in the USA Is a 'Pipe Dream'," *USA Today*, July 28, 2019.
8. "New Study: Trade Supported Over 40 Million Jobs," *Business Roundtable*, October 5, 2020.
9. "U.S. Trade in Goods and Services—Balance of Payments (BOP) Basis," U.S. Census Bureau.
10. "World Economic Outlook, January 2021," The International Monetary Fund.
11. "Canada – Country Commercial Guide," International Trade Association, August 3, 2020.
12. "Trade in Goods with European Union," U.S. Census Bureau.
13. "Trade in Goods with South and Central America," U.S. Census Bureau.
14. "Trade in Goods with Africa," U.S. Census Bureau.
15. Chuck Cartmill, "Lights and Insights: Streetlight Company Expands into New Solutions," Export Development Canada, blog, November 2, 2020.
16. Szu Ping Chan, "When Pepsi Was Swapped for Soviet Warships," BBCNews, June 13, 2019.
17. "About Us," Dunkin'.
18. Elizabeth Paton and Sapna Maheshwari, "H&M's Different Kind of Clickbait," *The New York Times*, December 18, 2019; "Supplier List," H&M Group.
19. James Bamford, Gerard Baynham, and David Ernst, "Joint Ventures and Partnerships," *Harvard Business Review*, September–October 2020, pp. 116–124.
20. "GM, Honda Announce North America Car Alliance," *Yahoo Finance*, September 3, 2020.
21. "U.S. Aluminum Industry Files Unfair Trade Cases Against Imports of Aluminum Foil from Five Countries," Globe Newswire, press release, September 29, 2020.
22. Josh Zumbrun and Bob Davis, "Tariffs on China Fail to Aid U.S. Factories," *The Wall Street Journal*, October 26, 2020, p. A1.
23. "World Outlook Database," International Monetary Fund, October 2020.
24. Scott A. Burns, "Banking the Unbanked—Lessons from the Developing World," *American Institute for Economic Research*, February 29, 2020.
25. Dylan Lyons, "Brands in Translation: 9 Cringeworthy Language Fails," *Babbel*, June 25, 2020.
26. Andrew Chatzkey, James McBride, and Mohammed Aly Sergie, "NAFTA and the USMCA: Weighing the Impact of North American Trade," Council on Foreign Relations, July 1, 2020; "Fast Facts: U.S. Trade with Canada and Mexico," USMCA Coalition.
27. Katie Lobosco, Brian Fung, and Tami Luhby, "6 Key Differences Between NAFTA and the USMCA Deal that Replaces It," *CNN*, December 17, 2019; Ana Swanson, "As New NAFTA Takes Effect, Much Remains Undone," *The New York Times*, July 1, 2020; "U.S. Relations with Canada," U.S. Department of State, July 16, 2020; and "Fast Facts: U.S. Trade with Canada and Mexico."
28. "Trade and Export," Texas Economic Development.
29. "About Citi," Citi Group.
30. "Keeping America Strong," Export-Import Bank of the United States, 2019 Annual Report.
31. The World Bank, www.worldbank.org (accessed January 20, 2021).
32. Based on information in Past To Future, "Honda History - How Soichiro Honda Started Company," *YouTube*, February 20, 2019; Honda, "History"; Honda, "Company Overview"; Michael Wayland, "GM, Honda Partner to Develop Two New All-Electric Vehicles," *CNBC*, April 2, 2020; "Honda Accelerates Its 'Electric Vision' Strategy With New 2022 Ambition," *Automotive World*, October 23, 2019; Roberto Baldwin, "Honda Kills Clarity EV, Its Only All-Electric Car in U.S.," *Car and Driver*, March 9, 2020.

Chapter 4

1. Based on information in Netflix Research, "Personalization & Search"; Jeremy Bowman, "Netflix Is Killing the Competition in This One Key Category," *The Motley Fool*, September 15, 2020; Tara Lachapelle, "Netflix Investors, We Need to Talk About Churn," *Bloomberg*, January 19, 2021.
2. Social Media Fact Sheet," Pew Research.
3. Brent Barnhart, "Social Media Demographics to Inform Your Brand's Strategy in 2021," Sprout Social, March 9, 2021.
4. "2020 National Customer Rage Study," Customer Care Measurement and Consulting.
5. "The Top 10 Super Bowl 2020 Commercials by Digital Share of Voice," Ad Age.
6. Rosie Murphy, "Local Consumer Review Survey 2020," BrightLocal.
7. Ibid.
8. The Wyndham Hotel website.
9. Kiva, www.kiva.org (accessed March 13, 2021).
10. "PwC Global Crisis Survey," PricewaterhouseCoopers.
11. Nina Solis, "How to Respond to a Negative Online Review," Broadly.
12. "Generation Z News," *Business Insider*.
13. Kavya Ravi, "6 Ways Nike Built a Strong Brand on Social Media," Unmetric.
14. Ibid.
15. Alexander Santo, "The Ultimate List of Marketing Spend Statistics," Brafton.
16. "More Smiles in 2020: Lay's Kicks Off Search for People Creating Joy Across the Country; Unveils Three New Flavors to Smile About," Frito-Lay.
17. "Lego Ideas," The Lego Group, March 12, 2021.
18. LinkedIn, www.linkedin.com (accessed March 3, 2021).
19. Melissa Barker, Donald Barker, Nicholas Bormann, and Krista

E. Neher. *Social Media Marketing: A Strategic Approach* (Mason, OH: Cengage Publishing, 2017).
20. Emily Heaslip, "9 Wildly Successful Crowdfunded Startups," U.S. Chamber of Commerce.
21. SAP, https://www.sap.com/community.html (accessed March 5, 2021).
22. Daniela Coppola, "E-Commerce in the United States—Statistics & Facts," Statista.com.
23. Jullia Andjelic, "47 Mobile Marketing Statistics to Transform Your Business," Smallbizgenius.
24. "Quarterly Retail E-Commerce Sales," *U.S. Census Bureau News*.
25. Natalie Colarossi, "Online Black Friday Shoppers Increase Nearly 45 Percent Amid COVID-19 Pandemic," Newsweek.
26. Internet World Stats, https://www.internetworldstats.com/ (accessed March 16, 2021).
27. Ibid.
28. Brent Barnhart, "Social Media Demographics to Inform Your Brand's Strategy in 2021," Sprout Social.
29. Eugene Lee, "Can My Employer Monitor My Web Surfing or Emails at work? (2020)," California Labor and Employer Law.
30. Jacquelyn Bulao, "How Many Cyber Attacks Happen Per Day in 2020?," TechJury.
31. "Seena Gressin, " Identity Theft Awareness Week Starts Today," Federal Trade Commission.
32. Eugene Bekker, "2020 Data Breaches," IdentityForce.
33. Based on information in Melissa Repko, "Target Aims to Make Its Booming Online Business More Profitable With New Technology, Small Sort Centers," *CNBC*, May 20, 2020; Jackie Crosby, "Target CEO: $7 Billion Investment in Stores and Technology Is Paying Off," *Star Tribune*, March 2, 2019; Shelley E. Kohan, "Target's Big Investments, From Small-Format Stores To Digital, Prove Successful," *Forbes*, March 4, 2020.

Chapter 5

1. Based on information in Derek Loosvelt, "Pros and Cons of Working for the Big 4 and Other Top Accounting Firms," *Vault*, March 20, 2019; KPMG, "Your Career," March 11, 2021; PwC, "Employee Benefits," March 11, 2021; Will Kenton, "The Big 4," Investopedia, January 7, 2021.
2. Wolf Richter, "Accounting Fraud & Freight Recession Topple Celadon, Largest Truckload-Carrier Bankruptcy In US History," Wolfstreet.
3. Matthew Heller, "Power Solutions Fined for Accounting Fraud," CFO.
4. "Welcome to Sarbanes Oxley 101," Sarbanes Oxley 101.
5. *Occupational Outlook Handbook*, U.S. Bureau of Labor Statistics.
6. Based on information in Oracle, "Oracle Cloud Economics," March 1, 2021; Oracle, "Oracle Security, Identity, and Compliance," March 1, 2021; Oracle, "Oracle Corporate Facts," March 1, 2021; Todd Bishop, "Oracle's Larry Ellison Looks to One-up Amazon, Offering Full Cloud Inside Customer Data Centers," *Geekwire*, July 9, 2020; Bob Evans, "Hello, IBM and Microsoft: Larry Ellison's Big Plans for Oracle Autonomous Database," *Cloud Wars*, September 16, 2019; Fox Business, "Oracle Database, Not Amazon Has Most of the World's Data: Larry Ellison," *YouTube*, October 25, 2018; Oracle, "Oracle Ups the Ante in Cloud with World's First Autonomous Operating System," September 16, 2019; and Silicon Valley Historical Association, "Oracle," 2008.

Chapter 6

1. Based on information in Adam Levine-Weinberg, "Southwest Airlines Takes a Different Path Through the Pandemic," *The Motley Fool*, July 27, 2020; Southwest, "Southwest Corporate Fact Sheet," March 21, 2021; "Southwest Airlines Reports Fourth Quarter and Annual 2020 Results," *PR Newswire*, January 28, 2021.
2. Priya Merchant, "Pivoting During the Pandemic: How These Businesses Succeeded," Entrepreneur.
3. The *Occupational Outlook Handbook*, U.S. Bureau of Labor Statistics.
4. "Income Statement," Intel.
5. S. Lock, "McDonald's: Ad Spend," Statista.com.
6. "Uber Agrees to Buy Food-Delivery Service Postmates for $2.65 Billion in Stock," CNBC.
7. Jonathan Stempel, "Warren Buffett Gives Up on Newspapers; Berkshire Sells Unit to Lee Enterprises," Reuters.
8. Chris Isidore, "As JC Penney Exits Bankruptcy, Its Long-Term Outlook Remains Grim," *CNN.com*.
9. Laura Kim, Raynil Kumar, and Shaun O'Brien, "2020 Findings from the Diary of Consumer Payment Choice," Federal Reserve Bank of San Francisco.
10. John Ulzheimer, "How Many Credit Cards Does the Average American Have?" CardRates.com.
11. Frank Vinluan, "Legend Biotech's Upsized IPO Lands $424M for Multiple Myeloma Drug," Xconomy.
12. Procter & Gamble, https://s1.q4cdn.com/695946674/files/doc_financials/2020/ar/PG-2020-Annual-Report.pdf (accessed March 5, 2021).
13. Based on information in CNBC Television, "DoorDash Releases IPO Filing, Reports $149 Million Loss Through September," *YouTube*, November 13, 2020; Jessica Bursztynsky, "DoorDash Skyrockets in Market Debut, Closes up 85%," *CNBC*, December 9, 2020; Megan Rose Dickey, "DoorDash Is Buying Caviar From Square in a Deal Worth $410 Million," TechCrunch, August 1, 2019.

Glossary 术语表

absolute advantage the ability to produce a specific product more efficiently than any other nation

accounting the process of systematically collecting, analyzing, and reporting financial information

accounting equation the basis for the accounting process: *Assets = Liabilities + Owners' equity*

affirmative action program a plan designed to increase the number of employees from underrepresented groups at all levels within an organization

angel investor a wealthy investor who provides financial backing for small business start-ups or entrepreneurs

annual report a report distributed to stockholders and other interested parties that describes the firm's operating activities and its financial condition

assets the resources that a business owns

audit an examination of a company's financial statements and the accounting practices that produced them

balance of payments the total flow of money into a country minus the total flow of money out of that country over a specified period of time

balance of trade the total value of a nation's exports minus the total value of its imports over a specified period of time

balance sheet (or **statement of financial position)** a summary of the dollar amounts of a firm's assets, liabilities, and owners' equity accounts at the end of a specific accounting period

banker's acceptance a written order for a bank to pay a third party a stated amount of money on a specific date

blog a website that allows a company to share information to increase the customer's knowledge about its products and services, and to build trust

bond indenture a legal document that details all the conditions relating to a bond issue

budget a financial statement that projects income, expenditures, or both over a specified future period

business the organized effort of individuals to produce and sell, for a profit, the goods and services that satisfy society's needs

business cycle the recurrence of periods of growth and recession in a nation's economic activity

business ethics the application of moral standards to business situations

business model a model that represents a group of common characteristics and methods of doing business to generate sales revenues and reduce expenses

business-to-business (or **B2B) model** a model used by firms that conduct business with other businesses

business-to-consumer (or **B2C) model** a model used by firms that focus on conducting business with individual consumers

capital budget a financial statement that estimates a firm's expenditures for major assets and its long-term financing needs

capitalism an economic system in which individuals own and operate the majority of businesses that provide goods and services

cash budget a financial statement that estimates cash receipts and cash expenditures over a specified period

cash flow the movement of money into and out of an organization

caveat emptor a Latin phrase meaning "let the buyer beware"

certificate of deposit (CD) a document stating that the bank will pay the depositor a guaranteed interest rate on money left on deposit for a specified period of time

certified public accountant (CPA) an individual who has met state requirements for accounting education and experience and has passed a rigorous accounting examination

cloud computing a type of computer usage in which services stored on the internet are provided to users on a temporary basis

code of ethics a guide to acceptable and ethical behavior as defined by the organization

collateral real estate or property pledged as security for a loan

command economy an economic system in which the government decides *what* goods and services will be produced, *how* they will be produced, *for whom* available goods and services will be produced, and *who* owns and controls the major factors of production

commercial paper a short-term promissory note issued by a large corporation

common stock the most basic form of corporate ownership and whose owners may vote on corporate policies

comparative advantage the ability to produce a specific product more efficiently than any other product

compensation the payment employees receive in return for their labor

competition rivalry among businesses for sales to potential customers

conflict of interest when businesspeople take advantage of a situation for their own personal interest rather than for the employer's interest

consumer price index (CPI) a monthly index that measures the changes in prices of a fixed basket of goods purchased by a typical consumer in an urban area

consumer products goods and services purchased by individuals for personal consumption

consumerism all activities undertaken to protect the rights of consumers

contract manufacturing an arrangement in which one firm contracts with another business, often in another country, to manufacture products or product components to its specifications

convertible bond a bond that can be exchanged, at the owner's option, for a specified number of shares of the corporation's common stock

cookie a small piece of software sent by a website that tracks an individual's internet use

corporate bond a corporation's written pledge that it will repay a specified amount of money with interest

corporate citizenship adopting a strategic approach to fulfilling economic, ethical, environmental, and social responsibilities

cost of goods sold the dollar amount equal to beginning inventory *plus* net purchases less ending inventory

countertrade an international barter transaction

crowdfunding a method of raising money to fund a project for a business, a nonprofit organization, or an individual

crowdsourcing outsourcing tasks to a group of people in order to tap into the ideas of the crowd

cultural (or **workplace) diversity** a system that recognizes and respects the differences among people because of their age, race, ethnicity, gender, sexual orientation, and ability

currency devaluation the reduction of the value of a nation's currency relative to the currencies of other countries

current liabilities debts that will be repaid in one year or less

current ratio a financial ratio computed by dividing current assets by current liabilities

data numerical or verbal descriptions that usually result from some sort of measurement

data mining the practice of searching through data records looking for useful information

data processing the transformation of data into a form that is useful for a specific purpose

database a single collection of data and information stored in one place that can be used by people throughout an organization to make decisions

debenture bond a bond backed only by the reputation of the issuing corporation

debit card a card that electronically subtracts the amount of a purchase from a customer's bank account at the moment the purchase is made

debt capital borrowed money obtained through loans of various types

decision-support system (DSS) a type of software program that provides relevant data and information to help a firm's employees make decisions

deflation a general decrease in the level of prices

demand the quantity of a product that buyers are willing to purchase at each of various prices

depression a severe recession that lasts longer than a typical recession and has a larger decline in business activity when compared to a recession

domestic system a method of manufacturing in which an entrepreneur distributes raw materials to various homes, where families process them into finished goods to be offered for sale by the entrepreneur

double-entry bookkeeping system a system in which each financial transaction is recorded as two separate accounting entries to maintain the balance shown in the accounting equation

dumping exportation of large quantities of a product at a price lower than that of the same product in the home market

e-business (or **electronic business)** the organized effort of individuals to produce and sell, for a profit, the goods and services that satisfy society's needs through the facilities available on the internet

e-commerce a part of e-business and usually refers only to buying and selling activities conducted online

economic community an organization of nations formed to promote the free movement of resources and products among its members and to create common economic policies

economic model of social responsibility the view that society will benefit most when business is left alone to produce and market profitable products that society needs

economics the study of how wealth is created and distributed

economy the way in which people deal with the creation and distribution of wealth

electronic funds transfer (EFT) system a means of performing financial transactions through a computer terminal

embargo a complete halt to trading with a particular nation or in a particular product

entrepreneur a person who risks time, effort, and money to start and operate a business

Equal Employment Opportunity Commission (EEOC) a government agency with the power to investigate complaints of employment discrimination and the power to sue firms that practice it

equity capital money received from the owners or from the sale of shares of ownership in a business

ethics the study of right and wrong and of the morality of the choices individuals make

exchange control a restriction on the amount of a particular foreign currency that can be purchased or sold

expert system a type of computer program that uses artificial intelligence to imitate a human's ability to think

Export-Import Bank of the United States an independent agency of the U.S. government whose function is to assist in financing the exports of American firms

exporting selling and shipping raw materials or products to other nations

factor a firm that specializes in buying other firms' accounts receivables

factors of production inputs and resources used to produce goods and services

factory system a system of manufacturing in which all the materials, machinery, and workers required to manufacture a product are assembled in one place

federal deficit a shortfall created when the federal government spends more in a fiscal year than it receives

financial accounting generates financial statements and reports for interested people outside an organization

financial leverage the use of borrowed funds to increase the return on owners' equity

financial management all the activities concerned with obtaining money and using it effectively

financial plan a plan for obtaining and using the money needed to implement an organization's goals and objectives

financial ratio a number that shows the relationship between two elements of a firm's financial statements

fiscal policy government influence on the amount of savings and expenditures; accomplished by altering the tax structure and by changing the levels of government spending

forum an interactive version of a community bulletin board that focuses on threaded discussions

free enterprise the system of business in which individuals are free to decide what to produce, how to produce it, and at what price to sell it

General Agreement on Tariffs and Trade (GATT) an international organization of nations dedicated to reducing or eliminating tariffs and other barriers to world trade

generally accepted accounting principles (GAAPs) an accepted set of guidelines and practices for U.S. companies reporting financial information and for the accounting profession

green IT a term used to describe all of a firm's activities to support a healthy environment and sustain the planet

green marketing the process of creating, making, delivering, and promoting products that are environmentally safe

gross domestic product (GDP) the total dollar value of all goods and services produced by all people within the boundaries of a country during a specified time period—usually a one-year period

gross profit a firm's net sales less the cost of goods sold

gross sales the total dollar amount of all goods and services sold during the accounting period

hard-core unemployed workers with little education or vocational training and a long history of unemployment

hashtag a word or a short phrase preceded by the pound sign (#), to identify different topics

import quota a limit on the amount of a particular good that may be imported into a country during a given period of time

importing purchasing raw materials or products in other nations and bringing them into one's own country

inbound marketing a marketing term that describes new ways of gaining attention and ultimately customers by creating content on a website that pulls customers in

income statement a summary of a firm's revenues and expenses during a specified accounting period

inflation a general rise in the level of prices

influencer a person known on social media who has an influence over a large number of followers

information data presented in a form that is useful for a specific purpose

initial public offering (IPO) occurs when a corporation sells common stock to the general public for the first time

international business all business activities that involve exchanges across national boundaries

International Monetary Fund (IMF) a 190-member international bank that makes short-term loans to developing countries experiencing balance-of-payment deficits

inventory turnover a financial ratio calculated by dividing the cost of goods sold in one year by the average value of the inventory

investment banking firm an organization that assists corporations in raising funds, usually by helping to sell new issues of stocks, bonds, or other financial securities

invisible hand a term created by Adam Smith to describe how an individual's personal gain benefits others and a nation's economy

key performance indicators (KPIs) measurements that define and measure the progress of an organization toward achieving its objectives

knowledge management (KM) a firm's procedures for generating, using, and sharing important data and information

letter of credit a legal document issued by a bank or other financial institution guaranteeing to pay a seller a stated amount for a specified period of time if certain conditions or requirements are met

liabilities a firm's debts and obligations

licensing a contractual agreement in which one firm permits another to produce and market its product and to use its brand name in return for a royalty or other compensation

line of credit a loan that is approved before the money is actually needed

liquidity the ease with which an asset can be converted into cash

long-term financing money that will be used for longer than one year

long-term liabilities debts that need not be repaid for at least one year

macroeconomics the study of the national economy and the global economy

malware a general term that describes software designed to infiltrate a computer system without the user's consent

management information system (MIS) a system that provides managers and employees with the information they need to perform their jobs as effectively as possible

managerial accounting provides managers and employees with the information needed to make decisions about a firm's financing, investing, marketing, and operating activities

market economy an economic system in which businesses and individuals decide what to produce and buy, and the market determines prices and quantities sold

market price the price at which the quantity demanded is exactly equal to the quantity supplied

maturity date the date on which a corporation is to repay borrowed money

media sharing sites websites which allow users to upload photos, videos, and podcasts

microeconomics the study of the decisions made by individuals and businesses

mixed economy an economy that exhibits elements of both capitalism and socialism

mobile marketing communicating with and selling to customers through mobile devices

mobile payment allows customers to use an electronic device or app to pay for a product or service

monetary policies Federal Reserve's actions to promote maximum employment, stabilize prices, and increase or decrease interest rates

monopolistic competition a market situation in which there are many buyers along with a relatively large number of sellers who differentiate their products from the products of competitors

monopoly a market (or industry) with only one seller, and customers can only buy the product or service from that seller

mortgage bond a corporate bond secured by various assets of the issuing firm

multilateral development bank (MDB) an internationally supported bank that provides loans to developing countries to help them grow

multinational corporation a firm that operates on a worldwide scale without ties to any specific nation or region

national debt the total of all federal deficits

net income occurs when revenues exceed expenses

net loss occurs when expenses exceed revenues

net profit margin (or **return on sales)** a financial ratio calculated by dividing net income after taxes by net sales

net sales the actual dollar amounts received by a firm for the goods and services it has sold after adjustment for returns, allowances, and discounts

nontariff barrier a nontax measure imposed by a government to favor domestic over foreign suppliers

oligopoly a market (or industry) in which there are few sellers

operating expenses all business costs other than the cost of goods sold

outsourcing an arrangement in which one firm contracts manufacturing or other activities to a firm in another country that specializes in those activities and can offer them at a lower cost than domestic firms

over-the-counter (OTC) market a network of dealers who buy and sell the stocks of corporations that are not listed on a securities exchange

owners' equity the difference between a firm's assets and its liabilities

perfect (or **pure) competition** the market situation in which there are many buyers and sellers of a product, and no single buyer or seller is powerful enough to affect the price of that product

plagiarism knowingly taking someone else's words, ideas, or other original material without acknowledging the source

podcasts digital audio or video files that people listen to or watch online on tablets, computers, smartphones, or other mobile devices

pollution the contamination of water, air, or land through the actions of people in an industrialized society

primary market a market in which an investor purchases financial securities (via an investment bank) directly from the issuer of those securities

prime interest rate the lowest rate charged by a bank for a short-term loan

private placement occurs when stock and other corporate securities are sold directly to wealthy investors, banks and financial firms, insurance companies, pension funds, large institutional investors, or mutual funds

producer price index (PPI) a monthly index that measures prices that producers receive for their finished goods

product differentiation the process of developing and promoting differences between a company's products and all competitive products

productivity the average level of output per worker per hour

profit what remains after all business expenses have been deducted from sales revenue

promissory note a written pledge by a borrower to pay a certain sum of money to a creditor at a specified future date

qualitative social media measurement the process of accessing the opinions and beliefs about a brand

quantitative social media measurement using numerical measurements, such as counting the number of website visitors, number of fans and followers, number of leads generated, and the number of new customers

recession two or more consecutive three-month periods of decline in a country's GDP

recycling converting used materials into new products or components for new products in order to prevent their unnecessary disposal

registered bond a bond registered in the owner's name by the issuing company

retained earnings the portion of a business's profits not distributed to stockholders

revenue stream a source of revenue flowing into a firm

revenues the dollar amounts earned by a firm from selling goods, providing services, or performing business activities

revolving credit agreement a guaranteed line of credit

risk–return ratio a ratio based on the principle that a highrisk decision should generate higher financial returns for a business and more conservative decisions often generate lower returns

Sarbanes-Oxley Act of 2002 provides sweeping legal protection for employees who report corporate misconduct

secondary market a market for existing financial securities that are traded between investors

securities exchange a marketplace where member brokers meet to buy and sell securities

sentiment analysis a measurement that uses technology to detect the mood, attitudes, or emotions of people who experience a social media activity

serial bonds bonds of a single issue that mature on different dates

service economy an economy in which more effort is devoted to the production of services than to the production of goods

short-term financing money that will be used for one year or less

sinking fund a sum of money to which deposits are made each year for the purpose of redeeming a bond issue

social audit a comprehensive report of what an organization has done and is doing with regard to social issues that affect it

social content sites websites which allow companies to create and share information about their products and services

social media the online interaction that allows people and businesses to communicate and share ideas, personal information, and information about products or services

social media communities groups of people who share common interests and who want to use technology and the internet to connect with people with similar interests

social media community manager a high-level executive who is responsible for all of a company's social media activities

social media marketing the utilization of software, c technology, and the internet to provide information ab firm's products and services, increase sales revenues, a improve customer service

social responsibility the recognition that business activities have an impact on society and the consideration of that impact in business decision making

socioeconomic model of social responsibility the concept that business should emphasize not only profits but also the impact of its decisions on society

specialization the separation of a manufacturing process into distinct tasks and the assignment of different tasks to different individuals

speculative production the time lag between the actual production of goods and when the goods are sold

stakeholders all the different people or groups of people who are affected by an organization's policies, decisions, and activities

standard of living a loose, subjective measure of how well off an individual or a society is, mainly in terms of want satisfaction through goods and services

statement of cash flows a statement that illustrates how the company's operating, investing, and financing activities affect cash during an accounting period

statistic a measure that summarizes a particular characteristic of an entire group of numbers

strategic alliance a partnership formed to create competitive advantage on a worldwide basis

supply the quantity of a product that producers are willing to sell at each of various prices

sustainability the ability to create and maintain conditions under which present and future generations can exist in productive harmony, and permit fulfilling the social, economic, and other requirements of future and present generations

tariff a tax levied on a particular foreign product entering a country

term-loan agreement a promissory note that requires a borrower to repay a loan in monthly, quarterly, semiannual, or annual installments

trade credit a type of short-term financing extended by a seller who does not require immediate payment after delivery of merchandise

trade deficit a negative balance of trade

trading company provides a link between buyers and sellers in different countries

trustee an individual or an independent firm that acts as a bond owner's representative

unemployment rate the percentage of a nation's labor force unemployed at any time

unsecured financing financing that is not backed by collateral

whistle-blowing informing the press or government officials about unethical practices within one's organization

…rking space that enables members
…n be shared with other people
…anking institution with 189 member

…ation (WTO)** a 164-member powerful successor to GATT that facilitates world trade among member nations by mediating disputes and fostering efforts to reduce trade barriers

zero-base budgeting a budgeting approach in which every expense in every budget must be justified

图书在版编目（CIP）数据

信息、会计和理财：第7版：双语教学版：英、汉 /（美）威廉·普赖德，（美）罗伯特·休斯，（美）杰克·卡普尔著；孔小磊译注. -- 北京：商务印书馆，2024.

ISBN 978-7-100-24578-4

Ⅰ. F232；TS976.15

中国国家版本馆CIP数据核字第2024HE1532号

权利保留，侵权必究。

信息、会计和理财（第7版，双语教学版）

〔美〕威廉·普赖德　罗伯特·休斯　杰克·卡普尔　著

孔小磊　译注

商　务　印　书　馆　出　版

（北京王府井大街36号　邮政编码100710）

商　务　印　书　馆　发　行

人卫印务（北京）有限公司印刷

ISBN 978-7-100-24578-4

2025年1月第1版　开本 850×1092　1/16

2025年1月北京第1次印刷　印张 14

定价：68.00元